MODERN
LITERARY THEORY

MODERN LITERARY THEORY

A READER

Second Edition

Philip Rice
Lecturer in Communication Studies, Coventry University
and
Patricia Waugh
Lecturer in English, University of Durham

Edward Arnold
A member of the Hodder Headline Group
LONDON   NEW YORK   MELBOURNE   AUCKLAND

Edward Arnold is a division of Hodder Headline PLC
338 Euston Road, London NW1 3BH

© 1989, 1992 Selection and editiorial matter
Philip Rice and Patricia Waugh

First published in the United Kingdom 1989
Second edition 1992

5 7 9 8 6
94 96 98 97 95

Distributed in the USA by Routledge, Chapman and Hall, Inc.
29 West 35th Street, New York, NY 10001

British Library Cataloguing in Publication Data
Rice, Philip
Modern Literary Theory: Reader. 2Rev. ed
I. Title   II. Waugh, Patricia
801

ISBN 0 340 57599 9

Library of Congress Cataloging-in-Publication Data
Modern literary theory: a reader/[edited by]
Philip Rice and Patricia Waugh. - 2nd ed.
p.   cm.
Includes bibliographical references (p.   ) and index.
ISBN 0 340 57599 9: $17.95
1. Literature-History and criticism-Theory, etc
I. Rice, Philip.   II. Waugh, Patricia.
PN81.M54 1992
801'.95'09045-dc20   91-19707
CIP

Typeset by Saxon Printing Ltd, Derby
Printed and bound in the United Kingdom by
J W Arrowsmith Ltd, Bristol

CONTENTS

ACKNOWLEDGEMENTS

We would like to thank Barbara Rasmussen, Barry Jordan and Jenny Rice for reading and commenting on various versions of the manuscript; and our editor at Edward Arnold, who has obviously realized that patience is a virtue.

The Publisher would like to thank the following for their permission to use copyright material:

Associated Book Publishers (UK) for the extract from *The Subject of Tragedy* by Catherine Belsey published by Methuen & Co. Associated Book Publishers (UK) and W W Norton & Company Inc for the extract from *Ecrits* by Jacques Lacan translated by Alan Sheridan, published by Tavistock Publications and W W Norton & Company, © 1977 by Tavistock Publications Ltd. Associated Book Publishers (UK) and the University of Chicago Press for the extract from *Writing and Difference* by Jacques Derrida, translated by Alan Bass, published by Routledge & Kegan Paul and the University of Chicago Press. Associated Book Publishers (UK) for 'Literature as an ideological form' by Pierre Macherey and Etienne Balibar in *Untying the Text* by Robert Young, published by Routledge & Kegan Paul. Associated Book Publishers (UK) for 'Analysis & Interpretation of the Realist Text' by David Lodge from *Working with Structuralism*, published by Routledge & Kegan Paul. Jonathan Cape Ltd and Macmillan Publishing Company and the Executor of the Estate of Ernest Hemingway for 'Cat in the Rain' by Ernest Hemingway. Croom Helm Ltd for 'Towards a Feminist Poetics' by Elaine Showalter published in *Women Writing about Women* by Mary Jacobus. Drake Marketing Services and Bay Press for 'Opponents, Audiences, Constituencies and Community' by Edward Said for *The Anti-Aesthetic: Essays on Post-Modern Culture* ed by Hal Foster. Dr Ian Hunter for 'Reading Character'. The Johns Hopkins University Press for 'To Write: An Intransitive Verb?' by Roland Barthes published in *The Structuralist Controversy* by Macksey and Donato. The Johns Hopkins University Press for 'Literary History as a Challenge to Literary Theory' by Hans Robert Jauss, reprinted from *New Literary History* Vol 2, 1970, 7–37. The Johns Hopkins University Press for an extract from *The Implied Reader* by Wolfgang

Iser. The MIT Press for 'Mimicry and Man: The Ambivalence of Colonial Discourse' Homi Bhabha, *October* 28 (1984), 125–133. The University of Nebraska Press for 'Art as Technique' by Victor Shklovsky reprinted from *Russian Formalist Criticism: Four Essays* translated and with an introduction by Lee T Lemon and Marion Reiss, by permission of the University of Nebraska Press, © 1965. Peter Owen Ltd for the extract from *Course in General Linguistics* by Ferdinand de Saussure edited by Charles Bally and Albert Sechehaye, translated by Wade Baskin. Editions Du Seuil and Collins for the extract from *Image-Music-Text* by Roland Barthes. 'The Text, the Poem and the Problem of Historical Method', © Jerome J. McGann 1985. Reprinted from *The Beauty of Inflections* by Jerome J. McGann (1985) by permission of Oxford University Press. The Society for Education in Film & Television Ltd and Colin, MacCabe for 'Realism and the Cinema. Notes on some Brechtian Theses' *Screen* (1974) Vol 15, no 2. The University of Minnesota Press for Fredric Jameson, 'Periodizing The Sixties', from *The Sixties Without Apology*, eds. S Saynes et al. (1984). The University of Texas Press for 'Discourse in the Novel' by Mikhail Bakhtin, reprinted from *The Dialogic Imagination: Four Essays* by M M Bakhtin, ed by Michael Holquist, translated by Carl Emerson and Michael Holquist, by permission of the University of Texas Press, Austin, © 1981. Verso Press for 'Criticism and Ideology' by Terry Eagleton and 'Lenin and Philosophy' by L Althusser, published in *New Left Books* translated by Ben Brewster. The University Press of Virginia for 'Past Significance and Present Meaning in Literary History', from *Structure and Society in Literary History*, by Robert Weimann (1976).

PREFACE

The success of the first edition of this anthology has fulfilled original hopes that it would form the basis for a pedagogic introduction to and clarification of the immense volume and diversity of theoretical writing that, over the past twenty-five years, has so radically questioned our understanding and construction of literature as an object of critical study and the methods and presuppositions of criticism itself. When we wrote the preface to the first edition (in 1988), it was evident that the rapid growth of literary theory since the mid-sixties and the mass of work devoted to theoretical discussion of literature had produced a radical transformation in literary studies. Critics and philosophers have always theorised about literature and literary criticism, but the recent erosion of boundaries between philosophy, political theory, psychoanalysis, social theory and literary criticism would seem to represent something of a 'paradigm shift' in literary studies. The very foundations of the Anglo-American literary tradition have been challenged. Since then, *all* foundations of Western thought and representation have increasingly been held up to critical gaze and for that reason we have included a revised and expanded section on Postmodernism to reflect this most recent development. Along with this change has occurred the rise of another critical practice referring to itself as the 'New Historicism' and, like Postmodernists, its practitioners tend to work with an eclectic mix of theories and to eschew the allure of holistic or 'totalising' theoretical models which claim to account for all aspects of human experience. We have included a new section, therefore, on the New Historicism. Anyone reading the essays reprinted here in the context of the material gathered in the reader as a whole will recognise that New Historicism is more a practice of reading than a theory of literature, but one which draws loosely and extensively on shifting combinations of many of the theoretical positions represented in earlier parts of the book. Any reflection upon Postmodernism or New Historicism inevitably raises questions about the compatibility or otherwise of different theoretical models and about their philosophical presuppositions. It seems likely that these are issues which will continue to be central to literary theoretical debates in the future.

The task of selection for this anthology has not been an easy one, for the field which has to be mapped continuously changes its boundaries as new relations and combinations move in and out of the foreground. A book which attempted to be totally inclusive would be well beyond the means of the readers we hope to reach. Our aims, therefore, have been modest rather than ambitious: to introduce a broad and diverse selection of works which might be seen as conceptual 'keys' to the theoretical revolution; to draw out some of the implications of the theoretical positions offered and, in particular, to offer an anthology through which the reader can get a foothold on the map of contemporary theory and become acquainted with some of the principal theories and theorists involved.

The book is organized into two parts which are subdivided into sections, each one representing a major area in contemporary literary theory. In most sections we have tried to include an extract which gives an account of the theory and, where appropriate, a contribution which uses that theoretical paradigm as a critical approach to literary texts. Editorial commentary has been kept to a minimum in order to devote as much space as possible to the source material, but commentary is nevertheless required for the field only partially organizes itself, and then more on the basis of history than of nature. If contemporary theory teaches us anything it is that the orders of the world are not 'natural' but constructed. Our commentary is thus offered more as an attempt to rationalize the organization of the material rather than to provide an exhaustive critical explanation of it. Indeed the anthology might usefully be seen as a supplement to the various critical accounts of literary theory that have appeared in the last few years (Eagleton 1983; Jefferson and Robey 1982; Selden 1985). Again, to save space, the bibliography is selective and indicative only, though it should prove an adequate starting point for further research.

We hope that the experience of reading the book will stimulate further interest and help to clarify the major theoretical positions and their relations to each other. But beyond that (and in the spirit of contemporary theory) we hope that it will encourage readers to contest and challenge the very structures of knowledge and understanding we have used in compiling this book.

PART ONE

INTRODUCTION

Though literary theory is not a recent phenomenon it often appears that way. Its rapid growth since the mid 1960s, and the mass of work devoted to theoretical discourse about and around literature has produced what can only be described as a radical transformation. If literary theory seems new it is not because theorizing about literature is new, but because of the quantitative and qualitative difference of contemporary work. What characterizes contemporary theory is, on the one hand, its heterogeneity and on the other, its unprecedented attack on the grounding assumptions of the Anglo-American critical tradition.

Literary studies has always been a pluralistic discipline. The various practices that constituted the Anglo-American tradition, such as literary history, literary biography, moral-aesthetic criticism and even the New Criticism had, until recently, managed to coexist in a state of fairly 'stable disequilibrium' based on a broad consensus about the author, the nature of the literary work, and the purpose of criticism. Critics might have argued about the inclusion of this or that piece of writing in the canon of literature, but the notion that something called 'literature' existed was never in doubt; nor was the sense that the author was the originator of the work, or that the act of criticism was subordinate to the literature it studied. All of this and more has come in for rigorous interrogation and re-evaluation from a theoretical discourse no longer consigned to the margins.

Contemporary critical theory has asserted itself in the everyday life of literary studies, refusing to accept its marginalization as a peripheral concern more akin to philosophy. It sees itself as existing at the heart of the critical enterprise, insisting that there is no critical act that can transcend theory. As numerous theorists have pointed out, the traditional forms of criticism through which literature is and has been studied are not 'theory free' responses to great literary works, nor are they pure scholastic endeavours. All forms of criticism are founded upon a theory, or an admix of theories, whether they consciously acknowledge that or not. Theoretical writings have recognized that what are often taken to be 'natural' and 'commonsensical' ways of studying literature actually rest upon a set of theoretical injunctions which have been naturalized to the point at which they no longer have to justify their own practices.

The way that theory has been inflected into the everyday workings of the literary discipline has often proved a source of passionate debate. Responses have taken many different forms, from irate dismissal to enthusiastic development. If theory seems to some critics to be deeply implicated in the everyday pursuits and routines of the discipline, to others it seems not to be addressing the object of study directly and to be operating in the realms of the abstract and the abstruse, divorced from that close reading and intimate study of literary works that has so characterized the discipline. Much of the theory *is* abstract, and does not offer a method for approaching literary texts directly, however, it has important implications for the way we study literature, implications that cannot be dismissed simply because the theory is of no immediate pragmatic value. The discipline of literary criticism is largely founded on the basis of an immediate relation with its objects of study, but this is historically determined, not inevitable or natural. Part of the attack on the critical orthodoxy has been concerned with the undermining of that sense of a 'natural' way to study literature. And if literary theory sometimes appears to caricature the tradition it attacks, and to make it seem more singular than it actually is, that is because its attack has often been targeted not at the manifest plurality of critical practices that constitute the tradition but at its roots, at that set of founding assumptions which traditional criticism often obdurately refuses to acknowledge as anything other than the 'natural' and 'sensible' way of criticism.

The critical orthodoxy is undoubtedly a plurality of practices; from literary history and literary biography, to myth criticism and psychoanalytic criticism, to the New Criticism and moral-aesthetic criticism. But this plurality is grounded in a broad consensus focused on an epistemological and ontological certainty regarding the nature of the relation between the author, the text and the reader, and upon the definition of the text itself. Each form of criticism leans in a different direction: psychoanalytic/ biographical emphasizes the author; historical/sociological emphasizes the context; New Criticism emphasizes the text-in-itself; moral-aesthetic criticism the relation between the text and the reality it portrays. However, they all accept a broadly mimetic view of literature where literature in some way or other, reflects and delivers up 'truths' about life and the human condition (even if, as in the case of New Criticism, the mimetic view is not foregrounded). The task of literature is to render life, experience, and emotion in a potent way; the job of criticism is to reveal the true value and meaning of the rendition – a rendition at once contained within the literary work and yet, paradoxically, needing the critical act to reveal it.

The mimetic perspective depends upon a view of language as a transparent medium, a medium through which reality can be transcribed and re-presented in aesthetic form, and reality, self-contained and coherent, transcends its formulation in words. This view of language is, in turn, related to a general conception of the world which is 'man-centred', and to an epistemology that Catherine Belsey has characterized as 'empiricist-idealist' (1980, p7).

> . . . common sense urges that 'man' is the origin and source of meaning, of action and of history (*humanism*). Our concepts and our knowledge are held to be the product of experience (*empiricism*), and this experience is preceded and interpreted by the mind, reason or thought, the property of a transcendent human nature whose essence is the attribute of each individual (*idealism*).

The grounding assumptions of humanism presuppose that experience is prior to its expression in language and conceive of language as a mere tool used to express the way that experience is felt and interpreted by the unique individual. The existence of the unique individual is the cornerstone of the humanist ideology and provides the grid on which traditional literary criticism enacts its particular studies of the literary text. Inscribed in this ideology is the notion that literature is the collective product of especially gifted individuals who are able to capture the elusive universal and timeless truths of the human condition through the sensuous and sensitive use of the tool of language. Contemporary literary theory addresses and interrogates this set of founding assumptions in various ways and from a number of different perspectives. Through its interrogation the consensus around literary studies, and the ideological grid which underwrites it, has fragmented.

One of the principal focuses for the attack on Anglo-American critical practices has centred on language and derives largely from the linguistic theory of Ferdinand de Saussure. Language, according to Saussure, is not a mere tool devised for the re-presentation of a pre-existent reality. It is, rather, a constitutive part of reality, deeply implicated in the way the world is constructed as meaningful. According to this view language cannot be regarded as transparent, as it has to be if the mimetic tradition is to sustain its validity. Saussure's theory offers the possibility of a different perspective and gives rise to a wholly different epistemology. This perspective has been referred to as 'post-Saussurean'; it generally includes structuralist and/or post-structuralist theories.

However, initial challenges to the orthodoxy did not come only from structuralism. Other perspectives had an important influence – feminism brought a cultural politics to literary studies, as did the particular mode of Marxism dominant in the 1960s/70s (though this mode of Marxism is closely related to structuralism). Reader theory also disturbed the orthodoxy by shifting the object of study from the author/text to the text/reader nexus (again some of this work was closely allied to structuralist thought). In general the critical perspectives that emerged strongly in the post-1960s period exhibited a much more self-conscious and reflexive tendency, and a more rigorous and coherent attitude to the study and analysis of literature. However, the more radical versions of theory, usually post-structuralist, took the issue further. They posed not just a new set of approaches and/or a revised understanding of literature and the world, but also a profoundly different mode of existence for the text, for discourse, for the individual and for the discipline of literary studies and literary criticism itself.

Part One of this book deals with the initial break with the orthodoxies of literary studies. The material for this part has been selected to exemplify its less radical questioning and undermining of the literary studies enterprise. But while it is less radical it does prepare the ground for the work represented in Part Two which generally adopts a more interrogative and disrupting perspective. It is in this sense that the book has been divided into two parts – but this division is not meant to imply an historical progression from, for instance, the inadequacies of structuralism to a more satisfactory post-structuralism. This is not a matter of simple causal development or progression through the gradual accretion of knowledge. It is, rather, a matter of different trajectories and different directions that have been taken or refused.

This second edition of the Reader has a new section on New Historicism and a revised section on Postmodernism. It is interesting that in both these most recent critical developments, theory as coherent 'grand narrative', begins to break down. In its place, a hybrid and shifting mix of aspects of and insights from earlier, more 'totalizing' theoretical systems are brought together in a new practice of textual criticism or analysis of cultural meaning. In New Historicism and Postmodernism, there is a shift from the pleasures of pure and coherent theory to an engagement with contingency, plurality, the fragment and a loss of clear distinction between text and context, depth and surface. Within the terms of both of them, there can be no transcendent theoretical 'view from nowhere', for in each case the object of theoretical enquiry is seen inevitably to be a construction of theoretical discourses arising out of specific cultural situations.

The field of literary studies is currently a heterogeneous configuration of competing practices and epistemologies ranging from the traditional forms of literary criticism such as New Criticism and moral-aesthetic criticism, to the more recent structuralism, reader theory, feminism, and various post-structuralisms. Within this configuration individuals do not always align themselves with one or other of the theoretical positions, rather, they often debate, support, argue against, believe in, deny and utilize a number of them; readers and critics, in other words, occupy multiple, and sometimes contradictory positions in relation to the theories. It is up to the reader of this book to evaluate the various positions represented here and though we have our own preferences our job is not to foist these on others. We would urge, though, a critical assessment of the various theories on the basis of the arguments they offer and an openness to the more radical positions offered in Part Two.

SECTION ONE
SAUSSURE

The work of the Swiss linguist Ferdinand de Saussure has played a crucial and formative role in the recent transformation in literary theory. Saussure's influence rests on a single book which records his seminal theory of language, the *Course in General Linguistics*. This was compiled by students and colleagues, after his death in 1913, from notes taken at lectures he delivered between 1907 and 1911 when he taught at the University of Geneva.

Though not as well known as Marx or Freud, Saussure has been ranked with them in terms of the influence they have had on systems of thought developed in the twentieth century. Like Freud and Marx, Saussure considered the manifest appearance of phenomena to be underpinned and made possible by underlying systems and structures; for Marx, it was the system of economic and social relations; for Freud, the unconscious; for Saussure, the system of language. The most radical implications of their work profoundly disrupt the dominant, humanist conception of the world for they undermine the notion that 'man' is the centre, source and origin of meaning. Saussure's influence on literary theory came to the fore in structuralism and post-structuralism, though his work had had significant influence prior to that, notably on the structural linguistics of the Prague Circle and on the structural anthropology of Lévi-Strauss.

It is worth reviewing the main tenets of Saussurean theory since they form the necessary grounding for much of the theory represented in this book. Saussure argued that the object of study for linguistics is the underlying system of conventions (words and grammar) by virtue of which a sign (word) can 'mean'. Language is a system of signs, the sign being the basic unit of meaning. The sign comprises a signifier and signified, the signifier is the 'word image' (visual or acoustic) and the signified the 'mental concept'. Thus the signifier *tree* has the signified *mental concept of a tree*. It is important to note that Saussure is not referring here to the distinction between a name and a thing but to a distinction between the *word image* and the *concept*. The signifier and signified, however, are only separable *the sign is arbitrary* ✱

on the analytic level, they are not separable at the level of thought – the word image cannot be divorced from the mental concept and *vice versa*.

The first principle of Saussure's theory is that the sign is arbitrary. It is useful to consider this at two levels; firstly at the level of the signifier, secondly at the level of the signified. At the level of the signifier, the sign is arbitrary because there is no *necessary* connection between the signifier *tree* and the signified *concept of tree*; any configuration of sounds or written shapes could be used to signify *tree* – for instance, *arbre*, *baum*, *arbor* or even *fnurd* (example used by Hawkes 1977). The relation between the signifier and the signified is a matter of convention; in the English language we conventionally associate the word 'tree' with the concept 'tree'. The arbitrary nature of the sign at this level is fairly easily grasped, but it is the arbitrary nature of the sign at the level of the signified that is more difficult to see and that presents us with the more radical implications of Saussure's theory.

Not only do different languages use different signifiers, they also 'cut up' the phenomenal world differently, articulating it through language-specific concepts – that is, they use different signifieds. The important point to grasp here is that language is not a simple naming process, language does not operate by naming things and concepts that have an independently meaningful existence. Saussure points out that '. . . if words stood for pre-existing entities they would all have exact equivalents in meaning from one language to the next, but this is not true' (1974, p116). One of the most commonly referred-to illustrations of this is the colour spectrum. The colours of the spectrum actually form a continuum; so, for instance, that part of the spectrum which runs from blue through to red does not consist of a series of different colours – blue, green, yellow, orange, red – existing independently of each other. The spectrum is, rather, a continuum which our language divides up in a particular way.

Just as there is nothing 'natural' about the way we divide up the colour continuum (indeed, other languages divide it up differently), so there is nothing natural or inevitable about the way we divide up and articulate our world in other ways. Each language cuts up the world differently, constructing different meaningful categories and concepts. It is sometimes difficult to see that our everyday concepts are arbitrary and that language does not simply name pre-existing things. We tend to be so accustomed to the world our language system has produced that it comes to seem natural – the correct and inevitable way to view the world. Yet the logic of Saussure's theory suggests that our world is constructed for us by our language and that 'things' do not have fixed essences or cores of meaning which pre-exist linguistic representation.

Returning to the colour spectrum, we can see that orange is not an independently existing colour, not a point on the spectrum but a range on the continuum: we can also see how the colour orange depends, for its existence, on the other colours around it. We can define 'orange' only by what it is not. There is no essence to the colour, only a differentiation. We know that it is orange because it is not yellow and not red. Orange depends for its meaning on what it is not, i.e. orange is produced by the system of difference we employ in dividing up the spectrum.

For Saussure the whole of our language works in this way. It is a system of difference where any one term has meaning only by virtue of its differential place within that system. If we consider the sign 'food', it could not mean anything without the concept of *not* food. In order to 'cut up' the world, even at this crude level, we need a system of difference, i.e. a basic binary system – food/not food. Language is a far more complex version of this simple binary system. This led Saussure to emphasize the *system* of language, for without the system the individual elements (the signs) could not be made to mean.

An important distinction follows from this: that between *langue* and *parole*. Langue is the system of language, the system of forms (the rules, codes, conventions) and parole refers to the actual speech acts made possible by the langue. Utterances (paroles) are many and varied and no linguist could hope to grasp them all. What linguists could do was to study what made them all possible – the latent, underlying system or set of conventions. Saussure then adds a further distinction, that between synchronic and diachronic aspects. The synchronic is the structural aspect of language, the system at a particular moment; the diachronic relates to the history of the language – the changes in its forms and conventions over time. Because signs do not have any essential core of meaning they are open to change, however, in order to 'mean' the sign must exist within a system that is complete at any one moment. This led Saussure to assert that the proper object of study for linguistics was langue (the system which made any one act of speech possible), in its synchronic aspect.

The extract we have chosen to represent the work of Saussure deals, for the most part, with the arbitrary nature of the signified and with that aspect of a sign's meaning which is given by virtue of its place in the system.

1   Ferdinand de Saussure,
From *Course in General Linguistics*

p111–119, 120–121

1 Language as Organized Thought Coupled with Sound

To prove that language is only a system of pure values, it is enough to consider the two elements involved in its functioning: ideas and sounds.

Psychologically our thought – apart from its expression in words – is only a shapeless and indistinct mass. Philosophers and linguists have always agreed in recognizing that without the help of signs we would be unable to make a clear-cut, consistent distinction between two ideas. Without language, thought is a vague, uncharted nebula. There are no pre-existing ideas and nothing is distinct before the appearance of language.

Against the floating realm of thought, would sounds by themselves yield predelimited entities? No more so than ideas. Phonic substance is neither more fixed nor more rigid than thought; it is not a mold into which thought must of necessity fit but a plastic substance divided in turn into distinct parts to furnish the signifiers needed by thought. The linguistic fact can therefore be pictured in its totality – i.e. language – as a series of contiguous subdivisions marked off on both the indefinite plane of jumbled ideas (*A*) and the equally vague plane of sounds (*B*). The following diagram gives a rough idea of it:

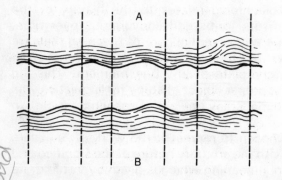

The characteristic role of language with respect to thought is not to create a material phonic means for expressing ideas but to serve as a link between thought and sound, under conditions that of necessity bring about the reciprocal delimitations of units. Thought, chaotic by nature, has to become ordered in the process of its decomposition. Neither are thoughts given material form nor are sounds transformed into mental entities; the somewhat mysterious fact is rather that 'thought sound' implies division and that language works out its units while taking shape between two shapeless masses. Visualize the air in contact with a sheet of water; if the atmospheric pressure changes, the surface of the water will be broken up into a series of divisions, waves; the waves resemble the union or coupling of thought with phonic substance.

Language might be called the domain of articulations, using the word as it was defined earlier. Each linguistic term is a member, an *articulus* in which an idea is fixed in a sound and a sound becomes the sign of an idea.

Language can also be compared with a sheet of paper: thought is the front and the sound the back; one cannot cut the front without cutting the back at the same time; likewise in language, one can neither divide sound from thought nor thought from sound; the division could be accomplished only abstractedly, and the result would be either pure psychology or pure phonology.

Linguistics then works in the borderland where the elements of sound and thought combine; *their combination produces a form, not a substance.*

These views give a better understanding of what was said before about the arbitrariness of signs. Not only are the two domains that are linked by the linguistic fact shapeless and confused, but the choice of a given slice of sound to name a given idea is completely arbitrary. If this were not true, the notion of value would be compromised, for it would include an externally imposed element. But actually values remain entirely relative, and that is why the bond between the sound and the idea is radically arbitrary.

The arbitrary nature of the sign explains in turn why the social fact alone can create a linguistic system. The community is necessary if values that owe their existence solely to usage and general acceptance are to be set up; by himself the individual is incapable of fixing a single value.

In addition, the idea of value, as defined, shows that to consider a term as simply the union of a certain sound with a certain concept is grossly misleading. To define it in this way would isolate the term from its system; it would mean assuming that one can start from the terms and construct the system by adding them together when, on the contrary, it is from the interdependent whole that one must start and through analysis obtain its elements.

To develop this thesis, we shall study value successively from the viewpoint of the signified or concept (Section 2), the signifier (Section 3), and the complete sign (Section 4).

Being unable to seize the concrete entities or units of language directly, we shall work with words. While the word does not conform exactly to the definition of the linguistic unit, it at least bears a rough resemblance to the unit and has the advantage of being concrete; consequently, we shall use words as specimens equivalent to real terms in a synchronic system, and the principles that we evolve with respect to words will be valid for entities in general.

2 Linguistic Value from a Conceptual Viewpoint

When we speak of the value of a word, we generally think first of its property of standing for an idea, and this is in fact one side of linguistic value. But if this is true, how does *value* differ from *signification*? Might the two words be synonyms? I think not, although it is easy to confuse them, since the confusion results not so much from their similarity as from the subtlety of the distinction that they mark.

From a conceptual viewpoint, value is doubtless one element in signification, and it is difficult to see how signification can be dependent upon value and still be distinct from it. But we must clear up the issue or risk reducing language to a simple naming-process.

Let us first take signification as it is generally understood and as it was pictured on page 67. As the arrows in the drawing show, it is only the counterpart of the sound-image. Everything that occurs concerns only the sound-image and the concept when we look upon the word as independent and self-contained.

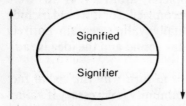

But here is the paradox: on the one hand the concept seems to be the counterpart of the sound-image, and on the other hand the sign itself is in turn the counterpart of the other signs of language.

Language is a system of interdependent terms in which the value of each term results solely from the simultaneous presence of the others, as in the diagram:

How, then, can value be confused with signification, i.e. the counterpart of the sound-image? It seems impossible to liken the relations represented here by horizontal arrows to those represented above (p. 10) by vertical arrows. Putting it another way – and again taking up the example of the sheet of paper that is cut in two (see p. 9) – it is clear that the observable relation between the different pieces A, B, C, D, etc. is distinct from the relation between the front and back of the same piece as in A/A′, B/B′, etc.

To resolve the issue, let us observe from the outset that even outside language all values are apparently governed by the same paradoxical principle. They are always composed:

(1) of a *dissimilar* thing that can be *exchanged* for the thing of which the value is to be determined; and

(2) of *similar* things that can be *compared* with the thing of which the value is to be determined.

Both factors are necessary for the existence of a value. To determine what a five-franc piece is worth one must therefore know: (1) that it can be exchanged for a fixed quantity of a different thing, e.g. bread; and (2) that it can be compared with a similar value of the same system, e.g. a one-franc piece, or with coins of another system (a dollar, etc.). In the same way a word can be exchanged for something dissimilar, an idea; besides, it can be compared with something of the same nature, another word. Its value is therefore not fixed so long as one simply states that it can be 'exchanged' for a given concept, i.e. that it has this or that signification: one must also compare it with similar values, with other words that stand in opposition to it. Its content is really fixed only by the concurrence of everything that exists outside it. Being part of a system, it is endowed not only with a signification but also and especially with a value and this is something quite different.

A few examples will show clearly that this is true. Modern French *mouton* can have the same signification as English *sheep* but not the same value, and this for several reasons, particularly because in speaking of a piece of meat ready to be served on the table, English uses *mutton* and not *sheep*. The difference in value between *sheep* and *mouton* is due to the fact that *sheep* has beside it a second term while the French word does not.

Within the same language, all words used to express related ideas limit each other reciprocally; synonyms like French *redouter* 'dread,' *craindre* 'fear,' and *avoir peur* 'be afraid' have value only through their opposition: if *redouter* did not exist, all its content would go to its competitors. Conversely, some words are enriched through contact with others: e.g. the new element introduced in *décrépit* (un vieillard *décrépit*) results from the co-existence of *décrépi* (un mur *décrépi*). The value of just any term is accordingly determined by its environment; it is impossible to fix even the value of the word signifying 'sun' without first considering its surroundings: in some languages it is not possible to say 'sit in the *sun*'.

Everything said about words applies to any term of language, e.g. to grammatical entities. The value of a French plural does not coincide with that of a Sanskrit plural even though their signification is usually identical; Sanskrit has three numbers instead of two (*my eyes, my ears, my arms, my legs*, etc. are dual);[1] it would be wrong to attribute the same value to the plural in Sanskrit and in French; its value clearly depends on what is outside and around it.

If words stood for pre-existing concepts, they would all have exact equivalents in meaning from one language to the next; but this is not true. French uses *louer* (*une maison*) 'let (a house)' indifferently to mean both 'pay for' and 'receive payment for', whereas German uses two words, *mieten* and *vermieten*; there is obviously no exact correspondence of values. The German verbs *schätzen* and *urteilen* share a number of significations, but that correspondence does not hold at several points.

Inflection offers some particularly striking examples. Distinctions of time, which are so familiar to us, are unknown in certain languages. Hebrew does not recognize even the fundamental distinctions between the past, present, and future. Proto-Germanic has no special form for the future; to say that the future is expressed by the present is wrong, for the value of the present is not the same in Germanic as in languages that have a future along with the present. The Slavic languages regularly single out two aspects of the verb: the perfective represents action as a point, complete in its totality; the imperfective represents it as taking place, and on the line of time. The categories are difficult for a Frenchman to understand, for they are unknown in French; if they were predetermined, this would not be true. Instead of pre-existing ideas then, we find in all the foregoing examples *values* emanating from the system. When they are said to correspond to concepts, it is understood that the concepts are purely differential and defined not by their positive content but negatively by their relations with the other terms of the system. Their most precise characteristic is in being what the others are not.

Now the real interpretation of the diagram of the signal becomes apparent. Thus

---

[1] The use of the comparative form for two and the superlative for more than two in English (e.g. *may the* better *boxer win: the* best *boxer in the world*) is probably a remnant of the old distinction between the dual and the plural number. [Tr.]

means that in French the concept 'to judge' is linked to the sound-image *juger*; in short, it symbolizes signification. But it is quite clear that initially the concept is nothing, that is only a value determined by its relations with other similar values, and that without them the signification would not exist. If I state simply that a word signifies something when I have in mind the associating of a sound-image with a concept, I am making a statement that may suggest what actually happens, but by no means am I expressing the linguistic fact in its essence and fullness.

3 Linguistic Value from a Material Viewpoint

The conceptual side of value is made up solely of relations and differences with respect to the other terms of language, and the same can be said of its material side. The important thing in the word is not the sound alone but the phonic differences that make it possible to distinguish this word from all others, for differences carry signification.

This may seem surprising, but how indeed could the reverse be possible? Since one vocal image is no better suited than the next for what it is commissioned to express, it is evident, even *a priori*, that a segment of language can never in the final analysis be based on anything except its noncoincidence with the rest. *Arbitrary* and *differential* are two correlative qualities.

The alteration of linguistic signs clearly illustrates this. It is precisely because the terms *a* and *b* as such are radically incapable of reaching the level of consciousness – one is always conscious of only the *a/b* difference – that each term is free to change according to laws that are unrelated to its signifying function. No positive sign characterizes the genitive plural in Czech *žen*; still the two forms *žena*: *žen* function as well as the earlier forms *žena*: *ženb*; *žen* has value only because it is different.

Here is another example that shows even more clearly the systematic role of phonic differences: in Greek, *éphēn* is an imperfect and *éstēn* an aorist although both words are formed in the same way; the first belongs to the system of the present indicative of *phēmí* 'I say,' whereas there is no present *stēmi*; now it is precisely the relation *phēmí*: *éphēn* that corresponds to the relation between the present and the imperfect (cf. *déiknūmi: edéikūn,* etc.). Signs function, then, not through their intrinsic value but through their relative position.

In addition, it is impossible for sound alone, a material element, to belong to language. It is only a secondary thing, substance to be put to use. All our conventional values have the characteristic of not being confused with the tangible element which supports them. For instance, it is not the metal in a piece of money that fixes its value. A coin nominally worth five francs may contain less than half its worth of silver. Its value will vary according to the amount stamped upon it and according to its use inside or outside a political boundary. This is even more true of the linguistic signifier, which is not phonic but incorporeal – constituted not by its material substance but by the differences that separate its sound-image from all others.

The foregoing principle is so basic that it applies to all the material elements of language, including phonemes. Every language forms its words on the basis of a system of sonorous elements, each element being a clearly delimited unit and one of a fixed number of units. Phonemes are characterized not, as one might think, by their own positive quality but simply by the fact that they are distinct. Phonemes are above all else opposing, relative, and negative entities.

Proof of this is the latitude that speakers have between points of convergence in the pronunciation of distinct sounds. In French, for instance, general use of a dorsal *r* does not prevent many speakers from using a tongue-tip trill; language is not in the least disturbed by it; language requires only that the sound be different and not, as one might imagine, that it have an invariable quality. I can even pronounce the French *r* like German *ch* in *Bach, doch*, etc., but in German I could not use *r* instead of *ch*, for German gives recognition to both elements and must keep them apart.

. . . .

4 The Sign Considered in Its Totality

Everything that has been said up to this point boils down to this: in language there are only differences. Even more important: a difference generally implies positive terms between which the difference is set up; but in language there are only differences *without positive terms*. Whether we take the signified or the signifier, language has neither ideas nor sounds that existed before the linguistic system, but only conceptual and phonic differences that have issued from the system. The idea or phonic substance that a sign contains is of less importance than the other signs that surround it. Proof of this is that the value of a term may be modified without either its meaning or its sound being affected, solely because a neighboring term has been modified (see p. 11).

But the statement that everything in language is negative is true only if the signified and the signifier are considered separately; when we consider the sign in its totality, we have something that is positive in its own class. A linguistic system is a series of differences of sound combined with a series of differences of ideas; but the pairing of a certain number of acoustical signs with as many cuts made from the mass of thought engenders a system of values; and this system serves as the effective link between the phonic and psychological elements within each sign. Although both the signified and the signifier are purely differential and negative when considered separately, their combination is a positive fact; it is even the sole type of facts that language has, for maintaining the parallelism between the two classes of differences is the distinctive function of the linguistic institution.

SECTION TWO
RUSSIAN FORMALISM

Terry Eagleton has suggested that '. . . if one wanted to put a date on the beginnings of the transformation which has overtaken literary theory in this century, one could do worse than settle on 1917, the year in which the young Russian Formalist Viktor Shklovsky published his pioneering essay ("Art as Device" ' (1983). Though formalist work predates the recent theoretical revolution by some forty-odd years, its stress on the systematic study of literature links it with the work which initially broke with the traditional critical orthodoxy in the 1960s. Indeed, Formalist work only became more widely available and influential in the post-60s period.

Russian Formalism is the name now given to a mode of criticism that emerged from two groups, The Moscow Linguistic Circle (1915) and the _Opojaz_ group (standing for The Society for the Study of Poetic Language) (1916). The main figures in the movement were Roman Jakobson, Viktor Shklovsky, Boris Eichenbaum, Boris Tomashevsky and Yuri Tynyanov. Jakobson was also involved in the later Prague Linguistic Circle (1926–39), which developed some of the Formalist's concerns. Influenced by Futurism and Futurist poetry, and reacting against Symbolism's mystification of poetry (though not against its emphasis on form), they sought to place the study of literature on a scientific basis; their investigation concentrated on the language and the formal devices of literary works.

Although Russian Formalism is often likened to the American New Criticism of the 1950s because of a similar emphasis on close critical attention to the text, the Russian Formalists were, in fact, more interested in method and a scientific approach. Russian Formalism emphasized a differential definition of literature, as opposed to the New Criticism's isolation and objectification of the single text; they also rejected the mimetic/expressive function of literature more strongly. The New Criticism, while challenging some of the views of the traditional orthodoxy, remained within the humanist problematic (Belsey 1980). Russian Formalism moves away from the view of the text as reflecting an essential unity which is ultimately one of moral or humanistic significance. The central focus of the movement was not literature *per se*, but *literariness*, that which makes a given work a 'literary' work. In this sense they sought to uncover the system of the literary discourse, the system that made literature possible. Their interests in texts centred on the functioning of literary devices rather than on content; literariness was to do with a special use of language.

Shklovsky's essay 'Art as Technique' was one of the first important contributions to the Russian Formalist movement. In it he develops the key notion of 'defamiliarization' (*ostranenie* – making strange). What literary language does is to 'make strange' or defamiliarize habituated perception and ordinary language. The key to defamiliarization is the literary device, for the 'device' impedes perception, draws attention to the artifice of the text and de-habituates automatized perception. (Formalists tend to be more interested in texts which 'lay bare the device' and which eschew realistic motivation, hence their privileging of difficult or modernist works).

One of the most important implications of this is that logically it must lead to a view of literature as a *relational* system rather than an absolute one, and a system that is bound to change through history. Literary devices cannot remain strange for all time, they too become automatized, so that new literature has to produce new defamiliarizational devices to avoid habituated perception. Such a view must see the literary tradition not as a seamless continuity, but as discontinuity, where breaks and reformations in form and formal devices continually renew the system.

The work of the Russian Formalists has proved fertile ground for later transformations in critical practice. In defining the object of inquiry as that of 'literariness' they gave a systematic inflection to the study of literature, one that went beyond intrinsic study of the individual text.

---

2   Victor Shklovsky,

From 'Art as Technique', *Russian Formalist Criticism*; *Four Essays,* **trans & ed L.T. Lemon & M.J. Reis**

p11–15, 18.

If we start to examine the general laws of perception, we see that as perception becomes habitual, it becomes automatic. Thus, for example, all of our habits retreat into the area of the unconsciously automatic; if one remembers the sensations of holding a pen or of speaking in a foreign language for the first time and compares that with his feeling at performing the action for the ten thousandth time, he will agree with us. Such habituation explains the principles by which, in ordinary speech, we leave phrases unfinished and words half expressed. In this process, ideally realized in algebra, things are replaced by symbols. Complete words are not expressed in rapid speech; their initial sounds are barely perceived. Alexander Pogodin offers the example of a boy considering the sentence 'The Swiss mountains are beautiful' in the form of a series of letters: *T, S, m, a, b.*[1]

This characteristic of thought not only suggests the method of algebra, but even prompts the choice of symbols (letters, especially initial letters). By this 'algebraic' method of thought we apprehend objects only as shapes with imprecise extensions; we do not see them in their entirety but rather recognize them by their main characteristics. We see the object as though it were enveloped in a sack. We know what it is by its con-figuration, but we see only its silhouette. The object, perceived thus in the manner of prose perception, fades and does not leave even a first impression; ultimately even the essence of what it was is forgotten. Such perception explains why we fail to hear the prose word in its entirety (see Leo Jakubinsky's article[2]) and, hence, why (along with other slips of the tongue) we fail to pronounce it. The process of 'algebrization', the over-automatization of an object, permits the greatest economy of perceptive effort. Either objects are assigned only one proper feature – a number, for example – or else they function as though by formula and do not even appear in cognition:

> I was cleaning a room and, meandering about, approached the divan and couldn't remember whether or not I had dusted it. Since these movements are habitual and unconscious, I could not remember and felt that it was impos-sible to remember – so that if I had dusted it and forgot – that is, had acted unconsciously, then it was the same as if I had not. If some conscious person had been watching, then the fact could be established. If, however, no one was looking, or looking on unconsciously, if the whole complex lives of many people go on unconsciously, then such lives are as if they had never been.[3]

And so life is reckoned as nothing. Habitualization devours works, clothes, furniture, one's wife, and the fear of war. 'If the whole complex lives of many people go on unconsciously, then such lives are as if they had never been.' And art exists that one may recover the sensation of life;

---

[1] Alexander Pogodin, *Yazyk, kak tvorchestvo* (*Language as Art*) (Kharkov, 1913), p. 42. (The original sentence was in French, '*Les montaignes de la Suisse sont belles,*' with the appropriate initials.)

[2] Jakubinsky, *Sborniki*, I (1916).

[3] Leo Tolstoy's *Diary*, entry dated February 29, 1987. (The date is transcribed incorrectly; it should read March 1, 1897).

it exists to make one feel things, to make the stone *stony*. The purpose of art is to impart the sensation of things as they are perceived and not as they are known. The technique of art is to make objects *'unfamiliar,'* to make forms difficult, to increase the difficulty and length of perception because the process of perception is an aesthetic end in itself and must be prolonged. *Art is a way of experiencing the artfullness of an object; the object is not important.*

The range of poetic (artistic) work extends from the sensory to the cognitive, from poetry to prose, from the concrete to the abstract: from Cervantes' Don Quixote – scholastic and poor nobleman, half consciously bearing his humiliation in the court of the duke – to the broad but empty Don Quixote of Turgenev; from Charlemagne to the name "king" (in russian "Charles" and "king" obviously derive from the same root, *korol*). The meaning of a work broadens to the extent that artfulness and artistry diminish; thus a fable symbolizes more than a poem, and a proverb more than a fable. Consequently, the least self-contradictory part of Potebnya's theory is his treatment of the fable, which, from his point of view, he investigated thoroughly. But since his theory did not provide for 'expressive' works of art, he could not finish his book. As we know, *Notes on the Theory of Literature* was published in 1905, thirteen years after Potebnya's death. Potebnya himself completed only the section on the fable.[4]

After we see an object several times, we begin to recognize it. The object is in front of us and we know about it, but we do not see it[5] – hence we cannot say anything significant about it. Art removes objects from the automatism of perception in several ways. Here I want to illustrate a way used repeatedly by Leo Tolstoy, that writer who, for Merezhkovsky at least, seems to present things as if he himself saw them, saw them in their entirety, and did not alter them.

Tolstoy makes the familiar seem strange by not naming the familiar object. He describes an object as if he were seeing it for the first time, an event as if it were happening for the first time. In describing something he avoids the accepted names of its parts and instead names corresponding parts of other objects. For example, in 'Shame' Tolstoy 'defamiliarizes' the idea of flogging in this way: 'to strip people who have broken the law, to hurl them to the floor, and to rap on their bottoms with switches,' and, after a few lines, 'to lash about on the naked buttocks.' Then he remarks:

> Just why precisely this stupid, savage means of causing pain and not any other – why not prick the shoulders or any part of the body with needles, squeeze the hands or the feet in a vise, or anything like that?

[4] Alexander Potebnya, *Iz lektsy po teorii slovesnosti* (*Lectures on the Theory of Language*) (Kharkov, 1914).

[5] Victor Shklovsky, *Voskresheniye slova* (*The Resurrection of the Word*) (Petersburg, 1914).

I apologize for this harsh example, but it is typical of Tolstoy's way of pricking the conscience. The familiar act of flogging is made unfamiliar both by the description and by the proposal to change its form without changing its nature. Tolstoy uses this technique of 'defamiliarization' constantly. The narrator of 'Kholstomer', for example, is a horse, and it is the horse's point of view (rather than a person's) that makes the content of the story seem unfamiliar. Here is how the horse regards the institution of private property:

> I understood well what they said about whipping and Christianity. But then I was absolutely in the dark. What's the meaning of 'his own', 'his colt'? From these phrases I saw that people thought there was some sort of connection between me and the stable. At the time I simply could not understand the connection. Only much later, when they separated me from the other horses, did I begin to understand. But even then I simply could not see what it meant when they called me 'man's property'. The words 'my horse' referred to me, a living horse, and seemed as strange to me as the words 'my land', 'my air', 'my water'.
>
> But the words made a strong impression on me. I thought about them constantly, and only after the most diverse experiences with people did I understand, finally, what they meant. They meant this: In life people are guided by words, not by deeds. It's not so much that they love the possibility of doing or not doing something as it is the possibility of speaking with words, agreed on among themselves, about various topics. Such are the words 'my' and 'mine', which they apply to different things, creatures, objects, and even to land, people, and horses. They agree that only one may say 'mine' about this, that, or the other thing. And the one who says 'mine' about the greatest number of things is, according to the game which they've agreed to among themselves, the one they consider the most happy. I don't know the point of all this, but it's true. For a long time I tried to explain it to myself in terms of some kind of real gain, but I had to reject that explanation because it was wrong.
>
> Many of those, for instance, who called me their own never rode on me – although others did. And so with those who fed me. Then again, the coachman, the veterinarians, and the outsiders in general treated me kindly, yet those who called me their own did not. In due time, having widened the scope of my observations, I satisfied myself that the notion 'my', not only in relation to us horses, has no other basis than a narrow human instinct which is called a sense of or right to private property. A man says 'this house is mine' and never lives in it; he only worries about its construction and upkeep. A merchant says 'my shop', 'my dry goods shop', for instance, and does not even wear clothes made from the better cloth he keeps in his own shop.
>
> There are people who call a tract of land their own, but they never set eyes on it and never take a stroll on it. There are people who call others their own, yet never see them. And the whole relationship between them is that the so-called 'owners' treat the others unjustly.
>
> There are people who call women their own, or their 'wives', but their women live with other men. And people strive not for the good in life, but for goods they can call their own.
>
> I am now convinced that this is the essential difference between people and

ourselves. And therefore, not even considering the other ways in which we are superior, but considering just this one virtue, we can bravely claim to stand higher than men on the ladder of living creatures. The actions of men, at least those with whom I have had dealings, are guided by *words* – ours, by deeds.

The horse is killed before the end of the story, but the manner of the narrative, its technique, does not change:

> Much later they put Serpukhovsky's body, which had experienced the world, which had eaten and drunk, into the ground. They could profitably send neither his hide, nor his flesh, nor his bones anywhere.
>
> But since his dead body, which had gone about in the world for twenty years, was a great burden to everyone, its burial was only a superfluous embarrassment for the people. For a long time no one had needed him, for a long time he had been a burden on all. But nevertheless, the dead who buried the dead found it necessary to dress this bloated body, which immediately began to rot, in a good uniform and good boots; to lay it in a good new coffin with new tassels at the four corners, then to place this new coffin in another of lead and ship it to Moscow; there to exhume ancient bones and at just that spot, to hide this putrefying body, swarming with maggots, in its new uniform and clean boots, and to cover it over completely with dirt.

Thus we see that at the end of the story Tolstoy continues to use the technique even though the motivation for it (the reason for its use) is gone.

. . . .

The technique of defamiliarization is not Tolstoy's alone. I cited Tolstoy because his work is generally known.

Now, having explained the nature of this technique, let us try to determine the approximate limits of its application. I personally feel that defamiliarization is found almost everywhere form is found. In other words, the difference between Potebnya's point of view and ours is this: An image is not a permanent referent for those mutable complexities of life which are revealed through it; its purpose is not to make us perceive meaning, but to create a special perception of the object – *it creates a 'vision' of the object instead of serving as a means for knowing it.*

SECTION THREE
STRUCTURALISM

Though structuralism developed out of Saussure's pioneering work on language, it was not until the 1960s and 1970s that it found its most widespread influence and application. Generally recognized as 'arriving' in France in the mid-1960s, it gradually made an impact on Anglo-American investigation in the human sciences, including literature. This mode of investigation has been called semiotics as well as structuralism and though these terms are virtually synonymous some difference in orientation is apparent (see Eagleton 1983, p. 100). Literary Structuralism of this period finds its most powerful advocates in such figures as Roland Barthes, Umberto Eco, Tzvetan Todorov, A.J. Greimas and Gérard Gennette. Saussure's influence is readily apparent in the terms and concepts literary structuralism deploys, however, the impetus for its development was also provided by such work as the structural anthropology of Lévi-Strauss and Roman Jakobson's studies of language (see Hawkes 1977).

In the *Course in General Linguistics*, Saussure had proposed, in a couple of programmatic statements, a 'general science of signs' based on his theory of language. He called this putative science 'semiology' and suggested that the method it inaugurates could be applied to more than just the language system. Recognizing that verbal language, although the most important, was only one among many sign systems, semiology would be widely applicable. Indeed, Saussure's suggestions are taken up in structuralism, where his theory of language is used as the basis for a critical model which investigates a diverse range of cultural phenomena.

However, structuralism is more than a methodology; its debt to Saussure goes beyond an analytic model, for inscribed in his theory is the potential for a radical epistemology. Saussure, as we have seen in section 1, viewed the linguistic sign as arbitrary and as having meaning only because it participates in a system of conventions. Meaning is dependent upon differential relations among elements within a system, i.e. it is *diacritical* not *referential*. In fact, structuralism is not particularly interested in meaning *per se*, but rather in attempting to describe and understand the conventions and modes of signification which make it possible to 'mean'; that is, it seeks to discover the *conditions* of meaning. So *langue* is more important than *parole* – system is more important than individual utterance. Concentration on the system led Todorov to advocate a 'poetics' which would provide a general grammar of literature, or a 'langue' of which the individual work is a 'parole'. Barthes, in *Elements of Semiology* (1964) and *Système de la Mode* (1967), working on broader cultural phenomena, assumes that an individual utterance – whether the wearing of clothes or the articulation of verbal sounds in a conversation – presupposes a system (of fashion or of language) which generates the possibility of meaning for those utterances. The first task of structuralism is to describe and analyse that system so structuralists usually begin their analysis by seeking general principles in individual works, though there is also a tendency to explain/interpret individual works by referring to those general principles.

Like Russian Formalism, structuralism believes in the possibility of a 'science' of literature, one based on form rather than content. For structuralism, such a science means it could potentially master and explain the world of signs through exhaustive detailing and analysing of the systems that allowed those signs to speak. Though this science would itself have to be carried out in language (the dominant sign system) the language of criticism was deemed to be a 'metalanguage' – that is, a language that can speak about and explain the workings of 'object' languages (languages that seem to speak directly about the world). Structuralism's claim to be operating through a metalanguage cannot, however, overcome the criticism that it is actually no more than a powerful interpretive schema for analysing texts. Moreover, while rejecting the idea of a unified meaning occupying the text, structuralism still seeks unity or unification in the literary system as a whole, recourse to which can then 'explain' the individual work. It also tends to treat the text as a function of the system of literature, divorcing it from historical and social context.

In the initial break with orthodox critical practice structuralism tended to be caught between being used simply as a method for analysing literature and the literary text, and being adopted as an epistemology – as a way of understanding the mode of existence of literature and the text. The two essays reprinted here illustrate, through their different inflections, the two sides of this moment of structuralism. Roland Barthes's essay dates from 1966; this was the beginning of the period when his work was undergoing transformation from a structuralist to a post-structuralist orientation, and elements of both can be traced in this article. We have included it here for that reason and because it outlines the grounds on which the epistemological break with traditional criticism was made. Though David Lodge's essay dates from 1980, we have placed this before the Barthes piece since it provides a clear and concise summary of the methods and approaches that structuralist and formalist-structuralist work offered and because it quite explicitly assesses the usefulness of those methods as interpretive tools.

---

3   David Lodge,
'Analysis and Interpretation of the Realist Text', *Poetics Today*, Vol 1;4 (1980)*

p5–22

I

It is a commonplace that the systematic study of narrative was founded by Aristotle, and scarcely an exaggeration to say that little of significance was added to those foundations until the twentieth century. Narrative theory in the intervening period was mainly directed (or misdirected) at deducing from Aristotle's penetrating analysis of the system of Greek tragedy a set of prescriptive rules for the writing of epic. The rise of the novel as a distinctive and eventually dominant literary form finally exposed the poverty of neoclassical narrative theory, without for a long time generating anything much more satisfactory. The realistic novel set peculiar problems for any formalist criticism because it worked by disguising or denying its own conventionality. It therefore invited – and received – criticism which was interpretative and evaluative rather than analytical. It was not until the late nineteenth and early twentieth centuries that something like a poetics of fiction began to evolve from the self-conscious experiments of novelists themselves, and was elaborated by literary critics. At about the same time, developments in linguistics, folklore and anthropology stimulated a more broad-ranging study of narrative, beyond the boundaries of modern literary fiction. For a long time these investigations were pursued on parallel tracks which seldom

* Paper presented at *Synopsis* 2: 'Narrative Theory and Poetics of Fiction,' an international symposium held at The Porter Institute for Poetics and Semiotics, Tel Aviv University, and the Van Leer Jerusalem Foundation, 16–22 June 1979. For the text of the story – see Appendix.

converged. In the last couple of decades, however, the Anglo-American tradition of formalist criticism, essentially empirical and text-based, theoretically rather underpowered but critically productive, has encountered the more systematic, abstract, theoretically rigorous and 'scientific' tradition of European structuralist criticism. The result has been a minor 'knowledge explosion' in the field of narrative theory and poetics of fiction.

The question I wish to raise in this paper is whether progress in theory and methodology means progress in the critical reading of texts.[1] Is it possible, or useful, to bring the whole battery of modern formalism and structuralism to bear upon a single text, and what is gained by so doing? Does it enrich our reading by uncovering depths and nuances of meaning we might not otherwise have brought to consciousness, help us to solve problems of interpretation and to correct misreadings? Or does it merely encourage a pointless and self-indulgent academicism, by which the same information is shuffled from one set of categories to another, from one jargon to another, without any real advance in appreciation or understanding? The analysis offered here of a short story by Ernest Hemingway is intended to support a positive answer to the first set of questions, a negative answer to the second set. But first it may be useful to remind ourselves of the range and variety of theories, methodologies and 'approaches' now available to the critic of fiction. I would group them into three categories, according to the 'depth' at which they address themselves to narrative structure.

1 Narratology and Narrative Grammar – i.e., the effort to discover the *langue* of narrative, the underlying system of rules and possibilities of which any narrative *parole* (text) is the realization. With a few arguable exceptions – e.g., Northrop Frye (1957) and Frank Kermode (1966) – this enterprise has been almost exclusively dominated by European scholars – Propp, Bremond, Greimas, Lévi-Strauss, Todorov and Barthes, among others. Crucial to this tradition of enquiry are the ideas of function and transformation. In the theory of Greimas for instance, all narrative consists essentially of the transfer of an object or value from one actant to another. An actant performs a certain function in the story which may be classified as Subject or Object, Sender or Receiver, Helper or Opponent, and is involved in doing things which may be classified as performative (tests, struggles, etc.), contractual (establishment and breaking of contracts) and disjunctional (departure and returns). These functions are not simply identifiable from the structure of a narrative text: for instance, several characters may perform the function of one

---

[1] I do not mean to imply that theory can only be justified on such grounds. Theoretical research may have a purpose and value quite independent of its application to particular problems. I merely wish to consider whether exponents of 'practical', or descriptive and interpretative, criticism have anything useful to learn from recent developments in the theory of narrative and poetics of fiction.

actant, or one character may combine the functions of two actants. All concepts are semantically defined by a binary relationship with their opposites (e.g., Life/Death) or negatives (e.g., Life : Death::Non-Life : Non-Death), so that all narrative can be seen as the transformation into actants and actions of a thematic four-term homology (Greimas, 1966, 1970, 1976).

It is often said that this kind of approach is more rewarding when applied to narratives of a traditional, formulaic and orally transmitted type, rather than sophisticated literary narratives; and the exponents of narratology themselves frequently remind us that their aim is not the explication of texts but the uncovering of the system that allows narrative texts to be generated and competent readers to make sense of them. Narratology does however bring to the attention of the literary critic factors involved in reading narrative that are important, but in a sense so obvious that they tend to be overlooked. Roland Barthes (1975, 1977) has very fruitfully applied to the analysis of literary fictions the idea, derived from structuralist narratology, that narrative is divisible into sequences that open or close possibilities for the characters, and thus for the reader. The interest of these openings and closures may be either retrospective, contributing to the solution of some enigma proposed earlier in the text (the hermeneutic code) or prospective, making the audience wonder what will happen next (the proairetic code). Suspense and curiosity are therefore the two basic 'affects' aroused by narrative. A story of any sophistication will also, as Kermode points out (1966:18), make use of what Aristotle called peripeteia, or reversal, when a possibility is closed in a way that is unexpected and yet plausible and instructive. The reversal tends to produce an effect of irony, especially if it is anticipated by the audience.

Two problems arise in applying this kind of approach to realistic fiction. If we segment a text into its smallest units of information, how do we identify those which are functional on the basic narrative level, and what do we do with those units (the majority) which are not? Roland Barthes suggests one solution in his 'Introduction to the Structural Analysis of Narratives' (1977) where, drawing his illustrations mainly from Ian Fleming's *Goldfinger*, he classifies the narrative units as either *nuclei* or *catalyzers*. Nuclei open or close alternatives that are of direct consequence for the subsequent development of the narrative and cannot be deleted without altering the story. Catalyzers are merely consecutive units which expand the nuclei or fill up the space between them. They can be deleted without altering the narrative, though not, in the case of realistic narrative, without altering its meaning and effect, since segments which connect not, or not only, with segments at the same level, but with some more generalized concept such as the psychological make-up of the characters, or the atmosphere of the story, function as *indices*, or (if merely factual) *informants*. Jonathan Culler has suggested that our ability to distinguish nuclei from catalyzers intuitively and to rank them in order of importance is a typical manifestation of reader-competence, verified by the fact that different readers will tend to summarize the plot of a given story in the same way. The intuitive recognition or ranking of nuclei is 'governed by readers' desire to reach an ultimate summary in which plot as a whole is grasped in a satisfying form' (1975:139). In short, the structural coherence of narratives is inseparable from their meaning, and reading them is inseparable from forming hypotheses about their overall meaning.

2 *Poetics of Fiction* Under this head I include all attempts to describe and classify techniques of fictional representation. The great break-through in this field in the modern era was undoubtedly the Russian Formalists' distinction between *fabula* and *sjuzhet*: on the one hand the story in its most neutral, objective, chronological form – the story as it might have been enacted in real time and space, a seamless continuum of innumerable contiguous events; and on the other hand, the actual text in which this story is imitated, with all its inevitable (but motivated) gaps, elisions, emphases and reorderings. Work along these lines in Europe, culminating in Gérard Genette's 'Discours du Récit' (1972), established two principal areas in which *sjuzhet* significantly modifies *fabula*: time, and what is generally called 'point of view' in Anglo-American criticism – though Genette correctly distinguishes here between 'per-spective' (who sees the action) and 'voice' (who speaks the narration of it). He also distinguishes most suggestively three different categories in the temporal organization (or deformation) of the *fabula* by the *sjuzhet*: order, duration and frequency.

The choices made by the narrative artist at this level are in a sense prior to, or 'deeper' than, his stylistic choices in composing the surface structure of the text, though they place important constraints upon what he can achieve in the surface structure. They are also of manifest impor-tance in the realistic novel which, compared to other, earlier narrative forms, is characterized by a carefully discriminated, pseudo-historical treatment of temporality, and a remarkable depth and flexibility in its presentation of consciousness.

A good deal of Anglo-American critical theorizing about the novel, from Percy Lubbock's *The Craft of Fiction* (1921) to Wayne Booth's *The Rhetoric of Fiction* (1961) was implicitly, if unconsciously, based on the same distinction between *fabula* and *sjuzhet*, between 'story' and 'way of telling it'. The cross-fertilization of the two critical traditions has produced much interesting and illuminating work, analyzing and classi-fying novelistic techniques and covering such matters as tense, person, speech and indirect speech in fictional narrative; and we are now, it seems to me, within sight of a truly comprehensive taxonomy of fictional form at this level. Two recent books which have made particularly

valuable contributions in this respect are Seymour Chatman (1978) and
the more narrowly focused work of Dorrit Cohn (1978).

3 *Rhetorical Analysis* By this I mean analyzing the surface structure of
narrative texts to show how the linguistic mediation of a story determines
its meaning and effect. This is a kind of criticism in which Anglo-
American tradition is comparatively strong, because of the close-reading
techniques developed by New Criticism. Mark Shorer's essays (1948)
and (1949) are classic statements of this approach. The stylistics that
developed out of Romance Philology, represented at its best by Spitzer
and Auerbach, also belongs in this category. When I wrote my first book
of criticism, *Language of Fiction* (1966), this seemed the best route by
which to achieve a formalist critique of the realistic novel.

The underlying aim of this criticism was to demonstrate that what
looked like redundant or random detail in realistic fiction was in fact
functional, contributing to a pattern of motifs with expressive and thematic significance. Much of this criticism was therefore concerned with
tracing symbolism and keywords in the verbal texture of novels. Though
very few of the New Critics were aware of the work of Roman Jakobson,
he provided a theoretical justification for this kind of criticism in his
famous definition of literariness, or the poetic function of language, as
'the projection of the principle of equivalence from the axis of selection
to the axis of combination' (1960:358). What the New Critics called
'spatial form' (Joseph Frank, 1948) was precisely a pattern of paradigmatic equivalences concealed in the narrative syntagm. Furthermore,
as I tried to show in my book *The Modes of Modern Writing* (1977), in
his distinction between metaphor and metonymy, Jakobson (1965) provided a key to understanding how the realistic novel contrives to build up
a pattern of equivalences without violating its illusion of life.

The argument is briefly as follows: metaphor and metonymy (or
synecdoche) are both figures of equivalence, but generated by different
processes, metaphor according to similarity between things otherwise
different, metonymy according to continuity or association between part
and whole, cause and effect, thing and attribute, etc. Thus, if I transform the literal sentence 'Ships sail the sea' into 'Keels plough the deep',
plough is equivalent to 'sail' because of the similarity between the movement of a plough through the earth and/or a ship through the sea, but
keel is equivalent to 'ship' because it is part of a ship (synecdoche) and
deep equivalent to 'sea' because it is an attribute of the sea (metonymy).
In fact, metonymy is a non-logical (and therefore foregrounded or rhetorical) condensation achieved by transformations of kernel sentences by
deletion (*the keels of the ships* condensed to *keels* rather than *ships*, deep
sea to *deep* rather than *sea*). Metonymy thus plays with the combination
axis of language as metaphor plays with the selection axis of language,
and together they epitomize the two ways by which any discourse

connects one topic with another: either because they are similar or because they are contiguous. Jackobson's distinction thus allows the analyst to move freely between deep structure and surface structure.

Realistic fiction is dominantly metonymic in a double sense: it connects actions that are contiguous in time and space and connected by cause and effect, but since it cannot describe exhaustively, the narrative *sjuzhet* is always in a metonymic relation to the *fabula*. The narrative text necessarily selects certain details and suppresses or deletes others. The selected details are thus foregrounded by being selected, and their recurrence and interrelation with other selected details in the text become aesthetically significant (what the Prague School calls systematic internal foregrounding). If these selected details are rhetorically mediated, through the use of the actual figures of metonymy and synecdoche, or of metaphor and simile a denser and more overt pattern of equivalences is generated, but such rhetoric is not essential to the process, which is usually called symbolism in Anglo-American criticism. Barthes defined it as connotation, the device by which one signified acts as the signifier of another signified. Jakobson's distinction enables us to distinguish four different ways in which it operates:

A. Metonymic Signified I metonymically evokes Signified II (e.g., hearth fires in Charlotte Bronte's *Jane Eyre* symbolize domestic comfort, intimacy, security, etc.).

B. Metonymic Signified I metaphorically evokes Signified II (e.g., mud and fog at the beginning of *Bleak House* symbolize obfuscation and degradation of goodness and justice by the law).

C. Metaphoric Signified I metonymically evokes Signified II (e.g., the description of the night in Llaregyb in Dylan Thomas's *Under Milk Wood* as 'bible-black' symbolizes the Protestant chapel-going religious culture of the community).

D. Metaphoric Signified II metaphorically evokes Signified I (e.g., in the opening lines of Yeats's poem, 'The Second Coming':

Turning and turning in the widening gyre
The falcon cannot hear the falconer

the metaphor *gyre* applied to the spiraling movement of the falcon also symbolizes the cyclical movement of history. Realistic fiction relies principally upon symbolism of types A and B.

II

No choice of a text for illustrative purposes is innocent, and no analysis of a single text could possibly provide universally valid answers to the questions posed at the beginning of this paper. These questions will

not be settled until we have a significant corpus of synthetic or pluralistic readings of narrative texts of various types. Two distinguished
achievements of this kind come to mind: Barthes' *S/Z* and Christine
Brooke-Rose's study of *The Turn of the Screw* (1976-7). The following discussion of Hemingway's short story 'Cat in the Rain' (1958) is
necessarily much more modest in scope and scale. Two considerations
prompted the choice of this story, apart from its convenient brevity:
(1) A staff seminar on it in my own Department at Birmingham revealed
that it presents certain problems of interpretation, though without being
quite so heavily encrusted with the deposits of previous readings and misreadings as *The Turn of the Screw*. (2) It is both realistic and modern,
cutting across that historicist and tendentious distinction between the
lisible and the *scriptible* which I personally find one of the less helpful
features of the work of Barthes and his disciples. The implied notion of
vraisemblance on which Hemingway's story depends, the assumed
relationship between the text and reality, is essentially continuous with
that of classic bourgeois realism, yet in the experience of readers it has
proved ambiguous, polyvalent and resistant to interpretative closure.

This is what Carlos Baker, in the standard critical work on Hemingway, had to say about 'Cat in the Rain' (he discusses it in the context of a
group of stories about men-women relationships):

> 'Cat in the Rain', another story taken in part from the woman's point of
> view, presents a corner of the female world in which the male is only tangen-
> tially involved. It was written at Rapallo in May, 1923. From the window of a
> hotel room where her husband is reading and she is fidgeting, a young wife
> sees a cat outside in the rain. When she goes to get it, the animal (which some-
> how stands in her mind for comfortable bourgeois domesticity) has dis-
> appeared. This fact is very close to tragic because of the cat's association in
> her mind with many other things she longs for: long hair she can do in a knot
> at the back of her neck; a candle-lighted dining table where her own silver
> gleams; the season of spring and nice weather; and of course, some new
> clothes. But when she puts these wishes into words, her husband mildly
> advises her to shut up and find something to read. 'Anyway', says the young
> wife, 'I want a cat. I want a cat. I want a cat now. If I can't have long hair or
> any fun, I can have a cat.' The poor girl is the referee in a face-off between the
> actual and the possible. The actual is made of rain, boredom, a preoccupied
> husband and irrational yearnings. The possible is made of silver, spring, fun,
> a new coiffure, and new dresses. Between the actual and the possible stands
> the cat. It is finally sent up to her by the kindly old inn-keeper, whose
> sympathetic deference is greater than that of the young husband.
>
> (1963:135-6)

There are several things to quibble with in this account of the story. Most
important perhaps is Baker's assumption that the cat sent up by the hotel
keeper at the end is the same as the one that the wife saw from her
window. This assumption is consistent with Baker's sympathy with the
wife as a character, implied by his reference to her as 'the poor girl' and

his description of the disappearance of the cat as 'very close to tragic'. The appearance of the maid with a cat is the main reversal, in Aristotelian terms, in the narrative. If it is indeed the cat she went to look for, then the reversal is a happy one for her, and confirms her sense that the hotel keeper appreciated her as a woman more than her husband. In Greimas's terms, the wife is the subject of the story and the cat the object. The hotel keeper and the maid enact the role of helper and George is the opponent. The story is disjunctive (departure and return) and concerns the transfer of the cat to the wife. *abstraction – fits into departure & return stories around world*

The description of the tortoiseshell cat as 'big', however, suggests that it is not the same as the one the wife referred to by the diminutive term 'kitty', and which she envisaged stroking on her lap. We might infer that the padrone, trying to humor a client, sends up the first cat he can lay hands on, which is in fact quite inappropriate to the wife's needs. This would make the reversal an ironic one at the wife's expense, emphasizing the social and cultural abyss that separates her from the padrone, and revealing her quasi-erotic response to his professional attentiveness as a delusion.

I shall return to this question of the ambiguity of the ending. One more point about Baker's commentary on the story: he says that the cat 'somehow stands in [the wife's] mind for comfortable bourgeois domesticity', and speaks of its 'association in her mind with many other things she longs for'. In other words, he interprets the cat as a metonymic symbol of type A above. Indeed he sees the whole story as turning on the opposition between two groups of metonymies. 'The actual is made of rain, boredom, a preoccupied husband, and irrational yearnings. The possible is made of silver, spring fun, a new coiffure, and new clothes'.

John V. Hagopian gives a very different reading of this story. It is, he says, about 'a crisis in the marriage . . . involving the lack of fertility, which is symbolically foreshadowed by the public garden (fertility) dominated by the war monument (death)' in the first paragraph. These again are metonymic symbols of type A, effect connoting cause; but Hagopian's reading of the story hinges on the identification of the cat as a symbol of a wanted child, and of the man in the rubber cape (lines 32–3) as a symbol of contraception – symbolism of type B, in which a metonymic signified evokes a second signified metaphorically, i.e., by virtue of similarity.

> As [the wife] looks out into the wet empty square, she sees a man in a rubber cape strolling to the café in the rain . . . The rubber cape is a protection from rain, and rain is a fundamental necessity for fertility and fertility is precisely what is lacking in the American wife's marriage. An even more precise interpretaton is possible but perhaps not necessary here (1975:231).

What Hagopian is presumably hinting at is that 'rubber' is an American colloquialism for contraceptive sheath, and that the wife notices the man in the rubber cape because of the subconscious association – a piece of

classic Freudian 'symbolism'. It is an ingenious interpretation and all the
more persuasive because there seems to be no very obvious reason for
introducing the man in the cape into the story – he is not an actant in the
narrative but an item of the descriptive background (Chatman,
1978:140), and his appearance does not tell us anything about the
weather or the square that we do not know already. Admittedly, the cape
does signify, by contrast, the wife's lack of protection from the rain, thus
emphasizing the padrone's thoughtfulness in sending the maid with the
umbrella. But if we accept Hagopian's reading then the umbrella itself,
opening with almost comical opportuneness and effortlessness behind
her, becomes a symbol of how the wife's way of life comes between her
and a vital, fertile, relationship with reality. Her later demands for new
clothes, a new hairstyle, a candlelit dining table are, according to Hagopian, expressions of a desire that never reaches full consciousness, for
'motherhood, a home with a family, an end to the strictly companionate
marriage with George.' And the cat, he says, is by this stage in the story
'an obvious symbol for a child' (p. 232).

Unlike Baker, Hagopian sees the final reversal in the story as ironic:

> The girl's symbolic wish is grotesquely fulfilled in painfully realistic terms. It
> is George, not the padrone, by whom the wife wants to be fulfilled, but the
> padrone has sent up the maid with a big tortoise-shell cat, a huge creature that
> swings down against her body. It is not clear whether this is exactly the same
> cat as the one the wife had seen from the window – probably not; in any case,
> it will most certainly not do. The girl is willing to settle for a child-surrogate,
> but the big tortoise-shell cat obviously cannot serve that purpose (1975:232).

The reason why this story is capable of providing these two very different interpretations might be expressed as follows: although it is a well-
formed narrative, with a clearly defined beginning, middle and end, the
primary action is not the primary vehicle of meaning. This can be
demonstrated by testing upon the story Jonathan Culler's hypothesis
that competent readers will tend to agree on what is and is not essential to
the plot of a narrative test. Before the seminar at Birmingham University
participants were invited to summarize the action of the story in not
more than 30 words of continuous prose.[2] All the contributors mentioned the wife, the cat, the rain, and the hotel manager; most mentioned
the nationality of the wife and her failure to find the cat under the table;
about half mentioned the husband, located the story in Italy, and made a
distinction between the two cats. None mentioned the maid, or the bickering between husband and wife.

These omissions are particularly interesting. The non-appearance of
the maid is easily explained: on the narrative level her function is
indistinguishable from that of the manager – both are 'helpers' and the

---

[2] My own effort was as follows: "Bored young American staying with husband at Italian hotel
fails to rescue a cat seen sheltering from the rain but is provided with a cat by the attentive manager."

narrative would not be significantly altered *qua* narrative if the maid were deleted from the story and her actions performed by the manager himself. She does contribute to the symmetry of the story both numerically and sexually: it begins by pairing husband and wife, then pairs wife and manager, then wife and maid, then (in the wife's thoughts) maid and manager, then wife and manager again, then wife and husband again, and ends by pairing husband and maid. But this seems to be a purely formal set of equivalences with no significance in the hermeneutic or proairetic codes (such as would obtain if, for instance, there were some intrigue linking the husband with the maid and the manager, the kind of plotting characteristic of the *lisible* text). The main function of the maid in the story is to emphasize the status of the wife as a client and expatriate, and thus to act as a warning or corrective against the wife's tendency to attribute to the padrone a deeply personal interest in herself.

Both Baker and Hagopian agree that the rift between husband and wife is what the story is essentially about, even if they disagree about the precise cause. That none of the synopses should make any allusion to the bickering between the couple is striking evidence that the meaning of the story does not inhere in its basic action. In trying to preserve what is essential to that action in a very condensed summary – the quest for the cat, the failure of the quest, the reversal – one has to discard what seems most important in the story as read: the relationship between husband and wife. Adopting Barthes' terminology in 'The Structural Analysis of Narratives' (1977), there are only four nuclei in the story, opening possibilities which might be closed in different ways: will the wife or the husband go to fetch the cat? will the wife get the cat? will she get wet? who is at the door?[3] The rest of the story consists of catalyzers that are indexical or informational, and since most of the information is given more than once, these too become indexical of mood and atmosphere (for instance, we are told more than once that it is raining). One might indeed describe the story generically as indexical: we infer its meaning indexically from its non-narrative components rather than hermeneutically or teleologically from its action. Another way of putting it would be to invoke Seymour Chatman's distinction between the resolved plot and the revealed plot:

> In the traditional narrative of resolution, there is a sense of problem solving . . . of a kind of ratiocinative or emotional teleology . . . 'What will happen?' is the basic question. In the modern plot of revelation, however, the emphasis is elsewhere, the function of the discourse is not to answer the question or even to pose it . . . It is not that events are resolved (happily or tragically) but rather that a state of affairs is revealed (1978:48).

[3] On further reflection, I am inclined to think that there is another "hidden" narrative nucleus in the story, related to the "marital rift" theme, though it is to be inferred only from George's body language as reported in lines 73–4, and his appreciative speech at line 75: namely, the possibility that he will put aside his book and make love to his wife. This possibility is closed, negatively, at line 85.

Chatman offers *Pride and Prejudice* and *Mrs. Dalloway* as examples of each kind of plot. 'Cat in the Rain' seems to share characterisitcs of both: it is, one might say, a plot of revelation (the relationship between husband and wife) disguised as a plot of resolution (the quest for the cat). The ambiguity of the ending is therefore crucial. By refusing to resolve the issue of whether the wife gets the cat she wants, the implied author indicates that this is not the point of the story.

There are several reasons why this ending is ambiguous. One, obviously, is that the story ends where it does, for if it continued for another line or two, or moment or two, it would become apparent from the wife's response whether the cat was the one she had seen from the window, whether she is pleased or disconcerted by its being brought to her, and so on. What I am doing here is comparing the *fabula* with the *sjuzhet*. The *sjuzhet* tantalizingly stops just short of that point in the *fabula* where we should, with our readerly desire for certainty, wish it to. In other respects there is nothing especially striking about the story's treatment of time, though we may admire the smooth transition in the first paragraph from summary of a state of affairs obtaining over a period of days or weeks to the state of affairs obtaining on a particular afternoon, and the subtle condensation of durational time in the final scene between husband and wife, marked by changes in the light outside the window. The order of events is strictly chronological (characteristic, Chatman observes, of the resolved plot (1978:48)). As regards what Genette calls frequency (the number of times an event is narrated), the story tends toward reiteration rather than summary, telling *n* times what happened *n* times or *n* times what happened once rather than telling once what happened *n* times. This is important because it reinforces the definition of the characters according to a very limited repertoire of gestures. Thus the wife is frequently described as looking out of the window, the husband as reading, the manager as bowing (and the weather as raining).

The story of the quest for the cat involves four characters, and in theory could be narrated from four points of view, each quite distinct and different in import. The story we have is written from the point of view of the American couple rather than that of the Italian hotel staff, and from the wife's point of view rather than the husband's. We must distinguish here between what Genette calls voice and perspective. The story is narrated throughout by an authorial voice which refers to the characters in the third person and uses the past tense. This is the standard mode of authorial narration and by convention the narrator is authoritative, reliable and within the fictional world of the discourse, omniscient. The authorial voice in this story, however, renounces the privilege of authorial omniscience in two ways: firstly, by abstaining from any comment, judgement or explanation of motive regarding the behaviour of the characters, and secondly by restricting itself to the perspective of only two of the characters, and, for part of the story, to the perspective of only one. By this I mean that the narrator describes nothing that is not seen by either husband or wife or both. Yet it is not quite true to say that the narrator has no independent angle of vision; he has. As in a film, we sometimes see the wife from the husband's angle, and the husband sometimes from the wife's angle, but much of the time we see them both from some independent, impersonal angle.

The first paragraph adopts the common perspective of the American couple, making no distinction between them. With the first sentence of the second paragraph, 'The American wife stood at the window looking out', the narrative adopts her perspective but without totally identifying with it. Note the deictic difference between '*her* husband' in line 18, which closely identifies the narration with her perspective, and '*the* husband' in line 20, '*the* wife' in line 23, which subtly reasserts the independence of the authorial voice. From this point onwards, however, for the next fifty lines the narration identifies itself closely with the wife's perspective, following her out of the room and downstairs into the lobby, and reporting what she thinks as well as what she sees. The anaphoric sequence of sentences beginning 'She liked' (lines 28–31) affects us as being a transcription rather than a description of her thoughts because they could be transposed into monologue (first person/present tense) without any illogicality or stylistic awkwardness. Sentences in free indirect speech, 'The cat would be round to the right. Perhaps she could go along under the eaves' (33–4) and 'of course, the hotel-keeper had sent her' (36–7), mark the maximum degree of identification of the narration with the wife's point of view. When she returns to the room the narration separates itself from her again. There is a lot of direct speech from now on, no report of the wife's thoughts, and occasionally the narration seems to adopt the husband's perspective alone, e.g., 'George looked up and saw the back of her neck, clipped like a boy's' (70), and – very importantly:

> Someone knocked on the door.
> 'Avanti', George said. He looked up from his book.
> In the doorway stood the maid. She held a big tortoise-shell cat . . . (92–4)

We can now fully understand why the ending of the story is so ambiguous: it is primarily because the narration adopts the husband's perspective at this crucial point. Since he did not rise from the bed to look out of the window at the cat sheltering from the rain, he has no way of knowing whether the cat brought by the maid is the same one – hence the non-committal indefinite article '*a* big tortoise-shell cat.' If, however, the wife's perspective had been adopted at this point and the text had read

> 'Avanti,' the wife said. She turned round from the window. In the doorway stood the maid. She held a big tortoise-shell cat . . .

a cat
the cat

then it would be clear that this was not the cat the wife had wanted to bring in from the rain (in which case the definite article would be used). It is significant that in the title of the story, there is no article before 'Cat', thus giving no support to either interpretation of the ending.

Carlos Baker's assumption that the tortoise-shell cat and the cat in the rain are one and the same is therefore unwarranted. Hagopian's reading of the ending as ironic is preferable but his assumption that the wife's desire for the cat is caused by childlessness is also unwarranted. Here, it seems to me, the structuralist notion of language as a system of differences and of meaning as the product of structural oppositions can genuinely help to settle a point of interpretation.[4] Hagopian's interpretation of the man in the rubber cape as a symbol of contraception depends in part on the association of rain with fertility. Now rain *can* symbolize fertility, when defined by opposition to drought. In this story, however (and incidentally, throughout Hemingway's work) it is opposed to 'good weather' and symbolizes the loss of pleasure and joy, the onset of discomfort and ennui. Hagopian's comments on the disappearance of the artists, 'The rain, ironically, inhibits creativity' (1975:230), is a strained attempt to reconcile his reading with the text: there is no irony here unless we accept his equation, rain = fertility.

The cat as a child-surrogate is certainly a possible interpretation in the sense that it is a recognized cultural stereotype, but again Hagopian tries to enlist in its support textual evidence that is, if anything, negative. He comments on the description of the wife's sensations as she passes the hotel keeper for the second time: ' "very small and tight inside . . . really important . . . of supreme importance" all phrases that might appropriately be used to describe a woman who is pregnant' (1975:231). But not, surely, to describe a woman who merely *wants* to be pregnant. Indeed, if we must have a gynecological reading of the story it is much more plausible to suppose that the wife's whimsical craving for the cat and for other things like new clothes and long hair is the result of her *being* pregnant. There is in fact some extratextual support for this hypothesis. In his biography of Hemingway, Carlos Baker states quite baldly that 'Cat in the Rain' was about Hemingway, his wife Hadley and the manager and chambermaid at the Hotel Splendide in Rapallo, where the story was written in 1923. He also states, without making any connection between the two items, that the Hemingways had left the chilly thaw of Switzerland and gone to Rapallo because Hadley had announced that

[4] Perhaps this is overconfident, since it is rarely possible to *disprove* interpretations. Among the more far-fetched interpretations of 'Cat in the Rain' are Horst Kruse's argument that the man in the rubber cape is an allusion to the mysterious man in the mackintosh in the 'Hades' episode of Joyce's *Ulysses*, and therefore a symbol of death ('The appearance of a man in a raincoat in both *Ulysses* and 'Cat in the Rain' seems clear indication of the dependence of Hemingway's short story on the work of the Irish writer' (Kruse, 1970:28); and Ramesh Srivastava's suggestion that 'the cat exists only in the imagination of the wife' (Srivastava, 1970:83), which presumably entails reading the second sentence in paragraph 2 as free indirect speech.

she was pregnant (1972:159, 161).

At about the same time, Hemingway was evolving 'a new theory that you could omit anything if you knew what you omitted, and the omitted part would strengthen the story and make people feel something more than they understood' (1972:165). This is, I think, a very illuminating description by Hemingway of his application of the metonymic mode of classical realism to modernist literary purposes. Metonymy, as I said earlier, is a device of non-logical deletion. Hemingway's word is 'omission'. By omitting the kind of motivation that classical realistic fiction provided, he generated a symbolist polysemy in his deceptively simple stories, making his readers 'feel more than they understood'. It would be a mistake, therefore, to look for a single clue, whether pregnancy or barrenness, to the meaning of 'Cat in the Rain'. That the wife's (and, for that matter, the husband's) behaviour is equally intelligible on either assumption is one more confirmation of the story's indeterminacy.

Hemingway's stories are remarkable for achieving a symbolist resonance without the use of rhetorical figures and tropes. Not only does 'Cat in the Rain' contain no metaphors and similes – it contains no metonymies and synecdoches either. The story is 'metonymic' in the structural sense defined above: its minimal semantic units are selected from a single context, a continuum of temporal and spatial contiguities, and are foregrounded simply by being selected, repeated and related to each other oppositionally. Consider, for example, the opening paragraph, which establishes the story's setting in diction that is apparently severely denotative, with no metaphors or metonymies, similes or synecdoches, no elegant variation or pathetic fallacies, yet is nevertheless highly charged with connotative meaning.

There were only two Americans stopping at the hotel. Americans opposed to other nationalities: index of cultural isolation.

They did not know any of the people they passed on the stairs on their way to and from their room. Index of social isolation and mutual dependence – vulnerability to breakdown in relationship.

Their room was on the second floor facing the sea. Culture faces nature.

It also faced the public garden and the war monument. Culture paired with nature (public: garden) and opposed to nature (monument: garden). Pleasure (garden) opposed to pain (war).

There were big palms and green benches in the public garden. Culture and nature integrated. Benches same color as vegetation.

In the good weather there was always an artist with his easel. Artists liked the way the palms grew and the bright colors of the hotels facing the garden and the sea. Culture and nature happily fused. Image of euphoria.

Italians came from a long way off to look up at the war monument.
Euphoria qualified. War monument attracts the living but commemo-
rates the dead. Looking associated with absence (of the dead). 'Italian'
opposed to 'American'.

It was made of bronze and glinted in the rain. Inert mineral (bronze)
opposed to organic vegetable (palm). Rain opposed to good weather.
Euphoria recedes.

It was raining. Rain dripped from the palm trees. Euphoria recedes
further. Garden uninviting.

Water stood in pools on the gravel paths. Image of stagnation.

*The sea broke in a long line in the rain and slipped back down the
beach to come up and break again in a long line in the rain.* Excess of
wetness. Monotony. Ennui.

*The motor cars were gone from the square by the war monument.
Across the square in the doorway of the café a waiter stood looking out
at the square.* Images of absence, loss, ennui.

The first paragraph, then, without containing a single narrative
nucleus, establishes the thematic core of the story through oppositions
between nature and culture, joy and ennui. Joy is associated with a har-
monious union of culture and nature. The wife, looking out of the
window at a scene made joyless by the rain, sees a cat with whose dis-
comfort she emotionally identifies. Her husband, though offering to
fetch it, implies his indifference to her emotional needs by not actually
moving. The husband is reading, a 'cultural' use of the eyes. The wife is
looking, a 'natural' use of the eyes. Her looking, through the window,
expresses a need for communion. His reading of a book is a substitute for
communion, and a classic remedy for ennui. It is worth noticing that he
is reading on the bed – a place made for sleeping and making love; and
the perversity of this behaviour is symbolized by the fact that he is lying
on the bed the wrong way round. As the story continues, the contrast
between looking and reading, both activities expressing the loss or
failure of love, becomes more insistent. Denied the kitty, a 'natural'
object (opposed to book) which she could have petted as a substitute for
being petted, the wife looks in the mirror, pining for a more natural feminine self. Then she looks out of the window again, while her husband,
who has not shifted his position (his immobility opposed to the
padrone's punctilious bowing) reads on and impatiently recommends
her to 'get something to read'. One could summarize this story in the
style of Greimas, as follows: loving is to quarrelling as stroking a cat is to
reading a book, a narrative transformation of the opposition between
joy and ennui, thus: –

Loving (Joy): Quarrelling (Ennui): stroking a cat (Non-joy, a giving but not
receiving of pleasure): reading a book (Non-ennui).

Such a summary has this to recommend it: that it brings together the overt action of the story (the quest for the cat) with its implicit subject (the relationship between husband and wife). Whether it, and the preceding comments, enhance our understanding and appreciation of Hemingway's story, I leave others to judge.

References

Baker, Carlos, 1963 (1952). *Hemingway: The Writer as Artist* (Princeton UP).
　1972 (1969) *Ernest Hemingway* (Harmondsworth: Penguin Books).
Barthes, Roland, 1975 (1970) *S/Z*, trans. Richard Miller (London: Cape).
　1977 (1966) 'Introduction to the Structural Analysis of Narratives' in *Image – Music – Text*, ed. and trans. Stephen Heath (London: Fontana).
Brooke-Rose, Christine, 1976–7. 'The Squirm of the True,' *PTL* 1, 265–94, & 513–46; 2, 517–61.
Chatman, Seymour, 1978. *Story and Discourse: Narrative Structure in Fiction and Film* (Ithaca NY: Cornell UP).
Cohn, Dorrit, 1978. *Transparent Minds: Narrative Modes for Presenting Consciousness in Fiction* (Princeton UP).
Culler, Jonathan, 1975. 'Defining Narrative Units' in: Roger Fowler, ed., *Style and Structure in Literature* (Oxford: Basil Blackwell), 123–142.
Frank, Joseph, 1948 (1945). 'Spatial Form in Modern Literature,' in: Mark Schorer, Josephine Miles and Gordon McKenzie, eds., *Criticism* (NY: Harcourt Brace), 379–392.
Frye, Northrop, 1957. *Anatomy of Criticism* (Princeton UP).
Genette, Gerard, 1972. *'Discours du Récit,'* in *Figures III* (Paris: Seuil).
Greimas, A.J., 1966. *Sémantique Structurale* (Paris: Larousse).
　1970 *Du Sens* (Paris: Seuil).
　1976 *Maupassant. La Sémiologie du Texte: Exercises Practiques* (Paris: Seuil).
Hagopian, John V., 1975 (1962). 'Symmetry in "Cat in the Rain",' in: *The Short Stories of Ernest Hemingway: Critical Essays*, ed. Jackson J. Benson (Durham NC: Duke UP).
Hemingway, Ernest, 1958 (1925). 'Cat in the Rain', in *In Our Time* (New York: Scribner).
Jakobson, Roman, 1956. 'Two Aspects of Language and Two Types of Linguistic Disturbances,' in Jakobson and Morris Halle, *Fundamentals of Language* (The Hague: Mouton).
——1960 'Closing Statement: Linguistics and Poetics' in: Thomas A. Sebeok, ed., *Style and Language* (Cambridge, Mass: MIT).
Kermode, Frank, 1966. *The Sense of an Ending* (New York-London: Oxford UP).
Kruse, Horst, 1970. 'Hemingway's "Cat in the Rain" and Joyce's *Ulysses*,' *Literatur in Wissenschaft und Unterricht* III, 28–30.
Lodge, David, 1966. *Language of Fiction* (London: Routledge & Kegan Paul).
——1977 *The Modes of Modern Writing* (London-Ithaca NY: Arnold-Cornell UP).
Schorer, Mark, 1948. 'Technique as Discovery,' *Hudson Review* I, 67–86.
　1949 'Fiction and the Analogical Matrix,' *Kenyon Review XI*, 539–560.

Srivastava, Ramesh, 1970. 'Hemingway's "Cat in the Rain": an inter-
  pretation,' *Literary Criterion* IX, 79–84.
Todorov, Tzvetan, 1977 (1971). *The Poetics of Prose*, trans. Richard Howard
  (Oxford: Blackwell).

APPENDIX

CAT IN THE RAIN*

There were only two Americans stopping at the hotel. They did not know any of the people they passed on the stairs on their way to and from their room. Their room was on the second floor facing the sea. It also faced the public garden and the war monument. There were big palms and green benches in the public garden. In the good weather there was always an artist with this easel. Artists liked the way the palms grew and the bright colors of the hotels facing the gardens and the sea. Italians came from a long way off to look up at the war monument. It was made of bronze and glistened in the rain. It was raining. The rain dripped from the palm trees. Water stood in pools on the gravel paths. The sea broke in a long line in the

10   rain and slipped back down the beach to come up and break again in a long line in the rain. The motor cars were gone from the square by the war monument. Across the square in the doorway of the café a waiter stood looking out at the empty square.

The American wife stood at the window looking out. Outside right under their

15   window a cat was crouched under one of the dripping green tables. The cat was trying to make herself so compact that she would not be dripped on.

"I'm going down and get that kitty," the American wife said.

"I'll do it," her husband offered from the bed.

"No, I'll get it. The poor kitty out trying to keep dry under a table."

20   The husband went on reading, lying propped up with the two pillows at the foot of the bed.

"Don't get wet," he said.

The wife went downstairs and the hotel owner stood up and bowed to her as she passed the office. His desk was at the far end of the office. He was an old man and

25   very tall.

"Il piove," the wife said. She liked the hotel-keeper.

"Si, si, Signora, brutto tempo. It is very bad weather."

He stood behind his desk in the far end of the dim room. The wife liked him. She liked the deadly serious way he received any complaints. She liked his dignity. She

30   liked the way he wanted to serve her. She liked the way he felt about being a hotel-keeper. She liked his old, heavy face and big hands.

Liking him she opened the door and looked out. It was raining harder. A man in a rubber cape was crossing the empty square to the café. The cat would be around to the right. Perhaps she could go along under the eaves. As she stood in the doorway

35   an umbrella opened behind her. It was the maid who looked after their room.

"You must not get wet," she smiled, speaking Italian. Of course, the hotel-keeper had sent her.

With the maid holding the umbrella over her, she walked along the gravel path until she was under their window. The table was there, washed bright green in the
40 rain, but the cat was gone. She was suddenly disappointed. The maid looked up at her.

"Ha perduto qualque cosa, Signora?"

"There was a cat," said the American girl.

"A cat?"
45 "Si, il gatto."

"A cat?" the maid laughed. "A cat in the rain?"

"Yes," she said, "under the table." Then, "Oh, I wanted it so much. I wanted a kitty."

When she talked English the maid's face tightened.
50 "Come, Signora," she said. "We must get back inside. You will be wet."

"I suppose so," said the American girl.

They went back along the gravel path and passed in the door. The maid stayed outside to close the umbrella. As the American girl passed the office, the padrone bowed from his desk. Something felt very small and tight inside the girl. The
55 padrone made her feel very small and at the same time really important. She had a momentary feeling of being of supreme importance. She went on up the stairs. She opened the door of the room. George was on the bed, reading.

"Did you get the cat?" he asked, putting the book down.

"It was gone."
60 "Wonder where it went to," he said, resting his eyes from reading.

She sat down on the bed.

"I wanted it so much," she said. "I don't know why I wanted it so much. I wanted that poor kitty. It isn't any fun to be a poor kitty out in the rain."

George was reading again.
65 She went over and sat in front of the mirror of the dressing table looking at herself with the hand glass. She studied her profile, first one side and then the other. Then she studied the back of her head and her neck.

"Don't you think it would be a good idea if I let my hair grow out?" she asked, looking at her profile again.
70 George looked up and saw the back of her neck, clipped close like a boy's.

"I like it the way it is."

"I get so tired of it," she said. "I get so tired of looking like a boy."

George shifted his position in the bed. He hadn't looked away from her since she started to speak.
75 "You look pretty darn nice," he said.

She laid the mirror down on the dresser and went over to the window and looked out. It was getting dark.

"I want to pull my hair back tight and smooth and make a big knot at the back that I can feel," she said. "I want to have a kitty to sit on my lap and purr when I
80 stroke her."

"Yeah?" George said from the bed.

"And I want to eat at a table with my own silver and I want candles. And I want it to be spring and I want to brush my hair out in front of a mirror and I want a kitty and I want some new clothes.
85 "Oh, shut up and get something to read," George said. He was reading again.

His wife was looking out of the window. It was quite dark now and still raining in the palm trees.

"Anyway, I want a cat," she said, "I want a cat. I want a cat now. If I can't have long hair or any fun, I can have a cat."

90   George was not listening. He was reading his book. His wife looked out of the window where the light had come on in the square.

Someone knocked at the door.

"Avanti," George said. He looked up from his book.

In the doorway stood the maid. She held a big tortoise-shell cat pressed tight
95   against her and swung down against her body.

"Excuse me," she said, "the padrone asked me to bring this for the Signora."

---

4   Roland Barthes,

'To Write: An Intransitive Verb?', *The Structuralist Controversy*, ed R. Macksey & E. Donato

p134–145

To Write: An Intransitive Verb?[1]

For centuries Western culture conceived of literature not as we do today, through a study of works, authors, and schools, but through a genuine theory of language. This theory, whose name, *rhetoric*, came to it from antiquity, reigned in the Western world from Gorgias to the Renaissance – for nearly two thousand years. Threatened as early as the sixteenth century by the advent of modern rationalism, rhetoric was completely ruined when rationalism was transformed into positivism at the end of the nineteenth century. At that point there was no longer any common ground of thought between literature and language: literature no longer regarded itself as language except in the works of a few pioneers such as Mallarmé, and linguistics claimed very few rights over literature, these being [limited to] a secondary philological discipline of uncertain status – stylistics.

As we know, this situation is changing, and it seems to me that it is in part to take cognizance of this change that we are assembled here: literature and language are in the process of finding each other again. The

---

[1] 'Ecrire: Verbe intransitif?' The translation which follows is a composite of the communication which M. Barthes distributed in advance to the Symposium participants and the actual transcription of his address. The footnotes have been supplied by the translator.

factors of this *rapprochement* are diverse and complex; I shall cite the most obvious. On one hand, certain writers since Mallarmé, such as Proust and Joyce, have undertaken a radical exploration of writing, making of their work a search for the total Book. On the other hand, linguistics itself, principally following the impetus of Roman Jakobson, has developed to include within its scope the poetic, or the order of effects linked to the message and not to its referent. Therefore, in my view, we have today a new perspective of consideration which, I would like to emphasize, is common to literature and linguistics, to the creator and the critic, whose tasks until now completely self-contained, are beginning to inter-relate, perhaps even to merge. This is at least true for certain writers whose work is becoming more and more a critique of language. It is in this perspective that I would like to place the following observations (of a prospective and not of a conclusive nature) indicating how the activity of writing can be expressed [*énoncée*] today with the help of certain linguistic categories.

This new union of literature and linguistics, of which I have just spoken, could be called, provisionally and for lack of a better name, *semio-criticism*, since it implies that writing is a system of signs. Semio-criticism is not to be identified with stylistics, even in a new form; it is much more than stylistics. It has a much broader perspective; its object is constituted not by simple accidents of form, but by the very relationships between the writer [*scripteur, not écrivain*] and language. This perspective does not imply a lack of interest in language but, on the contrary, a continual return to the 'truths' – provisional though they may be – of linguistic anthropology. I will recall certain of these truths because they still have a power of challenge in respect to a certain current idea of literature.

One of the teachings of contemporary linguistics is that there is no archaic language, or at the very least that there is no connection between simplicity and the age of a language: ancient languages can be just as complete and as complex as recent languages; there is no progressive history of languages. Therefore, when we try to find certain fundamental categories of language in modern writing, we are not claiming to reveal a certain archaism of the 'psyche'; we are not saying that the writer is returning to the origin of language, but that language is the origin for him.

A second principle, particularly important in regard to literature, is that language cannot be considered as a simple instrument, whether utilitarian or decorative, of thought. Man does not exist prior to language, either as a species or as an individual. We never find a state where man is separated from language, which he then creates in order to 'express' what is taking place within him: it is language which teaches the definition of man, not the reverse.

Moreover, from a methodological point of view, linguistics accustoms us to a new type of objectivity. The objectivity that has been required in the human sciences up until now is an objectivity of the given, a total acceptance of the given. Linguistics suggests, on the one hand, that we distinguish levels of analysis and that we described the distinctive elements of each of these levels; in short, that we establish the distinctness of the fact and not the fact itself. On the other hand, linguistics asks us to recognize that unlike physical and biological facts, cultural facts are always double, that they refer us to something else. As Benveniste remarked, the discovery of the 'duplicity' of language gives Saussure's reflection all its value.[2]

These few preliminaries are contained in one final proposition which justifies all semio-critical research. We see culture more and more as a general system of symbols, governed by the same operations. There is unity in this symbolic field: culture, in all its aspects, is a language. Therefore it is possible today to anticipate the creation of a single, unified science of culture, which will depend on diverse disciplines, all devoted to analyzing, on different levels of description, culture as language. Of course semio-criticism will be only a part of this science, or rather of this discourse on culture. I feel authorized by this unity of the human symbolic field to work on a postulate, which I shall call a postulate of *homology*: the structure of the sentence, the object of linguistics, is found again, homologically, in the structure of works. Discourse is not simply an adding together of sentences: it is, itself, one great sentence. In terms of this hypothesis I would like to confront certain categories of language with the situation of the writer in relation to his writing.

The first of these categories is *temporality*. I think we can all agree that there is a linguistic temporality. This specific time of language is equally different from physical time and from what Benveniste calls 'chronicle time' [*temps chronique*], that is, calendar time.[3] Linguistic time finds quite different expression and *découpages* in various languages. For example, since we are going to be interested in the analysis of myths, many languages have a particular past tense of the verb to indicate the past time of myth. One thing is sure: linguistic time always has its primary center [*centre générateur*] in the present of the statement [*énonciation*]. This leads us to ask whether there is, homological to linguistic time, a specific time of discourse. On this point we may take Benveniste's explanation that many languages, especially in the Indo-European group, have a double system of time. The first temporal system is that of the discourse itself, which is adapted to the temporality of the speaker

[2] Emile Benveniste, *Problèmes de la linguistique générale* (Paris, 1966), p. 40. 'Qu'est-ce donc que cet object, que Saussure érige sur une table rase de toutes les notions reçues? Nous touchons ici à ce qu'il y a de primordial dans la doctrine saussurienne, à un principe qui présume une intuition totale du language, totale à la fois parce qu'elle embrasse la totalité de son objet. Ce principe est que *le langage*, sous quelque point de vue qu'on l'étudie, *est toujours un objet double*, formé de deux parties dont l'une ne vaut que par l'autre.

[3] Cf. Benveniste, 'Les Relations de temps dans le verbe français,' *ibid.*, pp. 237–50.

[*énonciateur*] and for which the *énonciation* is always the point of origin [*moment générateur*]. The second is the system of history or of narrative, which is adapted to the recounting of past events without any intervention by the speaker and which is consequently deprived of present and future (except periphrastically). The specific tense of this second system is the aorist or its equivalent, such as our *passé simple* or the preterit. This tense (the aorist) is precisely the only one missing from the temporal system of discourse. Naturally the existence of this a-personal system does not contradict the essentially logocentric nature of linguistic time that I have just affirmed. The second system simply lacks the characteristics of the first.

Understood thus as the opposition of two radically different systems, temporality does not have the morphological mark of verbs for its only sign; it is marked by all the signs, often very indirect, which refer either to the a-personal tense of the event or to the personal tense of the locutor. The opposition in its fullness permits us first to account for some pure, or we might say classic, cases: a popular story and the history of France retold in our manuals are purely aoristic narratives; on the contrary, Camus' *L'Etranger*, written in the compound past, is not only a perfect form of autobiography (that of the narrator, and not of the author) but, what is more valuable, it permits us to understand better the apparently anomalous cases.[4] Being a historian, Michelet made all historical time pivot around a point of discourse with which he identified himself – the Revolution. His history is a narrative without the aorist, even if the simple past abounds in it; inversely, the preterit can very well serve to signify not the objective *récit*, but the depersonalization of the discourse – a phenomenon which is the object of the most lively research in today's literature.

What I would like to add to this linguistic analysis, which comes from Benveniste, is that the distinction between the temporal system of discourse and the temporal system of history is not at all the same distinction as is traditionally made between objective discourse and subjective discourse. For the relationship between the speaker [*énonciateur*] and the referent on the one hand and that between the speaker and his utterance [*énonciation*] on the other hand are not to be confused, and it is only the second relationship which determines the temporal system of discourse.

It seems to me that these facts of language were not readily perceptible so long as literature pretended to be a transparent expression of either objective calendar time or of psychological subjectivity, that is to say, as long as literature maintained a totalitarian ideology of the referent, or more commonly speaking, as long as literature was realistic. Today, however, the literature of which I speak is discovering fundamental

---

[4] Cf. Jean-Paul Sartre, 'Explication de *L'Etranger*', *Situations* I (Paris, 1947), pp. 99–121.

subtleties relative to temporality. In reading certain writers who are engaged in this type of exploration we sense that what is recounted in the aorist doesn't seem at all immersed in the past, in what has taken place, but simply in the impersonal [*la non-personne*], which is neither history, nor discursive information [*la science*], and even less the *one* of anonymous writing. (The *one* is dominated by the indefinite and not by the absence of person. I would even say that the pronoun *one* is marked in relation to person, while, paradoxically, *he* is not.) At the other extreme of the experience of discourse, the present-day writer can no longer content himself with expressing his own present, according to a lyrical plan, for example. He must learn to distinguish between the present of the speaker, which is grounded on a psychological fullness, and the present of what is spoken [*la locution*] which is mobile and in which the event and the writing become absolutely coincidental. Thus literature, at least in some of its pursuits, seems to me to be following the same path as linguistics when, along with Gustave Guillaume (a linguist not presently in fashion but who may become so again), it concerns itself with operative time and the time proper to the utterance [*énonciation*] itself.[5]

A second grammatical category which is equally important in linguistics and in literature is that of *person*. Taking linguists and especially Benveniste as my basis once more, I would like to recall that person (in the grammatical sense of the term) certainly seems to be a universal of language, linked to the anthropology of language. Every language, as Benveniste has shown, organizes person into two broad pairs of opposites: a correlation of personality which opposes person (*I or thou*) to non-person, which is *il* (*he or it*), the sign of absence; and, within this first opposing pair, a correlation of subjectivity (once again in the grammatical sense) which opposes two persons, the *I* and the *non-I* (the *thou*). For our purposes we must, along with Benveniste, make three observations. First, the polarity of persons, a fundamental condition of language, is nevertheless peculiar and enigmatic, for this polarity involves neither equality nor symmetry: *I* always has a position of transcendence with respect to *thou*, I being interior to the *énoncé* and *thou* remaining exterior to it; however, *I* and *thou* are reversible – *I* can always become *thou* and vice versa. This is not true of the non-person (*he or it*) which can never reverse itself into person or vice versa. The second observation is that the linguistic *I* can and must be defined in a strictly a-psychological way: *I* is nothing other than 'la personne qui énonce la présente instance de discours contenant l'instance linguistique *je*' (Benveniste ["the person who utters the present instance of discourse containing the linguistic

---

[5] Gustave Guillaume, *L'Architectonique du temps dans les langues classiques* (Copenhagen, 1945). The work of Guillaume (who died in 1960) toward a 'psycho-systématique' has been continued in the contributions of Roch Valin (*Petite introduction à la psychomécanique du langage* [Québec, 1954]). For a statement by Guillaume about his relation to the tradition of Saussure, see *La langue est-elle ou n'est-elle pas un système? Cahiers de linguistique structurale de l'Université de Québec*, I (1952), p. 4.

instance *I* ']).[6] The last remark is that the *he* or the non-person never reflects the instance of discourse; *he* is situated outside of it. We must give its full weight to Benveniste's recommendation not to represent the *he* as a more or less diminished or removed person: *he* is absolutely non-person, marked by the absence of what specifically constitutes, linguistically, the *I* and the *thou*.

The linguistic explanation provides several suggestions for an analysis of literary discourse. First, whatever varied and clever forms person may take in passing from the level of the sentence to that of discourse, the discourse of the literary work is rigorously submitted to a double system of person and non-person. This fact may be obscured because classical discourse (in a broad sense) to which we are habituated is a mixed discourse which alternates – very quickly, sometimes within the same sentence – personal and a-personal *énonciation*, through a complex play of pronouns and descriptive verbs. In this type of classical or bourgeois story the mixture of person and non-person produces a sort of ambiguous consciousness which succeeds in keeping the personal quality of what is stated while, however, continuously breaking the participation of the *énonciateur* in the *énoncé*.

Many novelistic utterances, written with *he* (in the third person), are nevertheless discourses of the *person* each time that the contents of the statement depend on its subject. If in a novel we read '*the tinkling of the ice against the glass seemed to give Bond a sudden inspiration,*' it is certain that the subject of the statement cannot be Bond himself – not because the sentence is written in the third person, since Bond could very well express himself through a *he*, but because of the verb *seem* which becomes a mark of the absence of person. Nevertheless, in spite of the diversity and often even the ruse of the narrative signs of the person, there is never but one sole and great opposition in the discourse, that of the person and the non-person; every narrative or fragment of a narrative is obliged to join one or the other of these extremes. How can we determine this division? In 're-writing' the discourse. If we can translate the *he* into *I* without changing anything else in the utterance, the discourse is in fact personal. In the sentence which we have cited, this transformation is impossible; we cannot say '*the tinkling of the ice seemed to give me a sudden inspiration*'. The sentence is impersonal. Starting from there, we catch a glimpse of how the discourse of the traditional novel is made; on the one hand it alternates the personal and the impersonal very rapidly, often even in the course of the same sentence, so as to produce, if we can speak thus, a proprietary consciousness which retains the mastery of what it states without participating in it; and on the other hand, in this type of novel, or rather, according to our perspective, in this type of discourse, when the narrator is explicitly an *I* (which has happened many times), there is confusion between the subject of the discourse and the

[6] Benveniste, *Problèmes*, p. 252.

subject of the reported action, as if – and this is a common belief – he who is speaking today were the same as he who acted yesterday. It is as if there were a continuity of the referent and the utterance through the person, as if the declaring were only a docile servant of the referent.

Now if we return to the linguistic definition of the first person (the one who says 'I' in the present instance of discourse), we may better understand the effort of certain contemporary writers (in France I think of Philippe Sollers's latest novel *Drame*) when they try to distinguish, at the level of the story, psychological person and the author of the writing. When a narrator recounts what has happened to him, the *I* who recounts is no longer the same *I* as the one that is recounted. In other words – and it seems to me that this is seen more and more clearly – the *I* of discourse can no longer be a place where a previously stored-up person is innocently restored. Absolute recourse to the instance of discourse to determine person is termed *nyn-egocentrism* by Damourette and Pichon (*nyn* from the greek *nun*, 'now').[7] Robbe-Grillet's novel *Dans le labyrinthe* begins with an admirable declaration of nyn-egocentrism: 'Je suis seul ici maintenant'. [I am alone here now.][8] This recourse, imperfectly as it may still be practiced, seems to be a weapon against the general "bad faith" of discourse which would make literary form simply the expression of an interiority constituted previous to and outside of language.

To end this discussion of person, I would like to recall that in the process of communication the course of the *I* is not homogenous. For example, when I use [*libéré*] the sign, *I*, I refer to myself inasmuch as I am talking: here there is an act which is always new, even if it is repeated, an act whose sense is always new. However, arriving at its destination, this sign is received by my interlocutor as a stable sign, product of a complete code whose contents are recurrent. In other words, the *I* of the one who writes *I* is not the same as the *I* which is read by *thou*. This fundamental dissymmetry of language, linguistically explained by Jespersen and then by Jakobson under the name of 'shifter' [*embrayeur*] or an overlapping of message and code, seems to be finally beginning to trouble literature in showing it that intersubjectivity, or rather interlocution, cannot be accomplished simply by wishing, but only by a deep, patient, and often circuitous descent into the labyrinths of meaning.[9]

[7] J. Damourette and E. Pichon, *Des mots à la pensée: Essai de grammaire de la langue française* (Paris, 1911–36), V, #1604 and VII, #2958. 'Le langage est naturellement centré sur le moi-ici-maintenant, c'est-à-dire sur la personne qui parle s'envisageant au moment même où elle parle; c'est ce qu'on peut appeler le *nynégocentrisme* naturel du langage' [#1604].

[8] *Dans le labyrinthe* (Paris: Editions de Minuit, 1959). For essays by Roland Barthes bearing on the fictional method and theory of Robbe-Grillet, see *Essais critiques* (Paris, 1964), pp. 29–40, 63–70, 198–205.

[9] Cf. Jakobson, *Shifters, Verbal Categories, and the Russian Verb* (Cambridge [Mass.], 1957). [Translated into French by Nicolas Ruwet in *Essais de linguistique générale* (Paris, 1963), pp. 176–96.] For the origin of the term 'shifter,' see Otto Jespersen, *Language, its Nature, Development and Origin* (London, 1922), p.123, and *ibid.*, *The Philosophy of Grammar* (London, 1923), pp. 83–84.

There remains one last grammatical notion which can, in my opinion, further elucidate the activity of writing at its center, since it concerns the verb *to write* itself. It would be interesting to know at what point the verb *to write* began to be used in an apparently intransitive manner, the writer being no longer one who writes *something*, but one who writes, absolutely. (How often now we hear in conversations, at least in more or less intellectual circles: 'What is he doing?' – 'He's writing.') This passage from the verb *to write*, transitive, to the verb *to write*, apparently intransitive, is certainly the sign of an important change in mentality. But is it really a question of intransitivity? No writer, whatever age he belongs to, can fail to realize that he always writes *something*: one might even say that it was paradoxically at the moment when the verb *to write* appeared to become intransitive that its object, the book or the text, took on a particular importance. It is not, therefore, in spite of the appearances, on the side of intransitivity that we must look for the definition of the modern verb *to write*. Another linguistic notion will perhaps give us the key: that of *diathesis*, or, as it is called in classical grammars, *voice* (active, passive, middle). Diathesis designates the way in which the subject of the verb is affected by the action [*procès*]; this is obvious for the passive (if I say "I am beaten," it is quite obvious that I am profoundly affected by the action of the verb *to beat*). And yet linguists tell us that, at least in Indo-European, the diathetical opposition is actually not between the active and the passive, but between the active and the middle. According to the classic example, given by Meillet and Benveniste, the verb *to sacrifice* (ritually) is active if the priest sacrifices the victim in my place for me, and it is middle voice if, taking the knife from the priest's hands, I make the sacrifice for myself.[10] In the case of the active, the action is accomplished outside the subject, because, although the priest makes the sacrifice, he is not affected by it. In the case of the middle voice, on the contrary, the subject affects himself in acting; he always remains inside the action, even if an object is involved. The middle voice does not, therefore, exclude transitivity. Thus defined, the middle voice corresponds exactly to the state of the verb *to write*: today to write is to make oneself the center of the action of speech [*parole*]; it is to effect writing in being affected oneself; it is to leave the writer [*scripteur*] inside the writing, not as a psychological subject (the Indo-European priest could very well overflow with subjectivity in actively sacrificing for his client), but as the agent of the action.

I think the diathetical analysis of the modern verb *to write*, which I have just tried to show a verb of middle voice, can be carried even

---

[10] Benveniste, 'Actif et moyen dans le verbe,' *Problèmes*, pp. 168–75. Cf. the distinction initiated by Pānini (fl. 350 BC): *parasmaipada*, 'word for another,' i.e., active, and *āmanepada*, 'word for self, i.e., middle. Thus *yajati* ('he sacrifices' [for another, *qua* priest]) vs. *yajate* ('he sacrifices' [for himself, *qua* offering]). Cf. Berthold Delbrück, *Vergleichende Syntax der Indogermanischen Sprachen* (Strassburg, 1893).

further. You know that in French – for I am obliged to refer to strictly French examples – certain verbs have an active meaning in the simple form, for example, *aller, arriver, rentrer, sortir* [to go, to arrive, to return, to go out], but, curiously, these active verbs take the passive auxiliary, the verb *être* [to be] in the forms of the *passé composé*. Instead of saying *j'ai allé*, we say *je suis allé, je suis sorti, je suis arrivé, je suis rentré*, etc. To explain this bifurcation peculiar to the middle voice, Guillaume distinguishes between two *passés composés*. The first, which he calls *diriment*, 'separated,' is a *passé composé* with the auxiliary *avoir* [to have]; this tense supposes an interruption of the action due to the initiative of the speaker. Take for example the verb *marcher* [to walk], an entirely commonplace active verb: *'je marche; je m'arrête de marcher; j'ai marché* [I walk; I stop walking (by my own initiative); I have walked] – this is the *passé composé diriment*. The other *passé composé* that he calls *intégrant* is constructed with the verb *être* [to be]; it designates a sort of semantic entity which cannot be delivered by the simple initiative of the subject. *'Je suis sorti'* or *'il est mort'* ['I went out' or 'he died'] (for I can't say 'I am dead') never refer to an interruption that would be at all like the *diriment* of the going out or the dying. I believe that this is an important opposition, for we see very well that the verb *to write* was traditionally an active verb and that its past tense is still today, formally a *diriment* past: *j'écris un livre; je le termine; je l'ai écrit.'* [I write a book; I end it; I have written it.] But in our literature, it seems to me, the verb is changing status, if not form, and the verb *to write* is becoming a middle verb with an *intégrant* past. This is true inasmuch as the modern verb *to write* is becoming a sort of indivisible semantic entity. So that if language followed literature – which, for once perhaps, has the lead – I would say that we should no longer say today *'j'ai écrit'* but, rather, *'je suis écrit,'* just as we say *je suis né, il est mort, elle est éclose.'* There is no passive idea in these expressions, in spite of the verb *to be*, for it is impossible to transform *'je suis écrit'* (without forcing things, and supposing that I dare to use this expression at all) into *'on m'a écrit'* ['I have been written' or 'somebody wrote me']. It is my opinion that in the middle verb *to write* the distance between the writer and the language diminishes asymptotically. We could even say that it is subjective writings, like romantic writing, which are active, because in them the agent is not interior but *anterior* to the process of writing. The one who writes here does not write for himself, but, as if by proxy, for a person who is exterior and antecedent (even if they both have the same name). In the modern verb of middle voice *to write*, however, the subject is immediately contemporary with the writing, being effected and affected by it. The case of the Proustian narrator is exemplary: he exists only in writing.

These remarks suggest that the central problem of modern writing exactly coincides with what we could call the problematic of the verb in linguistics; just as temporality, person, and diathesis define the positional field of the subject, so modern literature is trying, through various experiments, to establish a new status in writing for the agent of writing. The meaning or the goal of this effort is to substitute the instance of discourse for the instance of reality (or of the referent), which has been, and still is, a mythical 'alibi' dominating the idea of literature. The field of the writer is nothing but writing itself, not as the pure 'form' conceived by an aesthetic of art for art's sake, but, much more radically, as the only area [*espace*] for the one who writes.

It seems to me to be necessary to remind those who might be tempted to accuse this kind of inquiry of solipsism, formalism, or, inversely, of scientism, that in returning to the fundamental categories of language, such as person, tense, and voice, we place ourselves at the very heart of a problematic of *inter*locution. For these categories are precisely those in which we may examine the relationships between the *je* and that which is deprived of the mark of *je*. Inasmuch as person, tense, and voice imply those remarkable linguistic beings – the 'shifters' – they oblige us to conceive language and discourse no longer in terms of an instrumental and reified nomenclature but in the very exercise of language [*parole*]. The pronoun, for example, which is without doubt the most staggering of the 'shifters', belongs structurally to speech [*parole*]. That is its scandal, if you like, and it is on this scandal that we must work today, in linguistics and literature. We are all trying, with different methods, styles, perhaps even prejudices, to get to the core of this linguistic pact [*pacte de parole*] which unites the writer and the other, so that – and this is a contradiction which will never be sufficiently pondered – each moment of discourse is both absolutely new and absolutely understood. I think that, with a certain amount of temerity, we could even give a historical dimension to this research. We know that the medieval *septenium*, in its grandiose classification of the universe, prescribed two great areas of exploration: on the one hand, the secrets of nature (the *quadrivium*) and, on the other, the secrets of language [*parole*] (the *trivium: grammatica, rhetorica, dialectica*). From the end of the Middle Ages to the present day, this opposition was lost, language being considered only as an instrument in the service of either reason or the heart. Today, however, something of this ancient opposition lives again: once again the exploration of language, conducted by linguistics, psychoanalysis, and literature, corresponds to the exploration of the cosmos. For literature is itself a science, or at least knowledge, no longer of the 'human heart' but of human language [*parole*]. Its investigation is not, however, addressed to the secondary forms and figures that were the object of rhetoric, but to the fundamental categories of language. Just as in Western culture grammar was not born until long after rhetoric, so it is only after having made its way for centuries through *le beau littéraire* that literature can begin to ponder the fundamental problems of language, without which it would not exist.

SECTION FOUR
MARXISM

Broadly speaking, as an approach to literature, Marxism attempts to draw conclusions about the relations between the literary and the social. Recent Marxist literary theory has been heavily influenced by the work of the French philosopher Louis Althusser and the literary critic, Pierre Macherey. Whilst these figures claim not to be structuralists, and have explicitly criticized structuralism, their theories exhibit striking similarities to aspects of structuralist thought (see Harland 1987). Indeed Raman Selden, in his account of contemporary literary theory, considers them under the heading of 'structuralist Marxism' (1985) and critics who have drawn upon Althusser's work are likely also to draw upon structuralist/semiotic theories.

The initial influence of structuralist Marxism on literary theory centred mainly around the concept of ideology, though Althusser's notion of 'Ideological State Apparatus' and of the construction ('interpellation') of the human subject has been taken up in some post-structuralist work. The extract reprinted here comes from Althusser's seminal essay 'Ideology and the State' (1977b) and whilst a full account of his work is not possible some contextualizing remarks seem necessary. We can start by saying that 'ideology' reproduces 'subjects' who are willing workers in the capitalist system. Capitalism requires not only the hands of labour, but also the willingness of workers to subject themselves to the system – to accept the 'status quo' – and it is in this area that ideology works. The central feature of Althusser's Marxism and one of the key areas of differences between his and previous Marxisms, is the way in which he conceived ideology.

For Althusser, ideology is not a matter of conscious beliefs, attitudes and values, nor is it a matter of 'false consciousness' – sets of false ideas imposed on individuals to persuade them that there is no real contradiction between capital and labour or, more crudely, between the interests of the working class and ruling class. It is, rather, a matter of the representation of imaginary versions of the real social relations that people live. These imaginary versions of the real relations are necessary for the perpetuation of the capitalist system. Ideology imposes itself not simply through consiousness nor through disembodied ideas but through systems and structures; ideology is inscribed in the representations (the signs) and the practices (the rituals) of everyday life. Most importantly, though, it is through ideology that individuals are constituted as 'subjects' – (*mis*)recognizing themselves as free and autonomous beings with unique subjectivities.

The main agencies for the reproduction of ideology and the subject are what Althusser calls the 'Ideological State Apparatuses' (ISAs), which include the church, the family, the media, and the cultural ISAs (Literature, the Arts, sports, etc.). The extract reprinted here begins with a consideration of Ideological State Apparatuses.

Balibar and Macherey take up Althusser's notion of ISAs. They examine the way that literature functions in the reproduction of ideology within the ISAs of the French education system. Literature, in their article, is seen in terms of the acquisition and distribution of what the French sociologist of culture, Pierre Bourdieu, has called 'cultural capital'. However, a residue of Macherey's previous work in *A Theory of Literary Production* (1966) can be seen in the discussion of the relation between the literary text and social reality. *A Theory of Literary Production* had been an influential book offering a model of textual analysis based on Althusser's notion of 'symptomatic' reading. This model involved uncovering the significant absences of the texts, the ideological presuppositions on which the text was at once founded but of which it could not speak. It is a difficult model to grasp but a good account can be found in Jefferson and Robey (1982) and an interesting adaptation of the model appears in Belsey (1980).

Terry Eagleton, in *Criticism and Ideology* (1976), draws on the work of Althusser and Macherey to provide a general framework for understanding the relation between the literary text and the social world, and for a model of textual analysis which will reveal the 'ideology of the text'. Literary works are scrutinized for the symptoms of the ideology that form the raw material of their production. Such a critical enterprise is now frequently undertaken, often in conjunction with a version of semiotics which looks at the 'representations' inscribed in texts. This mode of analysis owes a debt also to Roland Barthes, who had woven a notion of ideology into the semiotic model in *Mythologies* (1957).

Aspects of both Althusser's and Macherey's work would seem to be more in line with material represented in Part Two of this book – Althusser's notion of the interpellation of the subject, and his radical attack on humanism; Macherey's concern with 'absences' and with the practices of the institution of literary studies. However, their belief in a scientific procedure which would yield knowledge and explanation, their placing of literature between the realms of ideology and science, and their reification of structure, all connect them, if not wholly satisfactorily, to the material of Part One. Additionally, their initial influence on literary theory produced a critical practice that, in its endeavour to analyse and understand texts, belongs to the less radical break with the critical orthodoxy.

---

5 Louis Althusser,

From 'Ideology and the State', *Lenin and Philosophy and other essays*, trans B. Brewster

p136–8; 152–3; 154–5; 155–6; 160–2; 162–4; 168–9

What are the ideological State apparatuses (ISAs)?

They must not be confused with the (repressive) State apparatus. Remember that in Marxist theory, the State Apparatus (SA) contains: the Government, the Administration, the Army, the Police, the Courts, the Prisons, etc., which constitute what I shall in future call the Repressive State Apparatus. Repressive suggests that the State Apparatus in question 'functions by violence' – at least ultimately (since repression, e.g. administrative repression, may take non-physical forms).

I shall call Ideological State Apparatuses a certain number of realities which present themselves to the immediate observer in the form of distinct and specialized institutions. I propose an empirical list of these which obviously have to be examined in detail, tested, corrected and reorganized. With all the reservations implied by this requirement, we can for the moment regard the following in situations as Ideological State Apparatuses (the order in which I have listed them has no particular significance):

- the religious ISA (the system of the different Churches),
- the educational ISA (the system of the different public and private 'Schools'),
- the family ISA,[1]
- the legal ISA,[2]

---

[1] The family obviously has other 'functions' than that of an ISA. It intervenes in the reproduction of labour power. In different modes of production it is the unit of production and/or the unit of consumption.

[2] The 'Law' belongs both to the (Repressive) State Apparatus and to the system of the ISAs.

- the political ISA (the political system, including the different Parties),
- the trade-union ISA,
- the communications ISA (press, radio and television, etc.),
- the cultural ISA (Literature, the Arts, sports, etc.).

I have said that the ISAs must not be confused with the (Repressive) State Apparatus. What constitutes the difference?

As a first moment, it is clear that while there is *one* (Repressive) State Apparatus, there is a *plurality* of Ideological State Apparatuses. Even presupposing that it exists, the unity that constitutes this plurality of ISAs as a body is not immediately visible.

As a second moment, it is clear that whereas the – unified – (Repressive) State Apparatus belongs entirely to the *public* domain, much the larger part of the Ideological State Apparatuses (in their apparent dispersion) are part, on the contrary, of the *private* domain. Churches, Parties, Trade Unions, families, some schools, most newspapers, cultural ventures, etc., etc., are private.

We can ignore the first observation for the moment. But someone is bound to question the second, asking me by what right I regard as Ideological *State* Apparatuses, institutions which for the most part do not possess public status, but are quite simply *private* institutions. As a conscious Marxist, Gramsci already forestalled this objection in one sentence. The distinction between the public and the private is a distinction internal to bourgeois law, and valid in the (subordinate) domains in which bourgeois law exercises its 'authority'. The domain of the State escapes it because the latter is 'above the law': the State, which is the State of the ruling class is neither public nor private; on the contrary, it is the precondition for any distinction between public and private. The same thing can be said from the starting-point of our State Ideological Apparatuses. It is unimportant whether the institutions in which they are realized are 'public' or 'private'. What matters is how they function. Private institutions can perfectly well 'function' as Ideological State Apparatuses. A reasonably thorough analysis of any one of the ISAs proves it.

But now for what is essential. What distinguishes the ISAs from the (Repressive) State Apparatus is the following basic difference: the Repressive State Apparatus functions 'by violence', whereas the Ideological State Apparatuses *function 'by ideology'*.

I can clarify matters by correcting this distinction. I shall say rather that every State Apparatus, whether Repressive or Ideological, 'functions' both by violence and by ideology, but with one very important distinction which makes it imperative not to confuse the Ideological State Apparatuses with the (Repressive) State Apparatus.

This is the fact that the (Repressive) State Apparatus functions massively and predominantly *by repression* (including physical repression), while functioning secondarily by ideology. (There is no such thing as a purely repressive apparatus.) For example, the Army and the Police also function by ideology both to ensure their own cohesion and reproduction, and in the 'values' they propound externally.

In the same way, but inversely, it is essential to say that for their part the Ideological State Apparatuses function massively and pre-dominantly *by ideology*, but they also function secondarily by repression, even if ultimately, but only ultimately, this is very attentuated and concealed, even symbolic. (There is no such thing as purely ideological apparatus.) Thus Schools and Churches use suitable methods of punishment, expulsion, selection, etc., to 'discipline' not only their shepherds, but also their flocks. The same is true of the Family. . . . The same is true of the cultural IS Apparatus (censorship, among other things), etc.

. . . .

Ideology is a 'Representation' of the Imaginary Relationship of Individuals to their Real Conditions of Existence

In order to approach my central thesis on the structure and functioning of ideology, I shall first present two theses, one negative, the other positive. The first concerns the object which is 'represented' in the imaginary form of ideology, the second concerns the materiality of ideology.

THESIS I Ideology represents the imaginary relationship of individuals to their real conditions of existence.

We commonly call religious ideology, ethical ideology, legal ideology, political ideology, etc., so many 'world outlooks'. Of course, assuming that we do not live one of these ideologies as the truth (e.g. 'believe' in God, Duty, Justice, etc. . . .), we admit that the ideology we are discussing from a critical point of view, examining it as the ethnologist examines the myths of a 'primitive society', that these 'world outlooks' are largely imaginary, i.e. do not 'correspond to reality'.

However, while admitting that they do not correspond to reality, i.e. that they constitute an illusion, we admit that they do make allusion to reality, and that they need only be 'interpreted' to discover the reality of the world behind their imaginary representation of that world (ideology = *illusion/allusion*).

. . . .

Now I can return to a thesis which I have already advanced: it is not their real conditions of existence, their real world, that 'men' 'represent to themselves' in ideology, but above all it is their relation to those conditions of existence which is represented to them there. It is this relation which is at the centre of every ideological, i.e. imaginary, representation of the real world. It is this relation that contains the 'cause' which has to explain the imaginary distortion of the ideological representation of the real world. Or rather, to leave aside the language of causality it is necessary to advance the thesis that it is the *imaginary nature of this relation* which underlies all the imaginary distortion that we can observe (if we do not live in its truth) in all ideology.

To speak in a Marxist language, if it is true that the representation of the real conditions of existence of the individuals occupying the posts of agents of production, exploitation, repression, ideologization and scientific practices, does in the last analysis arise from the relations of production, and from relations deriving from the relations of production, we can say the following: all ideology represents in its necessarily imaginary distortion not the existing relations of production (and the other relations that derive from them), but above all the (imaginary) relationship of individuals to the relations of production and the relations that derive from them. What is represented in ideology is therefore not the system of the real relations which govern the existence of individuals, but the imaginary relation of those individuals to the real relations in which they live.

. . . .

THESIS II   Ideology has a material existence.

I have already touched on this thesis by saying that the 'ideas' or 'representations', etc., which seem to make up ideology do not have an ideal (*idéale* and *idéelle*) or spiritual existence, but a material existence. I even suggested that the ideal (*idéale, idéelle*) and spiritual existence of 'ideas' arises exclusively in an ideology of the 'idea' and of ideology, and let me add, in an ideology of what seems to have 'founded' this conception since the emergence of the sciences, i.e. what the practicians of the sciences represent to themselves in their spontaneous ideology as 'ideas', true or false. Of course, presented in affirmative form, this thesis is unproven. I simply ask that the reader be favourably disposed towards it, say, in the name of materialism. A long series of arguments would be necessary to prove it.

This hypothetical thesis of the not spiritual but material existence of 'ideas' or other 'representations' is indeed necessary if we are to advance in our analysis of the nature of ideology. Or rather, it is merely useful to us in order the better to reveal what every at all serious analysis of any ideology will immediately and empirically show to every observer, however critical.

While discussing the ideological State apparatuses and their practices, I said that each of them was the realization of an ideology (the unity of these different regional ideologies – religious, ethical, legal, political, aesthetic, etc. – being assured by their subjection to the ruling ideology). I now return to this thesis: an ideology always exists in an apparatus, and its practice, or practices. This existence is material.

Of course, the material existence of the ideology in an apparatus and its practices does not have the same modality as the material existence of a paving-stone or a rifle. But, at the risk of being taken for a Neo-Aristotelian (NB Marx had a very high regard for Aristotle), I shall say that 'matter is discussed in many senses', or rather that it exists in different modalities, all rooted in the last instance in 'physical' matter.

. . . .

Ideology Interpellates Individuals as Subjects

This thesis is simply a matter of making my last proposition explicit: there is no ideology except by the subject and for subjects. Meaning, there is no ideology except for concrete subjects, and this destination for ideology is only made possible by the subject: meaning, *by the category of the subject* and its functioning.

By this I mean that, even if it only appears under this name (the subject) with the rise of bourgeois ideology, above all with the rise of legal ideology,[3] the category of the subject (which may function under other names: e.g., as the soul in Plato, as God, etc.) is the constitutive category of all ideology, whatever its determination (regional or class) and whatever its historical date – since ideology has no history.

I say: the category of the subject is constitutive of all ideology, but at the same time and immediately I add that *the category of the subject is only constitutive of all ideology insofar as all ideology has the function (which defines it) of 'constituting' concrete individuals as subjects*. In the interaction of this double constitution exists the functioning of all ideology, ideology being nothing but its functioning in the material forms of existence of that functioning.

In order to grasp what follows, it is essential to realize that both he who is writing these lines and the reader who reads them are themselves subjects, and therefore ideological subjects (a tautological proposition), i.e. that the author and the reader of these lines both live 'spontaneously' or 'naturally' in ideology in the sense in which I have said that 'man is an ideological animal by nature'.

That the author, insofar as he writes the lines of a discourse which claims to be scientific, is completely absent as a 'subject' from 'his' scientific discourse (for all scientific discourse is by definition a subject-less

[3] Which borrowed the legal category of 'subject in law' to make an ideological notion: man is by nature a subject.

discourse, there is no 'Subject of science' except in an ideology of science) is a different question which I shall leave on one side for the moment.

As St Paul admirably put it, it is in the 'Logos', meaning in ideology, that we 'live, move and have our being'. It follows that, for you and for me, the category of the subject is a primary 'obviousness' (obviousnesses are always primary): it is clear that you and I are subjects (free, ethical, etc. . . . .). Like all obviousnesses, including those that make a word 'name a thing' or 'have a meaning' (therefore including the obviousness of the 'transparency' of language), the 'obviousness' that you and I are subjects – and that that does not cause any problems – is an ideological effect, the elementary ideological effect.[4] It is indeed a peculiarity of ideology that it imposes (without appearing to do so, since these are 'obviousnesses') obviousnesses as obviousnesses, which we cannot *fail to recognize* and before which we have the inevitable and natural reaction of crying out (aloud or in the 'still, small voice of conscience'): 'That's obvious! That's right! That's true!'

At work in this reaction is the ideological *recognition* function which is one of the two functions of ideology as such (its inverse being the function of *misrecognition – méconnaissance*).

To take a highly 'concrete' example, we all have friends who, when they knock on our door and we ask, through the door, the question 'Who's there?', answer (since 'it's obvious') It's me'. And we recognized that 'it is him', or 'her'. We open the door, and 'it's true, it really was she who was there'. To take another example, when we recognize somebody of our (previous) acquaintance (*(re) – connaissance*) in the street, we show him that we have recognized him (and have recognized that he has recognized us) by saying to him 'Hello, my friend', and shaking his hand (a material ritual practice of ideological recognition in everyday life – in France, at least; elsewhere, there are other rituals).

In this preliminary remark and these concrete illustrations, I only wish to point out that you and I are *always already* subjects, and as such constantly practice the rituals of ideological recognition, which guarantee for us that we are indeed concrete, individual, distinguishable and (naturally) irreplaceable subjects. The writing I am currently executing and the reading you are currently[5] performing are also in this respect rituals of ideological recognition, including the 'obviousness' with which the 'truth' or 'error' of my reflections may impose itself on you.

. . . .

[4] Linguists and those who appeal to linguistics for various purposes often run up against difficulties which arise because they ignore the action of the ideological effects in all discourses – including even scientific discourses.

[5] NB: this double 'currently' is one more proof of the fact that ideology is 'eternal', since these two 'currentlys' are separated by an indefinite interval; I am writing these lines on 6 April 1969, you may read them at any subsequent time.

As a first formulation I shall say: *all ideology hails or interpellates concrete individuals as concrete subjects*, by the functioning of the category of the subject.

This is a proposition which entails that we distinguish for the moment between concrete individuals on the one hand and concrete subjects on the other, although at this level concrete subjects only exist insofar as they are supported by a concrete individual.

I shall then suggest that ideology 'acts' or 'functions' in such a way that it 'recruits' subjects among the individuals (it recruits them all), or 'transforms' the individuals into subjects (it transforms them all) by that very precise operation which I have called *interpellation* or hailing, and which can be imagined along the lines of the most commonplace everyday police (or other) hailing: 'Hey, you there!'[6]

Assuming that the theoretical scene I have imagined takes place in the street, the hailed individual will turn round. By this mere one-hundred-and-eighty-degree physical conversion, he becomes a *subject*. Why? Because he has recognized that the hail was 'really' addressed to him, and that 'it was *really him* who was hailed' (and not someone else). Experience shows that the practical telecommunication of hailings is such that they hardly ever miss their man: verbal call or whistle, the one hailed always recognizes that it is really him who is being hailed. And yet it is a strange phenomenon, and one which cannot be explained solely by 'guilt feelings', despite the large numbers who 'have something on their consciences'.

Naturally for the convenience and clarity of my little theoretical theatre I have had to present things in the form of a sequence, with a before and an after, and thus in the form of a temporal succession. There are individuals walking along. Somewhere (usually behind them) the hail rings out: 'Hey, you there!' One individual (nine times out of ten it is the right one) turns round, believing/suspecting/knowing that it is for him, i.e. recognizing that 'it really is he' who is meant by the hailing. But in reality these things happen without any succession. The existence of ideology and the hailing or interpellation of individuals as subjects are one and the same thing.

I might add: what thus seems to take place outside ideology (to be precise, in the street), in reality takes place in ideology. What really takes place in ideology seems therefore to take place outside it. That is why those who are in ideology believe themselves by definition outside ideology: one of the effects of ideology is the practical *denegation* of the ideological character of ideology by ideology: ideology never says, 'I am ideological'. It is necessary to be outside ideology, i.e. in scientific knowledge, to be able to say: I am in ideology (a quite exceptional case) or (the

---

[6] Hailing as an everyday practice subject to a precise ritual takes a quite 'special' form in the policeman's practice of 'hailing' which concerns the hailing of 'suspects'.

general case): I was in ideology. As is well known, the accusation of being in ideology only applies to others, never to oneself (unless one is really a Spinozist or a Marxist, which, in this matter, is to be exactly the same thing). Which amounts to saying that ideology *has no outside* (for itself), but at the same time *that it is nothing but outside* (for science and reality).

. . . .

Let me summarize what we have discovered about ideology in general. The duplicate mirror-structure of ideology ensures simultaneously:

1. the interpellation of 'individuals' as subjects;
2. their subjection to the Subject;
3. the mutual recognition of subjects and Subject, the subjects' recognition of each other, and finally the subject's recognition of himself;[7]
4. the absolute guarantee that everything really is so, and that on condition that the subjects recognize what they are and behave accordingly, everything will be all right: Amen – *'So be it'*.

Result: caught in this quadruple system of interpellation as subjects, of subjection to the Subject, of universal recognition and of absolute guarantee, the subjects 'work', they 'work by themselves' in the vast majority of cases, with the exception of the 'bad subjects' who on occasion provoke the intervention of one of the detachments of the (repressive) State apparatus. But the vast majority of (good) subjects work all right 'all by themselves', i.e. by ideology (whose concrete forms are realized in the Ideological State Apparatuses). They are inserted into practices governed by the rituals of the ISAs. They 'recognize' the existing state of affairs (*das Bestehende*), that 'it really is true that it is so and not otherwise', and that they must be obedient to God, to their conscience, to the priest, to de Gaulle, to the boss, to the engineer, that thou shalt 'love thy neighbour as thyself', etc. Their concrete, material behaviour is simply the inscription in life of the admirable words of the prayer: '*Amen – So be it*'.

Yes, the subjects 'work by themselves'. The whole mystery of this effect lies in the first two moments of the quadruple system I have just discussed, or, if you prefer, in the ambiguity of the term *subject*. In the ordinary use of the term, subject in fact means: (1) a free subjectivity, a centre of initiatives, author of and responsible for its actions; (2) a subjected being, who submits to a higher authority, and is therefore stripped of all freedom except that of freely accepting his submission. This last

[7] Hegel is (unknowingly) an admirable 'theoretician' of ideology insofar as he is a 'theoretician' of Universal Recognition who unfortunately ends up in the ideology of Absolute Knowledge. Feuerbach is an astonishing 'theoretician' of the mirror connexion, who unfortunately ends up in the ideology of the Human Essence. To find the material with which to construct a theory of the guarantee, we must turn to Spinoza.

note gives us the meaning of this ambiguity, which is merely a reflection of the effect which produces it: the individual *is interpellated as a (free) subject in order that he shall submit freely to the commandments of the Subject*, i.e. *in order that he shall (freely) accept his subjection*, i.e. in order that he shall make the gestures and actions of his subjection 'all by himself'. *There are no subjects except by and for their subjection*. That is why they 'work all by themselves'.

---

6   E. Balibar & P. Macherey,

From 'Literature as an Ideological Form', *Oxford Literary Review*, Vol 3;1, 1978

p6; 8; 10; 11–12

Literature as an ideological form

It is important to 'locate' the production of literary effects historically as part of the ensemble of social practices. For this to be seen dialectically rather than mechanically , it is important to understand that the relationship of 'history' to 'literature' is not like the relationship or 'correspondence' of *two 'branches'*, but concerns the developing forms of an internal *contradiction*. Literature and history are not each set up externally to each other (not even as the history *of* literature, social and political history), but are in an intricate and connected relationship, the historical conditions of existence of anything like a literature. Very generally, this internal relationship is what constitutes the definition of literature as an ideological form.

But this definition is significant only in so far as its implications are then developed. Ideological forms, to be sure, are not straightforward systems of 'ideas' and 'discourses', but are manifested through the workings and history of determinate *practices* in determinate social relations, what Althusser calls the *Ideological State Apparatus* (ISA). The objectivity of literary production therefore is inseparable from given social practices in a given ISA. More precisely, we shall see that it is inseparable from a given *linguistic practice* (there is a 'French' literature because there is a linguistic practice 'French', i.e., a contradictory ensemble making a national tongue), in itself inseparable from an *academic or schooling practice* which defines both the conditions for the consumption of literature and the very conditions of its production also.

By connecting the objective existence of literature to this ensemble of practices, one can define the material anchoring points which *make* literature an historic and social reality.

First, then, literature is historically constituted *in the bourgeois epoch* as an ensemble of language – or rather of specific linguistic practices – inserted in a general schooling process so as to provide appropriate fictional effects, thereby reproducing bourgeois ideology as the dominant ideology. Literature submits to a threefold determination: 'linguistic', 'pedagogic', and 'fictive' [*imaginaire*] (we must return to this point, for it involves the question of a recourse to psycho-analysis for an explanation of literary effects). There is a linguistic determination because the work of literary production depends on the existence of a common language codifying linguistic exchange, both for its material and for its aims – insomuch as literature *contributes* directly to the *maintenance* of a '*common* language'. That it has this starting point is proved by the fact that divergences from the common language are not arbitrary but determined. In our introduction to the work of R. Balibar and D. Laporte,[1] we sketched out an explanation of the historical process by which this 'common language' is set up. Following their thought, we stressed that the common language, i.e. the *national language*, is bound to the political form of 'bourgeois democracy' and is the historical outcome of particular class struggles. Like bourgeois *right*, its parallel, the common national language is needed to unify a new class domination thereby universalising it and providing it with progressive forms throughout its epoch. It refers therefore to a social *contradiction* perpetually reproduced via the process which surmounts it. What is the basis of this contradiction?

It is the effect of the historic conditions under which the bourgeois class established its political, economic and ideological dominance. To achieve hegemony, it had not only to transform the base, the relations of production, but also radically to transform the superstructure the ideological formations. This transformation could be called the bourgeois 'cultural revolution' since it involves not only the formation of a new ideology, but its realisation as the dominant ideology, through new ISAs and the remoulding of the relationships between the different ISAs. This revolutionary transformation, which took more than a century but which was preparing itself for far longer, is characterised by making the school apparatus the means of forcing submission to the dominant ideology – individual submission, but also, and more importantly, the submission of the very ideology of the dominated classes. Therefore in the last analysis, all the ideological contradictions rest on the contradictions

[1] R, Balibar and D. Laporte, *Le Français National: constitution de la langue nationale commune a l'époque de la revolution démocratique bourgeoise,* introduction by E. Balibar and P. Macherey, Éditions Hachette 1974, in *Analyses*.

of the school apparatus, and become contradictions subordinated to the form of schooling, within the form of schooling itself.

. . . .

The specific complexity of literary formations-ideological contradictions and linguistic conflicts

The first principle of a materialist analysis would be: literary productions must not be studied from the standpoint of their *unity* which is illusory and false, but from their material *disparity*. One must not look for unifying effects but for signs of the contradictions (historically determined) which produced them and which appear as unevenly resolved conflicts in the text.

So, in searching out the determinant contradictions, the materialist analysis of literature rejects on principle the notion of 'the word' – i.e., the illusory presentation of the unity of a text, its totality, self-sufficiency and perfection (in both senses of the word: success and completion). More precisely, it recognises the notion of 'the work' (and its correlative, 'the author') only in order to identify both as necessary illusions written into *the ideology of literature*, the accompaniment of all literary production. The text is produced under conditions which represent it as a finished work providing a requisite order, expressing either a subjective theme or the spirit of the age, according to whether the reading is a naive or a sophisticated one. Yet in itself the text is none of these things: on the contrary, it is materially incomplete, disparate and diffuse from being the outcome of the conflicting contradictory effect of superimposing real processes which cannot be abolished in it except in an imaginary way.[2]

To be more explicit: literature is produced finally through the effect of one or more ideological contradictions precisely because these contradictions cannot be solved within the ideology, i.e., in the last analysis through the effect of contradictory class positions within the ideology, as such irreconcilable. Obviously these contradictory ideological positions are not in themselves 'literary' – that would lead us back into the closed circle of 'literature'. They are ideological positions within theory and practice, covering the whole field of the ideological class struggle, i.e. religious, judicial, and political, and they correspond to the conjunctures of the class struggle itself. But it would be pointless to look in the texts for the 'original' bare discourse of these ideological positions, as they were 'before' their 'literary' realisation, *for these ideological*

---

[2] Rejecting the mythical unity and completeness of a work of art does not mean adopting a reverse position, i.e. the work of art as anti-nature, a violation of order (cf. *Tel Quel*). Such reversals are characteristic of conservative ideology: 'For oft a fine disorder stems from art' (Boileau)!

positions can only be formed in the materiality of the literary text. That is, they can only appear in a form which provides their *imaginary solution*, or better still, which displaces them by substituting imaginary contradictions soluble within the ideological practice of religion, politics, morality, aesthetics and psychology.

Let us approach this phenomenon more closely. We shall say that literature 'begins' with the imaginary solution of implacable ideological contradictions, with the representation of that solution: not in the sense of representating i.e. 'figuring' (by images, allegories, symbols or arguments) a solution which is really there (to repeat, literature is produced because such a solution is impossible) but in the sense of providing a 'mise en scene', a *presentation as solution* of the very terms of an insurmountable contradiction, by means of various displacements and substitutions. For there to be a literature, it must be the very terms of the contradiction (and hence of the contradictory ideological elements) that are enunciated in a special language, a language of 'compromise' realising in advance the fiction of a forthcoming conciliation. Or better still (it finds a language of 'compromise' which presents the conciliation as 'natural' and so both necessary and inevitable.

. . . .

Fiction and realism: the mechanism of identification in literature

Here we must pause, even if over-schematically, to consider a characteristic literary effect which has already been briefly mentioned: the identification effect. Brecht was the first marxist theoretician to focus on this by showing how the ideological effects of literature (and of the theatre, with the specific transformations that implies) *materialise* via an indentification process between the reader or the audience and the hero or anti-hero, the simultaneous mutual constitution of the fictive 'consciousness' of the character with the ideological 'consciousness' of the reader.

But it is obvious that any process of identification is dependent on the constitution and recognition of the individual as 'subject' – to use a very common ideological notion lifted by philosophy from the juridical and turning up under various forms in all other levels of bourgeois ideology. Now, all ideology, as Althusser shows in his essay 'Ideology and Ideological State Apparatuses',[3] must in a practical way 'hail or interpellate individuals as subjects': so that they perceive themselves as such, with rights and duties, the obligatory accompaniments. Each ideology has its specific mode: each gives to the 'subject' – and therefore to other real or

---

[3] In *La Pensée* no. 151, June 1970; *Lenin and Philosophy*, trans. B. Brewster, NLB, 1971.

imaginary subjects who confront the individual and present him with his ideological identification in a personal form – one or more appropriate names. In the ideology of literature the nomenclature is: Authors (i.e. signatures), Works (i.e. titles), Readers, and Characters (with their social background, real or imaginary). But in literature, the process of constituting subjects and setting up their relationships of mutual recognition necessarily takes a detour via the fictional world and its values, because that process (i.e. of constitution and setting-up) embraces within its circle the 'concrete' or 'abstract' 'persons' which the text stages. We now reach a classic general problem: what is specifically 'fictional' about literature?

. . . .

Literature is not fiction, a fictive image of the real, because it cannot define itself simply as a figuration, an appearance of reality. By a complex process, literature is the production of a certain reality, not indeed (one cannot over-emphasise this) an autonomous reality, but a material reality, and of a certain social effect (we shall conclude with this). Literature is not therefore fiction, but *the production of fictions*: or better still, the production of fiction-effects (and in the first place the provider of the material means for the production of fiction-effects).

Similarly, as the 'reflection of the life of a given society', historically given (Mao), literature is still not providing a 'realist' reproduction of it, even and least of all when it proclaims itself to be such, because even then it cannot be reduced to a straight mirroring. But it is true that the text does produce a *reality-effect*. More precisely it produces simultaneously a reality-effect and a fiction-effect, emphasising first one and then the other, interpreting each by each in turn but always *on the basis of their dualism*.

So, it comes to this once more: fiction and realism are not *the concepts for* the production of literature but on the contrary the notions produced by literature. But this leads to remarkable consequences for it means that the *model*, the real referent 'outside' the discourse which both fiction and realism presuppose, has no function here as a non-literary non-discursive anchoring point predating the text. (We know by now that this anchorage, the primacy of the real, is different from and more complex than a 'representation'.) But it does function as an effect of the discourse. *So, the literary discourse itself institutes and projects the presence of the 'real' in the manner of an hallucination.*

How is this materially possible? How can the text so control what it says, what it describes, what it sets up (or 'those' it sets up) with its sign of hallucinatory reality, or contrastingly, its fictive sign, diverging, infinitesimally perhaps, from the 'real'? On this point too, in parts of their deep analysis, the works we have used supply the material for an answer. Once more they refer us to the effects and forms of the fundamental linguistic conflict.

In a study of 'modern' French literary texts, carefully dated in each case according to their place in the history of the common language and of the educational system, R. Balibar refers to the production of 'imaginary French' [*français fictif*]. What does this mean? Clearly not pseudo-French, elements of a pseudo-language, seeing that these literary instances do also appear in certain contexts chosen by particular individuals, e.g. by compilers of dictionaries who illustrate their rubrics only with literary quotations. Nor is it simply a case of the language being produced *in* fiction (with its own usages, syntax and vocabulary), i.e. that of the characters in a narrative making an imaginary discourse in an imaginary language. Instead, it is a case of expressions which *always* diverge in one or more salient details from those used in practice outside the literary discourse, even when both are grammatically 'correct'. These are linguistic 'compromise formations', compromising between usages which are socially contradictory in practice and hence mutually exclude each other. In these compromise formations there is an essential place, more or less disguised but *recognisable*, for the reproduction of 'simple' language, 'ordinary' language, French 'just like that', i.e. the language which is taught in elementary school as the 'pure and simple' expression of 'reality'. In R. Balibar's book there are numerous examples which 'speak' to everyone, re-awakening or reviving memories which are usually repressed (it is their presence, their reproduction – the reason for a character or his words and for what the 'author' makes himself responsible for without naming himself – which produces the effect of 'naturalness' and 'reality', even if it is only by a single phrase uttered as if in passing). In comparison, all other expressions seem 'arguable', 'reflected' in a subjectivity. It is necessary that first of all there should be expressions which seem *objective*: these are the ones which in the text itself produce the imaginary referent of an elusive 'reality'.

Finally, to go back to our starting point: the ideological effect of identification produced by literature or rather by literary texts, which Brecht, thanks to his position as a revolutionary and materialist dramatist, was the first to theorise. But there is only ever identification *of one subject with another* (potentially with 'oneself': 'Madame Bovary, c'est moi', familiar example, signed Gustave Flaubert). And there are only ever subjects through the interpellation of the individual into a subject *by* a Subject who names him, as Althusser shows: 'tu es Un tel, et c'est à toi que je m'adresse': 'Hypocrite lecteur, mon semblable, mon frère', another familiar example, signed Charles Baudelaire. Through the endless functioning of its texts, literature unceasingly 'produces' *subjects*, on display for everyone. So paradoxically using the same schema we can say: literature endlessly transforms (concrete) individuals into subjects and endows them with a quasi-real hallucinatory individuality.

According to the fundamental mechanism of the whole of bourgeois ideology, to produce subjects ('persons' and 'characters') *one must oppose them to objects*, i.e. to *things*, by placing them *in* and *against* a world of 'real' things, outside it but always *in relation* to it. The realistic effect is the basis of this interpellation which makes characters or merely discourse 'live' and which makes readers take up an attitude towards imaginary struggles as they would towards real ones, though undangerously. They flourish here, the subjects we have already named: the Author and his Readers, but also the Author and his Characters, and the Reader and his Characters via the mediator, the Author – the Author identified with his Characters, or 'on the contrary' with one of their Judges, and likewise for the Reader. And from there, the Author, the Reader, the Characters opposite their universal abstract subjects: God, History, the People, Art. The list is neither final nor finishable: the work of literature is by definition to prolong and expand it indefinitely.

. . . .

The aesthetic effect of literature as ideological domination-effect

Here is the index of the structure of the process of reproduction in which the literary effect is inserted. What is in fact 'the primary material' of the literary text? (But a raw material which always seems to have been already transformed by it). It is the ideological contradictions which are *not* specifically literary but political, religious, etc.; in the last analysis, contradictory ideological realisations of determinate class positions in the class struggle. And what is the 'effect' of the literary text? (*at least* on those readers who recognise it as such, those of the *dominant* cultured class). Its effect is to provoke other ideological discourses which can sometimes be recognised as literary ones but which are usually merely aesthetic, moral, political, religious discourses in which the dominant ideology is realised.

We can now say that the literary text is the *agent* for the *reproduction* of ideology in its ensemble. In other words, it induces by the literary effect the production of 'new' discourses which always reproduce (under constantly varied forms) the *same* ideology (with its contradictions). It enables individuals to *appropriate* ideology and make themselves its 'free' *bearers* and even its 'free' *creators*. The literary text is a privileged operator in the concrete relations between the individual and ideology in bourgeois society and ensures its reproduction. To the extent that it induces the ideological discourse to leave its subject matter which has always already been invested as the aesthetic effect, in the form of the work of art, it does not seem a mechanical imposition, forced, revealed like a religious dogma, on individuals who must repeat it faithfully. Instead it appears as if offered for interpretations, a free choice, for the subjective private use of individuals. It is the privileged agent of ideological subjection, in the democratic and 'critical' form of 'freedom of thought'.[4]

Under these conditions, the aesthetic effect is also inevitably an effect of *domination*: the subjection of individuals to the dominant ideology, the dominance of the ideology of the ruling class.

It is inevitably therefore an *uneven* effect which does not operate uniformly on individuals and particularly does not operate in the same way on different and antagonistic social classes. 'Subjection' must be felt by the dominant class as by the dominant but in two different ways. Formally, literature as an ideological formation realised in the common language, is provided and destined for all and makes no distinctions between readers but for their own differing tastes and sensibilities,' natural or acquired. But concretely, subjection means one thing for the members of the educated dominant class: 'freedom' to think within ideology, a submission which is experienced and practised as if it were a mastery, another for those who belong to the exploited classes: manual workers or even skilled workers, employees, those who according to official statistics never 'read' or rarely. These find in reading nothing but the confirmation of their inferiority: subjection means domination and repression by the literary discourse of a discourse deemed 'inarticulate' and 'faulty' and inadequate for the expression of complex ideas and feelings.

This point is vital to an analysis. It shows that the difference is not set up *after the event* as a straightforward inequality of reading power and assimilation, conditioned by other social inequalities. It is implicit in the very production of the literary effect and materially inscribed in the constitution of the text.

But one might say, how is it clear that what is implicit in the structure of the text is not just the discourse of those who practice literature but also, *most significantly*, the discourse of those who do not know the text and whom it does not know; i.e. the discourse of those who 'write' (books) and 'read' them, and the discourse of those who do not know how to do it although quite simply they 'know how to read and write' – a play of words and a profoundly revealing double usage. One can understand this only by reconstituting and analysing the linguistic conflict in its determinant place as that which produces the literary text and which opposes two antagonistic usages, equal but inseparable of the common

---

[4] One could say that there is no proper *religious literature*; at least that there was not before the bourgeois epoch, by which time religion has been instituted as a form (subordinant and contradictory) of the bourgeois ideology itself. Rather, literature itself and the aesthetic ideology played a decisive part in the struggle against religion, the ideology of the dominant feudal class.

language: on one side, 'literary' French which is studied in higher education (l'enseignement secondaire et supérieur) and on the other 'basic',
'ordinary' French which, far from being natural, is also taught at the
other level (a l'école primaire). It is 'basic' only by reason of its *unequal
relation* to the other, which is 'literary' by the same reason. This is
proved by a comparative and historical analysis of their lexical and
syntactical forms – which R. Balibar is one of the first to undertake
systematically.

So, if in the way things are, literature can and must be used in secondary education both to fabricate and simultaneously dominate, isolate
and repress the 'basic' language' of the dominated classes, it is only on
condition that that same basic language should be present in literature,
as one of the terms of its constitutive contradiction – disguised and
masked, but also necessarily given away and exhibited in the fictive
reconstructions. And ultimately this is because literary French embodied
in literary texts is both tendentially *distinguished from* (and opposed to)
the common language and *placed with* its constitution and historic
development so long as this process characterises general education
because of its material importance to the development of bourgeois
society. That is why it is possible to assert that the use of literature in
schools and its place in education is only the converse of the *place of
education in literature* and that therefore the basis of the production of
literary effects is the very structure and historical role of the currently
dominant ideological state apparatus. And that too is why it is possible
to denounce as a den of their own real practice the claims of the writer
and his cultured readers to rise above simple classroom exercises, and
evade them.

The effect of domination realised by literary production presupposes
the presence of the dominated ideology within the dominant ideology
itself. It implies the constant 'activation' of the contradiction and its
attendant ideological risk – it thrives on this very risk which is the source
of its power. That is why, dialectically, in bourgeois democratic society,
the agent of the reproduction of ideology moves tendentially via the
effects of literary 'style' and linguistic forms of compromise. Class
struggle is not abolished in the literary text and the literary effects which
it produces. They bring about the reproduction, as dominant, of the
ideology of the dominant class.

7 Terry Eagleton,
From *Criticism and Ideology*

p157–161

D.H. Lawrence

Of all the writers discussed in this essay, D.H. Lawrence, the only one of proletarian origin, is also the most full-bloodedly 'organicist' in both his social and aesthetic assumptions. As a direct twentieth-century inheritor of the 'Culture and Society' Romantic humanist tradition, Lawrence's fiction represents one of the century's most powerful literary critiques of industrial capitalism, launched from a deep-seated commitment to an organic order variously located in Italy, New Mexico, pre-industrial England and, metaphorically, in the novel-form itself. The novel for Lawrence is a delicate, labile organism whose elements are vitally inter-related; it spurns dogma and metaphysical absolutes, tracing instead the sensuous flux of its unified life-forms.[1] Yet Lawrence is also a dogmatic, metaphysically absolutist, radically dualistic thinker, fascinated by mechanism and disintegration; and it is in this contradiction that much of his historical significance lies.

What Lawrence's work dramatises, in fact, is a contradiction within the Romantic humanist tradition itself, between its corporate and individualist components. An extreme form of individualism is structural to Romantic humanist ideology – an application, indeed, of organicism to the individual self, which becomes thereby wholly autotelic, spontaneously evolving into 'wholeness' by its own uniquely determining laws. This ideological component – at once an idealised version of common place bourgeois individualism and a 'revolutionary' protest against the 'reified' society it produces – is strongly marked in Lawrence's writing, and enters into conflict with the opposing imperatives of impersonality and organic order. His social organicism decisively rejects the atomistic, mechanistic ideologies of industrial capitalism, yet at the same time subsumes the values of the bourgeois liberal tradition: sympathy, intimacy, compassion, the centrality of the 'personal'. These contradictions come to a crisis in Lawrence with the First World War, the most traumatic event of his life. The war signifies the definitive collapse of the liberal humanist heritage, with its benevolistic idealism and 'personal' values, clearing the way for the 'dark gods' of discipline, action, hierarchy, individual separateness, mystical impersonality – in short,

[1] See 'The Novel', *Phoenix II* (London, 1968).

for a social order which rejects the 'female' principle of compassion and sexual intimacy for the 'male' principle of power. 'The reign of love is passing, and the reign of power is coming again.'[2]

In this sense Lawrence was a major precursor of fascism, which is not to say that he himself unqualifiedly accepted fascist ideology. He unequivocally condemned Mussolini, and correctly identified fascism as a spuriously 'radical' response to the crisis of capitalism.[3] Lawrence was unable to embrace fascism because, while it signified a form of Romantic organistic reaction to bourgeois liberalism, it also negated the individualism which was for him a crucial part of the same Romantic heritage. This is the contradiction from which he was unable to escape, in his perpetual oscillation between a proud celebration of individual autonomy and a hunger for social integration; he wants men to be drilled soldiers but *individual* soldiers, desires to 'rule' over them but not 'bully' them.[4] To 'resolve' this contradiction, Lawrence had recourse to a metaphysic which dichotomised reality into 'male' and 'female' principles and attempted to hold them in dialectical tension. The male principle is that of power, consciousness, spirit, activism, individuation; the female principle that of flesh, sensuality, permanence, passivity.[5] The male principle draw sustenance from the female, but must avoid collapsing inertly into it. Yet Lawrence's dualist metaphysic is ridden with internal contradictions, for a significant biographical reason: his mother, symbol of primordial sensual unity, was in fact petty-bourgeois, and so also represented individuation, aspiring consciousness and active idealism in contrast to the mute, sensuous passivity of his working-class father. This partial inversion of his parents' sexual roles, as defined by Lawrence, contorts and intensifies the contradictions which his metaphysic tries to resolve.[6] The mother, as symbol of the nurturing yet cloying flesh, is subconsciously resented for inhibiting true masculinity (as is the father's passivity), yet valued as an image of love, tenderness and personal intimacy. Conversely, her active, aspiring consciousness disrupts the mindless unity of sensual life symbolised by the father, but is preferred to his brutal impersonality. *Sons and Lovers* takes these conflicts as its subject-matter, on the whole rejecting the father and defending the mother;

---

[2] 'Blessed are the Powerful', *Phoenix II*.

[3] See his comment in *St. Mawr*: 'Try fascism. Fascism would keep the surface of life intact, and carry on the undermining business all the better.' Lawrence was not a fascist rather perhaps in the sense that he was not a homosexual. He thought both fascism and homosexuality immoral, but was subconsciously fascinated by both.

[4] *Fantasia of the Unconscious* (London, 1961), p. 84.

[5] This duality is imaged in Lawrence's work in a whole gamut of antinomies: love/law, light/dark, lion/unicorn, sun/moon, Son/Father, spirit/soul, sky/earth, and so on.

[6] A contortion evident in the *reversibility* of some of Lawrence's symbolic antinomies: the Father, symbol of sensual phallic consciousness, is identifiable with the *female*; the lion may signify both active power and sensuality; the sun is sometimes male intellect and sometimes sensuous female warmth, while the moon may suggest female passivity or the cold abstract consciousness of the male.

yet as Lawrence's fiction progresses, moving through and beyond the First World War, that priority is partly reversed. *Women in Love* struggles to complement a potentially claustrophobic sexual intimacy with the 'liberating' effect of a purely 'male' relationship; and the hysterical male chauvinism of the post-war novels (*Aaron's Rod, Kangaroo, The Plumed Serpent*) represents a strident rejection of sexual love for the male cult of power and impersonality. Lawrence's deepening hatred of women is a reaction both against bourgeois liberal values and the snare of a sensuality which violates individual autonomy; yet his commitment to sensual being as the source of social renewal contradictorily persists. In *Lady Chatterley's Lover*, the image of the father is finally rehabilitated in the figure of Mellors; yet Mellors combines impersonal male power with 'female' tenderness, working-class roughness with petty-bourgeois awareness, achieving a mythical resolution of the contradictions which beset Lawrence's work.

Lawrence's particular mode of relation to the dominant ideology, then, was in the first place a contradictory combination of proletarian and petty-bourgeois elements – a combination marked by a severe conflict between alternative ideological discourses which becomes encoded in his metaphysic. Yet this fact is of more than merely 'biographical' interest: for the ideological contradictions which the young Lawrence lives out – between power and love, community and autonomy, sensuality and consciousness, order and individualism – are a specific overdetermination of a deep-seated ideological crisis within the dominant formation as a whole. Lawrence's relation to that crisis is then doubly overdetermined by his expatriatism, which combines an assertive, deracinated individualism with a hunger for the historically mislaid 'totality'. The forms of Lawrence's fiction produce this ideological conjuncture in a variety of ways. The 'symptomatic' repressions and absences of the realist *Sons and Lovers* may be recuperated in the ultra-realist forms of *The Rainbow* – a text which 'explodes' realism in its letter, even as it preserves it in the 'totalising' organicism of its evolving generational structure. After the war, Lawrence's near-total ideological collapse, articulated with the crisis of aesthetic signification, presents itself in a radical rupturing and diffusion of literary form: novels like *Aaron's Rod* and *Kangaroo* are signally incapable of evolving a narrative, ripped between fragmentary plot, spiritual autobiography and febrile didacticism. But between these texts and *The Rainbow* occurs the unique moment of *Women in Love*. That work's break to synchronic form, away from the diachronic rhythms of *The Rainbow*, produces an 'ideology of the text' marked by stasis and disillusionment; yet it is precisely in its fissuring of organic form, in its 'montage' techniques of symbolic juxtaposition, that the novel enforces a 'progressive' discontinuity with a realist lineage already put into profound question by *Jude the Obscure*.

Conclusion

That the fissuring of organic form is a progressive act has not been a received position within a Marxist aesthetic tradition heavily dominated by the work of George Lukács. Yet to review a selection of English literary production from George Eliot to D.H. Lawrence in the light of the internal relations between ideology and literary form is to reactivate the crucially significant debate conducted in the 1930s between Lukács and Bertolt Brecht.[7] Brecht's rejection of Lukác's nostalgic organicism, his traditionalist preference for closed, symmetrical totalities, is made in the name of an allegiance to open, multiple forms which bear in their torsions the very imprint of the contradictions they lay bare. In English literary culture of the past century, the ideological basis of organic form is peculiarly visible, as a progressively impoverished bourgeois liberalism attempts to integrate more ambitious and affective ideological modes. In doing so, that ideology enters into grievous conflicts which its aesthetic forms betray in the very act of attempted resolution. The destruction of corporate and organicist ideologies in the political sphere has always been a central task for revolutionaries; the destruction of such ideologies in the aesthetic region is essential not only for a scientific knowledge of the literary past, but for laying the foundation on which the materialist aesthetic and artistic practices of the future can be built.

[7] See 'Brecht Against Lukács', *New Left Review* 84, March/April, 1974.

SECTION FIVE
READER THEORY

In contemporary literary theory the role of the reader has become increasingly prominent. An orientation toward the text/reader nexus has been taken up in structuralist, post-structuralist, formalist, feminist, and psychoanalytic criticism. However there has also been a body of work produced that specifically concentrates upon the reader and whose primary orientation is toward the process of reading.

Basically, two linked trajectories can be noted. The first, often called the 'Aesthetics of Reception', develops out of phenomenological philosophy and concerns itself with the reading process in relation to the reader's consciousness. The second, 'reader-response theory', is largely American in origin, comes in a variety of forms, and often lacks a fully coherent and cogent theoretical exposition. Reader-response theory includes the work of such figures as Norman Holland and David Bleich, working within a psychologistic frame, Michael Riffaterre working within semiotics, and Stanley Fish (see Holub 1984). Fish's initial theoretical position, 'affective stylistics', concentrated on reading as a temporal, experiential process but was later reworked in the light of the realization that the process he was describing could not be extrapolated out as *the* reading process, only as *a* reading process. In his reworking, he develops the more interesting notion of 'interpretive communities' – communities of readers with shared practices and competences. For Fish, it is the interpretive community that determines interpretations rather than the textual features of the work itself.

The essays chosen here to represent reader theory are by two of the prominent critics from the Aesthetics of Reception: Wolfgang Iser and Hans Robert Jauss. Iser draws extensively on the work of the phenomenologist aesthetician Roman Ingarden, sharing his view of the text as a potential structure which is 'concretized' by the reader. For Iser this is a process which takes place in relation to the extra-literary norms and values through which the reader makes sense of experience. Iser's writings reveal a considerable degree of ambiguity about the extent of the reader's freedom to fill in the blanks in the text's 'schemata' according to his/her own experiential norms, and the extent to which the text controls or determines the way it will be read. What is clear, however, is Iser's commitment to a phenomenological view of the reading experience; the reader realizes the text as an aesthetic object according to his/her own experience but the norms which structure that experience will inevitably be modified and shifted by the reading experience itself. As we read we continually perceive and evaluate events with regard to our expectations of what will happen in the text, and against the background of what has already happened. Unexpected textual occurences, however, will force us to reformulate our expectations and to reinterpret the significance which we have attributed to what has gone before. Iser sees the reader as someone who, above all, seeks coherence as the basis of sense-making and who will reconnect the different schemata of the text according to continual revisions which guarantee an overall meaning.

While Iser's theory presents us with a de-historicized reader confronting a de-contextualized text, Jauss's reception theory attempts a more historically situated understanding of the concretization process, positing an 'horizon of expectations' which lays down the criteria in each historical period according to which people read and evaluate literary works. The horizon of expectations at the original historical moment of production can only tell us something of how the work was understood and received at that time; it does not establish its absolute or universal meaning. Jauss draws extensively on the hermeneutic theory of Hans Gadamer, viewing the text as situated in an endless dialogue between past and present in which the present position of the interpreter will always influence how the past is understood and received. In attempting to make sense of the past we can only know it in the light of the present cultural horizon and thus Jauss argues for a 'fusion of horizons' which unite past and present. For Jauss the text's meaning and value is ultimately inseparable from the history of its reception.

The problem at the heart of this theory remains that of extrapolating from one's own concretization processes to a general reading and reception process, though Jauss circumscribes this to some extent through the historicizing notion of 'horizon of expectations'.

8 Wolfgang Iser,

From 'The Reading Process', *New Directions in Literary History* ed R. Cohen

p274-5; 276-7; 279-80; 281-2; 283-4; 285; 287-8; 290; 293-4; 294

THE READING PROCESS: A Phenomenological Approach

The phenomenological theory of art lays full stress on the idea that, in considering a literary work, one must take into account not only the actual text but also, and in equal measure, the actions involved in responding to that text. Thus Roman Ingarden confronts the structure of the literary text with the ways in which it can be *konkretisiert* (realised).[1] The text as such offers different 'schematised views'[2] through which the subject matter of the work can come to light, but the actual bringing to light is an action of *Konkretisation*. If this is so, then the literary work has two poles, which we might call the artistic and the esthetic: the artistic refers to the text created by the author, and the esthetic to the realization accomplished by the reader. From this polarity it follows that the literary work cannot be completely identical with the text, or with the realization of the text, but in fact must lie half-way between the two. The work is more than the text, for the text only takes on life when it is realized, and furthermore the realization is by no means independent of the individual disposition of the reader – though this in turn is acted upon by the different patterns of the text. The convergence of text and reader brings the literary work into existence, and this convergence can never be precisely pinpointed, but must always remain virtual, as it is not to be identified either with the reality of the text or with the individual disposition of the reader.

It is the virtuality of the work that gives rise to its dynamic nature, and this in turn is the precondition for the effects that the work calls forth. As the reader uses the various perspectives offered him by the text in order to relate the patterns and the 'schematised views' to one another, he sets the work in motion, and this very process results ultimately in the awakening of responses within himself. Thus, reading causes the literary work to unfold its inherently dynamic character.

. . . .

[1] Cf. Roman Ingarden, *Vom Erkennen des literarischen Kunstwerks* (Tübingen, 1968), pp. 49ff.
[2] For a detailed discussion of this term see Roman Ingarden, *Das literarische Kunstwerk* (Tübingen,[2]1960), pp. 270ff.

As a starting point for a phenomenological analysis we might examine the way in which sequent sentences act upon one another. This is of especial importance in literary texts in view of the fact that they do not correspond to any objective reality outside themselves. The world presented by literary texts is constructed out of what Ingarden has called *intentionale Satzkorrelate* (intentional sentence correlatives):

> Sentences link up in different ways to form more complex units of meaning that reveal a very varied structure giving rise to such entities as a short story, a novel, a dialogue, a drama, a scientific theory. . . . In the final analysis, there arises a particular world, with component parts determined in this way or that, and with all the variations that may occur within these parts – all this as a purely intentional correlative of a complex of sentences. If this complex finally forms a literary work, I call the whole sum of sequent intentional sentence correlatives the 'world presented' in the work.[3]

This world, however, does not pass before the reader's eyes like a film. The sentences are 'components parts' insofar as they make statements, claims, or observations, or convey information, and so establish various perspectives in the text. But they remain only 'component parts' – they are not the sum total of the text itself. For the intentional correlatives disclose subtle connections which individually are less concrete than the statements, claims, and observations, even though these only take on their real meaningfulness through the interaction of their correlatives.

How is one to conceive the connection between the correlatives? It marks those points at which the reader is able to 'climb aboard' the text. He has to accept certain given perspectives, but in doing so he inevitably causes them to interact. When Ingarden speaks of intentional sentence correlatives in literature, the statements made or information conveyed in the sentence are already in a certain sense qualified: the sentence does not consist solely of a statement – which, after all, would be absurd, as one can only make statements about things that exist – but aims at something beyond what it actually says. This is true of all sentences in literary works, and it is through the interaction of these sentences that their common aim is fulfilled. This is what gives them their own special quality in literary texts. In their capacity as statements, observations, purveyors of information, etc., they are always indications of something that is to come, the structure of which is foreshadowed by their specific content.

They set in motion a process out of which emerges the actual content of the text itself.

. . . .

As we have seen, the activity of reading can be characterized as a sort of kaleidoscope of perspectives, preintentions, recollections. Every sen-

---

[3] Ingarden, *Vom Erkenmen des literarischen Kunstwerks*, p. 29.

tence contains a preview of the next and forms a kind of viewfinder for what is to come; and this is turn changes the 'preview' and so becomes a 'viewfinder' for what has been read. This whole process represents the fulfillment of the potential, unexpressed reality of the text, but it is be seen only as a framework for a great variety of means by which the virtual dimension may be brought into being. The process of anticipation and retrospection itself does not by any means develop in a smooth flow. Ingarden has already drawn attention to this fact and ascribes a quite remarkable significance to it:

> Once we are immersed in the flow of *Satzdenken* (sentence-thought), we are ready, after completing the thought of one sentence, to think out the 'continuation', also in the form of a sentence – and that is, in the form of a sentence that connects up with the sentence we have just thought through. In this way the process of reading goes effortlessly forward. But if by chance the following sentence has no tangible connection whatever with the sentence we have just thought through, there then comes a blockage in the stream of thought. This hiatus is linked with a more or less active surprise, or with indignation. This blockage must be overcome if the reading is to flow once more.[4]

The hiatus that blocks the flow of sentences is, in Ingarden's eyes, the product of chance, and is to be regarded as a flaw; this is typical of his adherence to the classical idea of art. If one regards the sentence sequence as a continual flow, this implies that the anticipation aroused by one sentence will generally be realized by the next, and the frustration of one's expectations will arouse feelings of exasperation. And yet literary texts are full of unexpected twists and turns, and frustration of expectations. Even in the simplest story there is bound to be some kind of blockage, if only because no tale can ever be told in its entirety. Indeed, it is only through inevitable omissions that a story gains its dynamism. Thus whenever the flow is interrupted and we are led off in unexpected directions, the opportunity is given to us to bring into play our own faculty for establishing connections – for filling in the gaps left by the text itself.[5]

These gaps have a different effect on the process of anticipation and retrospection, and thus on the 'gestalt' of the virtual dimension, for they may be filled in different ways. For this reason, one text is potentially capable of several different realizations, and no reading can ever exhaust the full potential, for each individual reader will fill in the gaps in his own way, thereby excluding the various other possibilities; as he reads, he will make his own decision as to how the gap is to be filled. In this very act the

[4] Ingarden, *Vom Erkenmen des literarischen kunstwerks* p. 32.
[5] For a more detailed discussion of the function of 'gaps' in literary texts see Wolfgang Iser, 'Indeterminacy and the Reader's Response in Prose Fiction,' *Aspects of Narrative* (English Institute Essays), ed. J. Hillis Miller (New York, 1971), pp. 1–45.

dynamics of reading are revealed. By making his decision he implicitly acknowledges the inexhaustibility of the text; at the same time it is this very inexhaustibility that forces him to make his decision. With 'traditional' texts this process was more or less unconscious, but modern texts frequently exploit it quite deliberately. They are often so fragmentary that one's attention is almost exclusively occupied with the search for connections between the fragments; the object of this is not to complicate the 'spectrum' of connections, so much as to make us aware of the nature of our own capacity for providing links. In such cases, the text refers back directly to our own preconceptions – which are revealed by the act of interpretation that is a basic element of the reading process. With all literary texts, then, we may say that the reading process is selective, and the potential text is infinitely richer than any of its individual realizations. This is borne out by the fact that a second reading of a piece of literature often produces a different impression from the first. The reasons for this may lie in the reader's own change of circumstances, still, the text must be such as to allow this variation. On a second reading familiar occurrences now tend to appear is a new light and seem to be at times corrected, at times enriched.

. . . .

The manner in which the reader experiences the text will reflect his own disposition, and in this respect the literary text acts as a kind of mirror; but at the same time, the reality which this process helps to create is one that will be *different* from his own (since, normally, we tend to be bored by texts that present us with things we already know perfectly well ourselves). Thus we have the apparently paradoxical situation in which the reader is forced to reveal aspects of himself in order to experience a reality which is different from his own. The impact this reality makes on him will depend largely on the extent to which he himself actively provides the unwritten part of the text, and yet in supplying all the missing links, he must think in terms of experiences different from this own; indeed, it is only by leaving behind the familiar world of this own experience that the reader can truly participate in the adventure the literary text offers him.

. . . .

The 'picturing' that is done by our imagination is only one of the activities through which we form the 'gestalt' of a literary text. We have already discussed the process of anticipation and retrospection, and to this we must add the process of grouping together all the different aspects of a text to form the consistency that the reader will always be in search of. While expectations may be continually modified, and images continually expanded, the reader will still strive, even if unconsciously, to fit everything together in a consistent pattern. 'In the reading of images, as in the hearing of speech, it is always hard to distinguish what is given to us from what we supplement in the process of projection which is triggered off by recognition . . . it is the guess of the beholder that tests the medley of forms and colours for coherent meaning, crystallizing it into shape when a consistent interpretation has been found.[6] By grouping together the written parts of the text, we enable them to interact, we observe the direction in which they are leading us, and we project onto them the consistency which we, as readers, require. This 'gestalt' must inevitably be colored by our own characteristic selection process. For it is not given by the text itself; it arises from the meeting between the written text and the individual mind of the reader with its own particular history of experience, its own consciousness, its own outlook. The 'gestalt' is not the true meaning of the text; at best it is a configurative meaning; '. . . comprehension is an individual act of seeing-things-together, and only that.'[7] With a literary text such comprehension is inseparable from the reader's expectations, and where we have expectations, there too we have one of the most potent weapons in the writer's armory – illusion.

The process is virtually hermeneutic. The text provokes certain expectations which in turn we project onto the text in such a way that we reduce the polysemantic possibilities to a single interpretation in keeping with the expectations aroused, thus extracting an individual, configurative meaning. The polysemantic nature of the text and the illusion-making of the reader are opposed factors. If the illusion were complete, the polysemantic nature could vanish; if the polysemantic nature were all-powerful, the illusion would be totally destroyed. Both extremes are conceivable, but in the individual literary text we always find some form of balance between the two conflicting tendencies. The formation of illusions, therefore, can never be total, but it is this very incompleteness that in fact gives it its productive value.

. . . .

As we work out a consistent pattern in the text, we will find our 'interpretation' threatened, as it were, by the presence of other possibilities of 'interpretation', and so there arise new areas of indeterminacy (though

[6] E.H. Gombrich, *Art and Illusion* (London, 1962), p. 204.
[7] Louis O. Mink, 'History and Fiction as Modes of Comprehension,' *New Literary History* I (1970): 553.

we may only be dimly aware of them, if at all, as we are continually making 'decisions' which will exclude them). In the course of the novel, for instance, we sometimes find that characters, events, and backgrounds seem to change their significance; what really happens is that the other 'possibilities' begin to emerge more strongly, so that we become more directly aware of them. Indeed, it is this very shifting of perspectives that makes us feel that a novel is much more 'true-to-life'. Since it is we ourselves who establish the levels of interpretation and switch from one to another as we conduct our balancing operation, we ourselves impart to the text the dynamic lifelikeness which, in turn, enables us to absorb an unfamiliar experience into our personal world.

As we read, we oscillate to a greater or lesser degree between the building and the breaking of illusions. In a process of trial and error, we organize and reorganize the various data offered us by the text. These are the given factors, the fixed points on which we base our 'interpretation,' trying to fit them together in the way we think the author meant them to be fitted.

. . . .

The efficacy of a literary text is brought about by the apparent evocation and subsequent negation of the familiar. What at first seemed to be an affirmation of our assumptions leads to our own rejection of them, thus tending to prepare us for a re-orientation. And it is only when we have outstripped our preconceptions and left the shelter of the familiar that we are in a position to gather new experiences. As the literary text involves the reader in the formation of illusion and the simultaneous formation of the means whereby the illusion is punctured, reading reflects the process by which we gain experience. Once the reader is entangled, his own preconceptions are continually overtaken, so that the text becomes his 'present' while his own ideas fade into the 'past'; as soon as this happens he is open to the immediate experience of the text, which was impossible so long as his preconceptions were his 'present'.

. . . .

Text and reader no longer confront each other as object and subject, but instead the 'division' takes place within the reader himself. In thinking the thoughts of another, his own individuality temporarily recedes into the background, since it is supplanted by these alien thoughts which now become the theme on which his attention is focussed. As we read, there occurs an artificial division of our personality, because we take as a theme for ourselves something that we are not. Consequently when reading we operate on different levels. For although we may be thinking the thoughts of someone else, what we are will not disappear completely – it will merely remain a more or less powerful virtual force. Thus, in reading there are these two levels – the alien 'me' and the real, virtual 'me' – which are never completely cut off from each other. Indeed, we can only make someone else's thoughts into an absorbing theme for ourselves, provided the virtual background of our own personality can adapt to it. Every text we read draws a different boundary within our personality, so that the virtual background (the real 'me') will take on a different form, according to the theme of the text concerned. This is inevitable, if only for the fact that the relationship between alien theme and virtual background is what makes it possible for the unfamiliar to be understood.

. . . .

Herein lies the dialectical structure of reading. The need to decipher gives us the chance to formulate our own deciphering capacity – i.e., we bring to the fore an element of our being of which we are not directly conscious. The production of the meaning of literary texts – which we discussed in connection with forming the 'gestalt' of the text – does not merely entail the discovery of the unformulated, which can then be taken over by the active imagination of the reader; it also entails the possibility that we may formulate ourselves and so discover what has previously seemed to elude our consciousness. These are the ways in which reading literature gives us the chance to formulate the unformulated.

---

9   H.R. Jauss,

From 'Literary History as a Challenge to Literary Theory', *New Literary History*, **2, 1970**

p11–19

The analysis of the literary experience of the reader avoids the threatening pitfalls of psychology if it describes the response and the impact of a work within the definable frame of reference of the reader's expectations: this frame of reference for each work develops in the historical moment of its appearance from a previous understanding of the genre, from the form and themes of already familiar works, and from the contrast between poetic and practical language.

My thesis is opposed to a widespread skepticism that doubts that an analysis of the aesthetic impact can approach the meaning of a work of art or can produce at best more than a plain sociology of artistic taste. René Wellek directs such doubts against the literary theory of I.A. Richards. Wellek argues that neither the individual consciousness, since it is immediate and personal, nor a collective consciousness as J. Mukarovsky assumes the effect of an art work to be, can be determined by empirical means.[1] Roman Jakobson wanted to replace the 'collective consciousness' by a 'collective ideology.' This he thought of as a system of values which exists for each literary work as *langue* and which becomes *parole* for the respondent – although incompletely and never as a whole.[2] This theory, it is true, limits the subjectivity of the impact, but it leaves open the question of which data can be used to interpret the impact of a unique work on a certain public and to incorporate it into a system of values. In the meantime there are empirical means which had never been thought of before – literary data which give for each work a specific attitude of the audience (an attitude that precedes the psychological reaction as well as the subjective understanding of the individual reader). As in the case of every experience, the first literary experience of a previously unknown work demands a 'previous knowledge which is an element of experience itself and which makes it possible that anything new we come across may also be read, as it were, in some context of experience.[3]

A literary work, even if it seems new, does not appear as something absolutely new in an informational vacuum, but predisposes its readers to a very definite type of reception by textual strategies, overt and covert signals, familiar characteristics or implicit allusions. It awakens memories of the familiar, stirs particular emotions in the reader and with its 'beginning' arouses expectations for the 'middle and end', which can then be continued intact, changed, re-oriented or even ironically fulfilled in the course of reading according to certain rules of the genre or type of text. The psychical process in the assimilation of a text on the primary horizon of aesthetic experience is by no means only a random succession of merely subjective impressions, but the carrying out of certain directions in a process of [directed perception] which can be comprehended from the motivations which constitute it and the signals which set it off and which can be described linguistically. If, along with W.D. Stempel, one considers the previous horizon of expectations of a text as paradigmatic isotopy, which is transferred to an immanent syntactical horizon of expectations to the degree to which the message grows, the process

---

[1] R. Wellek, "The Theory of Literary History," *Études dédiées au quatrième Congrès de linguistes*, Travaux du Cercle Linguistique de Prague (Prague, 1936), p. 179.

[2] In *Slovo a slovenost*, I, 192, cited by Wellek. "The Theory of Literary History," pp. 179ff.

[3] G. Buck, *Lernen und Erfahrung* (Stuttgart, 1967), p. 56, who refers here to Husserl (*Erfahrung und Urteil*, esp. § 8) but goes farther than Husserl in a lucid description of negativity in the process of experience, which is of importance for the horizon structure of aesthetic experience.

of reception becomes describable in the expansion of a semiological procedure which arises between the development and the correction of the system.[4] A corresponding process of continuous horizon setting and horizon changing also determines the relation of the individual text to the succession of texts which form the genre. The new text evokes for the reader (listener) the horizon of expectations and rules familiar from earlier texts, which are then varied, corrected, changed or just reproduced. Variation and correction determine the scope, alteration and reproduction of the borders and structure of the genre.[5] The interpretative reception of a text always presupposes the context of experience of aesthetic perception. The question of the subjectivity of the interpretation and the taste of different readers or levels of readers can be asked significantly only after it has been decided which transsubjective horizon of understanding determines the impact of the text.

The ideal cases of the objective capability of such literary frames of reference are works which, using the artistic standards of the reader, have been formed by conventions of genre, style, or form. These purposely evoke responses so that they can frustrate them. This can serve not only a critical purpose but can even have a poetic effect. Thus Cervantes in *Don Quixote* fosters the expectations of the old tales of knighthood which the adventures of his last knight then parody seriously.[6] Thus Diderot in the beginning to *Jacques le Fataliste* evokes the expectations of the popular journey novel along with the (Aristotelian) convention of the romanesque fable and the providence peculiar to it, so that he can then confront the promised journey and love novel with a completely unromanesque 'verité de l'histoire': the bizarre reality and moral casuistry of the inserted stories in which the truth of life continually denies the lies of poetic fiction.[7] Thus Nerval in *Chimères* cites, combines, and mixes a quintessence of well-known romantic and occult motives to produce the expectation of a mythical metamorphosis of the world only in order to show his renunciation of romantic poetry. The mythical identification and relationships which are familiar to the reader dissolve in the unknown to the same degree as the attempted private myth of the lyrical 'I' fails; the law of sufficient information is broken

---

[4] W.D. Stempel, *Pour une description des genres littéraires*, in: *Actes du XIIe congrès internat. de linguistique Romane* (Bucharest, 1968), also in *Beiträge zur Texlinguistik*, ed. by W.D. Stempel (Munich, 1970).

[5] See also my treatment of this in "*Littérature médiévale et thorie des genres*," in *Poétique*, I (1970), 79–101, which will also shortly appear in expanded form in volume I of *Grundriss der romanischen Literaturen des Mittelalters*, (Heidelberg, 1970).

[6] According to the interpretation of H.J. Neuschäfer, *Der Sinn der Parodie im Don Quijote*, Studia *Romanica*, V (Heidelberg, 1963).

[7] According to the interpretation of R. Warning, *Allusion und Wirklichkeit in Tristram Shandy und Jacques le Fataliste,* Theorie und Geschichte der Literatur und der schönen Kunste, IV (Munich 1965), esp. pp. 80ff.

and the darkness which has become expressive gains a poetic function.[8]

There is also the possibility of objectifying the expectations in works which are historically less sharply delineated. For the specific reception which the author anticipates from the reader of a particular work can be achieved, even if the explicit signals are missing, by three generally acceptable means: first, by the familiar standards or the inherent poetry of the genre; second, by the implicit relationships to familiar works of the literary-historical context; and third, by the contrast between fiction and reality, between the poetic and the practical function of language, which the reflective reader can always realize while he is reading. The third factor includes the possibility that the reader of a new work has to perceive it not only within the narrow horizon of his literary expectations but also within the wider horizon of his experience of life.

. . . .

If the horizon of expectations of a work is reconstructed in this way, it is possible to determine its artistic nature by the nature and degree of its effect on a given audience. If the 'aesthetic distance' is considered as the distance between the given horizon of expectations and the appearance of a new work, whose reception results in a 'horizon change' because it negates familiar experience or articulates an experience for the first time, this aesthetic distance can be measured historically in the spectrum of the reaction of the audience and the judgment of criticism (spontaneous success, rejection or shock, scattered approval, gradual or later understanding).

The way in which a literary work satisfies, surpasses, disappoints, or disproves the expectations of its first readers in the historical moment of its appearance obviously gives a criterion for the determination of its aesthetic value. The distance between the horizon of expectations and the work, between the familiarity of previous aesthetic experiences and the 'horizon change'[9] demanded by the response to new works, determines the artistic nature of a literary work along the lines of the aesthetics of reception: the smaller this distance, which means that no demands are made upon the receiving consciousness to make a change on the horizon of unknown experience, the closer the work comes to the realm of 'culinary' or light reading. This last phrase can be characterized from the point of view of the aesthetics of reception in this way: it demands no horizon change but actually fulfills expectations, which are prescribed by a predominant taste, by satisfying the demand for the reproduction of familiar beauty, confirming familiar sentiments, encouraging dreams,

---

[8] According to the interpretation of K.H. Stierle, *Dunkelheit und Form in Gérard de Nervals 'Chimères,'* Theorie und Geschichte der Literatur und der schönen Künste, V (Munich, 1967), esp. pp. 55 and 91.

[9] See Buck, pp. 64 ff., about this idea of Husserl in *Lernen und Erfahrung*.

making unusual experiences palatable as 'sensations' or even raising moral problems, but only to be able to 'solve' them in an edifying manner when the solution is already obvious.[10] On the other hand, if the artistic character of a work is to be measured by the aesthetic distance with which it confronts the expectations of its first readers, it follows that this distance, which at first is experienced as a happy or distasteful new perspective, can disappear for later readers to the same degree to which the original negativity of the work has become self-evident and, as henceforth familiar expectation, has even become part of the horizon of future aesthetic experience. Especially the classic nature of so-called masterworks belongs to this second horizon change; their self-evident beauty and their seemingly unquestionable 'eternal significance' bring them, from the point of view of the aesthetics of reception, into dangerous proximity with the irresistable convincing and enjoyable 'culinary' art, and special effort is needed to read them 'against the grain' of accustomed experience so that their artistic nature becomes evident again.[11]

The relationship between literature and the public encompasses more than the fact that every work has its specific, historically and sociologically determined audience, that every writer is dependent upon the milieu, views and ideology of his readers and that literary success requires a book 'which expresses what the group expects, a book which presents the group with its own portrait. . . .'[12] The objectivist determination of literary success based on the congruence of the intent of a work and the expectation of a social group always puts literary sociology in an embarrassing position whenever it must explain later or continuing effects. This is why R. Escarpit wants to presuppose a 'collective basis in space or time' for the 'illusion of continuity' of a writer, which leads to an astonishing prognosis in the case of Molière: he 'is still young for the Frenchman of the 20th century because his world is still alive and ties of culture, point of view and language still bind us to him . . . but the ties

---

[10] Here I am incorporating the results of the discussion of 'Kitsch,' as a fringe manifestation of aesthetics, which took place during the third colloquium of the 'Forschungsgruppe Poetik und Hermeneutik' in the volume, *Die nicht mehr schönen Küste - Grenzphänomene des Ästhetischen,* ed. H.R. Jauss (Munich, 1968). For the 'culinary' approach which presupposes mere light reading, the same thing holds true as for 'Kitsch', namely, that the 'demands of the consumers are a *priori* satisfied' (P. Beylin), that 'the fulfilled expectation becomes the standard for the product' (W. Iser), or that 'a work appears to be solving a problem when in reality it neither has nor solves a problem' (M. Imdahl), pp. 651–67.

[11] As also 'Epigonentum' (Decadence), for this see B. Tomasevskij (in: *Théorie de la littérature. Texts des formalistes russes,* ed. by T. Todorov [Paris 1965], p. 306): 'L'apparition d'un génie équivaut toujours à une révolution littéraire qui détrône le canon dominant et donne le pouvoir aux procédés jusqu'alors subordonnés. [. . .] Les épigones répètent une combinaison usée des procédés, et d'originale et révolutionnaire qu'elle était, cette combinaison devient stéréotypée et traditionnelle. Ainsi les épigones tuent parfois pour longtemps l'aptitude des contemporains à sentir la force esthétique des exemples qu'ils imitent: ils discréditent leurs maîtres.'

[12] R. Escarpit, *Das Buch und der Leser: Entwurf einer Literatursoziologie* (Cologne and Opladen, 1961; first German expanded edition of *Sociologie de la littérature* [Paris, 1958], p. 116.

are becoming ever weaker and Molière will age and die when the things which our culture has in common with the France of Molière die' (p. 117). As if Molière had only reflected the manners of his time and had only remained successful because of this apparent intention! Where the congruence between work and social group does not exist or or longer exists, as for example in the reception of a work by a group which speaks a foreign language, Escarpit is able to help himself by resorting to a 'myth': 'myths which are invented by a later period which has become estranged from the reality which they represent' (p. 111). As if all reception of a work beyond the first socially determined readers were only 'distorted echoes', only a consequence of 'subjective myths' (p. 111) and did not have its objective *a priori* in the received work which sets boundaries and opens possibilities for later understanding! The sociology of literature does not view its object dialectically enough when it determines the circle of writers, work and readers so one-sidedly.[13] The determination is reversible: there are works which at the moment of their publication are not directed at any specific audience, but which break through the familiar horizon of literary expectations so completely that an audience can only gradually develop for them.[14] Then when the new horizon of expectations has achieved more general acceptance, the authority of the changed aesthetic norm can become apparent from the fact that readers will consider previously successful works as obsolete and reject them. It is only in view of such a horizon change that the analysis of literary effect achieves the dimension of a literary history of readers[15] and provides the statistical curves of the historical recognition of the bestseller.

A literary sensation from the year 1857 may serve as an example of this. In this year two novels were published: Flaubert's *Madame Bovary*, which has since achieved world-wide fame, and *Fanny* by his friend Feydeau, which is forgotten today. Although Flaubert's novel brought with it a trial for obscenity, *Madame Bovary* was at first overshadowed by Feydeau's novel: *Fanny* had thirteen editions in one year and success

[13] K. H. Bender, *König und Vasall: Untersuchungen zur Chanson de Geste des XII. Jahrhunderts,* Studia Romanica, XIII (Heidelberg, 1967), shows which step is necessary in order to escape from this one-sided determination. In this history of the early French epic the apparent congruence of feudal society and epic ideality is represented as a process which is maintained through a continually changing discrepancy between 'reality' and 'ideology', that is between the historical constellations of feudal conflict and the poetic answers of the epic.

[14] The much more sophisticated sociology of literature by Erich Auerbach brought to light this aspect in the variety of epoch-making disruptions of the relationship between author and reader. See also the evaluation of F. Schalk in his edition of E. Auerbach's *Gesämmelte Aufsätze zur romanischen Philologie* (Bern and Munich, 1967), pp. 11ff.

[15] See H. Weinrich, 'Für eine Literaturgeschichte des Lesers,' *Merkur,* XXI (November, 1967). Just as the linguistics of the speaker, which was earlier customary, has been replaced by the linguistics of the listener, Weinrich pleads for a methodical consideration for the perspective of the reader in literary history and thereby supports my aims. Weinrich shows especially how the empirical methods of literary sociology can be supplemented by the linguistic and literary interpretation of the role of the reader, which is implicit in the work.

the likes of which Paris had not seen since Chateaubriand's *Atala*. As far as theme is concerned, both novels fulfilled the expectations of the new audience, which – according to Baudelaire's analysis – had rejected anything romantic and scorned grand as well as naive passion.[16] They treated a trivial subject – adultery – the one in a bourgeois and the other in a provincial milieu. Both authors understood how to give a sensational twist to the conventional, rigid triangle which in the erotic scenes surpassed the customary details. They presented the worn-out theme of jealousy in a new light by reversing the expected relationship of the three classic roles. Feydeau has the youthful lover of the 'femme de trente ans' becoming jealous of his lover's husband, although he has already reached the goal of his desires, and perishing over this tormenting situation; Flaubert provides the adulteries of the doctor's wife in the provinces, which Baudelaire presents as a sublime form of 'dandysme', with a surprising ending, so that the ridiculous figure of the deceived Charles Bovary takes on noble traits at the end. In official criticism of the time there are voices which reject *Fanny* as well as *Madame Bovary* as a product of the new school of 'réalisme', which they accuse of denying all ideals and attacking the ideas on which the order of the society in the Second Empire was based.[17] The horizon of expectations of the public of 1857, here only sketched in, which did not expect anything great in the way of novels after the death of Balzac,[18] explains the differing success of the two novels only when these question of the effect of their narrative form is posed. Flaubert's innovation in form, his principle of "impersonal telling" *impassibilité* which Barbey d'Aurevilly attacked with this comparison: if a story-telling machine could be made of English steel, it would function the same as Monsieur Flaubert[19]), must have shocked the same audience which was offered the exciting contents of *Fanny* in the personable tone of a confessional novel. It could also have found in Feydeau's descriptions[20] popular ideals and frustrations of the level of

16 In '*Madame Bovary* par Gustave Flaubert,' Baudelaire, *Oeuvres complètes,* Pléiade ed. (Paris, 1951), p. 998: 'The last years of Louis-Philippe witnessed the last explosions of a spirit still excitable by the play of the imagination; but the new novelist found himself faced with a completely worn-out society – worse than worn-out – stupified and gluttonous, with a horror only of fiction and love only for possession.'

17 Cf. *ibid.*, p. 999, as well as the accusation, speech for the defense, and verdict of the *Bovary* trial in Flaubert, *Oeuvres,* Pléiade edition (Paris, 1951), 1, 649–717, esp. 717; also about *Fanny,* E. Montegut, "Le roman intime de la littérature réaliste," *Revue des deux mondes,* XVIII (1858), 196–213, esp. 201 and 209ff.

18 As Baudelaire testifies ('*Madame Bovary* par Gustave Flaubert,' p. 996): 'for since the disappearance of Balzac . . . all curiosity relative to the novel has been stilled and slumbers.'

19 For these and other contemporary verdicts see H.R. Jauss "Die beiden Fassungen von Flauberts 'Education Sentimentale,' " *Heidelberger Jahrbücher,* II (1958), 96–116, esp. 97.

20 See the excellent analysis by the contemporary critic E. Montegut (see note 17), who explains in detail why the dreams and the figures in Feydeau's novel are typical for the readers in the section between the *Bourse* and the boulevard Montmartre (p. 209): they need an "alcool poétique," enjoy seeing "their vulgar adventures of yesterday and their vulgar projects of tomorrow poeticized" (p. 210) and have an "idolatry of the material" by which term Montegut understands the ingredients of the "dream factory" of 1959 – "a sort of sanctimonious admiration, almost devout, for furniture, wallpaper, dress, escapes, like a perfume of patchouli, from each of its pages" (p. 201).

society which sets the style, and it could delight unrestrainedly in the lascivious main scene in which Fanny (without knowing that her lover is watching from the balcony) seduces her husband – for their moral indignation was forestalled by the reaction of the unfortunate witness. However, as *Madame Bovary,* which was understood at first only by a small circle of knowledgeable readers and called a turning point in the history of the novel, became a world-wide success, the group of readers who were formed by this book sanctioned the new canon of expectations, which made the weaknesses of Feydeau – his flowery style, his modish effects, his lyrical confessional clichés – unbearable and relegated *Fanny* to the class of bestsellers of yesterday.

. . . .

The reconstruction of the horizon of expectations, on the basis of which a work in the past was created and received, enables us to find the questions to which the text originally answered and thereby to discover how the reader of that day viewed and understood the work. This approach corrects the usually unrecognized values of a classical concept of art or of an interpretation that seeks to modernize, and it avoids the recourse to a general spirit of the age, which involves circular reasoning. It brings out the hermeneutic difference between past and present ways of understanding a work, points up the history of its reception – providing both approaches – and thereby challenges as platonizing dogma the apparently self-evident dictum of philological metaphysics that literature is timelessly present and that it has objective meaning, determined once and for all and directly open to the interpreter at any time.

SECTION SIX
FEMINISM

Perhaps more than any other mode of criticism, feminist theory has cut across and drawn on multiple and contradictory traditions whilst presenting what is arguably one of the most fundamental challenges to critical orthodoxies: its revaluation of subjectivity and the category of 'experience'.

Early feminist criticism drew extensively on Simone de Beauvoir's *The Second Sex* (1949), a work which had initiated the process of analysing the social construction of gender and of distinguishing between sex and gender; and on Kate Millett's *Sexual Politics* (1970) which analysed the system of sex-role stereotyping and the oppression of women under patriarchial social organization. Much of the criticism which drew on these texts and flourished, particulary in America, in the 1970s, concentrated its analysis on the 'images' of women represented in, or constructed through, cultural forms such as literature (Donovan 1975; Ellman 1979). Rarely did this writing seek explicitly to question the category of 'literature' itself or the dominant expressive-mimetic aesthetics. It has thus been viewed by later feminists (Kaplan 1986, Moi 1985) as often failing to offer an adequate analysis of the relationship between ideology and representation, and thus as inadvertently affirming the universalism and subjectivism of traditional liberal-humanist criticism.

In the article reprinted here, by the British Marxist-Feminist Collective, there is instead an attempt to study the literary text through an analysis of the *specific* articulations of patriarchy within capitalist society. Such an approach emphasizes the need to situate the text in relation to an analysis, for example, of the economic position of women as a consequence of the division of labour and the organization of the family; the effects of this on female authorship and reading habits; the control and organization of reproduction and sexuality; the role of cultural forms such as literature in this process, and the specific organization of the institution of literature according to masculine discourses and valuations.

By the mid-70s there was increasing attention from both broadly 'liberal' or broadly 'socialist' or 'radical' feminists to texts *by* women as opposed to the study of the representation of women in texts by male authors. This approach was explicitly advocated, in particular, by Elaine Showalter as the basis of 'Gynocriticism', and her *A Literature of their Own* (1977) attempted to construct an alternative tradition of women's writing, focusing specifically on female writing and experience. Although her work challenged the sexist bias of the liberal tradition, it failed to challenge its fundamental conception of the subject and of the literary text. Subjectivity was still conceived of in essential and unitary terms; tradition remained a continuous and seamless process and the text itself remained embedded in an expressive-mimetic aesthetic. In many ways, therefore, Showalter's work reaffirms the orthodox humanist belief in literature as the expression of a universal unity encompassing men *and* women and known as 'human nature'. The category is simply enlarged rather than undermined or deconstructed. Later feminists were to challenge this conception of the literary process, drawing on the insights of structuralist Marxism, psychoanalysis and deconstruction.

---

10 Elaine Showalter,
'Towards a Feminist Poetics', *Women Writing about Women*, ed M. Jacobus

p25–33; 34–36

Feminist criticism can be divided into two distinct varieties. The first type is concerned with *woman as reader* – with woman as the consumer of male-produced literature, and with the way in which the hypothesis of a female reader changes our apprehension of a given text, awakening us to the significance of its sexual codes. I shall call this kind of analysis the *feminist critique*, and like other kinds of critique it is a historically grounded inquiry which probes the ideological assumptions of literary phenomena. Its subjects include the images and stereotypes of women in literature, the omissions and misconceptions about women in criticism, and the fissures in male-constructed literary history. It is also concerned with the exploitation and manipulation of the female audience, especially in popular culture and film; and with the analysis of woman-as-sign in semiotic systems. The second type of feminist criticism is concerned with *woman as writer* – with woman as the producer of textual

[margin note: – woman as reader – woman as writer]

meaning, with the history, themes, genres and structures of literature by women. Its subjects include the psychodynamics of female creativity, linguistics and the problem of a female language; the trajectory of the individual or collective female literary career; literary history; and, of course, studies of particular writers and works. No term exists in English for such a specialised discourse, and so I have adapted the French term *la gynocritique:* '*gynocritics*' (although the significance of the male pseudonym in the history of women's writing also suggested the term 'georgics').

The feminist critique is essentially political and polemical, with theoretical affiliations to Marxist sociology and aesthetics; gynocritics is more self-contained and experimental, with connections to other modes of new feminist research. In a dialogue between these two positions, Carolyn Heilbrun, the writer, and Catherine Stimpson, editor of the American journal *Signs: Women in Culture and Society*, compare the feminist critique to the Old Testament, 'looking for the sins and errors of the past', and gynocritics to the New Testament, seeking 'the grace of imagination'. Both kinds are necessary, they explain, for only the Jeremiahs of the feminist critique can lead us out of the 'Egypt of female servitude' to the promised land of the feminist vision. That the discussion makes use of these Biblical metaphors points to the connections between feminist consciousness and conversion narratives which often appear in women's literature; Carolyn Heilbrun comments on her own text, 'when I talk about feminist criticism, I am amazed at how high a moral tone I take'.[1]

The Feminist Critique: Hardy

Let us take briefly as an example of the way a feminist critique might proceed, Thomas Hardy's *The Mayor of Casterbridge,* which begins with the famous scene of the drunken Michael Henchard selling his wife and infant daughter for five guineas at a country fair. In his study of Hardy, Irving Howe has praised the brilliance and power of this opening scene:

> To shake loose from one's wife; to discard the drooping rag of a woman, with her mute complaints and maddening passivity; to escape not by a slinking abandonment but through the public sale of her body to a stranger, as horses are sold at a fair; and thus to wrest, through sheer amoral wilfulness, a second chance out of life – it is with this stroke, so insidiously attractive to male fantasy, that *The Mayor of Casterbridge* begins.[2]

[1] 'Theories of Feminist Criticism' in Josephine Donovan (ed.), *Feminist Literary Criticism: Explorations in Theory* (Lexington, 1976), pp. 64, 68, 72.
[2] Irving Howe, *Thomas Hardy* (London, 1968), p. 84. For a more detailed discussion of this problem, see my essay 'The Unmanning of the Mayor of Casterbridge' in Dale Kramer (ed.), *Critical Approaches to Hardy* (London, 1979).

It is obvious that a woman, unless she has been indoctrinated into being very deeply identified indeed with male culture, will have a different experience of this scene. I quote Howe first to indicate how the fantasies of the male critic distort the text; for Hardy tells us very little about the relationship of Michael and Susan Henchard, and what we see in the early scenes does not suggest that she is drooping, complaining or passive. Her role, however, is a passive one; severely constrained by her womanhood, and further burdened by her child, there is no way that *she* can wrest a second chance out of life. She cannot master events, but only accommodate herself to them.

What Howe, like other male critics of Hardy, conveniently overlooks about the novel is that Henchard sells not only his wife but his child, a child who can only be female. Patriarchal societies do not readily sell their sons, but their daughters are all for sale sooner or later. Hardy wished to make the sale of the daughter emphatic and central; in early drafts of the novel Henchard has two daughters and sells only one, but Hardy revised to make it clearer that Henchard is symbolically selling his entire share in the world of women. Having severed his bonds with this female community of love and loyalty, Henchard has chosen to live in the male community, to define his human relationships by the male code of paternity, money and legal contract. His tragedy lies in realising the inadequacy of this system, and in his inability to repossess the loving bonds he comes desperately to need.

The emotional centre of *The Mayor of Casterbridge* is neither Henchard's relationship to his wife, nor his superficial romance with Lucetta Templeman, but his slow appreciation of the strength and dignity of his wife's daughter, Elizabeth-Jane. Like the other women in the book, she is governed by her own heart – man-made laws are not important to her until she is taught by Henchard himself to value legality, paternity, external definitions, and thus in the end to reject him. A self-proclaimed 'woman-hater', a man who has felt at best a 'supercilious pity' for womankind, Henchard is humbled and 'unmanned' by the collapse of his own virile façade, the loss of his mayor's chain, his master's authority, his father's rights. But in Henchard's alleged weakness and 'womanishness', breaking through in moments of tenderness, Hardy is really showing us the man at his best. Thus Hardy's female characters in *The Mayor of Casterbridge*, as in his other novels, are somewhat idealised and melancholy projections of a repressed male self.

As we see in this analysis, one of the problems of the feminist critique is that it is male-oriented. If we study stereotypes of women, the sexism of male critics, and the limited roles women play in literary history, we are not learning what women have felt and experienced, but what men have thought women should be. In some fields of specialisation, this may require a long apprenticeship to the male theoretician, whether he be Althusser, Barthes, Macherey or Lacan; and then an application of the theory of signs or myths or the unconscious to male texts or films. The temporal and intellectual investment one makes in such a process increases resistance to questioning it, and to seeing its historical and ideological boundaries. The critique also has a tendency to naturalise women's victimisation, by making it the inevitable and obsessive topic of discussion. One sees, moreover, in works like Elizabeth Hardwick's *Seduction and Betrayal,* the bittersweet moral distinctions the critic makes between women merely betrayed by men, like Hetty in *Adam Bede*, and the heroines who make careers out of betrayal, like Hester Prynne in *The Scarlet Letter*. This comes dangerously close to a celebration of the opportunities of victimisation, the seduction *of* betrayal.[3]

Gynocritics and Female Culture

In contrast to this angry or loving fixation on male literature, the programme of gynocritics is to construct a female framework for the analysis of women's literature, to develop new models based on the study of female experience, rather than to adapt male models and theories. Gynocritics begins at the point when we free ourselves from the linear absolutes of male literary history, stop trying to fit women between the lines of the male tradition, and focus instead on the newly visible world of female culture. This is comparable to the ethnographer's effort to render the experience of the 'muted' female half of a society, which is described in Shirley Ardener's collection, *Perceiving Women*.[4] Gynocritics is related to feminist research in history, anthropology, psychology and sociology, all of which have developed hypotheses of a female subculture including not only the ascribed status, and the internalised constructs of femininity, but also the occupations, interactions and consciousness of women. Anthropologists study the female subculture in the relationships between women, as mothers, daughters, sisters and friends; in sexuality, reproduction and ideas about the body; and in rites of initiation and passage, purification ceremonies, myths and taboos. Michelle Rosaldo writes in *Woman, Culture, and Society*,

> the very symbolic and social conceptions that appear to set women apart and to circumscribe their activities may be used by the women as a basis for female solidarity and worth. When men live apart from women, they in fact cannot control them, and unwittingly they may provide them with the symbols and social resources on which to build a society of their own.[5]

[3] Elizabeth Hardwick, *Seduction and Betrayal* (New York, 1974).

[4] Shirley Ardener (ed.), *Perceiving Women* (London, 1975).

[5] 'Women, Culture, and Society: A Theoretical Overview' in Louise Lamphere and Michelle Rosaldo (eds.), *Women, Culture and Society* (Stanford, 1974), p. 39.

Thus in some women's literature, feminine values penetrate and undermine the masculine systems which contain them; and women have imaginatively engaged the myths of the Amazons, and the fantasies of a separate female society, in genres from Victorian poetry to contemporary science fiction.

In the past two years, pioneering work by four young American feminist scholars has given us some new ways to interpret the culture of nineteenth-century American women, and the literature which was its primary expressive form. Carroll Smith-Rosenberg's essay. 'The Female World of Love and Ritual' examines several archives of letters between women, and outlines the homosocial emotional world of the nineteenth century. Nancy Cott's *The Bonds of Womanhood: Woman's Sphere in New England 1780–1835* explores the paradox of a cultural bondage, a legacy of pain and submission, which none the less generates a sisterly solidarity, a bond of shared experience, loyalty and compassion. Ann Douglas's ambitious book, *The Feminization of American Culture*, boldly locates the genesis of American mass culture in the sentimental literature of women and clergymen, two allied and 'disestablished' post-industrial groups. These three are social historians; but Nina Auerbach's *Communities of Women: An idea in Fiction* seeks the bonds of womanhood in women's literature, ranging from the matriarchal households of Louisa May Alcott and Mrs Gaskell to the women's schools and colleges of Dorothy Sayers, Sylvia Plath and Muriel Spark. Historical and literary studies like these, based on English women, are badly needed; and the manuscript and archival sources for them are both abundant and untouched.[6]

Gynocritics: Elizabeth Barrett Browning and Muriel Spark

Gynocritics must also take into account the different velocities and curves of political, social and personal histories in determining women's literary choices and careers. 'In dealing with women as writers,' Virginia Woolf wrote in her 1929 essay, 'Women and Fiction', 'as much elasticity as possible is desirable; it is necessary to leave oneself room to deal with other things besides their work, so much has that work been influenced by conditions that have nothing whatever to do with art.'[7] We might illustrate the need for this completeness by looking at Elizabeth Barrett Browning, whose verse-novel *Aurora Leigh* (1856) has recently been

---

[6] Carroll Smith-Rosenberg, 'The Female World of Love and Ritual: Relations Between Women in Nineteenth-Century America', *Signs: Journal of Women in Culture and Society*, vol i (Autumn 1975), pp. 1–30; Nancy Cott, *The Bonds of Womanhood* (New Haven, 1977); Ann Douglas, *The Feminization of American Culture* (New York, 1977); Nina Auerbach, *Communities of Women* (Cambridge, Mass., 1978).

[7] 'Women and Fiction' in Virginia Woolf, *Collected Essays*, vol. ii (London, 1967). p. 141.

handsomely reprinted by the Women's Press. In her excellent introduction Cora Kaplan defines Barrett Browning's feminism as romantic
and bourgeois, placing its faith in the transforming powers of love, art
and Christian charity. Kaplan reviews Barrett Browning's dialogue with
the artists and radicals of her time; with Tennyson and Clough, who had
also written poems on the 'woman question'; with the Christian
Socialism of Fourier, Owen, Kingsley and Maurice; and with such
female predecessors as Madame de Staël and George Sand. But in this
exploration of Barrett Browning's intellectual milieu, Kaplan omits discussion of the male poet whose influence on her work in the 1850s would
have been most pervasive: Robert Browning. When we understand how
susceptible women writers have always been to the aesthetic standards
and values of the male tradition, and to male approval and validation,
we can appreciate the complexity of a marriage between artists. Such a
union has almost invariably meant internal conflicts, self-effacement,
and finally obliteration for the women, except in the rare cases – Eliot
and Lewes, the Woolfs – where the husband accepted a managerial
rather than a competitive role. We can see in Barrett Browning's letters
of the 1850s the painful, halting, familiar struggle between her womanly
love and ambition for her husband and her conflicting commitment to
her own work. There is a sense in which she *wants* him to be the better
artist. At the beginning of the decade she was more famous than he; then
she notes with pride a review in France which praises him more; his work
on *Men and Women* goes well; her work on *Aurora Leigh* goes badly (she
had a young child and was recovering from the most serious of her four
miscarriages). In 1854 she writes to a woman friend,

> I am behind hand with my poem . . . Robert swears he shall have his book
> ready in spite of everything for print when we shall be in London for the pur-
> pose, but, as for mine, it must wait for the next spring I begin to see clearly.
> Also it may be better not to bring out the two works together.

And she adds wryly, 'If mine were ready I might not say so perhaps.[8]

Without an understanding of the framework of the female subculture,
we can miss or misinterpret the themes and structures of women's literature, fail to make necessary connections within a tradition. In 1852, in an
eloquent passage from her autobiographical essay 'Cassandra', Florence
Nightingale identified the pain of feminist awakening as its essence, as
the guarantee of progress and free will. Protesting against the protected
unconscious lives of middle-class Victorian women, Nightingale
demanded the restoration of their suffering:

> Give us back our suffering, we cry to Heaven in our hearts – suffering rather
> than indifferentism – for out of suffering may come the cure. Better to have

[8] Peter N. Heydon and Philip Kelley (eds.), *Elizabeth Barrett Browning's Letters to Mrs. David Ogilvy* (London, 1974), p. 115.

pain than paralysis: A hundred struggle and drown in the breakers. One discovers a new world.[9]

It is fascinating to see how Nightingale's metaphors anticipate not only her own medical career, but also the fate of the heroines of women's novels in the nineteenth and twentieth centuries. To waken from the drugged pleasant sleep of Victorian womanhood was agonising; in fiction it is much more likely to end in drowning than in discovery. It is usually associated with what George Eliot in *Middlemarch* calls 'the chill hours of a morning twilight', and the sudden appalled confrontation with the contingencies of adulthood. Eliot's Maggie Tulliver, Edith Wharton's Lily Barth, Olive Schreiner's Lyndall, Kate Chopin's Edna Pontellier wake to worlds which offer no places for the women they wish to become; and rather than struggling they die. Female suffering thus becomes a kind of literary commodity which both men and women consume. Even in these important women's novels – *The Mill on the Floss, Story of an African Farm, The House of Mirth* – the fulfilment of the plot is a visit to the heroine's grave by a male mourner.

According to Dame Rebecca West, unhappiness is still the keynote of contemporary fiction by English women.[10] Certainly the literary landscape is strewn with dead female bodies. In Fay Weldon's *Down Among the Women* and *Female Friends*, suicide has come to be a kind of domestic accomplishment, carried out after the shopping and the washing-up. When Weldon's heroine turns on the gas, 'she feels that she has been half-dead for so long that the difference in state will not be very great'. In Muriel Spark's stunning short novel of 1970, *The Driver's Seat*, another half-dead and desperate heroine gathers all her force to hunt down a woman-hating psychopath, and persuade him to murder her. Garishly dressed in a purposely bought outfit of clashing purple, green and white – the colours of the suffragettes (and the colours of the school uniform in *The Prime of Miss Jean Brodie*) – Lise goes in search of her killer, lures him to a park, gives him the knife. But in Lise's careful selection of her death-dress, her patient pursuit of her assassin, Spark has given us the devastated postulates of feminine wisdom: that a woman creates her identity by choosing her clothes, that she creates her history by choosing her man. That, in the 1970s, Mr Right turns out to be Mr Goodbar, is not the sudden product of urban violence, but a latent truth which fiction exposes. Spark asks whether men or women are in the driver's seat, and whether the power to choose one's destroyer is women's only form of self-assertion. To label the violence or self-destructiveness of these painful novels as neurotic expressions of a personal pathology, as many reviewers have done, is to ignore, Annette Kolodny suggests,

9 'Cassandra' in Ray Strachey (ed.), *The Cause* (London, 1928), p. 398.
10 Rebecca West, 'And They All Lived Unhappily Ever After', *TLS* (26 July 1974), p. 779.

the possibility that the worlds they inhabit may in fact be real, or true, and for them the only worlds available, and further, to deny the possibility that their apparently 'odd' or unusual responses, may in fact be justifiable or even necessary.[11]

But women's literature must go beyond these scenarios of compromise, madness and death. Although the reclamation of suffering is the beginning, its purpose is to discover the new world. Happily, some recent women's literature, especially in the United States where novelists and poets have become vigorously involved in the women's liberation movement, has gone beyond reclaiming suffering to its re-investment. This newer writing relates the pain of transformation to history. 'If I'm lonely,' writes Adrienne Rich in 'Song',

> it must be the loneliness
> of waking first, of breathing
> dawn's first cold breath on the city
> of being the one awake
> in a house wrapped in sleep[12]

Rich is one of the spokeswomen for a new women's writing which explores the will to change. In her recent book, *Of Woman Born: Motherhood as Experience and Institution*, Rich challenges the alienation from and rejection of the mother that daughters have learned under patriarchy. Much women's literature in the past has dealt with 'matrophobia' or the fear of becoming one's mother.[13] In Sylvia Plath's *The Bell Jar*, for example, the heroine's mother is the target for the novel's most punishing contempt. When Esther announces to her therapist that she hates her mother, she is on the road to recovery. Hating one's mother was the feminist enlightenment of the fifties and sixties; but it is only a metaphor for hating oneself. Female literature of the 1970s goes beyond matrophobia to a courageously sustained quest for the mother, in such books at Margaret Atwood's *Surfacing*, and Lisa Alther's recent *Kinflicks*. As the death of the father has always been an archetypal rite of passage for the Western hero, now the death of the mother as witnessed and transcended by the daughter has become one of the most profound occasions of female literature. In analysing these purposeful awakenings, these reinvigorated mythologies of female culture, feminist criticism finds its most challenging, inspiriting and appropriate task.

. . . .

[11] Annette Kolodny, 'Some Notes on Defining a "Feminist Literary Criticism" ', *Critical Inquiry*, vol. ii (1975), p. 84. For an illuminating discussion of *The Driver's Seat,* see Auerbach, *Communities of Women*, p. 181.

[12] Adrienne Rich,*Diving into the Wreck* (New York, 1973), p. 20.

[13] The term 'matrophobia' has been coined by Lynn Sukenick; see Rich, *Of Woman Born*, pp. 235 ff.

In *A Room of One's Own*, Virginia Woolf argued that economic independence was the essential precondition of an autonomous women's art. Like George Eliot before her, Woolf also believed that women's literature held the promise of a 'precious speciality', a distinctly female vision.

Feminine, Feminist, Female

All of these themes have been important to feminist literary criticism in the 1960s and 1970s but we have approached them with more historical awareness. Before we can even begin to ask how the literature of women would be different and special, we need to reconstruct its past, to rediscover the scores of women novelists, poets and dramatists whose work has been obscured by time, and to establish the continuity of the female tradition from decade to decade, rather than from Great Woman to Great Woman. As we recreate the chain of writers in this tradition, the patterns of influence and response from one generation to the next, we can also begin to challenge the periodicity of orthodox literary history, and its enshrined canons of achievement. It is because we have studied women writers in isolation that we have never grasped the connections between them. When we go beyond Austen, the Brontës and Eliot, say, to look at a hundred and fifty or more of their sister novelists, we can see patterns and phases in the evolution of a female tradition which correspond to the developmental phases of any subcultural art. In my book on English women writers, *A Literature of Their Own*, I have called these the Feminine, Feminist and Female stages.[14] During the Feminine phase, dating from about 1840 to 1880, women wrote in an effort to equal the intellectual achievements of the male culture, and internalised its assumptions about female nature. The distinguishing sign of this period is the male pseudonym, introduced in England in the 1840s, and a national characteristic of English women writers. In addition to the famous names we all know – George Eliot, Currer, Ellis and Acton Bell – dozens of other women chose male pseudonyms as a way of coping with a double literary standard. This masculine disguise goes well beyond the title page; it exerts an irregular pressure on the narrative, affecting tone, diction, structure and characterisation. In contrast to the English male pseudonym, which signals such clear self-awareness of the liabilities of female authorship, American women during the same period adopted super-feminine, little-me pseudonyms (Fanny Fern, Grace Greenwood, Fanny Forester), disguising behind these nominal bouquets their boundless energy, powerful economic motives and keen

---

[14] Elaine Showalter, *A Literature of Their Own: British Women Novelists from Brontë to Lessing* (Princeton, New Jersey, 1977).

professional skills. It is pleasing to discover the occasional English-woman who combines both these techniques, and creates the illusion of male authorship with a name that contains the encoded domestic message of femininity – such as Harriet Parr, who wrote under the pen name 'Holme Lee'. The feminist content of feminine art is typically oblique, displaced, ironic and subversive; one has to read it between the lines, in the missed possibilities of the text.

In the Feminist phase, from about 1880 to 1920, or the winning of the vote, women are historically enabled to reject the accommodating pos-tures of femininity and to use literature to dramatise the ordeals of wronged womanhood. The personal sense of injustice which feminine novelists such as Elizabeth Gaskell and Frances Trollope expressed in their novels of class struggle and factory life become increasingly and explicitly feminist in the 1880s, when a generation of New Women redefined the woman artist's role in terms of responsibility to suffering sisters. The purest examples of this phase are the Amazon Utopias of the 1890s, fantasies of perfect female societies set in an England or an America of the future, which were also protests against male govern-ment, male laws and male medicine. One author of Amazon Utopias, the American Charlotte Perkins Gilman, also analysed the preoccupations of masculine literature with sex and war, and the alternative possibilities of an emancipated feminist literature. Gilman's Utopian feminism carried George Eliot's idea of the 'precious speciality' to its matriarchal extremes. Comparing her view of sisterly collectivity to the beehive, she writes that

> the bee's fiction would be rich and broad, full of the complex tasks of comb-building and filling, the care and feeding of the young . . . It would treat of the vast fecundity of motherhood, the educative and selective processes of the group-mothers, and the passion of loyalty, of social service, which holds the hives together.[15]

This is Feminist Socialist Realism with a vengeance, but women novelists of the period – even Gilman, in her short stories – could not be limited to such didactic formulas, or such maternal topics.

In the Female phase, ongoing since 1920, women reject both imitation and protest – two forms of dependency – and turn instead to female experience as the source of an autonomous art, extending the feminist analysis of culture to the forms and techniques of literature. Representa-tives of the formal Female Aesthetic, such as Dorothy Richardson and Virginia Woolf, begin to think in terms of male and female sentences, and divide their work into 'masculine' journalism and 'feminine' fic-tions, redefining and sexualising external and internal experience. Their experiments were both enriching and imprisoning retreats into the cele-bration of consciousness; even in Woolf's famous definition of life: 'a

[15] Charlotte Perkins Gilman, *The Man-made World* (London, 1911), pp. 101-2.

luminous halo, a semi-transparent envelope surrounding us from the beginning of consciousness to the end',[16] there is a submerged metaphor of uterine withdrawal and containment. In this sense, the Room of One's Own becomes a kind of Amazon Utopia, population 1.

Note

I wish to thank Nina Auerbach, Kate Ellis, Mary Jacobus, Wendy Martin, Adrienne Rich, Helen Taylor, Martha Vicinus, Margaret Walters and Ruth Yeazell for sharing with me their ideas on feminist criticism.

[16] 'Modern Fiction', *Collected Essays*, vol. ii, p. 106.

---

11   The Marxist-Feminist Collective,
From 'Women Writing: Jane Eyre, Shirley, Villette, Aurora Leigh', *Ideology and Consciousness*, 3, Spring 1978

p30–35

In 1859, Charlotte Brontë made a final, impatient plea to Lewes:

> I wish you did not think me a woman. I wish all reviewers believed 'Currer Bell' to be a man; they would be more just to him. . . . I cannot, when I write, think always of myself and what you consider elegant and charming in femininity. . . .[1]

Criticism of women writers is in general divided between the extremes of gender-disavowal and gender-obsession. The second tendency, which Brontë struggles against in Lewes, patronises women writers as outsiders to literary history, without justifying this apartheid. The Brontës are considered important 'women novelists', not simply novelists. This kind of 'gender criticism' subsumes the text into the sexually-defined personality of its author, and thereby obliterates its literarity. To pass over the ideology of gender, on the other hand, ignores the fact that the conditions of literary production and consumption are articulated, in the Victorian period, in crucially different ways for women and men. Any rigorous Machereyan analysis must account for the ideology of gender as

[1] Wise, T.J. and Symington, J.A. (eds). *The Brontes: Their Lives, Friendships and Correspondence*, 4 Vols, Shakespeare Head, London, 1932. Vol iii, p. 31.

it is written into or out of texts by either sex. Women writers, moreover, in response to their cultural exclusion, have developed a relatively autonomous, clandestine tradition of their own.

Gender and genre come from the same root, and their connection in literary history is almost as intimate as their etymology. The tradition into which the woman novelist entered in the mid-19th century could be polarised as at once that of Mary Wollstonecraft and of Jane Austen, with the attendant polarisation of politics – between revolutionary feminism and conservatism – and of genre – between romanticism and social realism. Wollstonecraft and Austen between them pose the central question of access to male education and discourse on the one hand, on the other the annexing of women's writing to a special sphere, domestic and emotional.

Austen's refusal to write about anything she didn't know is as undermining to the patriarchal hegemony as Wollstonecraft's demand for a widening of women's choices: the very 'narrowness' of her novels gave them a subversive dimension of which she herself was unaware, and which has been registered in critics' bewilderment at what status to accord them.

Bourgeois criticism should be read symptomatically: most of its so-called 'evaluation' is a reinforcement of ideological barriers. Wollstonecraft's, and later Brontë's, ambivalent relation to Romanticism, usually described as clumsy Gothicism, is bound up with their feminism. Romanticism becomes a problem for women writers because of its assumptions about the 'nature of femininity'. The tidal rhythms of menstruation, the outrageous visibility of pregnancy, lead, by a non-sequitur common to all sexual analogy, to the notion that women exist in a state of unreflective bios, the victims of instincts, intuitions, and the mysterious pulsations of the natural world. Intuition is held to be a pre-lapsarian form of knowledge, associated especially with angels, children, idiots, 'rustics' and women. These excluded, or fabulous, groups act for the patriarchy as a mirror onto which it nostalgically projects the exclusions of its discourse. As a glorified, but pre-linguistic communion with nature, intuition lowers women's status while appearing to raise it.

While Wollstonecraft and Brontë are attracted to Romanticism because reluctant to sacrifice, as women writers, their privileged access to feeling, both are aware that full participation in society requires suppression of this attraction. The drive to female emancipation, while fuelled by the revolutionary energy at the origins of Romanticism, has an ultimately conservative aim – successful integration into existing social structures.

Romanticism, after the disappointments of the French Revolution, was gradually depoliticised, and it is only in the mid-nineteenth century, in a period of renewed revolutionary conflict, that it once again becomes a nexus of ideological tension where gender, genre, politics and feminism converge.

Jane Eyre: her hand in marriage

Charlotte Brontë's second preface to *Jane Eyre* states her authorial project as to "scrutinise and expose" what she calls "narrow human doctrines" of religion and morality.[2] Our reading of *Jane Eyre* identifies Charlotte Brontë's interrogation of the dominant ideology of love and marriage; but also suggests the Machereyan "not-said" of the novel – what it is not possible for her to "scrutinise and expose", woman as a desiring subject, a sexual subject seeking personal fulfilment within the existing structures of class and kinship, i.e. in a patriarchal capitalist society. *Jane Eyre* is *about* kinship, *about* the fact that the social position of a woman, whether rich or poor, pretty or plain, is mediated through the family – to which she may or may not belong.

The text of *Jane Eyre* speaks that desire in the interstices of the debate on woman's social role, between the romance/realism divide, the conflict between Reason and Imagination in her heroine's consciousness. It speaks of women's sexuality in Victorian England, opening the locked room of a tabooed subject – just as that part of the text which concerns Bertha Mason/Rochester disrupts the realistic narrative of Jane's search for an adequate kinship system, i.e. an opening into the family structure from which she is excluded. Charlotte Brontë's general fictional strategy is to place her heroines in varying degrees of marginality to the normative kinship patterns. Frances Henri, Crimsworth (a female surrogate), Jane, Shirley, Caroline Helstone and Lucy Snowe, all have a deviant socialisation, all confront the problem of a marriage not negotiated by a *pater familias*.

Why? By excluding them from a conventional family situation in which their socialisation and their exchange in marriage cannot follow the practice of Victorian middle-class women, Charlotte Bronte's fiction explores the constraints of the dominant ideology as they bear on female sexual and social identity.

'At the centre of Charlotte Brontë's novels is a figure who either lacks or deliberately cuts the bonds of kinship' (Eagleton, *Myths of Power*). But Eagleton, although stressing this structural characteristic, discusses it primarily in terms of class-mobility. This treatment of Jane Eyre herself

---

[2] Currer Bell, Preface to the Second Edition of *Jane Eyre,* Smith, Elder & Co., London, 1847.

as an asexual representative of the upwardly mobile bourgeoisie leads to a reductionist reading of the text. It neglects gender as a determinant, by subsuming gender under class. The meritocratic vision of "individual self-reliance", as Eagleton puts its, *cannot* be enacted by a woman character in the same way as it can be by a male. For a woman to become a member of the 'master-class' depends on her taking a sexual master whereby her submission brings her access to the dominant culture.

The social and judicial legitimacy of this relationship – its encoding within the law – is of primary importance; hence Jane's rejection of the role of Rochester's mistress. She would not merely *not* acquire access – she would forfeit the possibility of ever doing so. The structure of the novel, Jane's development through childhood and adolescence into womanhood does not simply represent an economic and social progression from penniless orphan to member of the landed gentry class; it represents a woman's struggle for access to her own sexual and reproductive potential – in other words, her attempts to install herself as a full subject within a male-dominated culture.

For example, the structure of the five locales of the novel is customarily seen as the articulation of the heroine's progress – a progress described in liberal criticism as the moral growth of the individual, in vulgar sociological terms as 'upward social mobility'. To foreground kinship provides a radically different reading.

Jane's progress is from a dependent orphan to the acquisition of the family necessary for her full integration into mid-nineteenth century culture as a woman. Her cousins, the Rivers, and the Madeira uncle who intervenes twice – once via his agent, Bertha's brother, to save her from becoming a 'fallen woman' as Rochester's bigamous wife, and again at the end of the novel with a legacy which is in effect a dowry – provide Jane with the necessary basis for her exchange into marriage.

Each of the five houses through which the heroine passes traces the variety and instability of a kinship structure at a transitional historical period, and the ideological space this offers to women.

At Gateshead, as the excluded intruder into the Reed family and at Thornfield as the sexually tabooed and socially ambiguous governess, Jane's lack of familial status renders her particularly vulnerable to oppression and exploitation. At Lowood, she acquires a surrogate sister and mother in Helen Burns and Miss Temple – only to lose them through death and marriage. The instability of kinship relations is imaged in the patterns of gain and loss, acceptance and denial, enacted at each 'home' – most dramatically in the loss of a lawful wedded husband, spiritually and sexually akin but socially tabooed. The subsequent flight from Thornfield reduces her to a homeless vagrant lacking both past and identity. Throughout the text, the symmetrical arrangement of Reed and Rivers cousins, the Reed and Eyre uncles, the patterns of metaphors about kinship, affinity and identification articulate the proposition that a woman's social identity is constituted within familial relationships. Without the kinship reading, the Rivers' transformation into long-lost, bona-fide blood-relations at Moor End appears a gross and unmotivated coincidence. This apparently absurd plot manipulation is in fact dictated by the logic of the not-said.

Like such violations of probability, the Gothic elements in the novel are neither clumsy interventions to resolve the narrative problems nor simply the residues of the author's earlier modes of discourse, the childhood fantasies of Angria. Their main function is to evade the censorship of female sexuality within the signifying practice of mid-Victorian realism. For the rights and wrongs of women in social and political terms, there existed a rationalist language, a political rhetoric, inherited from Mary Wollstonecraft. But for the 'unspeakable' sexual desires of women, Charlotte Brontë returned on the one hand to Gothic and Romantic modes, on the other to a metonymic discourse of the human body – hands and eyes for penises, 'vitals' or 'vital organs' for women's genitalia – often to comic effect:

> I am substantial enough – touch me.' . . . .
> He held out his hand, laughing. 'Is that a dream?' said he, placing it close to my eyes. He had a rounded, muscular, and vigorous hand, as well as a long, strong arm.[3]

The tale told of women's sexual possibilities is a halting, fragmented and ambivalent one. The libidinal fire of Jane Eyre's 'vital organs' is not denied, not totally repressed, as the refusal of St John Rivers suggests:

> At his side, always and always restrained, always checked – forced to keep the fire of my nature continually low, to compel it to burn inwardly, and never utter a cry, though the imprisoned flame consume vital after vital.[4]

The marriage proposed here, significantly, is an inter-familial one which denies the heroine's sexuality. If women's sexuality is to be integrated, reconciled with male patriarchal Law, a compromise must be achieved with the individual Law-bearer, in this case through a return to Edward Rochester.

[3] *Jane Eyre*, Penguin, Harmondsworth, 1966, pp. 306–7.
[4] Ibid, p. 433.

The alternative to either repression or integration is examined through that part of the text concerned with Bertha Mason/Rochester. Her initial intervention, the uncanny laughter after Jane surveys from the battlements of Thornfield the wider world denied her as a woman, signifies the return of the repressed, the anarchic and unacted desires of women. Bertha's appearances constitute a punctuating device or notation of the not-said – the Pandora's box of unleashed female libido. Bertha's tearing of the veil on the eve of Jane's wedding, for example, is a triumphant trope for the projected loss of Jane's virginity unsanctioned by legitimate marriage. Thus while other spectres were haunting Europe, the spectre haunting Jane Eyre, if not Victorian England, was the insurgence of women's sexuality into the signifying practice of literature.

The myth of unbridled male sexuality is treated through Rochester, whose name evokes that of the predatory Restoration rake, here modified by Byronic sensibility. In the vocabulary of Lacanian psychoanalysis, his maiming by the author is not so much a punitive castration, but represents his successful passage through the castration complex. Like all human subjects he must enter the symbolic order through a necessary acceptance of the loss of an early incestuous love object, a process he initially tries to circumvent through bigamy. His decision to make Jane his bigamous wife attempts to implicate the arch-patriarch, God himself ('I know my maker sanctions what I do'). The supernatural lightning which this presumption provokes is less a re-establishing of bourgeois morality than an expression of disapproval by the transcendental phallic signifier of Rochester's Oedipal rivalry. It is God at the end of the novel who refuses to sanction Jane's marriage to St John Rivers when invoked in its support, and who sends Rochester's supernatural cry to call Jane to him; and it is God's judgement which Rochester, in his maimed condition, finally accepts with filial meekness.

By accepting the Law, he accepts his place in the signifying chain and enters the Symbolic order, as bearer rather than maker of the Law. Sexuality in a reduced and regulated form is integrated – legitimised – within the dominant kinship structure of patriarchy and within the marriage which he (by Bertha's death-by-fire), and Jane (by her acquisition of a family) is now in a position to contract. *Jane Eyre* does not attempt to rupture the dominant kinship structures. The ending of the novel ('Reader, I married him') affirms those very structures. The feminism of the text resides in its 'not-said', its attempt to inscribe women as sexual subjects within this system.

PART TWO

INTRODUCTION

The term 'post-structuralism' does not refer to a body of work that represents a coherent school or movement. Indeed there is an extensive debate about what constitutes post-structuralism and about its relation to structuralism. For some it is a matter of a more radical reading of Saussure, for others it is the moment at which structuralism becomes self-reflective. It is sometimes taken as a critique of structuralism, sometimes a development of it. In some instances it has almost become synonymous with the name of Derrida and the mode of analysis he inaugurates – 'deconstruction'. However, it is usually used to refer to Derrida and the later Barthes, less certainly to Foucault and Lacan as the principal theorists in the field, and to work which develops out of the writings of these key figures. Our use of the term is related to the body of work that presupposes structuralism, but that distances itself from certain of its features, and that presents a more radical attack on critical orthodoxies (structuralism among them). In other words, while retaining a 'post-Saussurean' definition (see Belsey 1980) we have made the category as broad as possible, certainly not restricting it to the Derridean strand.

There are a number of problems with any attempt to classify work as either structuralist or post-structuralist. The material is not naturally self-categorizing, rather, it forms a network: a web of interconnections and antitheses around which it is difficult to draw simple boundaries. Some of the work covered in Part One of this anthology relates more closely at times to the trajectories typical of the work represented in Part Two, and, by the same token, work covered in Part Two often slips back into the kind of mastery of explanation and use of metalanguage characteristic of Part One.

The problem is further complicated by the moments of appearance of structuralism and post-structuralism. If one wanted to date the appearance of post-structuralism then 1966/7 would be a reasonable point to start. At the international symposium, 'The Languages of Criticism and the Sciences of Man', in 1966, a significant post-structuralist impetus emerged (Macksey and Donato 1972). Derrida published three books in 1967, among them *Of Grammatology* and

Writing and Difference. Barthes's work was undergoing a transition from the structuralism of *Elements of Semiology* (1964) to a post-structuralist position that can be traced in essays written between then and the publication of *S/Z* in 1972. Foucault's *Order of Things* and Lacan's *Ecrits* were published in 1966, and though these latter two might not be fully-fledged works of post-structuralism, they differ significantly from the structuralism represented in Part One of this book.

But if there was a visible post-structuralist impetus it became entangled (in Anglo-American theory at any rate) with structuralism, for the latter was itself only taking significant hold in the mid-70s. Indeed the books cited above were not published in English translation until the mid/late-70s, while Culler's *Structuralist Poetics* and Hawkes's *Structuralism and Semiotics* had only appeared in the mid-70s. The moment of structuralism and the moment of post-structuralism almost coincide in terms of their appearance and adoption in Anglo-American literary theory.

Roland Barthes's *S/Z* serves as a good illustration of the convergence and varying appropriations by Anglo-American criticism of structuralist and post-structuralist work. The five codes Barthes had used in his implosive analysis of a short story by Balzac were taken by many critics to be the codes out of which the text was structured and which could therefore be used in textual criticism to reveal an absolute textual structure and meaning. However, a more radical reading of *S/Z* saw it not as providing the structural grid of the text but as *processing* the textual web in an act of structuration. The difference can be captured in the distinction between a 'product' orientation, where criticism sets out to reveal the construction of the product, and a 'process' orientation, where the act of criticism is acknowledged to be a processing act – an act of structuration which is itself an active part of that construction. Here the text is not revealed and explained but worked upon. Colin MacCabe's notion of the classic realist text (see Part Two, section one) owes much to Barthes's *S/Z*, but it hesitates between the more formalist and more radical approach.

While there is a difficulty in simply ascribing certain writings to either a structuralist or a post-structuralist position certain features of post-structuralism do distinguish it from structuralism. Though language remains a central area of interest, post-structuralism takes up a more radical reading and/or critique of Saussurean theory. As we have seen, Saussure argued that 'language is a system of difference, with no positive terms'. Identities do not refer to essences and are not discrete but are articulated in difference; identities are events in language. Structuralism had tended to acknowledge this but only to a limited degree; it did not extend such reasoning to the

foundations of the literary discourse. In post-structuralism everything can be subjected to this formulation. All of the categories
which literary studies assumes, and which form the basis of the
critical act, are open to the re-evaluation and radical scepticism of a
post-structuralist perspective, including the category 'Literature'
itself. And if the categories of literature and literary study do not refer
to things-in-themselves, but are constructed in difference then the
act of criticism which articulates that difference cannot be viewed as
subordinate. Rather, it is of equal importance to the literature it
studies, for it is the very act that brings the 'literary' into being; it is
the necessary supplement that endows 'literature' with its special
and specific existence. In a Derridean inversion, the supplement
becomes, paradoxically, the more important term, for without criticism 'literature' would have no meaning. It is not only the category of
literature that can be subjected to such reasoning, but also that of
the author and the literary text itself. Post-structuralism effectively
undermines all the categories that had previously been taken for
granted as having an independent existence.

If this were all that post-structuralism amounted to then it would
not be altogether radical. Though identities might be arbitrary, once
they had been fixed in language then they would be defined and
stable; however, post-structuralism goes further. In the system of
difference proposed by Saussure the sign, made up of the signifier
and the signified, is arbitrary, fixed by social contract. Once formed,
the sign becomes a totality; signifier and signified are inseparable
and the sign's form and meaning are self-identical. In other words,
Saussure had argued that the continuum of the phenomenal world
was 'cut up' by language; but once this process was complete, then
the relationship between the arbitrary signifier and the arbitrary
signified was fixed and they achieved a stable one-to-one correspondence. Post-structuralism questions this assumption, arguing
that signifiers do not carry with them well–defined signifieds;
meanings are never as graspable or as 'present' as this suggests.
Any attempt to define the meaning of a word illustrates the point for
it inevitably ends up in a circularity of signifiers, with the signifiers
sliding over the continuum of the field of the signified. For example,
in the *Concise Oxford Dictionary* the meaning of the word 'meaning'
is given as 'what is meant; significance . . .'; 'meant' in turn refers
us to 'mean', 'mean' to 'signify'; meanwhile, 'significance' refers us
to 'significant' which is defined as 'having a meaning'. The meaning
of 'meaning' does not become present to us, it simply slips beneath a
circularity of signifiers. And, of course, these signifiers are open to
multiple meaning areas; 'mean' also refers us to 'inferior, poor'; 'not
generous'; 'the mathematical mean', etc. Post-structuralism
argues, then, that the sign is not stable, that there is an

indeterminacy or undecidability about meaning and that it is subject to 'slippage' from signifier to signifier. So, if literature, the author and the text no longer have an identity outside of difference, neither do they have *a* single, fixed and determinate meaning; they are relativized and unstable.

Post-structuralism, whilst continuing the attack on humanist ideology and the Anglo-American critical tradition, also applies its perspectives to structuralism. It argues that, in its claim to explain by unveiling an underlying structure, structuralism is in the grip of another form of essentialism in that it presupposes a latent centre or core which gives rise to surface, manifest forms. Structuralism's appeal to a metalanguage of explanation cannot avoid the problems of interpretation and meaning. The signs of that metalanguage are themselves subject to slippage and indeterminacy; they can no more offer a full and final presence of meaning than the signs of an object language. And the metalanguage itself is always open, in its turn, to the gaze of an alternative metalanguage. Indeed, the distinction between an object language and a metalanguage breaks down in post-structuralism. From this position, the claim of structuralism to effect a mastery and explanation of the world through the scientific investigation of sign systems is undermined and compromised.

The radical de-centring of identities and an emphasis on the signifier over the signified, form two central characteristics of post-structuralism. However, these characteristics are not evenly distributed throughout the work we have classified under the post-structuralism heading. Neither are they all that post-structuralism concerns itself with. In order to map out the areas that it has encompassed we have organized the second part of the book according to three primary domains of post-structuralist work – the 'subject', 'textuality', and 'discourse'. Additionally, a final section, 'postmodernism', indicates a recent development in critical theory. Though it has sometimes been seen as an antithesis to post-structuralism, it undoubtedly depends on post-structural work for its impetus.

Unlike the material represented in Part One, the work covered in Part Two cannot be seen in terms of schools or movements. However, certain key figures are significant and demand attention. To a large extent our introductions to each section revolve around these figures, since they provide landmarks on the map; they are used to locate areas of post-structuralist work and should be treated in this light rather than as the authoritative subjects of original theories. The first three sections can be seen to be informed principally by the work of Lacan, Derrida, and Foucault respectively but, as Young has pointed out, these '. . . are the names of problems, not "authors" of doctrines' (1981, p. 9). It is also important to recognize that, although we have grouped work under section headings, that work should not be seen as 'belonging' in any simple sense to particular classifications. Post-structuralism is a network of inter-connected notions and concepts, and work we have categorized in one section is often pertinent to another. Our categorizations should be seen, therefore, as convenient ways to locate work and as convenient ways of introducing themes.

However, we would contend that two distinct trajectories have developed in which both the object of enquiry and the way it is conceptualized, fundamentally differ. These trajectories we have called 'language' and 'discourse'. The former is concerned with the figures of language in abstraction, the latter situates language in the context of its use by (and use of) speaking and listening subjects. The language trajectory is concerned primarily with deconstructing the principles of ordering and the 'metaphysics of presence' (see section two) that are inescapably built into our language. It views all language as a web of signifiers bound up in an endless play of textuality (textuality being the condition of existence of signifiers where they refer endlessly to other textual occurrences, rather than to a pre-text). The discourse trajectory considers language as a practical activity intimately connected with the context in which it appears. Though the sign is unstable in both trajectories, here it is constantly being fixed and unfixed, or refixed, by different users and communities of users of the language. In this trajectory the actual mode of existence of language is central; it is seen to relate immediately to the socio-cultural formation in which it appears, and to the exercise of power.

Few critics or theorists would subscribe to one or other of these trajectories in any simply way. They represent the two poles of the post-structural enterprise rather than either/or positions to be adopted. However, it is clear that where Derrida tends toward language, Foucault tends toward discourse. It is also clear that some of the 'deconstructionist' work that owes most to Derrida is firmly located at the language-end of the continuum.

We have chosen Roland Barthes's essay, 'The Death of the Author' to introduce our survey because it provides a short and useful introduction to some of the significant themes developed in post-structuralism. It is an essay which has achieved notoriety for its polemical stance in displacing the author from the centre of the critical act.

12 Roland Barthes,

'The Death of the Author', *Image, Music, Text,* trans & ed
S. Heath,

p142–148

In his story *Sarrasine* Balzac, describing a castrato disguised as a woman,
writes the following sentence: *'This was woman, herself, with her sudden
fears, her irrational whims, her instinctive worries, her impetuous bold-
ness, her fussings, and her delicious sensibility.'* Who is speaking thus? Is
it the hero of the story bent on remaining ignorant of the castrato hidden
beneath the woman? Is it Balzac the individual, furnished by his personal
experience with a philosophy of Woman? Is it Balzac the author profes-
sing 'literary' ideas on femininity? Is it universal wisdom? Romantic
psychology? We shall never know, for the good reason that writing is the
destruction of every voice, of every point of origin. Writing is that
neutral, composite, oblique space where our subject slips away, the
negative where all identity is lost, starting with the very identity of the
body writing.

No doubt it has always been that way. As soon as a fact is *narrated* no
longer with a view to acting directly on reality but intransitively, that is to
say, finally outside of any function other than that of the very practice of
the symbol itself, this disconnection occurs, the voice loses its origin, the
author enters into his own death, writing begins. The sense of this phenomenon, however, has varied; in ethnographic societies the responsibility
for a narrative is never assumed by a person but by a mediator, shaman
or relator whose 'performance' – the mastery of the narrative
code – may possibly be admired but never his 'genius'. The author is a
modern figure, a product of our society insofar as, emerging from the
Middle Ages and English empiricism, French rationalism and the personal faith of the Reformation, it discovered the prestige of the individual, of, as it is more nobly put, the 'human person'. It is thus logical
that in literature it should be this positivism, the epitome and culmination of capitalist ideology, which has attached the greatest importance to
the 'person' of the author. The *author* still reigns in histories of literature, biographies of writers, interviews, magazines, as in the very
consciousness of men of letters anxious to unit their person and their
work through diaries and memoirs. The image of literature to be found
in ordinary culture is tyrannically centred on the author, his person, his
life, his tastes, his passions, while criticism still consists for the most part
in saying that Baudelaire's work is the failure of Baudelaire the man,
Van Gogh's his madness, Tchaikovsky's his vice. The *explanation* of a

work is always sought in the man or woman who produced it, as if it were always in the end, through the more or less transparent allegory of the fiction, the voice of a single person, the *author* 'confiding' in us.

Though the sway of the Author remains powerful (the new criticism has often done no more than consolidate it), it goes without saying that certain writers have long since attempted to loosen it. In France, Mallarmé was doubtless the first to see and to foresee in its full extent the necessity to substitute language itself for the person who until then has been supposed to be its owner. For him, for us too, it is language which speaks, not the author; to write, is, through a prerequisite impersonality (not at all to be confused with the castrating objectivity of the realist novelist), to reach that point, where only language acts, 'performs' and not 'me'. Mallarmé's entire poetics consists in suppressing the author in the interests of writing (which is, as will be seen, to restore the place of the reader). Valéry, encumbered by a psychology of the Ego, considerably diluted Mallarmé's theory but, his taste for classicism leading him to turn to the lessons of rhetoric, he never stopped calling into question and deriding the Author; he stressed the linguistic and, as it were, 'hazardous' nature of his activity, and throughout his prose works he militated in favour of the essentially verbal condition of literature, in the face of which all recourse to the writer's interiority seemed to him pure superstition. Proust himself, despite the apparently psychological character of what are called his *analyses*, was visibly concerned with the task of inexorably blurring, by an extreme subtilization, the relation between the writer and his characters; by making of the narrator not he who has seen and felt nor even he who is writing, but he who *is going to write* (the young man in the novel – but, in fact, how old is he and who is he? – wants to write but cannot; the novel ends when writing at last becomes possible), Proust gave modern writing its epic. By a radical reversal, instead of putting his life into his novel, as is so often maintained, he made of his very life a work for which his own book was the model; so that it is clear to us that Charlus does not imitate Montesquiou but that Montesquiou – in his anecdotal, historical reality – is no more than a secondary fragment, derived from Charlus. Lastly, to go no further than this prehistory of modernity, Surrealism, though unable to accord language a supreme place (language being system and the aim of the movement being, romantically, a direct subversion of codes – itself moreover illusory: a code cannot be destroyed, only 'played off'), contributed to the desacrilization of the image of the Author by ceaselessly recommending the abrupt disappointment of expectations of meaning (the famous surrealist 'jolt'), by entrusting the hand with the task of writing as quickly as possible what the head itself is unaware of (automatic writing), by accepting the principle and the experience of several people writing together. Leaving aside literature itself (such distinctions really becoming invalid), linguistics has recently provided the destruction of the Author with a valuable analytical tool by showing that the whole of the enunciation is an empty process, functioning perfectly without there being any need for it to be filled with the person of the interlocutors. Linguistically, the author is never more than the instance writing, just as *I* is nothing other than the instance saying *I*: language knows a 'subject', not a 'person', and this subject, empty outside of the very enunciation which defines it, suffices to make language 'hold together', suffices, that is to say, to exhaust it.

The removal of the Author (one could talk here with Brecht of a veritable 'distancing', the Author diminishing like a figurine at the far end of the literary stage) is not merely an historical fact or an act of writing; it utterly transforms the modern text (or – which is the same thing – the text is henceforth made and read in such a way that at all its levels the author is absent). The temporality is different. The Author, when believed in, is always conceived of as the past of his own book: book and author stand automatically on a single line divided into a *before* and an *after*. The Author is thought to *nourish* the book, which is to say that he exists before it, thinks, suffers, lives for it, is in the same relation of antecedence to his work as a father to his child. In complete contrast, the modern scriptor is born simultaneously with the text, is in no way equipped with a being preceding or exceeding the writing, is not the subject wth the book as predicate; there is no other time than that of the enunciation and every text is eternally written *here and now*. The fact is (or, it follows) that *writing* can no longer designate an operation of recording, notation, representation, 'depiction' (as the Classics would say); rather, it designates exactly what linguists, referring to Oxford philosophy, call a performative, a rare verbal form (exclusively given in the first person and in the present tense) in which the enunciation has no other content (contains no other proposition) than the act by which it is uttered – something like the *I declare* of kings or the *I sing* of very ancient poets. Having buried the Author, the modern scriptor can thus no longer believe, as according to the pathetic view of his predecessors, that this hand is too slow for his thought or passion and that consequently, making a law of necessity, he must emphasize this delay and indefinitely 'polish' his form. For him, on the contrary, the hand, cut off from any voice, borne by a pure gesture of inscription (and not of expression), traces a field without origin – or which, at least, has no other origin than language itself, language which ceaselessly calls into question all origins.

We know now that a text is not a line of words releasing a single 'theological' meaning (the 'message' of the Author-God) but a multidimensional space in which a variety of writings, none of them original, blend and clash. The text is a tissue of quotations drawn from the innumerable centres of culture. Similar to Bouvard and Pécuchet, those eternal copyists, at once sublime and comic and whose profound ridiculousness indicates precisely the truth of writing, the writer can only imitate a gesture that is always anterior, never original. His only power is to mix writings, to counter the ones with the others, in such a way as never to rest on any one of them. Did he wish to *express himself*, he ought at least to know that the inner 'thing' he thinks to 'translate' is itself only a ready-formed dictionary, its words only explainable through other words, and so on indefinitely; something experienced in exemplary fashion by the young Thomas de Quincey, he who was so good at Greek that in order to translate absolutely modern ideas and images into that dead language, he had, so Baudelaire tells us (in *Paradis Artificiels*), 'created for himself an unfailing dictionary, vastly more extensive and complex than those resulting from the ordinary patience of purely literary themes'. Succeeding the Author, the scriptor no longer bears within him passions, humours, feelings, impressions, but rather this immense dictionary from which he draws a writing that can know no halt: life never does more than imitate the book, and the book itself is only a tissue of signs, an imitation that is lost, infinitely deferred.

Once the Author is removed, the claim to decipher a text becomes quite futile. To give a text an Author is to impose a limit on that text, to furnish it with a final signified, to close the writing. Such a conception suits criticism very well, the latter then allotting itself the important task of discovering the Author (or its hypostases: society, history, psyche, liberty) beneath the work: when the Author has been found, the text is 'explained' - victory to the critic. Hence there is no surprise in the fact that, historically, the reign of the Author has also been that of the Critic, nor again in the fact that criticism (be it new) is today undermined along with the Author. In the multiplicity of writing, everything is to be *disentangled,* nothing *deciphered*; the structure can be followed, 'run' (like the thread of a stocking) at every point and at every level, but there is nothing beneath: the space of writing is to be ranged over, not pierced; writing ceaselessly posits meaning ceaselessly to evaporate it, carrying out a systematic exemption of meaning. In precisely this way literature (it would be better from now on to say *writing*), by refusing to assign a 'secret', an ultimate meaning, to the text (and to the world as text), liberates what may be called an anti-theological activity, an activity that is truly revolutionary since to refuse to fix meaning is, in the end, to refuse God and his hypostases - reason, science, law.

Let us come back to the Balzac sentence. No one, no 'person', says it: its source, its voice, is not the true place of the writing, which is reading. Another - very precise - example will help to make this clear: recent research (J.-P. Vernant[1]) has demonstrated the constitutively ambiguous nature of Greek tragedy, its texts being woven from words with double

---

[1] [Cf. Jean-Pierre Vernant (with Pierre Vidal-Naquet), *Mythe et tragédie en Grèce ancienne*, Paris 1972, esp. pp. 19–40, 99–131.]

meanings that each character understands unilaterally (this perpetual misunderstanding is exactly the 'tragic'); there is, however, someone who understands each word in its duplicity and who, in addition, hears the very deafness of the characters speaking in front of him – this some-one being precisely the reader (or here, the listener). Thus is revealed the total existence of writing: a text is made of multiple writings, drawn from many cultures and entering into mutual relations of dialogue, parody, contestation, but there is one place where this multiplicity is focused and that place is the reader, not, as was hitherto said, the author. The reader is the space on which all the quotations that make up a writing are inscribed without any of them being lost; a text's unity lies not in its origin but in its destination. Yet this destination cannot any longer be personal: the reader is without history, biography, psychology; he is simply that *someone* who holds together in a single field all the traces by which the written text is constituted. Which is why it is derisory to con-demn the new writing in the name of a humanism hypocritically turned champion of the reader's rights. Classic criticism has never paid any attention to the reader; for it, the writer is the only person in literature. We are now beginning to let ourselves be fooled no longer by the arro-gant antiphrastical recriminations of good society in favour of the very thing it sets aside, ignores, smothers, or destroys; we know that to give writing its future, it is necessary to overthrow the myth: the birth of the reader must be at the cost of the death of the Author.

SECTION ONE
THE SUBJECT

The notion of the 'subject' has proved crucial to the post-structuralist enterprise; the concept can be traced in most varieties of post-structuralism and acts as a focal point for the critique of humanist ideology. Post-structuralism uses the term 'subject' rather than 'self' or 'individual' in an attempt to avoid the presupposition that the human being is in some way 'given' and fully-formed prior to its entrance into the symbolic order of language or discourse. The term plays ambiguously between, on the one hand, *subject* as in the opposition subject/object, or subject as in grammar; and on the other hand, *subject* as in subject of the state, or subject to the law – that is, *subject* is both central and at the same time de-centred.

Humanist ideology depends upon a fundamental assumption about the primacy of the autonomous and unified individual. For humanism, 'man' is at the centre of meaning and action; the world is oriented around the individual. Each individual is different, each possesses a unique subjectivity; yet also, paradoxically, each shares a common human nature. The combination of unique individuality and common human essence cohere around the idea of a sovereign self, whose essential core of being transcends the outward signs of environmental and social conditioning. Post-structuralism has sought to disrupt this man-centred view of the world, arguing that the subject, and that sense of unique subjectivity itself, is constructed in language and discourse; and rather than being fixed and unified, the subject is split, unstable or fragmented.

Of the post-structuralists to have written on the notion of the subject it is arguably the French psychoanalyst, Jacques Lacan, who has produced the most influential theory. His work is complex and the brief account given here concentrates on language. For fuller details see Coward and Ellis (1977); Wright (1984); Moi (1985). Lacan's theory of the subject owes much to Freud, however, he re-reads Freud in the light of post-Saussurean linguistics and it is the latter which gives the work its post-structuralist inflection. Language is a crucial element in the theory for it is only in the moment of entry into the symbolic order of language that full subjectivity comes into being.

Before it enters the symbolic through the acquisition of language, the infant goes through the mirror stage, entering the realm of the imaginary (which the subject never entirely leaves). In the mirror stage, Lacan argues, the infant begins to recognize a distinction between its own body and the outside world. This is illustrated in the child's relation to its own image in the mirror; the infant lacks control of its limbs and its experience is a jumbled mass but its image in the mirror appears unified and in control. The child recognizes its image and merges with it in a process of identification, creating an illusory experience of control of the self and the world – an imaginary correspondence of self and image. The two are perceived as self-identical. However, to achieve full distinction of the self, the subject has to enter the symbolic, where identity depends on difference rather than self-identicality. Language, the system of difference which articulates identities, constructs positions for the subject – notably the subject position 'I' – which allows differentiation from others, and identity for the self. However, in the necessary acceptance of the subject-positions offered by language, the individual experiences a loss or *lack* because it is *subject to* the positions that are predefined for it and beyond its control. The sense of a full and unified subject is contradicted by a sense of being defined by the law of human culture. At this point, desire and the unconscious are also created. The unconscious is, as it were, the repository of that which has to be repressed when the subject takes on the pre-defined positions available in language. Subject-positions, meaning and consciousness, made available through the symbolic order, depend on language as a system of difference and hence they entail a loss of the full presence that seemed to characterize the imaginary realm. The individual desires to control meaning but this is not possible because of the nature of language. Language, Lacan argued, is not a matter of a one-to-one correspondence between signifier and signified; the signifiers of language cannot fix the arbitrary field of the signified; signifiers slide across the continuum and hence the desire for mastery of meaning is unsatisfiable. The unified and stable subject of humanism is contradicted and de-stabilized by this primacy of the signifier and loss of apparent one-to-one correspondence between signifier and signified.

Lacan's work has been criticized for its universalizing and a-historical view of the construction of the subject – in other words, for a residual essentialism. This might seem to put his work into the first part of this book, however, it has provided a starting point for a set of concerns that have become a part of the post-structuralist enterprise and his view of language coincides with the post-structuralist view. Although Lacan's work had been available for some considerable time (indeed the essay reprinted dates from 1949), and had influenced Althusser's notion of interpellation, the attempt to use his psychoanalytic work in literary theory belongs more to the post-structuralist moment and impetus.

Lacan has also been taken to task, particularly by feminist theorists, for the phallocentric (male-centredness) orientation of his theory. However, his work has proved fertile ground for a number of feminist theorists. One of the foremost of these is Julia Kristeva, whose work encompasses and combines linguistics, literature and psychoanalysis. The interview reprinted here provides a brief illustration of one of the ways in which feminist writers have appropriated Lacanian theory to enable what Toril Moi has called a 'sexual/textual politics' (1986).

Colin MacCabe draws on Lacan's account of the construction of the subject to inform his theory of the 'classic realist text'. While his insistence on the subject as a construct articulated in the language of the text takes up Lacan in quite a suggestive way, the model of analysis he develops is rather formalist in its concentration on the immanent structure of the text itself.

Post-structuralism commonly discusses the subject as a construct articulated in the symbolic order of language, and though the discussion owes much to Lacan, his is not the only influence in this area. In recent years Foucault's work around the subject-positions inscribed in discursive formations, and their relations to configurations of knowledge and power, has had an increasingly influential impact, offering a more historically grounded theory of the subject. Catherine Belsey's book, *The Subject of Tragedy* (extract reprinted here), is more indebted to Foucault than to Lacan and illustrates another perspective deployed by feminist oriented post-structuralism, one that links closely with work covered in the section we have called 'discourse and the social'.

13 Jacques Lacan,

'The Mirror Stage as Formative of the Function of the I as revealed in Psychoanalytic Experience', *Ecrits, A Selection*, trans Alan Sheridan

p1–7

The conception of the mirror stage that I introduced at our last congress, thirteen years ago, has since become more or less established in the practice of the French group. However, I think it worthwhile to bring it again to your attention, especially today, for the light it sheds on the formation of the *I* as we experience it in psychoanalysis. It is an experience that leads us to oppose any philosophy directly issuing from the *Cogito*.

Some of you may recall that this conception originated in a feature of human behaviour illuminated by a fact of comparative psychology. The child, at an age when he is for a time, however short, outdone by the chimpanzee in instrumental intelligence, can nevertheless already recognize as such his own image in a mirror. This recognition is indicated in the illuminative mimicry of the *Aha-Erlebnis*, which Köhler sees as the expression of situational apperception, an essential stage of the act of intelligence.

This act, far from exhausting itself, as in the case of the monkey, once the image has been mastered and found empty, immediately rebounds in the case of the child in a series of gestures in which he experiences in play the relation between the movements assumed in the image and the reflected environment, and between this virtual complex and the reality it reduplicates – the child's own body, and the persons and things, around him.

This event can take place, as we have known since Baldwin, from the age of six months, and its repetition has often made me reflect upon the startling spectacle of the infant in front of the mirror. Unable as yet to walk, or even to stand up, and held tightly as he is by some support human or artificial (what, in France, we call a *'trotte-bébé'*), he nevertheless overcomes, in a flutter of jubilant activity, the obstructions of his support and, fixing his attitude in a slightly leaning-forward position, in order to hold it in his gaze, brings back an instantaneous aspect of the image.

For me, this activity retains the meaning I have given it up to the age of eighteen months. This meaning discloses a libidinal dynamism, which has hitherto remained problematic, as well as an ontological structure of the human world that accords with my reflections on paranoiac knowledge.

We have only to understand the mirror stage *as an identification*, in the full sense that analysis gives to the term: namely, the transformation that takes place in the subject when he assumes an image – whose pre-destination to this phase-effect is sufficiently indicated by the use, in analytic theory, of the ancient term *imago*. *– a baby is happy when she sees her image in a mirror*

This jubilant assumption of his specular image by the child at the *infans* stage, still sunk in his motor incapacity and nursling dependence, would seem to exhibit in an exemplary situation the symbolic matrix *early form of development* in which the *I* is precipitated in a primordial form, before it is objectified in the dialectic of identification with the other, and before language restores to it, in the universal, its function as subject.

This form would have to be called the Ideal-I,[1] if we wished to incorporate it into our usual register, in the sense that it will also be the source of secondary identifications, under which term I would place the functions of libidinal normalization. But the important point is that this form situates the agency of the ego, before its social determination, in a fictional direction, which will always remain irreducible for the individual alone, or rather, which will only rejoin the coming-into-being (*le devenir*) of the subject asymptotically, whatever the success of the dialectical syntheses by which he must resolve as *I* his discordance with his own reality.

The fact is that the total form of the body by which the subject anticipates in a mirage the maturation of his power is given to him only as *Gestalt*, that is to say, in an exteriority in which this form is certainly more constituent than constitute, but in which it appears to him above all in a contrasting size (*un relief de stature*) that fixes it and in a symmetry that inverts it, in contrast with the turbulent movements that the subject feels are animating him. Thus, this *Gestalt* – whose pregnancy should be regarded as bound up with the species, though its motor style remains scarcely recognizable – by these two aspects of its appearance, symbolizes the mental permanence of the *I*, at the same time as it prefigures its alienating destination; it is still pregnant with the correspondences that unite the *I* with the statue in which man projects himself, with the phantoms that dominate him, or with the automaton in which, in an ambiguous relation, the world of his own making tends to find completion.

Indeed, for the *imagos* – whose veiled faces it is our privilege to see in outline in our daily experience and in the penumbra of symbolic efficacity[2] – the mirror-image would seem to be the threshold of the visible world, if we go by the mirror disposition that the *imago of one's own body* presents in hallucinations or dreams, whether it concerns its individual features, or even its infirmities, or its object-projections; or if we

[1] Throughout this article I leave in its peculiarity the translation I have adopted for Freud's *Ideal-Ich* [i.e., 'je-idéal'], without further comment, other than to say that I have not maintained it since.
[2] Cf. Claude Lévi-Strauss, *Structural Anthropology*, Chapter X.

observe the role of the mirror apparatus in the appearance of the *double*, in which psychical realities, however heterogeneous, are manifested.

That a *Gestalt* should be capable of formative effects in the organism is attested by a piece of biological experimentation that is itself so alien to the idea of psychical causality that it cannot bring itself to formulate its results in these terms. It nevertheless recognizes that it is a necessary condition for the maturation of the gonad of the female pigeon that it should see another member of its species, of either sex; so sufficient in itself is this condition that the desired effect may be obtained merely by placing the individual within reach of the field of reflection of a mirror. Similarly, in the case of the migratory locust, the transition within a generation from the solitary to the gregarious form can be obtained by exposing the individual, at a certain stage, to the exclusively visual action of a similar image, provided it is animated by movements of a style sufficiently close to that characteristic of the species. Such facts are inscribed in an order of homeomorphic identification that would itself fall within the larger question of the meaning of beauty as both formative and erogenic.

But the facts of mimicry are no less instructive when conceived as cases of heteromorphic identification, in as much as they raise the problem of the signification of space for the living organism – psychological concepts hardly seem less appropriate for shedding light on these matters than ridiculous attempts to reduce them to the supposedly supreme law of adaptation. We have only to recall how Roger Caillois (who was then very young, and still fresh from his breach with the sociological school in which he was trained) illuminated the subject by using the term '*legendary psychasthenia*' to classify morphological mimicry as an obsession with space in its derealizing effect.

I have myself shown in the social dialectic that structures human knowledge as paranoiac[3] why human knowledge has greater autonomy than animal knowledge in relation to the field of force of desire, but also why human knowledge is determined in that 'little reality' (*ce peu de réalité*), which the Surrealists, in their restless way, saw as its limitation. These reflections lead me to recognize in the spatial captation manifested in the mirror-stage, even before the social dialectic, the effect in man of an organic insufficiency in his natural reality – in so far as any meaning can be given to the word 'nature'.

I am led, therefore, to regard the function of the mirror-stage as a particular case of the function of the *imago*, which is to establish a relation between the organism and its reality – or, as they say, between the *Innenwelt* and the *Umwelt*.

In man, however, this relation to nature is altered by a certain dehiscence at the heart of the organism, a primordial Discord betrayed by the

---

[3] Cf. 'Aggressivity in Psychoanalysis', p. 8 and *Écrits*, p. 180.

signs of uneasiness and motor unco-ordination of the neo-natal months. The objective notion of the anatomical incompleteness of the pyramidal system and likewise the presence of certain humoral residues of the maternal organism confirm the view I have formulated as the fact of a real *specific prematurity of birth* in man.

It is worth noting, incidentally, that this is a fact recognized as such by embryologists, by the term *foetalization*, which determines the prevalence of the so-called superior apparatus of the neurax, and especially of the cortex, which psycho-surgical operations lead us to regard as the intra-organic mirror.

This development is experienced as a temporal dialectic that decisively projects the formation of the individual into history. The *mirror stage* is a drama whose internal thrust is precipitated from insufficiency to anticipation - and which manufactures for the subject, caught up in the lure of spatial identification, the succession of phantasies that extends from a fragmented body-image to a form of its totality that I shall call orthopaedic - and, lastly, to the assumption of the armour of an alienating identity, which will mark with its rigid structure the subject's entire mental development. Thus, to break out of the circle of the *Innenwelt* into the *Umwelt* generates the inexhaustible quadrature of the ego's verifications.

This fragmented body - which term I have also introduced into our system of theoretical references - usually manifests itself in dreams when the movement of the analysis encounters a certain level of aggressive disintegration in the individual. It then appears in the form of disjointed limbs, or of those organs represented in exoscopy, growing wings and taking up arms for intestinal persecutions - the very same that the visionary Hieronymus Bosch has fixed, for all time, in painting, in their ascent from the fifteenth century to the imaginary zenith of modern man. But this form is even tangibly revealed at the organic level, in the lines of 'fragilization' that define the anatomy of phantasy, as exhibited in the schizoid and spasmodic symptoms of hysteria.

Correlatively, the formation of the *I* is symbolized in dreams by a fortress, or a stadium - its inner arena and enclosure surrounded by marshes and rubbish-tips, dividing it into two opposed fields of contest where the subject flounders in quest of the lofty, remote inner castle whose form (sometimes juxtaposed in the same scenario) symbolizes the id in a quite startling way. Similarly, on the mental plane, we find realized the structures of fortified works, the metaphor of which arises spontaneously, as if issuing from the symptoms themselves, to designate the mechanisms of obsessional neurosis - inversion, isolation, reduplication, cancellation and displacement.

But if we were to build on these subjective givens alone - however little we free them from the condition of experience that makes us see them as partaking of the nature of a linguistic techique - our theoretical attempts would remain exposed to the charge of projecting themselves into the unthinkable of an absolute subject. This is why I have sought in the present hypothesis, grounded in a conjunction of objective data, the guiding grid for a *method of symbolic reduction*.

It establishes in the *defences of the ego* a genetic order, in accordance with the wish formulated by Miss Anna Freud, in the first part of her great work, and situates (as against a frequently expressed prejudice) hysterical repression and its return at a more archaic stage than obsessional inversion and its isolating processes, and the latter in turn as preliminary to paranoic alienation, which dates from the deflection of the specular *I* into the social *I*.

This moment in which the mirror-stage comes to an end inaugurates, by the identification with the *imago* of the counterpart and the drama of primordial jealousy (so well brought out by the school of Charlotte Bühler in the phenomenon of infantile *transitivism*), the dialectic that will henceforth link the *I* to socially elaborated situations.

It is this moment that decisively tips the whole of human knowledge into mediatization through the desire of the other, constitutes its objects in an abstract equivalence by the co-operation of others, and turns the I into that apparatus for which every instinctual thrust constitutes a danger, even though it should correspond to a natural maturation – the very normalization of this maturation being henceforth dependent, in man, on a cultural mediation as exemplified, in the case of the sexual object, by the Oedipus complex.

In the light of this conception, the term primary narcissism, by which analytic doctrine designates the libidinal investment characteristic of that moment, reveals in those who invented it the most profound awareness of semantic latencies. But it also throws light on the dynamic opposition between this libido and the sexual libido, which the first analysts tried to define when they invoked destructive and, indeed, death instincts, in order to explain the evident connection between the narcissistic libido and the alienating function of the *I*, the aggressivity it releases in any relation to the other, even in a relation involving the most Samaritan of aid.

In fact, they were encountering that existential negativity whose reality is so vigorously proclaimed by the contemporary philosophy of being and nothingness.

But unfortunately that philosophy grasps negativity only within the limits of a self-sufficiency of consciousness, which as one of its premises, links to the *méconnaissances* that constitute the ego, the illusion of autonomy to which it entrusts itself. This flight of fancy, for all that it draws, to an unusual extent, on borrowings from psychoanalytic experience, culminates in the pretention of providing an existential psychoanalysis.

At the culmination of the historical effort of a society to refuse to recognize that it has any function other than the utilitarian one, and in the anxiety of the individual confronting the 'concentrational'[4] form of the social bond that seems to arise to crown this effort, existentialism must be judged by the explanations it gives of the subjective impasses that have indeed resulted from it; a freedom that is never more authentic than when it is within the walls of a prison; a demand for commitment, expressing the impotence of a pure consciousness to master any situation; a voyeuristic-sadistic idealization of the sexual relation; a personality that realizes itself only in suicide; a consciousness of the other that can be satisfied only by Hegelian murder.

These propositions are opposed by all our experience, in so far as it teaches us not to regard the ego as centred on the *perception–consciousness system*, or as organized by the 'reality principle' – a principle that is the expression of a scientific prejudice most hostile to the dialectic of knowledge. Our experience shows that we should start instead from the *function of méconnaissance* that characterizes the ego in all its structures so markedly articulated by Miss Anna Freud. For, if the *Verneinung* represents the patent form of that function, its effects will, for the most part, remain latent, so long as they are not illuminated by some light reflected on to the level of fatality, which is where the id manifests itself.

We can thus understand the inertia characteristic of the formation of the *I*, and find there the most extensive definition of neurosis – just as the captation of the subject by the situation gives us the most general formula for madness, not only the madness that lies behind the walls of asylums, but also the madness that deafens the world with its sound and fury.

The sufferings of neurosis and psychosis are for us a schooling in the passions of the soul, just as the beam of the psychoanalytic scales, when we calculate the tilt of its threat to entire communities, provides us with an indication of the deadening of the passions in society.

At this junction of nature and culture, so persistently examined by modern anthropology, psychoanalysis alone recognizes this knot of imaginary servitude that love must always undo again, or sever.

For such a task, we place no trust in altruistic feeling, we who lay bare the aggressivity that underlies the activity of the philanthropist, the idealist, the pedagogue, and even the reformer.

In the recourse of subject to subject that we preserve, psychoanalysis may accompany the patient to the ecstatic limit of the '*Thou art that*', in which is revealed to him the cipher of his mortal destiny, but it is not in our mere power as practitioners to bring him to that point where the real journey begins.

---

4 '*Concentrationnaire*', an adjective coined after World War II (this article was written in 1949) to describe the life of the concentration-camp. In the hands of certain writers it became, by extension, applicable to many aspects of 'modern' life [Tr.].

14 Julia Kristeva,

'A Question of Subjectivity – an Interview', *Women's Review*, no 12

p19–21

Susan Sellers: As a professor of linguistics, and with publications on subjects ranging from philosophy to literary criticism, what led you also to train as a psychoanalyst?

Julia Kristeva: I don't believe one commits oneself to psychoanalysis without certain secret motivations . . . difficulties living, a suffering which is unable to express itself. I talked to my psychoanalyst about this aspect of things and so today can speak about these motives for my work.

I wanted to examine the states at the limits of language; the moments where language breaks up in psychosis for example, or the moments where language doesn't yet exist such as during a child's apprenticeship to language. It seemed to me to be impossible to content oneself with a description which held itself to be objective and neutral in these two cases, because already the selection of examples presupposes a particular type of contact with the people who talk to you.

Also the interpretation of people's speech presupposes that you apply yourself to the meaning of what they say. I saw that there was no neutral objectivity possible in descriptions of language at its limits and that we are constantly in what psychoanalysis calls a 'transfer'. It seemed to me dishonest to apply this transfer without having myself undergone the experience of psychoanalysis.

Susan Sellers: An important part of your psychoanalytic research has been the process by which the individual acquires language. What does this 'process' entail?

Julia Kristeva: I used the term 'process' whilst I was working on the texts of Antonin Artaud. Artaud is an extremely disturbing writer in modern French literature, partly because he underwent a dramatic experience of madness and partly because he thought carefully about the music in language. Anyone who reads Artaud's texts will realize that all identities are unstable: the identity of linguistic signs, the identity of meaning and, as a result, the identity of the speaker. And in order to take account of this de-stabilization of meaning and of the subject I thought the term 'subject in process' would be appropriate. 'Process' in the sense of process but also in the sense of a legal proceeding where the subject is committed to trial, because our identities in life are constantly called into question, brought to trial, over-ruled.

I wanted to examine the language which manifests these states of instability because in ordinary communication – which is organized, civilized – we repress these states of incandescence. Creativity as well as suffering comprises these moments of instability, where language, or the signs of language, or subjectivity itself are put into 'process'. And one can extrapolate this notion and use it not just for the texts of Artaud but for every 'proceeding' in which we move outside the norms.

Susan Sellers: Writing about this process, one of the distinctions you have drawn in order to chart the development from non-differentiated infant to speaking subject is the distinction between 'the semiotic' and 'the symbolic'. Can you explain this distinction?

Julia Kristeva: In order to research this state of instability – the fact that meaning is not simply a structure or process, or that the subject is not simply a unity but is constantly called into question – I proposed to take into account two modalities or conditions of meaning which I called 'the semiotic' and 'the symbolic'. What I call 'the semiotic' takes us back to the pre-linguistic states of childhood where the child babbles the sounds s/he hears, or where s/he articulates rhythms, alliterations, or stresses, trying to imitate her/his surroundings. In this state the child doesn't yet possess the necessary linguistic signs and thus there is no meaning in the strict sense of the term. It is only after the mirror phase or the experience of castration in the Oedipus complex that the individual becomes subjectively capable of taking on the signs of language, of articulation as it has been prescribed – and I call that 'the symbolic'.

Susan Sellers: What actually happens during the mirror phase and the Oedipus complex?

Julia Kristeva: Identification takes place. What I call 'the semiotic' is a state of disintegration in which patterns appear but which do not have any stable identity: they are blurred and fluctuating. The processes which are at work here are those which Freud calls 'primary': processes of transfer. We have an example of this if we refer once again to the melodies and babblings of infants which are a sound image of their bodily instability. Babies and children's bodies are made up of erotogenic zones which are extremely excitable, or, on the contrary, indifferent, in a state of constant change, of excitation, or extinction, without there being any fixed identity.

A 'fixed identity': it's perhaps a fiction, an illusion – who amongst us has a 'fixed' identity? It's a phantasm; we do nevertheless arrive at a certain type of stability. There are several steps which lead to this stability and one step which has been accentuated by the French psychoanalyst Jacques Lacan is the specular identification which he calls 'the mirror phase'. In this phase one recognizes one's image in a mirror as one's self-image. It is a first identification of the chaotic, fragmented body, and is both violent and jubilatory. The identification comes about under the domination of the maternal image, which is the one nearest to the child and which allows the child both to remain close and to distance itself.

I see a face. A first differentiation takes place, and thus a first self-identity. This identity is still unstable because sometimes I take myself to be me, sometimes I confuse myself with my mother. This narcissistic instability, this doubt persists and makes me ask 'who am I?', 'is it me or is it the other?' The confusion with the maternal image as first other remains.

In order for us to be able to get out of this confusion, the classical pattern of development leads us to a confrontation inside the Oedipal triangle between our desire for the mother and the process of loss which is the result of paternal authority. In the ideal case, this finishes by stabilising the subject, rendering her/him capable both of pronouncing sentences which conform to the rules, to the law, and of telling her/his own story – of giving her/his account.

These are symbolic acquisitions that are pre-conditioned by a certain psychic experience which is the stabilization of the self in relation to the other.

Susan Sellers: One of the images you have used to clarify this semiotic relationship to the maternal is that of the 'chora'. Could you explain this image?

Julia Kristeva: I believe that this archaic semiotic modality that I have referred to as infantile babblings, in order to give it clearer definition, is a modality which bears the most archaic memories of our link with the maternal body – Of the dependence that all of us have vis-à-vis the maternal body, and where a sort of self-eroticism is indissociable from the experience of the (m)other. We repress the vocal or gestural inscription of this experience under our subsequent acquisitions and this is an important condition for autonomy.

Nevertheless there may be different ways of repressing this experience. There may be a dramatic repression, after which we are building on sand because the foundation has been destroyed, suppressed. Or there may be an attempt to transpose this continent, this receptacle beyond the symbolic. In other words after the mirror phase, and Oedipal castration. (The word 'chora' means receptacle in Greek, which refers us to Winnicott's idea of 'holding': mother and child are in a permanent stricture in which one holds the other, there's a double entrance, the child is held but so is the mother.)

At that point we witness the possibility of creation, of sublimation. I think that every type of creation, even if it's scientific, is due to this possibility of opening the norms, towards pleasure, which refers to an archaic experience with a maternal pre-object.

Susan Sellers: What are the implications of this for literary creation? Do women, with their own real or potential experience of maternity, have a privileged relationship to the semiotic?

Julia Kristeva: What is obvious is that this experience of the semiotic chora in language produces poetry. It can be considered as the source of all stylistic effort, the modifying of banal, logical order by linguistic distortions such as metaphor, metonymy, musicality.

As far as women are concerned the question is rather complex. On the one hand many women – no matter what their particular case structure is: depressive, hysteric, or obsessional – complain that they experience language as something secondary, cold, foreign to their lives. To their passion. To their suffering. To their desire. As if language were a foreign body. And when they say this we are often given the impression that what they question is language as a logical exercise. This complaint can be heard two ways. There may be a refusal to submit to communication, which demands a sacrifice from everyone – from men as well as women. This refusal has often been interpreted by a certain type of romantic feminism as revolutionary, but this is not always the case. It can quite simply be an attempt to escape society and communication and to take refuge in a sort of mystical state which can be extremely regressive and narcissistic. I refuse logical communication; logical communication is a stranger to me and so I withdraw into my archaic experience where I seek the delights of the maternal body. And I give this out as a revolutionary challenge.

On the other hand I think we do have to listen to the truth of a certain suffering which these complaints translate. This consists in noting that often in the social code, in social communication, the basis for our identities which the semiotic forms within language is repressed, thrown into confusion, and the fact of not hearing it, of not giving it room, (thus in a way of killing the maternal and the primordial link every subject has with the maternal) exposes us to depression, to a feeling of strangeness. Many women and men experience this. As an analyst up against this depression I am often looking for two things. On the one hand I am looking to release the hatred which has not been able to express itself, to manifest itself (depression is often the result of hatred which has not been exhausted).

At the same time I am searching for the inscriptions in language of the archaic contact with the maternal body which has been forgotten. Where are these incriptions to be found? Often not in the meaning of what the patients say, because the meaning of their speech is frequently banal and clichéd, without real investment or relevance. They are to be found in the tempo of the voice, in the rapidity of the delivery, or in its monotony, or in certain musicalities. Or in certain alliterations, which mean that like *Alice in Wonderland* one has to cut the phrases up in order to look for the 'portmanteau words,' the real meaning of the wounded desire in which this archaic relation to the mother takes refuge. This is necessary in order to be able to rehabilitate them, to create for each individual, and for women in particular, a new point of departure.

Susan Sellers: Is is possible to distinguish a language or writing which is specific to women?

Julia Kristeva: I am very uncertain on this point because what asserts itself today as 'women's writing' distinguishes itself from 'men's writing' mainly by the choice of themes. For example we would talk about the care of children or maternity in a way men would not be able to because we don't have the same historical, social or family experiences.

As far as style is concerned – the actual dynamics of language, this recourse to the semiotic, the inscription of the archaic relation to the mother in language – it isn't the monopoly of women. Men writers such as Joyce, Mallarmé or Artaud are proof of this. It's a question of subjectivity. It's possible that in aesthetic creation we occupy several positions. Any creator necessarily moves through an identification with the maternal, which is why the resurgence of this semiotic dynamic is important in every act of creation.

The question is: do men and women identify in the same way with the archaic mother? Formally, I don't really see a difference. Psychologically, I would say it's more difficult for women, because a woman is confronted by something not differentiable; she is confronted by the same. Because we are two women. Whereas for a man she's an other. For men this identification with the maternal involves a perverse pleasure, whilst for women there are psychotic risks attached. I might lose myself, lose my identity.

This explains perhaps why it's more difficult for women to get out of hell, this descent: Orpheus manages it but Eurydice doesn't.

Susan Sellers: Does this explain why so much of your work in literature has tended to concentrate on male writers?

Julia Kristeva: I am currently working on melancholia and I am using the texts of Marguerite Duras as an example of modern writing about suffering. In Duras' texts there is a thematisation of suffering – a thematic description of suffering rather than any stylistic or linguistic research. Where stylistic innovation does occur it's mainly in the form of imperfection, awkwardness. It's through being imperfect that Duras' sentences translate suffering rather than in the fireworks of musical and vocal pleasure we find in Joyce. For Duras, the expression of pain is painful.

Susan Sellers: Your most recent work has explored the relationship between melancholy or depression and creativity. How did this particular area of your research come into being?

Julia Kristeva: It starts from the psychoanalytic observation that depression is virtually a sickness of our time. There are more and more people complaining about depression, and in psychoanalysis we note that many people who otherwise present themselves as hysteric, obsessional etc. have an underlying depression. Various important because it's a problem situated at the cross-over point between biological and psychological research.

A few years ago psychoanalysis was confronted by the science of language, now there is a new challenge: neuro-biology. There are many anti-depressants, and these anti-depressants have a certain effectiveness. But as a psychoanalyst I think that the work of relieving the anguish and clearing the depression is not done by these pills. The root of the problem remains.

As far as literary-aesthetic creation is concerned (which is what interests me), I would say that the creative act is released by an experience of depression without which we would not call into question the stability of meaning or the banality of expression. A writer must at one time or another have been in a situation of loss – of ties, of meaning – in order to write.

There is nevertheless something paradoxical about a writer, who experiences depression in its most acute and dramatic form, but who also has the possibility of lifting her/himself out of it. For example, the writer is able to describe her/his depression to us, and this is already a triumph over depression. The texts of Marguerite Duras are about suffering, the experience of sadness, death, suicide. As are the texts of Dostoyevsky. The texts of Nerval, with all their references to the cultural tradition, show us to what extent sadness and suffering can be themes.

Yet even when it's a question of celebratory writing, it very often transpires when one knows the biography of the writer that there is a contra-investment: it's the bright side of the black sun of melancholy. There is a possibility of getting out of depression by inverting the negative contents, through transposing them in a positive way. Like the clown whose laugh translates a profound sadness. It's in this optic that I examine the imaginary as essentially melancholic and as a combat against melancholy.

Imaginary creations are a powerful anti-depressant. Provided we are able to create them . . .　　　　　　　　　　　　　　　*Susan Sellers*

---

15 Colin MacCabe,

'Realism and the Cinema; Notes on some Brechtian Theses',
***Screen*, vol 15;2 1974. (in *Popular TV and Film*, ed T. Bennett et al)**

p216–221; 226–229

The Classic Realist Text

Criticism, at least Marxist criticism, must proceed methodically and concretely in each case, in short scientifically. Loose talk is of no help here, whatever its vocabulary. In no circumstances can the necessary guide-lines for a practical definition of realism be derived from literary works alone. (Be like Tolstoy – but without his weaknesses! Be like Balzac – only up-to-date!) Realism is an issue not only for literature: it is a major political, philosophical and practical issue and must be handled and explained as such – as a matter of general human interest. [Brecht, 1974, p. 45.]

One of the difficulties of any discussion about realism is the lack of any really effective vocabulary with which to discuss the topic. Most discussions turn on the problems of the production of discourse which will fully adequate the real. This notion of adequacy is accepted both by the realists and indeed by the anti-realists whose main argument is that no discourse can ever be adequate to the multifarious nature of the real. This notion of the real is, however, I wish to suggest, a notion which is tied to a particular type of literary production – the nineteenth century realist novel. The dominance of this novel form is such that people still tend to confuse the general question of realism with the particular forms of the nineteenth century realist novel. In order to make the discussion clearer I want therefore to attempt to define the structure which typifies the nineteenth century realist novel and to show how that structure can also be used to describe a great number of films. The detour through literature is necessary because, in many ways, the structure is much more obvious there and also because of the historical dominance of the classic realist novel over much film production. What to a large extent will be lacking in this article is the specific nature of the film form but this does

classic realist
text applies to
novels + film

not seem to me to invalidate the setting up of certain essential categories from which further discussion must progress. The structure I will attempt to disengage I shall call the classic realist text and I shall apply it to novels and films.

A classic realist text may be defined as one in which there is a hierarchy amongst the discourses which compose the text and this hierarchy is defined in terms of an empirical notion of truth. Perhaps the easiest way to understand this is through a reflection on the use of inverted commas within the classic realist novel. While those sections in the text which are contained in inverted commas may cause a certain difficulty for the reader – a certain confusion vis-à-vis what really is the case – this difficulty is abolished by the unspoken (or more accurately the unwritten) prose that surrounds them. In the classical realist novel the narrative prose functions as a metalanguage that can state all the truths in the object language – those words held in inverted commas – and can also explain the relation of this object language to the real. The metalanguage can thereby explain the relation of this object language to the world and the strange methods by which the object languages attempt to express truths which are straightforwardly conveyed in the metalanguage. What I have called an unwritten prose (or a metalanguage) is exactly that language which, while placing other languages between inverted commas and regarding them as certain material expressions which express certain meanings, regards those same meanings as finding transparent expression within the metalanguage itself. Transparent in the sense that the metalanguage is not regarded as material; it is dematerialised to achieve perfect representation – to let the identity of things shine through the window of words. For insofar as the metalanguage is treated itself as material – it, too, can be reinterpreted; new meanings can be found for it in a further metalanguage. The problem is the problem that has troubled western thought since the pre-Socratics recognised the separation between what was said and the act of saying. This separation must be thought both as time and space – as the space, which in the distance from page to eye or mouth to ear allows the possibility of misunderstanding – as the time taken to traverse the page or listen to an utterance which ensures the deferred interpretation of words which are always only defined by what follows. The problem is that in the moment that we say a sentence the meaning (what is said) seems fixed and evident but what is said does not exist solely for the moment and is open to further interpretations. Even in this formulation of the problem I have presupposed an original moment when there is strict contemporaneity between the saying and what is said, but the difficulty is more radical for there is no such original moment. The separation is always already there as we cannot locate the presence of what is said – distributed as it is through space – nor the present of what is said – distributed as it is through time.

metalanguage
object lang

This (separation) bears witness to the real as articulated. The thing represented does not appear in a moment of pure identity as it tears itself out of the world and presents itself, but rather is caught in an articulation in which each object is defined in a set of difference and oppositions.

It is this separation that the unwritten text attempts to *anneal*, to make whole, through denying its own status as writing – as marks of material difference distributed through time and space. Whereas other discourses within the text are considered as material which are open to reinterpretation, the narrative discourse simply allows reality to appear and denies its own status as articulation. This relationship between discourses can be clearly seen in the work of such a writer as George Eliot. In the scene in *Middlemarch* where Mr Brooke goes to visit the Dagleys' farm we read two different languages. One is the educated, well-meaning, but not very intelligent discourse of Mr Brooke and the other is the uneducated, violent and very nearly unintelligible discourse of the drunken Dagley. But the whole dialogue is surrounded by a metalanguage, which being unspoken is also unwritten, and which places these discourses in inverted commas and can thus discuss these discourses' relation to truth – a truth which is illuminatingly revealed in the metalanguage. The metalanguage reduces the object languages into a simple division between form and content and extracts the meaningful content from the useless form. One can see this process at work in the following passage which ends the scene:

> He [Mr Brooke] had never been insulted on his own land before, and had been inclined to regard himself as a general favourite (we are all apt to do so, when we think of our own amiability more than what other people are likely to want of us). When he had quarrelled with Caleb Garth twelve years before he had thought that the tenants would be pleased at the landlord's taking everything into his own hands.
>
> Some who follow the narrative of this experience may wonder at the midnight darkness of Mr Dagley; but nothing was easier in those times than for a hereditary farmer of his grade to be ignorant, in spite somehow of having a rector in the twin parish who was a gentleman to the backbone, a curate nearer at hand who preached more learnedly than the rector, a landlord who had gone into everything, especially fine art and social improvement, and all the lights of Middlemarch only three miles off. [Eliot, 1967, pp. 432–3.]

This passage provides the necessary interpretations for the discourses that we have read earlier in the chapter. Both the discourses of Dagley and Mr Brooke are revealed as springing from two types of ignorance which the metalanguage can expose and reveal. So we have Mr Brooke's attitude to what his tenants thought of him contrasted with the reality which is available through the narrative prose. No discourse is allowed to speak for itself but rather it must be placed in a context which will reduce it to a simple explicable content. And in the claim that the narrative prose has direct access to a final reality we can find the claim of the classic realist novel to present us with the truths of human nature. The ability to reveal the truth about Mr Brooke is the ability that guarantees the generalisations of human nature.

Thus then a first definition of the classic realist text – but does this definition carry over into films, where it is certainly less evident where to locate the dominant discourse? It seems to me that it does and in the following fashion. The narrative prose achieves its position of dominance because it is in the position of knowledge and this function of knowledge is taken up in the cinema by the narration of events. Through the knowledge we gain from the narrative we can split the discourses of the various characters from their situation and compare what is said in these discourses with what has been revealed to us through narration. The camera shows us what happens – it tells the truth against which we can measure the discourses. A good example of this classical realist structure is to be found in Pakula's film *Klute*. This film is of particular interest because it was widely praised for its realism on its release. Perhaps even more significantly it tended to be praised for its realistic presentation of the leading woman, Bree (played by Jane Fonda).

In *Klute* the relationship of dominance between discourses is peculiarly accentuated by the fact that the film is interspersed with fragments of Bree talking to her psychiatrist. This subjective discourse can be exactly measured against the reality provided by the unfolding of the story. Thus all her talk of independence is portrayed as finally an illusion as we discover, to no great surprise but to our immense relief, what she really wants is to settle down in the mid-West with John Klute (the detective played by Donald Sutherland) and have a family. The final sequence of the film is particularly telling in this respect. While Klute and Bree pack their bags to leave, the soundtrack records Bree at her last meeting with her psychiatrist. Her own estimation of the situation is that it most probably won't work but the reality of the image ensures us that this is the way it will really be. Indeed Bree's monologue is even more interesting – for in relation to the reality of the image it marks a definite advance on her previous statement. She has gained insight through the plot development and like many good heroines of classic realist texts her discourse is more nearly adequate to the truth at the end of the film than at the beginning. But if a progression towards knowledge is what marks Bree, it is possession of knowledge which marks the narrative, the reader of the film and John Klute himself. For Klute is privileged by the narrative as the one character whose discourse is also a discourse of knowledge. Not only is Klute a detective and thus can solve the problem of his friend's disappearance – he is also a man, and a man who because he has not come into contact with the city has not had his virility undermined. And it is as a full-blooded man that he can know not only the truth of the mystery of the murders but also the truth of the woman Bree. Far from being a film which goes any way to portraying a woman liberated from male definition (a common critical response), *Klute* exactly guarantees that the real essence of woman can only be discovered and defined by a man.

The analysis sketched here is obviously very schematic but what, hopefully, it does show is that the structure of the classic realist text can be found in film as well. That narrative of events – the knowledge which the film provides of how things really are – is the metalanguage in which we can talk of the various characters in the film. What would still remain to be done in the elaboration of the structure of the classic realist text in cinema is a more detailed account of the actual mechanisms by which the narrative is privileged (and the way in which one or more of the characters within the narrative can be equally privileged) and also a history of the development of this dominant narrative. On the synchronic level it would be necessary to attempt an analysis of the relationship between the various types of shot and their combination into sequences – are there for example certain types of shot which are coded as subjective and therefore subordinate to others which are guaranteed as objective? In addition how does music work as the guarantee or otherwise of truth? On the diachronic level it would be necessary to study how this form was produced – what relationship obtains between the classic realist text and technical advances such as the development of the talkie? What ideological factors were at work in the production and dominance of the classic realist text?

To return, however, to the narrative discourse. It is necessary to attempt to understand the type of relations that this dominant discourse produces. The narrative discourse cannot be mistaken in its identifications because the narrative discourse is not present as discourse – as articulation. The unquestioned nature of the narrative discourse entails that the only problem that reality poses is to go and look and see what *Things* there *are.* The relationship between the reading subject and the real is placed as one of pure specularity. The real is not articulated – it is. These features imply two essential features of the classic realist text:

1. The classic realist text cannot deal with the real as contradictory.
2. In a reciprocal movement the classic realist text ensures the position of the subject in a relation of dominant specularity.

. . . .

Freud's theory is a theory of the construction of the subject: the entry of the small infant into language and society and the methods by which it learns what positions, as subject, it can take up. This entry into the symbolic (the whole cultural space which is structured, like language, through a set of differences and oppositions) is most easily traced in the analytic situation through that entry which is finally determining for the infant – the problem of sexual difference. Freud's insight is that the

Freud—repression

unproblematic taking up of the position of the subject entails the repression of the whole mechanism of the subject's construction. The subject is seen as the founding source of meanings – unproblematically standing outside an articulation in which it is, in fact, defined. This view of the subject as founding source is philosophically encapsulated in Descartes' *cogito*: I think, therefore I am – the I in simple evidence to itself provides a moment of pure presence which can found the enterprise of analysing the world. Jacques Lacan, the French psychoanalyst, has read Freud as reformulating the Cartesian *cogito* and destroying the subject as source and foundation – Lacan rewrites the *cogito*, in the light of Freud's discoveries as: I think where I am not and I am where I do not think. We can understand this formulation as the indicating of the fundamental misunderstanding (*méconnaissance*) which is involved in the successful use of language (or any other area of the symbolic which is similarly structured) in which the subject is continually ignored as being caught up in a process of articulation to be taken as a fixed place founding the discourse. The unconscious is that effect of language which escapes the conscious subject in the distance between the act of signification in which the subject passes from signifier to signifer and what is signified in which the subject finds himself in place as, for example, the pronoun 'I'. The importance of phenomena like verbal slips is that they testify to the existence of the unconscious through the distance between what was said and what the conscious subject intended to say. They thus testify to the distance between the subject of the act of signification and the conscious subject (the ego). In this distance there is opened a gap which is the area of desire. What is essential to all of those psychic productions which Freud uses in the analytic interpretation is that they bear witness to the lack of control of the conscious subject over his discourses. The mechanisms of the unconscious can indeed be seen as the mechanisms of language. Condensation is the work of metaphor which brings together two signifieds under one signifier and displacement is the constant process along the signifying chain. The ego is constantly caught in this fundamental misunderstanding (*méconnaissance*) about language in which from an illusory present it attempts to read only one signified as present in the metaphor and attempts to bring the signifying chain to an end in a perpetually deferred present.

The relationship between the unconscious and desire, the subject and language is concisely summarised by Lacan in the following passage:

There is not *an* unconscious because then there would be an unconscious desire which was obtuse, heavy, caliban like, even animal like, an unconscious desire lifted up from the depths which would be primitive and would have to educate itself to the superior level of consciousness. Completely on the contrary there is desire because there is unconsciousness (*de l'inconscient*) – that's to say language which escapes the subject in its structure and in its effects and there is always at the level of language something which is beyond consciousness and it is there that one can situate the function of desire. [Lacan, cited in Wahl, 1968.]

It is clear that the classic realist text, as defined above, guarantees the position of the subject exactly outside any articulation – the whole text works on the concealing of the dominant discourse as articulation – instead the dominant discourse presents itself exactly as the presentation of objects to the reading subject. But within the classic realist text the dominant discourse can be subverted, brought into question – the position of the subject may be rendered problematic. If we return to our original example of George Eliot we can see this process of subversion at work in *Daniel Deronda*. Within the text there is a discourse, the writings of Mordecai in Hebrew which are unmastered by the dominant discourse. The text tells us that they are untranslatable and thus that there is an area outside the text's control. This area is exactly the area of the mother-tongue (Daniel's mother is Jewish) and this mother-tongue subverts the assured positions of both the characters in the text and the reading subject. My business here is not to give a full analysis of George Eliot's work but rather to indicate the possibility of *moments* within a classical realist text which subvert it and its evident status for subject and object. [. . .] These *moments* are those elements which escape the control of the dominant discourse in the same way as a neurotic symptom or a verbal slip attest to the lack of control of the conscious subject. They open up another area than that of representation – of subject and object caught in an eternal paralysed fixity – in order to investigate the very movement of articulation and difference – the movement of desire. [. . .] Over and above these *moments* of subversion, however, there are what one might call *strategies* of subversion. Instead of a dominant discourse which is transgressed at various crucial moments we can find a systematic refusal of any such dominant discourse. One of the best examples of a cinema which practices certain strategies of subversion are the films of Roberto Rossellini. In *Germany year Zero*, for example, we can locate a multitude of ways in which the reading subject finds himself without a position from which the film can be regarded. Firstly, and most importantly, the fact that the narrative is not privileged in any way with regard to the characters' discourses. The narrative does not produce for us the knowledge with which we can then judge the truth of those discourses. Rather than the narrative providing us with knowledge – it provides us with various settings. Just as in Brecht the 'fable' serves simply as a procedure to produce the various *gests*, so in Rossellini the story simply provides a framework for various scenes which then constitute the picture of Germany in year zero. [. . .] Secondly, Rossellini's narrative introduces many elements which are not in any sense resolved and which deny the possibility of regarding the film as integrated through a dominant discourse. The Allied soldiers, the street kids, the landlord, the Teacher's house – all these provide elements which stretch outside the narrative of the film and deny its dominance. [. . .]

It may be objected that it is deliberately perverse to tear Rossellini away from realism with which he has been firmly connected both through his own own statements and through critical reception. The realist element in Rossellini is not simply located in the subject matter, the traditional criterion of realism, for I have already argued that the subject matter is a secondary condition for realism. What typifies the classic realist text is the way the subject matter is ordered and articulated rather than its origins. To deal with the facts of the world is, in itself, not only a realist but also a materialist viewpoint. The materialist, however, must regard these materials as ordered within a certain mode of production, within which they find their definition. And it is here that one could begin to isolate that element of realist ideology which does figure in Rossellini's films as a certain block. If the reading subject is not offered any certain mode of entry into what is presented on the screen, he is offered a certain mode of entry to the screen itself. For the facts presented by the camera, if they are not ordered in fixed and final fashion amongst themselves, *are* ordered in themselves. The camera, in Rossellini's films, is not articulated as part of the productive process of the film. What it shows is in some sense beyond argument and it is here that Rossellini's films show the traditional realist weakness of being unable to deal with contradiction. In *Viva l'Italia* the glaring omission of the film is the absence of Cavour. It is wrong to attack this omission on purely political grounds for it is an inevitable result of a certain lack of questioning of the camera itself. Garibaldi can be contrasted with Francisco II of Naples because their different conceptions of the world are so specifically tied to different historical eras that the camera can cope with their contradictions within an historical perspective. Here is the way the world is now – there is the way the world was then. But to introduce Cavour would involve a simultaneous contradiction – a class contradiction. At this point the camera itself, as a neutral agent, would become impossible. For it would have to offer two present contradictory articulations of the world and thus reveal its own presence. This cannot happen within a Rossellini film where if we are continually aware of our presence in the cinema (particularly in his historical films) – that presence itself is not questioned in any way. We are not allowed any particular position to read the film but we are allowed the position of a reader – an unproblematic viewer – an eternally human nature working on the material provided by the camera.

A possible way of advancing on Rossellini's practice (there are no obvious films which have marked such an advance although some of Godard's early films might be so considered) would be to develop the possibility of articulating contradiction. Much in the way that James

Joyce in *Ulysses* and *Finnegans Wake* investigated the contradictory ways of articulating reality through an investigation of the different forms of language, one could imagine a more radical strategy of subversion than that practised by Rossellini in which the possibilities of the camera would be brought more clearly into play. What would mark such a cinema and indeed any cinema of subversion would be that feature quoted by Brecht at the beginning of this section – the fact that it would be ill at ease in the class struggle, always concerned with an area of contradiction beyond the necessity of the present revolution – the ineliminable contradictions of the sexes, the eternal struggle between Desire and Law, between articulation and position.

References

Brecht, B. (1974), 'Against Georg Lukàcs', *New Left Review*, no. 84, 1974.
Eliot, G. (1967), *Middlemarch*, London.
Wahl, F. (ed.) (1968), *Qu' est-ce que le structuralisme?*, Paris.

---

16 Catherine Belsey,
From *The Subject of Tragedy*

p215–221

Mary Astell's *Some Reflections upon Marriage* first appeared anonymously in 1700 (though in many respects it might have been written at any time since then). By the third edition in 1706 it included a preface (an appendix in later editions) which acknowledged that the author was a woman. The voice in the body of the text, however, is ostensibly masculine. None the less, in the following extract the third person pronouns invite the reader to take up a position in relation to the argument which differs radically from that offered by Dod and Cleaver. The passage identifies what a husband wants from marriage:

> He wants one to manage his family, an house-keeper, one whose interest it will be not to wrong him, and in whom therefore he can put greater confidence than in any he can hire for money. One who may breed his children, taking all the care and trouble of their education, to preserve his name and family. One whose beauty, wit, or good humour and agreeable conversation, will entertain him at home when he has been contradicted and disappointed abroad; who will do him that justice the ill-natur'd world denies him; that is, in any one's language but his own, sooth his pride and flatter his vanity, by having always so much good sense as to be on his side, to conclude him in the

right, when others are so ignorant, or so rude, as to deny it. Who will not be blind to his merit nor contradict his will and pleasure, but make it her business, her very ambition to content him; whose softness and gentle compliance will calm his passions, to whom he may safely disclose his troublesome thoughts; and in her breast discharge his cares; whose duty, submission and observance, will heal those wounds other people's opposition or neglect have given him. In a word, one whom he can entirely govern, and consequently may form her to his will and liking, who must be his for life, and therefore cannot quit his service, let him treat her how he will.

(Astell, 1730:24-5)

Half way through the passage 'his' (the husband's) 'language' is differentiated from anyone else's, so that the reader is invited to reinterpret ironically all that has gone before. In consequence, when the final sentence offers a summary 'in a word', in a language shared by reader and writer, it is clear that the perspective that has been offered is feminine – and feminist.

7.4 Women's speaking justified

Some Reflections upon Marriage is a remarkable book. It never explicitly challenges male sovereignty in marriage but it subjects it to various kinds of irony. How can women fail to admire men? 'Have they not founded empires and overturn'd them? Do they not make laws and continually repeal and amend them? Their vast minds lay kingdoms waste' (Astell, 1730:36). It is not obvious that Swift belongs on the English syllabus if Astell does not. Not only have men displayed their eminence in developing the arts of gambling and deep drinking; in addition,

Their subtlety in forming cabals and laying deep designs, their courage and conduct in breaking through all tyes, sacred and civil, to effect them, not only advances them to the post of honour, and keeps them securely in it for twenty or thirty years, but gets them a name, and conveys it down to posterity for some hundreds; and who would look any further?

(Astell, 1730:53).

As in the previous passage, the irony works here because the argument is so close to the claims actually made on behalf of patriarchy.

Locke in *Two Treatises of Government* had conceded that women had rights (Locke, 1967, II:82). But in his repudiation of the patriarchalist arguments of Filmer and others that the state needed a head in just the same way as a family did, he introduced a distinction between the modes of government in the family and the state. In transferring power from the sovereign to the social body, Locke saw no cause for altering the power of the husband over his wife. The husband, it was made clear in Locke's text, had 'to order the things of private concernment in his family, as proprietor of the goods and land there, and to have his will take place before that of his wife in all things of their common concernment'. But the husband's power was purely 'conjugal', and 'not a political power of life and death over her' (Locke, 1967, I: 48). Patriarchalism was a justification of absolute power in the family and in the state. In its insistence on the parallel between the two, patriarchalism included the family within the political. By breaking down the analogy between family and state, microcosm and macrocosm, Locke effectively removed the family from the sphere of politics – and consequently depoliticized the relationships within it. Astell challenges the logic of this position. 'If absolute sovereignty be not necessary in a state, how comes it to be so in a family? Or if in a family why not in a state; since no reason can be alledged for the one that will not hold more strongly for the other? . . . For if arbitrary power is evil in it self, and an improper method of governing rational and free agents, it ought not to be practis'd anywhere.' And more tersely, 'If *all men are born free*, how is it that all women are born slaves?' (Astell, 1730:66).

. . . .

Like Bathsua Makin's *Essay to Revive the Antient Education of Gentlewomen, Some Reflections* begins to acknowledge the social construction of the subject. Perhaps it is impossible to put the feminist case without making this fundamental break with liberal-humanist common sense. In Makin's version,

> Custom, when it is inveterate, hath a mighty influence: it hath the force of nature it self. The barbarous custom to breed women low, is grown general amongst us, and hath prevailed so far, that it is verily believed (especially amongst a sort of debauched sots) that women are not endued with such reason, as men; nor capable of improvement by education, as they are.
>
> (Makin, 1673:3)

As Mary Astell rather more laconically puts it, 'Sense is a portion that God himself has been pleased to distribute to both sexes with an impartial hand, but learning is what men have engross'd to themselves' (Astell, 1730:69).

It is evident in these texts, and others like Margaret Fell's *Women's Speaking Justified* (1666), that women had found a voice. There were, of course, earlier instances of women's writing in defence of women, but they are notably less radical, and the pseudonyms often make it difficult to be sure that the authors were not male pamphleteers eager to increase their incomes by writing replies to the anti-feminist tracts they themselves had produced. Constantia Munda and Esther Sowernam, both of whom replied in 1617 to Joseph Swetnam's *The Arraignment of Lewde,*

Idle, Froward, and Unconstant Women (1615), may well come into this category. Their pamphlets consists largely of invective. Mary Tattlewell and Joane Hit-Him-Home, authors of *The Womens Sharpe Revenge* (1640) may in practice have been John Taylor. Jane Anger's *Protection for Women* (1589) is a more serious contribution to the debate, arguing that men insist on women's inferiority because they know that in reality women are generally wiser and more moral. When women reprove men with good counsel, men resent it. And Rachel Speght in *A Mouzell for Melastomus* (1617), the first of the replies to Swetnam, puts a good deal of stress on the concept of women as companions, sharing their husbands' burdens. 'Marriage is a merri-age, and this worlds Paradise, where there is mutuall love . . . a joyfull union and conjunction, with such a creature as God hath made meete for man, for none was meete till she was made' (Speght, 1617:14).[1] But the distance between this position and Astell's is readily apparent.

What fills the space between them is the installation of women as subjects through the redefinition of the family. Loving partners, specialists in domesticity, nurturing, caring mothers, they progressively became autonomous, unified, knowing authors of their own choices. As subjects women were entitled to make a living – to become actresses on the Restoration stage, or even writers, like Aphra Behn who, not without a struggle, became a successful professional dramatist. In fiction too they are shown as entitled to speak without transgression. Behn herself rewrote *The Miseries of Enforced Marriage* as a Restoration comedy and *The Town Fop; or, Sir Timothy Tawdrey* (1676) shows women taking action to alleviate the miseries their counterparts had accepted patiently in the earlier play. While Clare Harcop killed herself on learning that William was married, Celinda, her equivalent in the later play, is seen dressed as a boy defending her lover in a fight at his wedding feast. Katherine, William's wife, waited and pleaded for his return to her: Diana, having failed to seduce the disguised Celinda in revenge, prevails on her uncle to arrange a divorce. William's sister marries Ilford to save the family: Phillis marries Sir Timothy Tawdrey to save her honour and secure a happy ending. Enforced marriage is not indissoluble, because it is not based on love, and women are not purely objects of exchange but agents of their own destinies.

The transformation is less startling when we remember that while *Miseries* is written largely in the mode of tragedy, *The Town Fop* is consistently and confidently comic, and the comic tradition since Medwall, or at least since Shakespeare, had permitted the presentation of women who were to some degree self-determining without being demonic. None the less, in conjunction with the decline of the witchcraze on the one

---

[1] The pamphlets from the period before the Revolution have been reprinted in modern spelling (Shepherd, 1985).

hand, and the rise of a recognizable feminism on the other, it is possible to read this text as marking a change in the discursive position of women.

It is hardly necessary to point out, of course, that the installation of women as subjects was not the end of our problems. Liberalism does not guarantee equality. People may be equal by nature, but excellence, age, virtue, birth or other distinguishing characteristics [gender, for instance] may justify inequalities (Locke, 1967, II: 54). To have a subject-position, however, is to occupy a place in discourse, to be able to speak – though it does not guarantee an audience. To be a subject is to be able to claim rights, to protest, and to be capable, therefore, of devising a mode of resistance more sharply focused than prophesying, witchcraft or murder. It is to be in a position to identify and analyse the nature of women's oppression.

The position allotted to women, the position of the subject in liberal humanism, is one in which unity, autonomy and choice are always imaginary. The gap between the 'I' of utterance and the uttering 'I', between the subject which speaks and the subject which is only represented – symbolized – in the symbolic order, is the location of a desire which cannot be satisfied. And the gap thus produced is the place of a resistance which it is the task of liberal humanism to depoliticize, privatize, psychologize or, in psychoanalysis and sexology, specifically to sexualize. Women as subjects find a position in the discourses about them and addressed to them, and are consequently able to speak. But their speech is predicated on an absence which a feminism that refuses the liberal-humanist modes of self-fulfilment is able to appropriate for politics. The installation of women as subjects is the production of a space in which to problematize the liberal-humanist alliance with patriarchy, to formulate a sexual politics, to begin the struggle for change.

References

The Town Fop; or, Sir Timothy Tawdrey (1676), Aphra Behn, *Works* ed. Montague Summers, New York Phaeton Press, 1967, vol. 3.

Anger, Jane (1589), *Jane Anger her Protection for Women*, London.

Astell, Mary (1730), *Some Reflections upon Marriage*, Dublin.

Fell, Margaret (1666), *Womens Speaking Justified*, London.

Locke, John (1967), *Two Treatises of Government*, ed. Peter Laslett, Cambridge, Cambridge University Press.

Makin, Bathsua, (1673), *An Essay to Revive the Antient Education of Gentlewomen*, London.

Speght, Rachel (1617), *A Mouzell for Melastomus*, London.

Swetnam, Joseph (1615), *The Arraignment of Lewde, Idle, Froward and Unconstant Women*, London.

Tattlewell, Mary and Hit-Him-Home, Joane (1640), *The Womens Sharpe Revenge*, London.

SECTION TWO
LANGUAGE AND TEXTUALITY

The work represented in this trajectory of post-structuralist criticism tends to concentrate on abstract philosophical argument and specu- lation around language and textuality. For this trajectory, the text is taken not as referring to a pre-text but as inscribed within a web of textuality and difference. Its characteristic mode of operation is a spectacular play of language game around the texts it interrogates; its most formidable exponent is the French philosopher Jacques Derrida.

Derrida has been seen as almost synonymous with the post- structuralist enterprise. He has consistently critiqued and extended structuralism, rigorously following through the most radical impli- cations of the Saussurean theory of language. Though Derrida is perhaps best known for inaugurating 'deconstruction', the various forms of textual analysis that claim to be 'deconstructing the text' often have only tenuous links with his consistent concern to undo the 'logocentric' impulse in texts. 'Logocentrism' is the term Derrida uses to cover that form of rationalism that presupposes a 'presence' behind language and text − a 'presence' such as an idea, an inten- tion, a truth, a meaning or a reference for which language acts as a subservient and convenient vehicle of expression. But at the same time as language and text exhibit logocentric impulses, *writing*, as textuality, undoes that logocentrism through its rhetorical and troping figures; while the text attempts to suppress textuality, textuality inevitably imposes itself on the scene of writing.

Logocentrism, the mark of a 'metaphysics of presence' is, for Derrida, the very foundation of Western thought; it is undermined by Saussure's theory of language in which identities result only from difference. But, as Derrida shows, Saussure himself falls into a logo- centrism. In *Of Grammatology* Derrida criticizes Saussure on the grounds that he privileges speech over writing. Speech becomes the authentic moment of language where meaning is identical to the speaker's intention and it thus bears the sign of presence, whereas writing is seen as a secondary and inferior form of speech. Typically, Derrida reverses the privileged term of the binary opposition, to show how speech can be seen as a form of writing (rather than *vice versa*), and how both exist in a mutually reciprocal dependence marked by différance.

Derrida reads Saussure radically, transposing difference to différance – where meaning is a matter of both difference and deferring. Meaning is never self-present in the sign, for if it were then the signifier would simply be the reference for the signified, the signifier 'standing-in' for the absent 'presence' of the concept that lies behind it. Meaning is a result of difference, but it is also deferred, there is always an element of 'undecidability' or 'play' in the unstable sign. This leads to an emphasis on the signifier and on textuality rather than the signified and meaning, since there is no point at which the slippage of signifiers can be stopped, no final resting point where the signifier yields up the truth of the signified, for that signified is just another signifier in a moment in différance.

Deconstruction is a twofold strategy of, on the one hand, uncovering and undoing logocentric rationality and on the other, drawing attention to the language of the text, to its figurative and rhetorical gestures and pointing up the text's existence in a web of textuality, in a network of signifiers where no final and transcendental signified can be fixed. If it is to sustain such a strategy then it must constantly refuse to set itself up as a systematic analysis independent of the text, a system that explains and masters, since to do so would be to fix the meaning of the text. Deconstruction appears, therefore, not as a rigid method or explanatory metalanguage, but more as a process and a performance closely tied to the texts it deconstructs. However, as Derrida notes, such strategies cannot ultimately escape logocentrism, they can only push at its limits; deconstructionist texts are themselves not beyond deconstruction, as Barbara Johnson has illustrated (in Young 1981).

For literary criticism the implications of deconstruction, and of Derrida's work in general, are profound. Literary studies has traditionally been concerned with the interpretation of texts, with revealing the 'meaning' behind the text (be that meaning the author's intention or the 'truth' of the human condition). Deconstructionist logic disrupts that interpretive mode. If the meaning of the text is unstable, undecidable, then the project of literary interpretation is compromised; interpretation is doomed to endlessly repeat the interpretive act, never able to reach that final explanation and understanding of the text – it is haunted by the continual play of différance. What is left to criticism is either a celebration of that play, or a rigorous argumentation around the logocentric versus textuality paradox. Both of these modes of criticism have been taken up directly by the American deconstructionists of the Yale School (Paul De Man, J. Hillis Miller, Geoffrey Hartman) (See Norris 1982).

Though Derrida's work has had a formative and direct influence on the American deconstructionists, it has also been highly influential in the development of post-structuralism in general. Indeed, it would be tempting to say that his 'presence' is pervasive in post-structuralist thought – but that would be wilfully logocentric. The essay by Derrida reprinted here interrogates the structuralist project and in particular the work of Lévi-Strauss, taking it to task over the notion of structure; for in structure, structuralism proposes a centre beyond the play of language. This essay is one of Derrida's most widely known pieces, one of the first to be translated into English.

Barthes's essay, 'From Work to Text' was first published in 1971, one year after his seminal work of criticism, *S/Z*. As in *S/Z*, Barthes works on the notion of the 'plurality' of meaning and text. However, there is some hesitation about whether the text itself is the site of plurality or whether reading and interpreting, necessarily a process of structuration, governs this plurality. Barthes seems here, as he does in *The Pleasure of the Text* (1976) to imply that some texts are better than others because they actively engage in the 'moving-play of signifiers' rather than attempting to constrain and repress plurality (as in realism). His elusiveness over this point reinforces that sense of Barthes as post-structuralist, not prepared to produce the definitive meaning, but quite prepared to play undecidably between two.

The Hillis Miller article acts as a representative illustration of deconstructive practice, while the subsequent exchange between Hillis Miller and Rimmon-Kenan usefully traces some of the differences between structuralism and deconstruction.

---

17 **Jacques Derrida,**
'Structure, Sign and Play in the Discourse of the Human Sciences', *Writing and Difference,* **trans Alan Bass**

p278–295

We need to interpret interpretations more than to interpret things.
(Montaigne)

Perhaps something has occurred in the history of the concept of structure that could be called an 'event', if this loaded word did not entail a meaning which it is precisely the function of structural – or structuralist – thought to reduce or to suspect. Let us speak of an 'event', nevertheless, and let us use quotation marks to serve as a precaution. What would this event be then? Its exterior form would be that of a *rupture* and a redoubling.

It would be easy enough to show that the concept of structure and even the word 'structure' itself are as old as the *epistēmē* – that is to say, as old as Western science and Western philosophy – and that their roots thrust deep into the soil of ordinary language, into whose deepest recesses the *epistēmē* plunges in order to gather them up and to make them part of itself in a metaphorical displacement. Nevertheless, up to the event which I wish to mark out and define, structure – or rather the structurality of structure – although it has always been at work, has always been neutralized or reduced, and this by a process of giving it a center or of referring it to a point of presence, a fixed origin. The function of this center was not only to orient, balance, and organize the structure – one cannot in fact conceive of an unorganized structure – but above all to make sure that the organizing principle of the structure would limit what we might call the *play* of the structure. By orienting and organizing the coherence of the system, the centre of a structure permits the play of its elements inside the total form. And even today the notion of a structure lacking any center represents the unthinkable itself.

Nevertheless, the center also closes off the play which it opens up and makes possible. As center, it is the point at which the substitution of contents, elements, or terms is no longer possible. At the center, the permutation or the transformation of elements (which may of course be structures enclosed within a structure) is forbidden. At least this permutation has always remained *interdicted* (and I am using this word deliberately). Thus it has always been thought that the center, which is by definition unique, constituted that very thing within a structure which while governing the structure, escapes structurality. This is why classical thought concerning structure could say that the center is, paradoxically, *within* the structure and *outside* it. The center is at the center of the totality, and yet, since the center does not belong to the totality (is not part of the totality), the totality *has its center elsewhere*. The center is not the center. The concept of centered structure – although it represents coherence itself, the condition of the *epistēmē* as philosophy or science – is contradictorily coherent. And as always, coherence in contradiction expresses the force of a desire.[1] The concept of centered structure is in fact the concept of a play based on a fundamental ground, a play constituted on the basis of a fundamental immobility and a

---

1. TN. The reference, in a restricted sense, is to the Freudian theory of neurotic symptoms and of dream interpretation in which a given symbol is understood contradictorily as both the desire to fulfill an impulse and the desire to suppress the impulse. In a general sense the reference is to Derrida's thesis that logic and coherence themselves can only be understood contradictorily, since they presuppose the suppression of *différance*, 'writing' in the sense of the general economy. Cf. 'La pharmacie de Platon', in *La dissemination*, pp. 125–26, where Derrida uses the Freudian model of dream interpretation in order to clarify the contractions embedded in philosophical coherence.

reassuring certitude, which itself is beyond the reach of play. And on the basis of this certitude anxiety can be mastered, for anxiety is invariably the result of a certain mode of being implicated in the game, of being caught by the game, of being as it were at stake in the game from the outset. And again on the basis of what we call the center (and which, because it can be either inside or outside, can also indifferently be called the origin or end, *archē* or *telos*), repetitions, substitutions, transformations, and permutations are always *taken* from a history of meaning [*sens*] – that is, in a word, a history – whose origin may always be reawakened or whose end may always be anticipated in the form of presence. This is why one perhaps could say that the movement of any archaeology, like that of any eschatology, is an accomplice of this reduction of the structurality of structure and always attempts to conceive of structure on the basis of a full presence which is beyond play.

If this is so, the entire history of the concept of structure, before the rupture of which we are speaking, must be thought of as a series of substitutions of center for center, as a linked chain of determinations of the center. Successively, and in a regulated fashion, the center receives different forms or names. The history of metaphysics, like the history of the West, is the history of these metaphors and metonymies. Its matrix – if you will pardon me for demonstrating so little and for being so elliptical in order to come more quickly to my principal theme – is the determination of Being as *presence* in all senses of this word. It could be shown that all the names related to fundamentals, to principles, or to the center have always designated an invariable presence – *eidos, archē, telos, energeia, ousia* (essence, existence, substance, subject) *alētheia*, transcendentality, consciousness, God, man, and so forth.

The event I called a rupture, the disruption I alluded to at the beginning of this paper, presumably would have come about when the structurality of structure had to begin to be thought, that is to say, repeated, and this is why I said that this disruption was repetition in every sense of the word. Henceforth, it became necessary to think both the law which somehow governed the desire for a center in the constitution of structure, and the process of signification which orders the displacements and substitutions for this law of central presence – but a central presence which has never been itself, has always already been exiled from itself into its own substitute. The substitute does not substitute itself for anything which has somehow existed before it. Henceforth, it was necessary to begin thinking that there was no center, that the center could not be thought in the form of a present-being, that the center had no natural site, that it was not a fixed locus but a function, a sort of nonlocus in which an infinite number of sign-substitutions came into play. This was the moment when language invaded the universal problematic, the moment when, in the absence of a center or origin, everything became discourse – provided we can agree on this word – that is to say, a system in which the central signified, the original or transcendental signified, is never absolutely present outside a system of differences. The absence of the transcendental signified extends the domain and the play of signification infinitely.

Where and how does this decentering, this thinking the structurality of structure, occur? It would be somewhat naïve to refer to an event, a doctrine, or an author in order to designate this occurrence. It is no doubt part of the totality of an era, our own, but still it has always already begun to proclaim itself and begun to *work*. Nevertheless, if we wished to choose several 'names', as indications only, and to recall those authors in whose discourse this occurrence has kept most closely to its most radical formulation, we doubtless would have to cite the Nietzschean critique of metaphysics, the critique of the concepts of Being and truth, for which were substituted the concepts of play, interpretation, and sign (sign without present truth); the Freudian critique of self-presence, that is, the critique of consciousness, of the subject, of self-identity and of self-proximity or self-possession; and, more radically, the Heideggerean destruction of metaphysics, of onto-theology, of the determination of Being as presence. But all these destructive discourses and all their analogues are trapped in a kind of circle. This circle is unique. It describes the form of the relation between the history of metaphysics and the destruction of the history of metaphysics. There is no sense in doing without the concepts of metaphysics in order to shake metaphysics. We have no language – no syntax and no lexicon – which is foreign to this history; we can pronounce not a single destructive proposition which has not already had to slip into the form, the logic, and the implicit postulations of precisely what it seeks to contest. To take one example from many: the metaphysics of presence is shaken with the help of the concept of *sign*. But, as I suggest a moment ago, as soon as one seeks to demonstrate in this way that there is no transcendental or privileged signified and that the domain or play of signification henceforth has no limit, one must reject even the concept and word 'sign' itself – which is precisely what cannot be done. For the signification 'sign' has always been understood and determined, in its meaning, as sign-of, a signifier referring to a signified, a signifier different from its signified. If one erases the radical difference between signifier and signified, it is the word 'signifier' itself which must be abandoned as a metaphysical concept. When Levi-Strauss says in the preface to *The Raw and the Cooked* that he has 'sought to transcend the opposition between the sensible and the intelligible by operating from the outset at the level of signs,'[2] the necessity, force, and legitimacy of his act cannot make us forget that the concept of the sign cannot in itself surpass this opposition between the sensible and the intelligible. The concept of the sign, in each

---

2. *The Raw and the Cooked*, trans. John and Doreen Wightman (New York: Harper & Row, 1969), p. 14.[Translation somewhat modified.]

of its aspects, has been determined by this opposition throughout the totality of its history. It has lived only on this opposition and its system. But we cannot do without the concept of the sign, for we cannot give up this metaphysical complicity without also giving up the critique we are directing against this complicity, or without the risk of erasing difference in the self-identity of a signified reducing its signifier into itself or, amounting to the same thing, simply expelling its signifier outside itself. For there are two heterogenous ways of erasing the difference between the signifier and the signified: one, the classic way, consists in reducing or deriving the signifier, that is to say, ultimately in *submitting* the sign to thought; the other, the one we are using here against the first one, consists in putting into question the system in which the preceding reduction functioned: first and foremost, the opposition between the sensible and the intelligible. For the *paradox* is that the metaphysical reduction of the sign needed the opposition it was reducing. The opposition is systematic with the reduction. And what we are saying here about the sign can be extended to all the concepts and all the sentences of metaphysics, in particular to the discourse on 'structure'. But there are several ways of being caught in this circle. They are all more or less naïve, more or less empirical, more or less systematic, more or less close to the formulation – that is, to the formalization – of this circle. It is these differences which explain the multiplicity of destructive discourses and the disagreement between those who elaborate them. Nietzsche, Freud, and Heidegger, for example, worked within the inherited concepts of metaphysics. Since these concepts are not elements or atoms, and since they are taken from a syntax and a system, every particular borrowing brings along with it the whole of metaphysics. This is what allows these destroyers to destroy each other reciprocally – for example, Heidegger regarding Nietzsche, with as much lucidity and rigor as bad faith and misconstruction, as the last metaphysician, the last 'Platonist'. One could do the same for Heidegger himself, for Freud, or for a number of others. And today no exercise is more widespread.

What is the relevance of this formal schema when we turn to what are called the 'human sciences'? One of them perhaps occupies a privileged place – ethnology. In fact one can assume that ethnology could have been born as a science only at the moment when a decentering had come about: at the moment when European culture – and, in consequence, the history of metaphysics and of its concepts – has been *dislocated*, driven from its locus, and forced to stop considering itself as the culture of reference. This moment is not first and foremost a moment of philosophical or scientific discourse. It is also a moment which is political, economic, technical, and so forth. One can say with total security that there is nothing fortuitous about the fact that the critique of ethnocentrism – the very condition for ethnology – should be systematically and historically contemporaneous with the destruction of the history of metaphysics. Both belong to one and the same era. Now, ethnology – like any science – comes about within the element of discourse. And it is primarily a European science employing traditional concepts, however much it may struggle against them. Consequently, whether he wants to or not – and this does not depend on a decision on his part – the ethnologist accepts into his discourse the premises of ethnocentrism at the very moment when he denounces them. This necessity is irreducible; it is not a historical contingency. We ought to consider all its implications very carefully. But if no one can escape this necessity, and if no one is therefore responsible for giving into it, however little he may do so, this does not mean that all the ways of giving in to it are of equal pertinence. The quality and fecundity of a discourse are perhaps measured by the critical rigor with which this relation to the history of metaphysics and to inherited concepts is thought. Here is a question both of a critical relation to the language of the social sciences and a critical responsibility of the discourse itself. It is a question of explicitly and systematically posing the problem of the status of a discourse which borrows from a heritage the resources necessary for the deconstruction of that heritage itself. A problem of *economy* and *strategy*.

If we consider, as an example, the texts of Claude Lévi-Strauss, it is not only because of the privilege accorded to ethnology among the social sciences, nor even because the thought of Lévi-Strauss weighs heavily on the contemporary theoretical situation. It is above all because a certain choice has been declared in the work of Lévi-Strauss and because a certain doctrine has been elaborated there, and precisely, in a *more or less explicit manner*, as concerns both this critique of language and this critical language in the social sciences.

In order to follow this movement in the text of Lévi-Strauss, let us choose as one guiding thread among others the opposition between nature and culture. Despite all its rejuvenations and disguises, this opposition is congenital to philosophy. It is even older than Plato. It is at least as old as the Sophists. Since the statement of the opposition *physis/nomos, physis/technē*, it has been relayed to us by means of a whole historical chain which opposes 'nature' to law, to education, to art, to technics – but also to liberty, to the arbitrary, to history, to society, to the mind, and so on. Now, from the outset of his researches, and from his first book (*The Elementary Structures of Kinship*) on, Lévi-Strauss simultaneously has experienced the necessity of utilizing this opposition and the impossibility of accepting it. In the *Elementary Structures*, he begins from this axiom or definition: that which is *universal* and spontaneous, and not dependent on any particular culture or on any determinate norm, belongs to nature. Inversely, that which depends upon a system of *norms* regulating society and therefore is capable of *varying* from one social structure to another, belongs to culture. These two definitions are of the traditional type. But in the very first pages of the *Elementary Structures* Lévi-Strauss, who has begun by giving credence to these concepts, encounters what he calls a *scandal*, that is to say, something which no longer tolerates the nature/culture opposition he has accepted, something which *simultaneously* seems to require the predicates of nature and of culture. This scandal is the *incest prohibition*. The incest prohibition is universal; in this sense one could call it natural. But it is also a prohibition, a system of norms and interdicts; in this sense one could call it cultural:

> Let us suppose then that everything universal in man relates to the natural order, and is characterized by spontaneity, and that everything subject to a norm is cultural and is both relative and particular. We are then confronted with a fact, or rather, a group of facts, which, in the light of previous definitions, are not far removed from a scandal: we refer to that complex group of beliefs, customs, conditions and institutions described succinctly as the prohibition of incest, which presents, without the slightest ambiguity, and inseparably combines, the two characteristics in which we recognize the conflicting features of two mutually exclusive orders. It constitutes a rule, but a rule which, alone among all the social rules, possesses at the same time a universal character.[3]

Obviously there is no scandal except within a system of concepts which accredits the difference between nature and culture. By commencing his work with the *factum* of the incest prohibition. Lévi-Strauss thus places himself at the point at which this difference, which has always been assumed to be self-evident, finds itself erased or questioned. For from the moment when the incest prohibition can no longer be conceived within the nature/culture opposition, it can no longer be said to be a scandalous fact, a nucleus of opacity within a network of transparent significations. The incest prohibition is no longer a scandal one meets with or comes up against in the domain of traditional concepts; it is something which escapes these concepts and certainly precedes them – probably as the condition of their possibility. It could perhaps be said that the whole of philosophical conceptualization, which is systematic with the nature/culture opposition, is designed to leave in the domain of the unthinkable the very thing that makes this conceptualization possible: the origin of the prohibition of incest.

This example, too cursorily examined, is only one among many others, but nevertheless it already shows that language bears within itself the necessity of its own critique. Now this critique may be undertaken along two paths, in two 'manners'. Once the limit of the nature/culture opposition makes itself felt, one might want to question systematically and rigorously the history of these concepts. This is a first action. Such a

---

3. *The Elementary Structures of Kinship*, trans. James Bell, John von Sturmer, and Rodney Needham (Boston: Beacon Press, 1969), p. 8.

systematic and historic questioning would be neither a philological nor a philosophical action in the classic sense of these words. To concern one-self with the founding concepts of the entire history of philosophy, to deconstitute them, is not to undertake the work of the philologist or of the classic historian of philosophy. Despite appearances, it is probably the most daring way of making the beginnings of a step outside of philosophy. The step 'outside philosophy' is much more difficult to conceive than is generally imagined by those who think they made it long ago with cavalier ease, and who in general are swallowed up in metaphysics by the entire body of discourse which they claim to have disengaged from it.

The other choice (which I believe corresponds more closely to Lévi-Strauss's manner), in order to avoid the possibly sterilizing effects of the first one, consists in conserving all these old concepts within the domain of empirical discovery while here and there denouncing their limits, treating them as tools which can still be used. No longer is any truth value attributed to them; there is a readiness to abandon them, if necessary, should other instruments appear more useful. In the meantime, their relative efficacy is exploited, and they are employed to destroy the old machinery to which they belong and of which they themselves are pieces. This is how the language of the social sciences criticizes *itself*. Lévi-Strauss thinks that in this way he can separate *method* from *truth*, the instruments of the method and the objective significations envisaged by it. One could almost say that this is the primary affirmation of Lévi-Strauss; in any event, the first words of the *Elementary Structures* are: 'Above all, it is beginning to emerge that this distinction between nature and society ('nature' and 'culture' seem preferable to us today), while of no acceptable historical significance, does contain a logic, fully justifying its use by modern sociology as a methological tool'.[4]

Lévi-Strauss will always remain faithful to this double intention: to preserve as an instrument something whose truth value he criticizes.

On the one hand, he will continue, in effect, to contest the value of the nature/culture opposition. More than thirteen years after the *Elementary Structures, The Savage Mind* faithfully echoes the text I have quoted: 'The opposition between nature and culture to which I attached much importance at one time . . . now seems to be of primarily methodological importance.' And this methodological value is not affected by its 'ontological' nonvalue (as might be said, if this notion were not suspect here): 'However, it would not be enough to reabsorb particular humanities into a general one. This first enterprise opens the way for others which . . . are incumbent on the exact natural sciences: the reintegration of culture in nature and finally of life within the whole of its physio-chemical conditions.'[5]

4. Ibid., p. 3.
5. *The Savage Mind* (London: George Weidenfeld and Nicolson; Chicago: The University of Chicago Press, 1966), p. 247.

On the other hand, still in *The Savage Mind*, he presents as what he calls *bricolage* what might be called the discourse of this method. The *bricoleur*, says Lévi-Strauss, is someone who uses 'the means at hand', that is, the instruments he finds at his disposition around him, those which are already there, which had not been especially conceived with an eye to the operation for which they are to be used and to which one tries by trial and error to adapt them, not hesitating to change them whenever it appears necessary, or to try several of them at once, even if their form and their origin are heterogenous – and so forth. There is therefore a critique of language in the form of *bricolage*, and it has even been said that *bricolage* is critical language itself. I am thinking in particular of the article of G. Genette. 'Structuralisme et critique littéraire', published in homage to Lévi-Strauss in a special issue of *L'Arc* (no. 26, 1965), where it is stated that the analysis of *bricolage* could 'be applied almost word for word' to criticism, and especially to 'literary criticism'.

If one calls *bricolage* the necessity of borrowing one's concepts from the text of a heritage which is more or less coherent or ruined, it must be said that every discourse is *bricoleur*. The engineer, whom Lévi-Strauss opposes to the *bricoleur*, should be the one to construct the totality of his language, syntax, and lexicon. In this sense the engineer is a myth. A subject who supposedly would be the absolute origin of his own discourse and supposedly would construct it 'out of nothing', 'out of whole cloth', would be the creator of the verb, the verb itself. The notion of the engineer who supposedly breaks with all forms of *bricolage* is therefore a theological idea; and since Lévi-Strauss tells us elsewhere that *bricolage* is mythopoetic, the odds are that the engineer is a myth produced by the *bricoleur*. As soon as we cease to believe in such an engineer and in a discourse which breaks with the received historical discourse, and as soon as we admit that every finite discourse is bound by a certain *bricolage* and that the engineer and the scientist are also species of *bricoleurs*, then the very idea of *bricolage* is menaced and the difference in which it took on its meaning breaks down.

This brings us to the second thread which might guide us in what is being contrived here.

Lévi-Strauss describes *bricolage* not only as an intellectual activity but also as a mythopoetical activity. One reads in *The Savage Mind*, 'Like *bricolage* on the technical plane, mythical reflection can reach brilliant unforeseen results on the intellectual plane. Conversely, attention has often been drawn to the mythopoetical nature of *bricolage*.'[6]

But Lévi-Strauss's remarkable endeavor does not simply consist in proposing, notably in his most recent investigations, a structural science of myths and of mythological activity. His endeavour also appears – I would say almost from the outset – to have the status which he accords to his own discourse on myths, to what he calls his 'mythologicals'. It is

6. Ibid., p. 17.

here that his discourse on the myth reflects on itself and criticises itself. And this moment, this critical period, is evidently of concern to all the languages which share the field of the human sciences. What does Lévi-Strauss say of his 'mythologicals'? It is here that we rediscover the mythopoetical virtue of *bricolage*. In effect, what appears most fascinating in this critical search for a new status of discourse is the stated abandonment of all reference to a *center*, to a *subject*, to a privileged *reference*, to an origin, or to an absolute *archia*. The theme of this decentering could be followed throughout the 'Overture' to his last book, *The Raw and the Cooked*. I shall simply remark on a few key points.

1 From the very start, Lévi-Strauss recognizes that the Bororo myth which he employs in the book as the 'reference myth' does not merit this name and this treatment. The name is specious and the use of the myth improper. This myth deserves no more than any other its referential privilege: 'In fact, the Bororo myth, which I shall refer to from now as the key myth, is, as I shall try to show, simply a transformation, to a greater or lesser extent, of other myths originating either in the same society or in neighboring or remote societies. I could, therefore, have legitimately taken as my starting point any one representative myth of the group. From this point of view, the key myth is interesting not because it is typical, but rather because of its irregular position within the group.'[7]

2 There is no unity or absolute source of the myth. The focus or the source of the myth are always shadows and virtualities which are elusive, unactualizable, and nonexistent in the first place. Everything begins with structure, configuration, or relationship. The discourse on the acentric structure that myth itself is, cannot itself have an absolute subject or an absolute center. It must avoid the violence that consists in centering a language which describes an acentric structure if it is not to shortchange the form and movement of myth. Therefore it is necessary to forego scientific or philosophical discourse, to renounce the *epistēmē* which absolutely requires, which is the absolute requirement that we go back to the source, to the center, to the founding basis, to the principle, and so on. In opposition to *epistemic* discourse, structural discourse on myths – *mythological* discourse – must itself be *mythomorphic*. It must have the form of that of which it speaks. This is what Lévi-Strauss says in *The Raw and the Cooked*, from which I would now like to quote a long and remarkable passage:

> The study of myths raises a methodological problem, in that it cannot be carried out according to the Cartesian principle of breaking down the difficulty into as many parts as may be necessary for finding the solution. There is no real end to methodological analysis, no hidden unity to be grasped once

7. *The Raw and the Cooked*, p .2.

the breaking-down process has been completed. Themes can be split up *ad infinitum*. Just when you think you have disentangled and separated them, you realize that they are knitting together again in response to the operation of unexpected affinities. Consequently the unity of the myth is never more than tendential and projective and cannot reflect a state or a particular moment of myth. It is a phenomenon of the imagination, resulting from the attempt at interpretation; and its function is to endow the myth with synthetic form and to prevent its disintegration into a confusion of opposites. The science of myths might therefore be termed "anaclastic," if we take this old term in the broader etymological sense which includes the study of both reflected rays and broken rays. But unlike philosophical reflection, which aims to go back to its own source, the reflections we are dealing with here concern rays whose only source is hypothetical . . . And in seeking to imitate the spontaneous movement of mythological thought, this essay, which is also both too brief and too long, has had to conform to the requirements of that thought and to respect its rhythm. It follows that this book on myths is itself a kind of myth.[8]

This statement is repeated a little further on: 'As the myths themselves are based on secondary codes (the primary codes being those that provide the substance of language), the present work is put forward as a tentative draft of a tertiary code, which is intended to ensure the reciprocal translatability of several myths. This is why it would not be wrong to consider this book itself as a myth: it is, as it were, the myth of mythology.'[9] The absence of a centre is here the absence of a subject and the absence of an author. 'Thus the myth and the musical work are like conductors of an orchestra, whose audience becomes the silent performers. If it is now asked where the real center of the work is to be found, the answer is that this is impossible to determine. Music and mythology bring man face to face with potential objects of which only the shadows are actualized. . . . Myths are anonymous'.[10] The musical model chosen by Lévi-Strauss for the composition of his book is apparently justified by this absence of any real and fixed center of the mythical or mythological discourse.

Thus it is at this point that ethnographic *bricolage* deliberately assumes its mythopoetic function. But by the same token, this function makes the philosophical or epistemological requirement of a center appear as mythological, that is to say, as a historical illusion.

Nevertheless, even if one yields to the necessity of what Lévi-Strauss has done, one cannot ignore its risks. If the mythological is mythomorphic, are all discourses on myths equivalent? Shall we have to abandon any epistemological requirement which permits us to distinguish between several qualities of discourse on the myth? A classic,

8. Ibid., pp. 5–6.
9. Ibid., p. 12.
10. Ibid., pp. 17–18.

but inevitable question. It cannot be answered – and I believe that Lévi-Strauss does not answer it – for as long as the problem of the relations between the philosopheme or the theorem, on the one hand, and the mytheme or the mythopoem, on the other, has not been posed explicitly, which is no small problem. For lack of explicitly posing this problem, we condemn ourselves to transforming the alleged transgression of philosophy into an unnoticed fault within the philosophical realm. Empiricism would be the genus of which these faults would always be the species. Transphilosophical concepts would be transformed into philosophical naïvetés. Many examples could be given to demonstrate this risk: the concepts of sign, history, truth, and so forth. What I want to emphasize is simply that the passage beyond philosophy does not consist in turning the page of philosophy (which usually amounts to philosophizing badly), but in continuing to read philosophers *in a certain way*. The risk I am speaking of is always assumed by Lévi-Strauss, and it is the very price of this endeavor. I have said that empiricism is the matrix of all faults menacing a discourse which continues, as with Lévi-Strauss in particular, to consider itself scientific. If we wanted to pose the problem of empiricism and *bricolage* in depth, we would probably end up very quickly with a number of absolutely contradictory propositions concerning the status of discourse in structural ethnology. On the one hand, structuralism justifiably claims to be the critique of empiricism. But at the same time there is not a single book or study by Lévi-Strauss which is not proposed as an empirical essay which can always be completed or invalidated by new information. The structural schemata are always proposed as hypotheses resulting from a finite quantity of information and which are subjected to the proof of experience. Numerous texts could be used to demonstrate this double postulation. Let us turn once again to the 'Overture' of *The Raw and the Cooked*, where it seems clear that if this postulation is double, it is because it is a question here of a language on language:

> If critics reproach me with not having carried out an exhaustive inventory of South American myths before analyzing them, they are making a grave mistake about the nature and function of these documents. The total body of myth belonging to a given community is comparable to its speech. Unless the population dies out physically or morally, this totality is never complete. You might as well criticize a linguist for compiling the grammar of a language without having complete records of the words pronounced since the language came into being, and without knowing what will be said in it during the future part of its existence. Experience proves that a linguist can work out the grammar of a given language from a remarkably small number of sentences. . . . And even a partial grammar or an outline grammar is a precious acquisition when we are dealing with unknown languages. Syntax does not become evident only after a (theoretically limitless) series of events has been recorded and examined, because it is itself the body of rules governing their production. What I have tried to give is an outline of the syntax of South American

mythology. Should fresh data come to hand, they will be used to check or modify the formulation of certain grammatical laws, so that some are abandoned and replaced by new ones. But in no instance would I feel constrained to accept the arbitrary demand for a total mythological pattern, since, as has been shown, such a requirement has no meaning.[11]

Totalization, therefore, is sometimes defined as *useless*, and sometimes as *impossible*. This is no doubt due to the fact that there are two ways of conceiving the limit of totalization. And I assert once more that these two determinations coexist implicitly in Lévi-Strauss's discourse. Totalization can be judged impossible in the classical style: one then refers to the empirical endeavor of either a subject or a finite richness which it can never master. There is too much, more than one can say. But nontotalization can also be determined in another way: no longer from the standpoint of a concept of finitude as relegation to the empirical, but from the standpoint of the concept of *play*. If totalization no longer has any meaning, it is not because the infiniteness of a field cannot be covered by a finite glance or a finite discourse, but because the nature of the field – that is, language and a finite language – excludes totalization. This field is in effect that of *play*, that is to say, a field of infinite substitutions only because it is finite, that is to say, because instead of being an inexhaustible field, as in the classical hypothesis, instead of being too large, there is something missing from it: a center which arrests and grounds the play of substitutions. One could say – rigorously using that word whose scandalous signification is always obliterated in French – that this movement of play, permitted by the lack or absence of a center or origin, is the movement of *supplementarity*. One cannot determine the center and exhaust totalization because the sign which replaces the center, which supplements it, taking the center's place in its absence – this sign is added, occurs as a surplus, as a *supplement*.[12] The movement of signification adds something, which results in the fact that there is always more, but this addition is a floating one because it comes to perform a vicarious function, to supplement a lack on the part of the signified. Although Lévi-Strauss in his use of the word 'supplementary' never emphasizes, as I do here, the two directions of meaning which are so strangely compounded within it, it is not by chance that he uses this word twice in his 'Introduction to the Work of Marcel Mauss', at one point where he is speaking of the 'overabundance of signifier, in relation to the signifieds to which this overabundance can refer':

11. Ibid., pp. 7–8.
12. TN. This double sense of supplement – to supply something which is missing, or to supply something additional – is at the center of Derrida's deconstruction of traditional linguistics in *De la grammatologie*. In a chapter entitled 'The Violence of the Letter: From Lévi-Strauss to Rousseau' (pp. 149ff.), Derrida expands the analysis of Lévi-Strauss begun in this essay in order further to clarify the ways in which the contradictions of traditional logic 'program' the most modern conceptual apparatuses of linguistics and the social sciences.

In this endeavor to understand the world, man therefore always has at his disposal a surplus of signification (which he shares out amongst things according to the laws of symbolic thought – which is the task of ethnologists and linguists to study). This distribution of a *supplementary* allowance [*ration supplémentaire*] – if it is permissible to put it that way – is absolutely necessary in order that on the whole the available signifier and the signified it aims at may remain in the relationship of complementarity which is the very condition of the use of symbolic thought'.[13]

(It could no doubt be demonstrated that this *ration supplémentaire* of signification is the origin of the *ratio* itself.) The word reappears a little further on, after Lévi-Strauss has mentioned 'this floating signifier, which is the servitude of all finite thought':

In other words – and taking as our guide Mauss's precept that all social phenomena can be assimilated to language – we see in *mana, Wakau, oranda* and other notions of the same type, the conscious expression of a semantic function, whose role it is to permit symbolic thought to operate in spite of the contradiction which is proper to it. In this way are explained the apparently insoluble antinomies attached to this notion. . . . At one and the same time force and action, quality and state, noun and verb; abstract and concrete, omnipresent and localized – *mana* is in effect all these things. But is it not precisely because it is none of these things that *mana* is a simple form, or more exactly, a symbol in the pure state, and therefore capable of becoming charged with any sort of symbolic content whatever? In the system of symbols constituted by all cosmologies, *mana* would simply be a zero symbolic value, that is to say, a sign marking the necessity of a symbolic content *supplementary* [my italics] to that with which the signified is already loaded, but which can take on any value required, provided only that this value still remains part of the available reserve and is not, as phonologists put it, a group-term'

Lévi-Strauss adds the note:

'Linguists have already been led to formulate hypotheses of this type. For example: 'A zero phoneme is opposed to all other phonemes in French in that it entails no differential characters and no constant phonetic value. On the contrary, the proper function of the zero phoneme is to be opposed to phoneme absence.' (R. Jakobson and J. Lutz, 'Notes on the French Phonemic Pattern', *Word* 5, no. 2 [August 1949]: 155). Similarly, if we schematize the conception I am proposing here, it could almost be said that the function of notions like *mana* is to be opposed to the absence of signification, without entailing by itself any particular signification'.[14]

The *overabundance* of the signifier, its *supplementary* character, is thus the result of a finitude, that is to say, the result of a lack which must be *supplemented*.

---

13. 'Introduction à l'oeuvre de Marcel Mauss,' in Marcel Mauss, *Sociologie et anthropologie* (Paris: P.U.F., 1950), p. xlix.
14. Ibid., pp. xlix-l.

It can now be understood why the concept of play is important in Lévi-Strauss. His references to all sorts of games, notably to roulette, are very frequent, especially in his *Conversations*,[15] in *Race and History*,[16] and in *The Savage Mind*. Further, the reference to play is always caught up in tension.

Tension with history, first of all. This is a classical problem, objections to which are now well worn. I shall simply indicate what seems to me the formality of the problem: by reducing history, Lévi-Strauss has treated as it deserves a concept which has always been in complicity with a teleological and eschatological metaphysics, in other words, paradoxically, in complicity with that philosophy of presence to which it was believed history could be opposed. The thematic of historicity, although it seems to be a somewhat late arrival in philosophy, has always been required by the determination of Being as presence. With or without etymology, and despite the classic antagonism which opposes these significations throughout all of classical thought, it could be shown that the concept of *epistēmē* has always called forth that of *historia*, if history is always the unity of a becoming, as the tradition of truth ·or the development of science of knowledge oriented toward the appropriation of truth in presence and self-presence, toward knowledge in consciousness-of-self. History has always been conceived as the movement of a resumption of history, as a detour between two presences. But if it is legitimate to suspect this concept of history, there is a risk, if it is reduced without an explicit statement of the problem I am indicating here, of falling back into an ahistoricism of a classical type, that is to say, into a determined moment of the history of metaphysics. Such is the algebraic formality of the problem as I see it. More concretely, in the work of Lévi-Strauss it must be recognized that the respect for structurality, for the internal originality of the structure, compels a neutralization of time and history. For example, the appearance of a new structure, of an original system, always comes about – and this is the very condition of its structural specificity – by a rupture with its past, its origin, and its cause. Therefore one can describe what is peculiar of the structural organization only by not taking into account, in the very moment of this description, its past conditions: by omitting to posit the problem of the transition from one structure to another, by putting history between brackets. In this 'structuralist' moment, the concepts of chance and discontinuity are indispensable. And Lévi-Strauss does in fact often appeal to them, for example, as concerns that structure of structures, language, of which he says in the 'Introduction to the Work of Marcel Mauss' that it 'could only have been born in one fell swoop':

> Whatever may have been the moment and the circumstances of its appearance on the scale of animal life, language could only have been born in

15. George Charbonnier, *Entretiens avec Claude Lévi-Strauss* (Paris: Plon, 1961).
16. *Race and History* (Paris: Unesco Publications, 1958).

one fell swoop. Things could not have set about acquiring signification progressively. Following a transformation the study of which is not the concern of the social sciences, but rather of biology and psychology, a transition came about from a stage where nothing had a meaning to another where everything possessed it.[17]

This standpoint does not prevent Lévi-Strauss from recognizing the slowness, the process of maturing, the continuous toil of factual transformations, history (for example, in *Race and History*). But, in accordance with a gesture which was also Rousseau's and Husserl's, he must 'set aside all the facts' at the moment when he wishes to recapture the specificity of a structure. Like Rousseau, he must always conceive of the origin of a new structure on the model of catastrophe – an overturning of nature in nature, a natural interruption of the natural sequence, a setting aside *of* nature.

Besides the tension between play and history, there is also the tension between play and presence. Play is the disruption of presence. The presence of an element is always a signifying and substitutive reference inscribed in a system of differences and the movement of a chain. Play is always play of absence and presence, but if it is to be thought radically, play must be conceived of before the alternative of presence and absence. Being must be conceived as presence or absence on the basis of the possibility of play and not the other way around. If Lévi-Strauss, better than any other, has brought to light the play of repetition and the repetition of play, one no less perceives in his work a sort of ethic of presence, an ethic of nostalgia for origins, an ethic of archaic and natural innocence, of a purity of presence and self-presence in speech – an ethic, nostalgia, and even remorse, which he often presents as the motivation of the ethnological project when he moves toward the archaic societies which are examplary societies in his eyes. These texts are well known.[18]

Turned towards the lost or impossible presence of the absent origin, this structuralist thematic of broken immediacy is therefore the saddened, *negative*, nostalgic, guilty, Rousseauistic side of the thinking of play whose other side would be the Nietzschean *affirmation*, that is the joyous affirmation of the play of the world and of the innocence of becoming, the affirmation of a world of signs without fault, without truth, and without origin which is offered to an active interpretation. *This affirmation then determines the noncenter otherwise than as loss of the center*. And it plays without security. For there is a *sure* play: that which is limited to the *substitution* of *given* and *existing, present*, pieces. In absolute chance, affirmation also surrenders itself to *genetic* indetermination, to the *seminal* adventure of the trace.

There are thus two interpretations of interpretation; of structure, of

17. 'Introduction à l'oeuvre de Marcel Mauss', p. xlvi.
18. TN. The reference is to *Tristes tropiques*, trans. John Russel (London: Hutchinson & Co., 1961).

sign, of play. The one seeks to decipher, dreams of deciphering a truth or an origin which escapes play and the order of the sign, and which lives the necessity of interpretation as an exile. The other, which is no longer turned toward the origin affirms play and tries to pass beyond man and humanism, the name of man being the name of that being who, throughout the history of metaphysics or of ontotheology – in other words, throughout his entire history – has dreamed of full presence, the reassuring foundation, the origin and the end of play. The second interpretation of interpretation, to which Nietzsche pointed the way, does not seek in ethnography, as Lévi-Strauss does, the 'inspiration of a new humanism' (again citing the 'Introduction to the Work of Marcel Mauss').

There are more than enough indications today to suggest we might perceive that these two interpretations of interpretation – which are absolutely irreconcilable even if we live them simultaneously and reconcile them in an obscure economy – together share the field which we call, in such a problematic fashion, the social sciences.

For my part, although these two interpretations must acknowledge and accentuate their difference and define their irreducibility, I do not believe that today there is any question of *choosing* – in the first place because here we are in a region (let us say, provisionally, a region of historicity) where the category of choice seems particularly trivial; and in the second, because we must first try to conceive of the common ground, and the *différance* of this irreducible difference. Here there is a kind of question, let us still call it historical, whose *conception, formation, gestation*, and *labor* we are only catching a glimpse of today. I employ these words, I admit, with a glance toward the operations of childbearing – but also with a glance toward those who, in a society from which I do not exclude myself, turn their eyes away when faced by the as yet unnamable which is proclaiming itself and which can do so, as is necessary whenever a birth is in the offing, only under the species of the nonspecies, in the formless, mute, infant, and terrifying form of monstrosity.

18 Roland Barthes,

'From Work to Text', *Image, Music, Text*, ed S. Heath

p155–164

It is a fact that over the last few years a certain change has taken place (or is taking place) in our conception of language and, consequently, of the literary work which owes at least its phenomenal existence to this same language. The change is clearly connected with the current development of (amongst other disciplines) linguistics, anthropology, Marxism and psychoanalysis (the term 'connection' is used here in a deliberately neutral way: one does not decide a determination, be it multiple and dialectical). What is new and which affects the idea of the work comes not necessarily from the internal recasting of each of these disciplines, but rather from their encounter in relation to an object which traditionally is the province of none of them. It is indeed as though the *interdisciplinarity* which is today held up as a prime value in research cannot be accomplished by the simple confrontation of specialist branches of knowledge. Interdisciplinarity is not the calm of an easy security; it begins *effectively* (as opposed to the mere expression of a pious wish) when the solidarity of the old disciplines breaks down – perhaps even violently, via the jolts of fashion – in the interests of a new object and a new language neither of which has a place in the field of the sciences that were to be brought peacefully together, this unease in classification being precisely the point from which it is possible to diagnose a certain mutation. The mutation in which the idea of the work seems to be gripped must not, however, be over-estimated: it is more in the nature of an epistemological slide than of a real break. The break, as is frequently stressed, is seen to have taken place in the last century with the appearance of Marxism and Freudianism; since then there has been no further break, so that in a way it can be said that for the last hundred years we have been living in repetition. What History, our History, allows us today is merely to slide, to vary, to exceed, to repudiate. Just as Einsteinian science demands that *the relativity of the frames of reference* be included in the object studied, so the combined action of Marxism, Freudianism and structuralism demands, in literature, the relativization of the relations of writer, reader and observer (critic). Over against the traditional notion of the *work*, for long – and still – conceived of in a, so to speak, Newtonian way, there is now the requirement of a new object, obtained by the sliding or overturning of former categories. That object is the *Text*. I know the word is fashionable (I am myself often led to use it) and therefore regarded by some with suspicion, but that is exactly why I should like to remind myself of the principal propositions at the intersection of which I see the Text as standing. The word 'proposition' is to be understood more in a grammatical than in a logical sense: the following are not argumentations but enunciations, 'touches', approaches that consent to remain metaphorical. Here then are these propositions; they concern method, genres, signs, plurality, filiation, reading and pleasure.

1 The Text is not to be thought of as an object that can be computed. It would be futile to try to separate out materially works from texts. In particular, the tendency must be avoided to say that the work is classic, the text avant-garde; it is not a question of drawing up a crude honours list in the name of modernity and declaring certain literary productions 'in' and others 'out' by virtue of their chronological situation: there may be 'text' in a very ancient work, while many products of contemporary literature are in no way texts. The difference is this: the work is a fragment of substance, occupying a part of the space of books (in a library for example), the Text is a methodological field. The opposition may recall (without at all reproducing term for term) Lacan's distinction between 'reality' and 'the real': the one is displayed, the other demonstrated; likewise, the work can be seen (in bookshops, in catalogues, in exam syllabuses), the text is a process of demonstration, speaks according to certain rules (or against certain rules); the work can be held in the hand, the text is held in language, only exists in the movement of a discourse (or rather, it is Text for the very reason that it knows itself as text); the Text is not the decomposition of the work, it is the work that is the imaginary tail of the Text; or again, *the Text is experienced only in an activity of production*. It follows that the Text cannot stop (for example on a library shelf); its constitutive movement is that of cutting across (in particular, it can cut across the work, several works).

2 In the same way, the Text does not stop at (good) Literature; it cannot be contained in a hierarchy, even in a simple division of genres. What constitutes the Text is, on the contrary (or precisely), its subversive force in respect of the old classifications. How do you classify a writer like Georges Bataille? Novelist, poet, essayist, economist, philosopher, mystic? The answer is so difficult that the literary manuals generally prefer to forget about Bataille who, in fact, wrote texts, perhaps continuously one single text. If the Text poses problems of classification (which is furthermore one of its 'social' functions), this is because it always involves a certain experience of limits (to take up an expression from Philippe Sollers). Thibaudet used already to talk – but in a very restricted sense – of limit-works (such as Chateaubriand's *Vie de Rancé*, which does indeed come through to us today as a 'text'); the Text is that which goes to the limit of the rules of enunciation (rationality, readability, etc.). Nor is this a rhetorical idea, resorted to for some 'heroic' effect: the Text tries to place itself very exactly *behind* the limit of the

doxa (is not general opinion – constitutive of our democratic societies and powerfully aided by mass communications – defined by its limits, the energy with which it excludes, its *censorship?*). Taking the word literally, it may be said that the Text is always *paradoxical*.

3 The Text can be approached, experienced, in reaction to the sign. The work closes on a signified. There are two modes of signification which can be attributed to this signified: either it is claimed to be evident and the work is then the object of a literal science, of philology, or else it is considered to be secret, ultimate, something to be sought out, and the work then falls under the scope of a hermeneutics, of an interpretation (Marxist, psychoanalytic, thematic, etc.); in short, the work itself functions as a general sign and it is normal that it should represent an institutional category of the civilization of the Sign. The Text, on the contrary, practices the infinite deferment of the signified, is dilatory; its field is that of the signifier and the signifier must not be conceived of as 'the first stage of meaning', its material vestibule, but, in complete opposition to this, as its *deferred action*. Similarly, the *infinity* of the signifier refers not to some idea of the ineffable (the unnameable signified) but to that of a *playing*; the generation of the perpetual signifier (after the fashion of a perpetual calender) in the field of the text (better, of which the text is the field) is realized not according to an organic progress of maturation or a hermeneutic course of deepening investigation, but, rather, according to a serial movement of disconnections, overlappings, variations. The logic regulating the Text is not comprehensive (define 'what the work means') but metonymic; the activity of associations, contiguities, carryings-over coincides with a liberation of symbolic energy (lacking it, man would die); the work – in the best of cases – is *moderately* symbolic (its symbolic runs out, comes to a halt); the Text is *radically* symbolic: *a work conceived, perceived and received in its integrally symbolic nature is a text*. Thus is the Text restored to language; like language, it is structured but off-centred, without closure (note, in reply to the contemptuous suspicion of the 'fashionble' sometimes directed at structuralism, that the epistemological privilege currently accorded to language stems precisely from the discovery there of a paradoxical idea of structure: a system with neither close nor centre).

4 The Text is plural. Which is not simply to say that it has several meanings, but that it accomplishes the very plurality of meaning: an *irreducible* (and not merely an acceptable) plural. The Text is not a co-existence of meanings but a passage, an overcrossing; thus it answers not to an interpretation, even a liberal one, but to an explosion, a dissemination. The plural of the Text depends, that is, not on the ambiguity of its contents but on what might be called the *stereographic plurality* of its weave of signifiers (etymologically, the text is a tissue, a woven fabric). The reader of the Text may be compared to someone at a loose end

(someone slackened off from any imaginary); this passably empty subject strolls – it is what happened to the author of these lines, then it was that he had a vivid idea of the Text – on the side of a valley, a *oued* flowing down below (*oued* is there to bear witness to a certain feeling of unfamiliarity); what he perceives is multiple, irreducible, coming from a disconnected, heterogeneous variety of substances and perspectives: lights, colours, vegetation, heat, air, slender explosions of noises, scant cries of birds, children's voices from over on the other side, passages, gestures, clothes of inhabitants near or far away. All these *incidents* are half identifiable: they come from codes which are known but their combination is unique, founding the stroll in a difference repeatable only as difference. So the Text: it can be it only in its difference (which does not mean its individuality), its reading is semelfactive (this rendering illusory any inductive-deductive science of texts – no 'grammar' of the text) and nevertheless woven entirely with citations, references, echoes, cultural languages (what language is not?), antecedent or contemporary, which cut across it through and through in a vast stereophony. The intertextual in which every text is held, it itself being the text-between of another text, is not to be confused with some origin of the text: to try to find the 'sources', the 'influences' of a work, is to fall in with the myth of filiation; the citations which go to make up a text are anonymous, untraceable, and yet *already read*: they are quotations without inverted commas. The work has nothing disturbing for any monistic philosophy (we know that there are opposing examples of these); for such a philosophy, plural is the Evil. Against the work, therefore, the text could well take as its motto the words of the man possessed by demons (*Mark* 5:9): 'My name is Legion: for we are many'. The plural of demoniacal texture which opposes text to work can bring with it fundamental changes in reading, and precisely in areas where monologism appears to be the Law: certain of the 'texts' of Holy Scripture traditionally recuperated by theological monism (historical or anagogical) will perhaps offer themselves to a diffraction of meanings (finally, that is to say, to a materialist reading), while the Marxist interpretation of works, so far resolutely monistic, will be able to materialize itself more by pluralizing itself (if, however, the Marxist 'institutions' allow it).

5 The work is caught up in a process of filiation. Three things are postulated: a *determination* of the work by the world (by race, then by History), a *consecution* of works amongst themselves, and a *conformity* of the work to the author. The author is reputed the father and the owner of his work: literary science therefore teaches *respect* for the manuscript and the author's declared intentions, while society asserts the legality of the relation of author to work (the '*droit d'auteur*' or 'copyright', in fact of recent date since it was only really legalized at the time of the French Revolution). As for the Text, it reads without the inscription of the Father. Here again, the metaphor of the Text separates from that of the

work: the latter refers to the image of an *organism* which grows by vital expansion, by 'development' (a word which is significantly ambiguous, at once biological and rhetorical); the metaphor of the Text is that of the *network*; if the Text extends itself, it is as a result of a combinatory systematic (an image, moreover, close to current biological conceptions of the living being). Hence no vital 'respect' is due to the Text: it can be *broken* (which is just what the Middle Ages did with two nevertheless authoritative texts – Holy Scripture and Aristotle); it can be read without the guarantee of its father, the restitution of the inter-text paradoxically abolishing any legacy. It is not that the Author may not 'come back' in the Text, in his text, but he then does so as a 'guest'. If he is a novelist, he is inscribed in the novel like one of his characters, figured in the carpet; no longer privileged, paternal, aletheological, his inscription is ludic. He becomes, as it were, a paper-author: his life is no longer the origin of his fictions but a fiction contributing to his work; there is a reversion of the work on to the life (and no longer the contrary); it is the work of Proust, of Genet which allows their lives to be read as a text. The word 'bio-graphy' re-acquires a strong, etymological sense, at the same time as the sincerity of the enunciation – a veritable 'cross' borne by literary morality – becomes a false problem: the *I* which writes the text, it too, is never more than a paper-*I*.

6 The work is normally the object of consumption; no demagogy is intended here in referring to the so-called consumer culture but it has to be recognized that today it is the 'quality' of the work (which supposes finally an appreciation of 'taste') and not the operation of reading itself which can differentiate between books: structurally, there is no difference between 'cultured' reading and casual reading in trains. The Text (if only by its frequent 'unreadability') decants the work (the work permitting) from its consumption and gathers it up as play, activity, production, practice. This means that the Text requires that one try to abolish (or at the very least to diminish) the distance between writing and reading, in no way by intensifying the projection of the reader into the work but by joining them in a single signifying practice. The distance separating reading from writing is historical. In the times of the greatest social division (before the setting up of democratic cultures), reading and writing were equally privileges of class. Rhetoric, the great literary code of those times, taught one to *write* (even if what was then normally produced were speeches, not texts). Significantly, the coming of democrary reversed the word of command: what the (secondary) School prides itself on is teaching to *read* (well) and no longer to write (consciousness of the deficiency is becoming fashionable again today: the teacher is called upon to teach pupils to 'express themselves', which is a little like replacing a form of repression by a misconception). In fact, *reading*, in the sense of consuming, is far from *playing* with the text. 'Playing' must be understood here in all its polysemy: the text itself *plays*

(like a door like a machine with 'play') and the reader plays twice over, playing the Text as one plays a game, looking for a practice which re-produces it, but, in order that that practice not be reduced to a passive, inner *mimesis* (the Text is precisely that which resists such a reduction), also playing the Text in the musical sense of the term. The history of music (as a practice, not as an 'art') does indeed parallel that of the Text fairly closely: there was a period when practising amateurs were numerous (at least within the confines of a certain class) and 'playing' and 'listening' formed a scarcely differentiated activity; then two roles appeared in sucession, first that of the performer, the interpreter to whom the bourgeois public (though still itself able to play a little – the whole history of the piano) delegated its playing, then that of the (passive) amateur, who listens to music without being able to play (the gramophone record takes the place of the piano). We know that today post-serial music has radically altered the role of the 'interpreter', who is called on to be in some sort the co-author of the score, completing it rather than giving it 'expression'. The Text is very much a score of this new kind: it asks of the reader a practical collaboration. Which is an important change, for who executes the work? (Mallarmé posed the question, wanting the audience to *produce* the book). Nowadays only the critic executes the work (accepting the play on words). The reduction of reading to a consumption is clearly responsible for the 'boredom' experienced by many in the face of the modern ('unreadable') text, the avant-garde film or painting: to be bored means that one cannot produce the text, open it out, *set it going*.

7   This leads us to pose (to propose) a final approach to the Text, that of pleasure. I do not know whether there has ever been a hedonistic aesthetics (eudaemonist philosophies are themselves rare). Certainly there exists a pleasure of the work (of certain works); I can delight in reading and re-reading Proust, Flaubert, Balzac, even – why not? – Alexandre Dumas. But this pleasure, no matter how keen and even when free from all prejudice, remains in part (unless by some exceptional critical effort) a pleasure of consumption; for if I can read these authors, I also know that I cannot *re-write* them (that it is impossible today to write 'like that') and this knowledge, depressing enough, suffices to cut me off from the production of these works, in the very moment their remoteness establishes my modernity (is not to be modern to know clearly what cannot be started over again?). As for the Text, it is bound to *jouissance*, that is to a pleasure without separation. Order of the signifier, the Text participates in its own way in a social utopia; before History (supposing the latter does not opt for barbarism), the Text achieves, if not the transparency of social relations, that at least of language relations: the Text is that space where no language has a hold over any other, where languages circulate (keeping the circular sense of the term).

These few propositions, inevitably, do not constitute the articulations of a Theory of the Text and this is not simply the result of the failings of the person here presenting them (who in many respects has anyway done no more than pick up what is being developed round about him). It stems from the fact that a Theory of the Text cannot be satisfied by a meta-linguistic exposition: the destruction of meta-language, or at least (since it may be necessary provisionally to resort to meta-language) its calling into doubt, is part of the theory itself: the discourse on the Text should itself be nothing other than text, research, textual activity, since the Text is that *social* space which leaves no language safe, outside, nor any subject of the enunciation in position as judge, master, analyst, confessor, decoder. The theory of the Text can coincide only with a practice of writing.

---

19 J. Hillis Miller,
'The Figure in the Carpet', *Poetics Today*, vol 1;3, 1980

p107–118

Images of filaments, *ficelles*, lines, figures drawn with lines, woven or embroidered cloth; thread themselves through the dense metaphorical texture of Henry James's prefaces.[1] These prefaces taken together no doubt form the most important treatise on the novel in English. A passage in the preface to *Roderick Hudson* is an appropriate place to begin, since it bears not only on the difficulty of beginning but on the even greater difficulty of stopping once one has begun. In the passage I cite, the issue is a double one: first, how, in writing a novel, to draw a line around the material to be treated, to give it an edge or border which appears as a natural stopping place in all directions beyond which there is nothing relevant to the subject, and, second, how, within those limits, to treat what is left inside the charmed circle totally and with total continuity, omitting nothing and establishing or articulating all the connec-

---

[1] This essay is drawn from a book in progress to be called *Ariadne's Thread*. The book is on the image of the line in narrative and in language about narrative. James's insight into the problems of continuity in story-telling finds an appropriate place in a study which is an extended effort to organize the unorganizable, to trace a sequential line making a figure through a tangled web of examples of linear imagery in narrative. This web extends in all directions from any given starting place in Daedalian complexity. On its surface innumerable figures might be traced, in the impossible attempt to achieve Apollonian reduction of Dionysiac materials. Such an attempt would be like that dance of the too rational Theseus, which marked out ever-changing, winding figures on the ground, compulsively retracing the labyrinth in an always frustrated desire to master it (see Damisch, 1966). The present essay is one more execution of the dance of Theseus.

tions, all of what Tolstoy, in a splendid phrase, called 'the labyrinth of linkages'.[2] Continuity and completeness, on the one hand, and finite form, on the other, this is the double necessity:

> Yet it must even then have begun for me too, the ache of fear, that was to become so familiar, of being unduly tempted and led on by 'developments'; which is but the desperate discipline of the question involved in them. They are of the very essence of the novelist's process, and it is by their aid, fundamentally, that his idea takes form and lives; but they impose on him, through the principle of continuity that rides them, a proportionate anxiety. They are the very condition of interest, which languishes and drops without them; the painter's subject consisting ever, obviously, of the related state, to each other, of certain figures and things. To exhibit these relations, once they have all been recognized, is to 'treat' his idea, which involves neglecting none of those that directly minister to interest; the degree of that directness remaining meanwhile a matter of highly difficult appreciation, and one on which the felicity of form and composition, as a part of the total effect, mercilessly rests. Up to what point is such and such a development *indispensable* to the interest? What is the point beyond which it ceases to be rigorously so? Where, for the complete expression of one's subject, does a particular relation stop – giving way to some other not concerned in that expression?[2]

Completeness; continuity; finite form – James here gives masterly expression to this triple necessity in the production of a literary text. Where is the edge of a given subject or relation within that subject? It is obviously a matter of degree, of nuance. What is the difference between 'directly' or 'rigorously' ministering to interest and only indirectly or loosely doing so, beyond the margin, peripherally? The edge is no sharp boundary but an indefinitely extending gray area, no longer quite so rigorously relevant, but not irrelevant either. At what point does a bit of accrued interest become so small that it can be dispensed with, rounded off to the nearest zero, so to speak? What does James mean here by 'figures'? The figures in the carpet? Figures of speech, embroidered flowers of rhetoric? Figures as the persons of the drama? Whatever the answers to these questions, it is clear that for James the necessity of completeness and continuity, reconciled with finite form, can never by any means other than a fictitious appearance be satisfied. The triple necessity is a triple bind.

The reasons for this are multiple. On the one hand, there is in fact no intrinsic limit to a given subject. To represent it completely would be to retrace an infinite web of relevant relations extending to the horizon and beyond, in every direction: 'Really, universally, relations stop nowhere' (P,5). It would appear, however, that this problem could be solved by the

---

[2] Cited by Erlich (1969: 241). Tolstoj was attacking critics who attempted to reduce *Anna Karenina* to a brief formula. Critics rather, he said, should inquire into 'the laws governing that labyrinth of linkages (*labirint sceplenij*) which is literary art'.

[3] Henry James (1950: 4–5). Further references to the prefaces will be identified by 'P', followed by page numbers in this text.

arbitrary drawing of a boundary line establishing an edge beyond which the writer will not allow himself to go. The fundamental act of form-giving is the establishment of a periphery. This periphery must be made to appear to be an absolutely opaque wall beyond which there is nothing, or not even a perceptible wall, but an invisible enclosure or reduction, like a piece of music in which the note C cannot appear, or like the limits, no limits, of universe which is finite but unbounded. In such a universe, one can go anywhere, in any direction, but one remains enclosed, without even encountering walls or boundaries. If 'relations stop nowhere', 'the exquisite problem of the artist is eternally but to draw, by a geometry of his own, the circle within which they shall happily *appear* to do so' (P,5).

Even when this reduction of the infinite to the finite has been accomplished, however, the problem of the limitless reforms itself within the magic circle. Continuity is everything for the novelist. This means that every possible relation must be retraced within the circle, every figure drawn on its surface. Since each entity, 'figure', or 'thing', for James, exists *as* its relations, to represent the figure or thing completely is to represent all its relations. The figure, by a cunning equivocation, is the figure made by the lines which may be drawn between it and other things, other figures. The multiplicity of these lines would be paralyzing if the writer consulted it directly. He has to know it and not to know it in order to focus on one relation without being distracted by all the others. Here is another way in which the narrative line may be described as spun out of its own impossibility. Even the tiniest temporal or spatial gap in the universal continuity would be a disaster. The writer has to be both aware of this necessity and force himself fiercely to ignore it. This is as impossible a task as being told *not* to think of something without being given a positive substitute: 'Don't think of your own name'. The artist, says James, 'is in the perpetual predicament that the continuity of things is the whole matter, for him, of comedy and tragedy; that this continuity is never, by the space of an instant or an inch, broken, and that, to do anything at all, he has at once intensely to consult and intensely to ignore it' (P,5).

The infinity and hence impossibility of the narrator's task reforms itself, then, within the arbitrary closed line which was drawn to make the infinite finite. One way to see this infinity of the finite is to recognize an equivocation in the concept of representation, an equivocation also to be encountered in the term *diegesis*. A *diegesis* is the following through of a line already there. A representation is a presenting again of something once present. Any telling is a retelling, a new line different from the first line. Therefore it contains within itself the potentiality of further repetition. One doubling invites endless redoublings.

In the passage which follows the one just quoted, James speaks of life as a featureless canvas. The novelist's work is the embroidery of figures on this surface. Life itself is a woven texture, but an undifferentiated or unfigured one. It contains the possibility of many figures rather than being a single unequivocal figure already present. Representation is the choice of one line to follow with the new thread interlaced from hole to hole on the already woven canvas of life. This new thread makes a figure, a flower on that ground. The same canvas contains the possibility, however, of an infinite number of slightly different variations on the 'original' flower, set side by side on the canvas like the figures on a quilt, but intrinsically present as possibilities of the original finite square or circle. They are in fact not only possibilities but necessities. The initial requirement was for total completeness in the retracing of all possible relations.

Here the figure of the embroidered canvas breaks down, like all such figures, and, in its breaking down, as in all such cases, reveals an impasse which was implicit as much as a conceptual as a figurative possibility in the 'original' idea to be expressed. The narrative line, word following word, episode following episode, in a linear sequence, makes a configuration, but the latent possibilities of relation in the elements of the presupposed subject demand an indefinite number of repetitive variations on any embroidered figure which happens to come first. These in fact must be thought of as superimposed or simultaneous, with no intrinsic priorities of originality and repetition, though in words they must make a line. In the spatial figure of embroidered canvas they must falsely be imaged as separate flowers side by side, extending outward in every direction on a canvas which, at first a figure for the finite surface enclosed within the charmed circle the artist has drawn by that 'geometry of his own', now must become 'boundless' once more, since it is the paradoxical unfolding of the infinity implicit in the finite. All the flowers possible on a single circle of canvas cannot be imaged in that circle but only thought of as an infinitely repeating pattern, each figure somewhat different from the last. 'All of which', says James of his claim that the demand for absolute continuity must be both intensely consulted and intensely ignored,

> will perhaps pass but for a supersubtle way of pointing the plain moral that a young embroiderer of the canvas of life soon began to work in terror, fairly, of the vast expanse of that surface, of the boundless number of its distinct perforations for the needle, and of the tendency inherent in his many-colored flowers and figures to cover and consume as many as possible of the little holes. The development of the flower, of the figure, involved thus an immense counting of holes and a careful selection among them. That would have been, it seemed to him, a brave enough process, were it not the very nature of the holes so to invite, to solicit, to persuade, to practise positively a thousand lures and deceits (P, 5–6).

The finite has here become magically infinite once more, according to the paradoxical law, which governs all James's fiction, whereby the more apparently narrow, restricted, and exclusive the focus, as for example on the relations of just four persons in *The Golden Bowl*, the more the novel is likely to extend itself to greater and greater length and even then to be unfinished in the sense of being disproportionate. Each work has what James called a 'misplaced middle', a lopsided shape seeking to be hidden by consummate dissimulation, so that the incomplete treatment of certain relations will not appear.

These 'flowers and figures', what are they? Is it a question of a single all-inclusive design encompassing the totality of the story, or is it a question of a repeating figure specified and then varied throughout the story? The figure of the flower is an ancient one for figure itself, that is, for 'flowers of rhetoric', for the anthology or bouquet of tropes in their use as the indispensable means of expressing by displacement what cannot be expressed properly, in literal language. Of what are James's flowers the figurative expression? What is the literal for these figures? The answers to these questions are impossible to give. It is a matter of both/and and at the same time of the logical impossibility of having both/and, of having something which is A and not A at once. James's figure is at once single and multiple. It is the figure of the whole and at the same time the figure of the repeated configuration of the detail. Figure is at once a name for the actual 'figure' or characters of the story, and at the same time it is the name for relation, for a design which emerges only from the retracing of 'the related state, to each other, of certain figures and things'.

'Flower' or 'figure' – the figure as flower – is James's metaphor for the configuration made by the 'realistically' treated human characters and relationships, with all their abundance of psychological and social detail. The realistic human story is the literal of which James's figure of the flower is the metaphor. On the other hand, the characters in their relationships are not the end of the story. They are themselves, in all their referential specificity, the material with which James creates the flowers or figures, the overall design of his story, like a repeated figure in a carpet. The human story is the metaphor of the figure, which, paradoxically, is the literal object of the story, though it is a literal which could never be described or named literally. It exists only in figure, as figure or flower, that is, as catachresis. Catachresis is the rhetorical name for the flower no flower which poisons the anthology of tropes, the odd man out. Catachresis is the name for that procedure whereby James uses all the realistic detail of his procedure as a novelist to name in figure, by a violent, forced, and abusive transfer, something else for which there is no literal name and therefore, within the convention of referentiality which the story as a realistic novel accepts, no existence. This something else is figure, design, the embroidered flower itself.

'The Figure in the Carpet' is James's most explicit allegorical narrative of this procedure, but it is of course the procedure of all his fiction, and in fact of fiction in general. It is not self-referentiality which subverts the assumptions and procedures of realistic fiction, since self-reference is still reference and therefore is assimilable into the assumptions of mimetic representation. This means that all those Anglo-American studies of the novel which trace the supposed gradual development within it or constant presence within it since Cervantes of self-reflection on its own procedures remain, in spite of their considerable sophistication, caught in the false assumptions of mimetic representationalism. Examples of such books are Robert Alter, 1975, Peter Garrett, 1969, Alan Friedman, 1967, and Frank Kermode, 1968. Self-referentiality is the mirror image of extra-referentiality. The former imperturbably reaffirms the assumption of the latter since the notion of self-reference depends for its definition on the assumption that there could be such a thing as a straightforwardly realistic novel, from which the self-referential novel is a deviation, modification, or development. The more or less hidden presence of catachresis in one way or another in any 'realistic' narrative, for example in the fact that there is no 'literal' language for the representation of states of consciousness and interior experience, does, however, constantly subvert the claims of literal reference of any realistic narrative, even the claims of straightforward mirroring made by the most apparently simple stories. This subversion makes all realistic narrative 'unreadable', undecidable, irreducible to any single unequivocal interpretation.

'The Figure in the Carpet' is a story which mimes this unreadability, on the thematic level, on the figurative level, and on the overall level of its organization as text. As Shlomith Rimmon has argued (1977),[4] 'The Figure in the Carpet' is fundamentally uncertain in meaning. It presents clues or narrative details supporting two incompatible readings. Therefore all those critics who have presented 'monological' readings of it have fallen into a trap set not so much by the story itself, in its presentation of an enigma which invites definitive clarification, as by their false presupposition that each work of literature has a single, logically unified meaning. Rimmon's definition of ambiguity, however, is too rational,

---

[4] See also Rimmon, 1973. Two other recent valuable discussions of James's story may be mentioned. One is Tsvetan Todorov, 1973. Though this essay does not discuss 'The Figure in the Carpet' in detail, but rather attempts to find a common theme in all James's tales, the figure in *his* carpet, so to speak, Todorov's formulation is close to my own: 'James's tales are based on the quest for an absolute and absent cause. . . . The secret of James's tales is, therefore, precisely this existence of an essential secret, of something which is not named, of an absent, overwhelming force which puts the whole machinery of the narrative into motion'. I differ from Todorov in arguing that James allows also for the possibility that the 'cause' may be not only absent but non-existent, a phantom projection. The other recent discussion of 'The Figure in the Carpet' is by Wolfgang Iser (1978: 3–10), who uses James's story as an opening illustration of the way readers have expected narratives to have kernel meanings which, once reached, will allow the reader to throw away the husk, so to speak, dismiss the surface details as superficial, mere means of access to the deeper significance. Once that is found, the story can be dispensed with as the vehicle of a separable meaning. Iser, of course, wants to argue that the meaning is in the details, but this too, as I have claimed, is part of the metaphysical paradigm.

too 'canny', too much an attempt to reduce the *mise en abîme* of any literary work, for example the novels and stories of James, to a logical scheme. The multiple ambiguous readings of James's fictions are not merely alternative possibilities. They are intertwined with one another in a system of unreadability, each possibility generating the others in an unstilled oscillation. Rimmon's concept of ambiguity, in spite of its linguistic sophistication, is a misleadingly logical schematization of the alogical in literature, that uncanny blind alley of unreadability encountered ultimately in the interpretation of any work.

The notion of unreadability must be distinguished, in one direction, from a definition of ambiguity in literature as plurisignificance or richness of meaning. In the other direction, the notion of unreadability must be distinguished from that perspectivism which holds that each reader bring something different to a text and so the text has a different meaning for each reader. Though the insight into ambiguity and irony in the New Critics, for example in Empson (from which, by the way, Rimmon distinguishes her concept of ambiguity), goes beyond the notion of plurisignificance, nevertheless, such insights tend to be covered over or controlled, within the New Criticism, by the notion of organic unity, the notion that a work has total and totalizable significance, even if that totalizing is an insight which the critic can never satisfactorily express in words. Though a literary text is seen as having a richness of meaning which is beyond paraphrase, nevertheless, for the New Criticism, that meaning makes a whole. 'Unreadability', on the other hand, is something intrinsic to the words of a work, an effect of the rhetoric or of the play of figure, concept, and narrative in the work, an effect the words of the work impose on the reader, not a result of 'reader response'. Moreover, instead of rich plurisignificance, the notion of 'unreadability' names the presence in a text of two or more incompatible or contradictory meanings which imply one another or are intertwined with one another, but which may by no means be felt or named as a unified totality. 'Unreadability' names the discomfort of this perpetual lack of closure, like a Möbius strip which has two sides, but only one side, yet two sides still, interminably.

There is nothing new about the experience of the working of language in literature to which the name 'unreadability' is sometimes today given. The great writers themselves through all the centuries of our tradition have tended to know this experience, as their works show. Readers, however, sometimes even writers in their readings of their own work, have tended to be beguiled by the lure of single and totalizable meaning, which is the lure of metaphysics as such. They have tended to believe in the presence of some *logos*, some single meaning for each work. This lure is always present as the other side of the coin of unreadability. Unreadability is the generation by the text itself of a desire for the possession of the *logos*, while at the same time the text itself frustrates this desire, in a torsion of undecidability which is intrinsic to language. The text itself leads the reader to believe that he ought to be able to say what it means, while at the same time making that saying impossible. This, I am arguing, is what 'The Figure in the Carpet' is about, though to claim that one can, in so many words, say what it is 'about' is of course to succumb to the lure, to take the bait. It might be better to say that the story dramatizes the experience of unreadability, or, rather, since this experience can only be named in figure, it presents figures for it, not least in the recurrent pattern of interpersonal relations which forms the human base for the story's allegorizing of its own unreadability.

The 'figure in the carpet' is on the 'literal' level the figure used by the narrator to formulate his understanding of Vereker's claim that all his work as a novelist is unified by the presence of a single all-inclusive design or meaning which none of his critics has noticed, though it is what all the work is written to reveal. The reader of this admirably comic story must therefore figure out what is meant by this figure in the carpet, and figure out also what is meant by the adjacent terms and figures for this figure which the narrator or Vereker, at one time or another, use:

> 'Isn't there', [asks Vereker in his midnight confidence to the narrator,] 'for every writer a particular thing of that sort, the thing that most makes him apply himself, the thing without the effort to achieve which he wouldn't write at all, the very passion of his passion, the part of the business in which, for him, the flame of art burns most intensely? Well, it's that! . . .
>
> . . . there's an idea in my work without which I wouldn't have given a straw for the whole job. It's the finest fullest intention of the lot, and the application of it has been, I think, a triumph of patience, of ingenuity. I ought to leave that to somebody else to say; but that nobody does say it is precisely what we're talking about. It stretches, this little trick of mine, from book to book, and everything else, comparatively, plays over the surface of it. The order, the form, the texture of my books will perhaps someday constitute for the initiated a complete representation of it. So it's naturally the thing for the critic to look for. It strikes me . . . even as the thing for the critic to find'.[5]

The unifying design is here spoken of as an 'idea' behind, or below, the work and yet 'in' it too. It existed first as a patronizing matrix in the mind of its author, father and mother at once, a generative 'passion' or 'intention', which was then 'applied'. What, however, was the base of this idea in the mind of the novelist? 'I wondered as I walked away', says the narrator, exasperated at their second meeting by Vereker's refusal to give him any clue to the figure in the carpet of his works, 'where he had got *his* tip' (241). After the 'idea' has been 'applied', the intention fulfilled, it exists as an immanent and yet transcendent pattern within and behind the work, present both in the part of it and in the whole, and

---

[5] Henry James (1909: 230–231). Further references to 'The Figure in the Carpet' will be identified by page numbers in this text.

at the same time above and beyond the work as its presiding paternal genius. The work as totality, its 'surface', or 'texture', or 'form', that is, what is superficially visible in it, is a gradually self-completing picture of the figure. The structure in question, one can see, is the basic meta-physical one of the *logos* of God, for example, as the creative word who is present in all his creations as their ground, as the signature written everywhere in the creation, but who is always present in veiled form, since he can manifest himself, by definition, only in disguised, delegated, or represented appearances. The figure in the carpet is visible, the overall pattern of Vereker's work which ought to stare any critic in the face. At the same time it is necessarily hidden, since anything visible is not it but the sign, signature, or trace of an 'it' which is always absent. In short, the figure is precisely a figure, a substitution.

The various figures for this figure, glyphs or hieroglyphs, are dispersed everywhere in 'The Figure in The Carpet', whether in local verbal clues, or in the design of interpersonal relations the story makes. All these figures reinforce or restate the traditional metaphysical paradox of the creative *logos*, as well as its always present subversive anaglyph, the 'idea' that there is no idea, the idea that the figure behind the surface is a phantasm generated by the play of superficial and visible figurative elements. Neither of these ideas is possible without the other. Each generates the other in a regular rhythm of unreadability, figure and ground reversing constantly.

The development of the story in 'The Figure in the Carpet' is punc-tuated by a wonderfully comic series of clues playing on the various con-tradictory possibilities latent in the 'logocentric' image: that it is within, as contained within container, that it is beneath, that it is behind, that it is a pervasive hidden thread, that it is all surface and no depth and so a fraud, that it does not exist at all, that it is abyss, that it is a fatal lure, the appearance of food or of satisfaction which destroys the one who yields to its promise. These clues are always figures, since the 'it' can only be expressed in figure. There are no literal terms for the 'it', which means that these figures are, once more, examples of the figure that explodes the distinction between literal and figurative: *catachresis*. Rhythm, ratio, or proportion, measure of all – the figure is an idea, a design, a general and organizing intention; subjective as latent theoretical possi-bility, and yet existing only as objective theatrical pattern; within, behind, below; hidden, and yet revealed; ground, groundless abyss, and yet surface pattern, all three; secret, perhaps phantasmal, thread, and yet the figure made by the visible beads strung on that thread – in short, *logos*.

'Is it a kind of esoteric message?' asks the delightfully obtuse narrator. To whch Vereker replies, 'Ha my dear fellow, it can't be described in cheap journalese!' (233). Vereker refuses to give any of his readers a clue to his labyrinth because, as he says, 'my whole lucid effort gives him the clue – every page and line and letter. The thing's as concrete there as a bird in a cage, a bait on a hook, a piece of cheese in a moustetrap. It's stuck into every volume as your foot is stuck into your shoe. It governs every line, it choses every word, it dots every i, it places every comma' (233). Immanent law which governs every detail and is therefore present in that detail, as contained with container, foot in shoe, this 'thing' has the power of punctuating the line of the narrative, establishing the rhythm of pauses in the chain of signs which is essential to its meaning. It also gives heads to what might otherwise be decapitated, without a ruling energy of capitalization. It dots every i. It gives a ruling law to the miniscule detail by establishing a pervasive law or figure of the whole. At the same time, the 'thing' leads the one who sees it by the false promise of satisfaction, of filling, a saturating of emptiness and blandness. This promise, however, leads to a diabolical satire of fulfillment. It leads in fact to the abyss of death. The beautiful caged bird changes in mid-chain of figures into the bait to trap the presumably safely theoretical spectator, watching at a distance, as in a theater. 'It' is a food which becomes a means of execution. Vereker's images are as much a warning as a promise. 'Give it up – give it up!' he mockingly but also 'earnestly' and 'anxiously' says to the narrator at the end of their midnight dialogue (235).

The 'general intention' of Vereker's work is, as the narrator guesses, 'a sort of buried treasure' (235), visible, audible, or detectable as a faint odor, as whiffs and hints, . . . faint wandering notes of a hidden music' (244). It is a veiled idol or goddess (251), and yet visible as a mode of behavior betraying the goddess in her mortal incarnation. This mode is the rhythm of movement in the text itself: *vera incessu patuit dea*! (251). 'It's the very string', says Vereker, 'that my pearls are strung on!' (241). In short, as the narrator guesses, it is 'something like a complex figure in a Persian carpet' (240). Inside, outside; visible, hidden, 'It' is also absent, hollow, a hoax, a vacancy: 'The buried treasure was a bad joke, the general intention a monstrous *pose*' (236), says the narrator, in exasperation, and later: 'I know what to think then. It's nothing!' (266).

The best, and most comic, expression for this last possibility is a significantly displaced one. It is shifted from the work of the strongly masculine, even male chauvinist, Vereker ('A woman will never find out', he says of his secret figure [239]), to the parody of that work in the first novel by Gwendolen Erme, the lady in the story who is fascinated by Vereker's work and who is passed from man to man among the critics who are fascinated by it in their turn. 'I got hold of "Deep Down" again', says the narrator, of her first novel; 'it was a desert in which she had lost herself, but in which too she had dug a wonderful hole in the sand – a cavity . . .' (250). The title and the figurative description of this novel, the title of Gwendolen Erme's second, slightly better, novel, *Overmastered*[!] ('As a tissue tolerably intricate it was a carpet with a figure of its own; but the figure was not the figure I was looking for' [267]), the title of Vereker's last work, *The Right of Way*, and the name of the journal for which the narrator, Corvick, and the others write reviews, *The Middle* – all these are dispersed clues, the names of absent and unattainable texts. These titles reinforce the image of a journey of penetration, crossing barriers, reaching depths, but remaining always, precisely, in the middle, on the way. With however much of a right of way one is never finally in the arcanum. One remains always face to face with some mediating sign, obstacle as well as promise, trace of an absence.

This structure is repeated in the chain of interpersonal relations which organizes James's story. It is a chain so absurd, when the reader thinks of it, as to be one of the major sources of comedy in the tale, what the narrator calls 'a series of phenomena so strangely interlaced' (260). Behind the whole series is Vereker's sick wife. Her illness, 'which has long kept her in retirement' (246), is the reason the great novelist goes south, never to be seen again by the narrator. His friend, Corvick, however, identifies the figure in the carpet of Vereker's work in a flash of intuition. Corvick visits Vereker in the south to have his insight confirmed. Presumably he passes his secret on to his wife Gwendolen (or does he?). She in turn may or may not have given her secret to her second husband, the egregious Drayton Deane, though Deane appears to be honest in his denials of knowledge. One by one, after Vereker's death, and then after the death of his wife (who probably, the narrator says, had never seen the figure in the carpet anyway), the possessors of the secret die. They die so abruptly and so fortuitously as to suggest that possession of this secret is deadly, like looking on the goddess naked. The newly-married Corvick falls from a dogcart on his head and is killed on the spot, leaving his critical essay on Vereker, which was to have revealed all, a mere useless fragment. Gwendolen, who has married Corvick and presumably received the secret as a wedding present, then marries Drayton Deane, but dies in childbirth without telling the narrator the secret and perhaps without having revealed it to her new husband either.

The passing on of the secret obviously has something to do with sexual intimacy and sexual knowledge. The narrator's 'impotence' (273) seems connected with his celibacy, though both he and Drayton Deane at the end of the story are left equally 'victims of unappeased desire' (277), in spite of the fact that Deane was not celibate. 'Corvick', says the narrator, 'had kept his information from his young friend till after the removal of the last barrier to their intimacy – then only had he let the cat out of the bag. Was it Gwendolen's idea, taking a hint from him, to liberate this animal only on the basis of the renewal of such a relation? Was the figure in the carpet traceable or describable only for husbands and wives – for lovers supremely united? (265). What *is* revealed in sexual knowledge? Is it nothing at all? Is sexual experience a figure of death, an absence, the absence of any heading power, any law able to put dots on the i's, or is it rather some ultimate presence, capital source or phallogocentric origin, yarn beam, loom (*istos*)[6], on which is woven the figure in the carpet? Is that figure the figure of nothing, or is it the figure of the *logos*? There is no way to know. James's story remains alogical, caught in the oscillation among these various possibilities. It remains a *mise en abîme* of analogies, not least important of which is the analogy between the frustrated activity of decipherment performed on Vereker's work by the narrator and that performed on James's own figure in the carpet by any reader.

To return, then, after this digression (or is 'The Figure in the Carpet' not smack in the middle of the right of way?), to James's preface to *Roderick Hudson*. There the figure of the figure in the carpet is, the reader will remember, both figurative and literal, both a name of the design of relations among the human figures in the story and the 'it' which is the literal goal of the story, as the young author works away month after month at his 'pale embroidery' (P, 6). The images of cloth and the figures woven on that cloth reappear, in fact, both before and after the passage I began with from the preface, in obedience to the law of that compulsion to repeat which seems intrinsic to signs. It seems as though signs must have a genetic life of their own, like some viral energy of replication appropriating foreign conceptual material to their own shape.

It is by way of the metaphor describing *Roderick Hudson* as his first adventure out of the shallow waters of the short story into deep water in the larger ship of the novel that the metaphor of canvas is first introduced: 'The subject of 'Roderick' figures [!] to me vividly this employment of canvas, and I have not forgotten, even after long years, how the blue southern sea seemed to spread immediately before me and the breath of the spice-islands to be already in the breeze' (P, 4). After this figure, introduced so casually and so artificially (in the sense that its figurative nature is made obvious), is fully exploited in the theoretical paragraph I discussed above, it reappears once more in the subsequent return to reminiscences about the writing of *Roderick Hudson*. It returns as an image of the fact that the novel had not been finished when it began to appear in monthly parts. This fact 'is one of the silver threads of the recoverable texture of that embarrassed phase' (P, 6). The sequence of paragraphs is like a quilt with squares in repeating patterns.

How can this series of compulsive duplications be stopped from proliferating endlessly? This is the question James addresses at the end of the theoretical development of the image of the embroidered flower. The image is of a seduction. The embroidering novelist, 'masculine' perhaps

---

[6] The Greek word ιστός means ship's mast; weaver's yarn-beam; loom; warp; web; tissue; spider's web; honeycomb; wand, rod, shaft, shank; penis.

in his activity of piercing all those little holes with his needle, is 'feminine' in his act of 'covering' them and in the passivity of his yielding to the invitation of the perforated surface. He follows it wherever it may lead. It is, the reader will remember, 'the very nature of the holes so to invite, to solicit, to persuade, to practise positively a thousand lures and deceits'. The problem, once the writer is led astray, seduced, is how ever to stop. He must initially assume that there is some loving fatherly power, paternal and patronizing. This father would govern the whole and give it visible boundaries, a beginning and an end. Such a power would act as the law or *logos* of the whole fabric.

Alas, no such power exists. The writer must act as his own father, in an act of self-generating which is at the same time a self-mutilation, an act of surrender and sacrifice. The writer can come to an end, make form, preserve himself from the abyss of the interminable, only by his willingness to practice a *découpage* at the moment of 'cruel crisis'. This crisis is an encounter at the crossroads which reverses the Oedipal murder. The artist as father, as patron, cuts off the potentially infinite power of the artist as son, as weaver, as artificer. Only this act of giving up can draw the line which makes narrative possible, defining narration as a feminine and at the same time masculine activity of embroidery. It pierces the little holes on the prepared canvas with a threaded needle and makes the figure in the carpet:

> The prime effect of so sustained a system, so prepared a surface, is to lead on and on; while the fascination of following resides, by the same token, in the presumability *somewhere* of a convenient, of a visibly-appointed stopping-place. Art would be easy indeed if, by a fond power disposed to "patronise" it, such conveniences, such simplifications, had been provided. We have, as the case stands, to invent and establish them, to arrive at them by a difficult, dire process of selection and comparison, of surrender and sacrifice. The very meaning of expertness is acquired courage to brace one's self for the cruel crisis from the moment one sees it grimly loom (P, 6).

References

Alter, Robert, 1975, *Partial Magic* (Berkeley: California UP).

Damisch, Hubert, 1966, 'Le Danse de Thésée', *Tel Quel* 26, 60–68.

Erlich, Victor, 1969, *Russian Formalism: History – Doctrine* (Hague, Paris: Mouton).

Garrett, P., 1969, *Scene and Symbol from George Eliot to James Joyce: Studies in Changing Fictional Mode* (New Haven: Yale UP).

Friedman, A., 1967, *Turn of the Novel* (New York: Oxford UP).

Iser, Wolfgang, 1978, *The Act of Reading: A Theory of Aesthetic Response* (London and Henley: Routledge and Kegan Paul).

James, Henry, 1909, *The Novels and Tales* XV (New York: Charles Scribner's Sons)
1950, *The Art of the Novel, Critical Prefaces*, R.P. Blackmur, ed. (New York: Charles Scribner's Sons).

Kermode Frank, 1968, *The Sense of an Ending* (Oxford UP).

Rimmon, Shlomith, 1973, 'Barthes' "Hermeneutic Code" and Henry James's Literary Detective: Plot-Composition in "The Figure in the Carpet", *HSL* 1, 183–207.

1977, *The Concept of Ambiguity: the Example of James* (Chicago UP).

Todorov, Tsvetan, 1973, 'The Structural Analysis of Literature: The Tales of Henry James,' in: David Robey, ed., *Structuralism: an Introduction* (Oxford: Clarendon Press), 73–103.

---

20 Shlomith Rimmon-Kenan,

Deconstructive Reflections on Deconstruction; In Reply to Hillis Miller', *Poetics Today*, vol 2;1b 1980/1

p185–188

Hillis Miller's fascinating text in the last issue of *Poetics Today* (1980: 107–118) discusses, among other things, a theory I proposed in *The Concept of Ambiguity: the Example of James* (1977). Although only a short section of his article is devoted to a direct disagreement with that theory, I undertake this reply, because what is at stake are not merely differences (and similarities) between two readings of James's 'The Figure in the Carpet', nor solely a distinction between 'ambiguity' and 'unreadability' but a confrontation between a structuralist (or structuralist-affiliated) and a deconstructive (or post-structuralist) approach. My purpose here is not to reject Miller's rejection of my analysis, but to show how his deconstructive stance inevitably leads to an inclusion of the opposed – "constructive" or structuralist – stance and vice-versa. Since the paradoxical interlocking of deconstruction and its opposite was best described by Miller himself in 'The Critic as Host' (1979: 217–253) – published before but perhaps written after 'The Figure in the Carpet' article – I shall enter into the intertextual game and answer Miller at least partly by quoting Miller. Moreover, in pointing out the necessary oscillation between Miller's view and mine, I am also tracing in the realm of theory a pattern similar to the one he has detected in 'The Figure in the Carpet'. It is thus not only with the help of his other article but also in the name of his own treatment of James's story that I would like to question his objection to my opposed view of the same text, and of ambiguity in general.

In my book (1977), I suggested a more sharply focused definition of 'ambiguity' than those currently used, and distinguished it from cognate phenomena like 'multiple meaning', 'complexity', 'irony', 'openness', 'indeterminacy'. Ambiguity, I argued, is the 'conjunction' of exclusive disjuncts, or – in less technical language – the co-existence of mutually exclusive readings.[1] In this restricted sense, the term was meant to characterize some, not all, literary texts (e.g., works by James, Gogol, Robbe-Grillet, Sarraute, Pynchon). By providing incompatible, yet equally tenable possibilities, ambiguity renders choice impossible and frustrates the reader's expectations of a univocal, definitive meaning. In spite of this challenge to univocality, ambiguity (in my sense of the term) remains a relatively closed phenomenon, subordinating most of the data to the mutually exclusive readings and restricting uncertainty to an insoluble oscillation between the opposed members of a logical contradiction ('a' and 'not a'). It is precisely this that Miller objects to:

> Rimmon's definition of ambiguity, however, is too rational, too 'canny', too much an attempt to reduce the *mise en abîme* of any literary work, for example the novels and stories of James, to a logical scheme. The multiple ambiguous readings of James's fictions are not merely alternative possibilities. They are intertwined with one another in a system of unreadability, each possibility generating the others in unstilled oscillation. Rimmon's concept of ambiguity, in spite of its linguistic sophistication, is a misleadingly logical schematization of the alogical in literature, that uncanny blind alley of unreadability encountered ultimately in the interpretation of any work (1980: 112).

Thus Miller replaces my notion of ambiguity by a notion of undecidability or unreadability. Furthermore, the applicability of his notion is not confined to one category of texts but promoted to a characteristic of all literary texts. I would like to question this move in two respects, the first regarding ambiguity in my narrow sense, the second relating to the broader notion of undecidability or unreadability.

An analysis of the so-called undecidability of a strictly ambiguous text is bound to yield the exclusive disjuncts from which it hoped to escape. Thus, many of Miller's statements about James's story fall into a pattern of mutual exclusives, and his very description of the 'rhythm of unreadability' as that of 'figure and ground reversing constantly' is identical to my description of ambiguity (1977: ix–xi). In order to show how the binary oppositions constitutive of ambiguity are inevitably repeated in Miller's own language, let me quote from his text at some length:

1) The figure in the carpet is visible, the overall pattern of Vereker's work which ought to stare any critic in the face. At the same time it is necessarily hidden, since anything visible is not it but the sign, signature, or trace of an 'it' which is always absent (p. 114).

---

[1] This is further specified for narrative as the co-existence of mutually exclusive *fabulas* in one *sjuzhet* which – closer to the surface – takes the form of the co-existence of mutually exclusive systems of gap-filling clues, but these technical details are not essential to my argument here.

2) All these figures reinforce or restate the traditional metaphysical paradox of the creative *logos*, as well as its always present subversive anaglyph, the 'idea' that there is no idea, the idea that the figure behind the surface is the phantasm generated by the play of superficial and visible figurative elements (p. 114).
3) Inside, outside; visible, hidden, 'It' is also absent, hollow, a hoax, a vacancy (p. 115).
4) Presumably he passes his secret on to his wife Gwendolen (or does he?). She in turn may or may not have given her secret to her second husband, the egregious Drayton Deane, though Deane appears to be honest in his denials of knowledge (p. 116).
5) What *is* revealed in sexual knowledge? Is it nothing at all? Is sexual experience a figure of death, an absence, the absence of any heading power, any law able to put dots on the i's, or is it rather some ultimate presence, capital source or phallogocentric origin, yarn, beam, loom (*istos*), on which is woven the figure in the carpet? (p. 117)

Miller's account of the unreadability of an ambiguous text thus often reduces it to the clash between mutual exclusives dictated by ambiguity. In fact, the above quotations are rather similar to several specific points which came up in the course of my analysis of the same story (1977: 99, 100, 102, 107, 108, 109). Such is the inescapable trap an ambiguous text sets for its readers.

But, Miller says, the conflicting possibilities are not only mutually exclusive: they generate each other in a regular rhythm of unreadability (p. 114). It is to the general concept of unreadability I turn now. As shown above, Miller replaces the narrow notion of ambiguity as a feature of some texts by the broad notion of unreadability as a characteristic of all texts. One drawback of such a procedure is that it would ultimately do away with the *differentia specifica* of those texts I labelled ambiguous, but this is not my main concern here. What is particularly interesting in the present context is that Miller's method of deconstruction, taken to its logical conclusion, cannot supplant ambiguity by unreadability. Instead, it produces a continuous alternation between the two, each inevitably leading to the other.

Unreadability, for Miller, 'names the presence in a text of two or more incompatible or contradictory meanings which imply each other or are intertwined with one another, but which may by no means be felt or named as a unified totality' (1980: 113). And yet his discussion of 'The Figure in the Carpet' as 'miming' or 'allegorizing' (112, 113) its own unreadability yields precisely that unified totality which unreadability is supposed to subvert:

Unreadability is the generation by the text itself of a desire for the possession of the *logos*, while at the same time the text itself frustrates this desire, in a torsion of undecidability which is intrinsic to language. The text itself leads the reader to believe that he ought to be able to say what it means, while at the same time making that saying impossible. This, I am arguing, is what 'The Figure in the Carpet' is about, though to claim that one can, in so many words, say that it is 'about' is of course to succumb to the lure, to take the bait (p. 113).

In spite of the reservation in the last sentence and of the reformulation in the sentence which follows, unreadability turns from an impossibility of stating meaning to a statement of this impossibility as the meaning of this particular text. This crystallization of unreadability into a kind of 'last word' paradoxically makes it more readable than the ambiguity which it was meant to replace. While ambiguity keeps oscillating between mutually exclusive possibilities, unreadability uncannily becomes the one and only possibility. Can one escape from such closure?

In 'The Critic as Host' (1979), Miller seems to find a way out (without directly confronting the above question), but it involves a re-instatement of indecidability within a binary opposition:

> This might be defined by saying that the critic can never show decisively whether or not the work of the writer is 'decidable', whether or not it is capable of being definitively interpreted (1979: 248).

In a different context, Barbara Johnson makes a similar point:

> If we could be sure of the difference between the determinable and the undeterminable, the undeterminable would be comprehended within the determinable. What is undecidable is precisely whether a thing is decidable or not (1977: 504).

If what is undecidable is whether a thing is decidable or not, we remain with two possibilities between which we cannot choose: 'a' – it is decidable; 'not a' – it is not decidable. And what is such a contradiction if not the 'a and not a' which I claim is the 'basic formula' of ambiguity (1977: 6, 8–9, and elsewhere)?

Just as in 'The Figure in the Carpet' the figurative and the literal are like figure and ground reversing constantly (Miller, 1980: 111, 112), so ambiguity and undecidability incessantly change positions. When an unequivocal statement of ambiguity (like mine) seems too 'decidable', undecidability is called upon (e.g., by Miller) to escape from this constrictive closure. But undecidability itself soon rigidifies into a meaning, i.e., another form of the decidable closure (as in Miller, 1980). What is then invoked is the very undecidability between decidability and undecidability (Miller, 1979). This, however, involves a logical deadlock between mutual exclusives which forms ambiguity (in my sense), and so on in infinite regress.

What is true of ambiguity and undecidability is also true of the two intellectual frameworks within which they are formulated: structuralism and deconstruction. Here Miller himself (1979:230) comes to my help. Emphasizing the 'inherence of metaphysics in nihilism and of nihilism in metaphysics', he then detects the same interdependence between the 'obvious' and the 'deconstructionist' readings of texts (what he says about the 'obvious' reading applies equally to a 'structuralist' analysis of the kind practised in my *The Concept of Ambiguity*):

> In fact, neither the 'obvious' reading nor the 'deconstructionist' reading is univocal. Each contains, necessarily, its enemy within itself, is itself both host and parasite. The deconstructionist reading contains the obvious one and vice versa (1979:226).

Thus a deconstructive reading need not supplant a structuralist reading, as it implicitly claims to do in Miller's article on 'The Figure in the Carpet' (1980). Instead, the two approaches appear to imply each other in a constant see-saw movement. Within this movement, the deconstructionist notion of undecidability or unreadability introduces the uncanny into a 'rational' notion like ambiguity, but ambiguity, in turn, can subvert the paradoxical univocality of the supposedly 'alogical' undecidability. In the realm of the uncanny, it is paradoxically the canny that becomes 'the uncanniest of all guests' (Nietzsche, 1968: 7, quoted by Miller, 1979:227, 253).

References

Johnson, Barbara, 1977, 'The Frame of Reference: Poe, Lacan, Derrida', *Yale French Studies* 55/56, 457–505.

Miller, J. Hillis, 1979, 'The Critic as Host', in: Harold Bloom *et al.*, eds., *Deconstruction and Criticism* (New York: The Seabury Press).

1980, 'The Figure in the Carpet', *Poetics Today* 1:3, 107–118.

Rimmon, Shlomith, 1977. *The Concept of Ambiguity: the Example of James* (Chicago UP).

21 J. Hillis Miller,

'A Guest in the House; Reply to Shlomith Rimmon-Kenan's Reply', *Poetics Today*, vol 2/1b, 1980/81

p189–191

I thank Shlomith Rimmon-Kenan for her courteous, intelligent, and penetrating comment on my 'The Figure in the Carpet', published in the Spring (1980) issue of *Poetics Today*. I much admire her *The Concept of Ambiguity, The Example of James* (1977) and was, in what I said of her book in my essay, attempting to measure the differences between us, as well as the similarities. Her reply gives me a chance to think about this again. In reading that reply I have had the experience, probably common in such cases, of feeling 'She's doing it again', that is, repeating those features of her original work which seemed to me to differ from my way of reading James's story. Those features are primarily forms of a schematizing rationality devoted to intellectual mastery, whereas I was attempting to 'express' the 'experience' (both words must be put in suspension) of the failure of an attempt at mastery.

No doubt I failed in this. No doubt my formulations, like all such formulations, are, as Shlomith Rimmon-Kenan says, too decisive, too canny, to avoid being recuperable within such concepts as 'ambiguity' or 'binary opposition'. Precisely. This was the point I was making. My own discourse is necessarily an example of the failure I was trying to identify. Had I succeeded I would have failed. Only by failing could I succeed, which is lucky, since, like everyone else playing this game, like the characters, including the narrator, in 'The Figure in the Carpet', like Henry James himself, I am certain to lose it. (No doubt at this point Shlomith Rimmon-Kenan, if she reads this, will say, 'He's doing it again.') Nevertheless, though losing is inevitable here, there are different forms of it, and I have one or two more remarks to make about the differences between Shlomith Rimmon-Kenan's procedures with 'The Figure in the Carpet' and mine. I shall try to make them as economically canny as possible. In these regions the traveler needs as much of the protective shield of logic as he can get.

First point: Shlomith Rimmon-Kenan is right to say that more is at stake between us than a question of slightly different ways of reading James's 'The Figure in the Carpet'. The two readings set against one another that form of criticism called 'structuralist' and that form called 'deconstructive'. To what she says of the differences I would add that the difference in 'tone' or 'style' of critical discourse (I don't know quite what to call it) is decisive here. Structuralism, as practiced for example by Shlomith Rimmon-Kenan in her book on James, is reasoned, more or less abstract, given to diagrams and tables. It is written from within an international community of researchers sharing the same goals, the same norms and procedures, and speaking the same language of analysis. The way of coding references to previous works in *Poetics Today* is a good example of this. Like the other features of tone and style in question it incorporates the essays in *Poetics Today* within the domain of linguistics and the other 'human sciences', those in turn within a larger domain including the social and physical sciences, as part of a world-wide collective enterprise of technicalization and scientific mastery. James's story is one more item in the vast inventory of items, physical, social, and linguistic; mesons, phonemes, and the customs of the Kwakiutl, offering themselves to be rationally mastered. The concept of ambiguity as developed by Shlomith Rimmon-Kenan in her admirable book (' "a" and "not a" ') is a specialized tool needed in this particular case to get hold of certain stories by James and other writers, just as the diffraction grating is needed for spectrum analysis.

The goal of 'deconstruction' is very different from this. The system of assumptions defining the collective enterprise of scientific mastery is one of the things it wants to put in question by disarticulating it or by showing that it disarticulates itself. This means showing that it contains contradictions and aporias makings its enterprise impossible. Deconstruction wants to show the impossibility of mastery, for example the impossibility of mastering James's story by means of such an analytical tool as Shlomith Rimmon-Kenan's concept of ambiguity. No doubt it fails in this. To that moment of failure it has sometimes given the names 'unreadability' or 'undecidability', which, as Shlomith Rimmon-Kenan notes, are to be defined as the impossibility of deciding whether or not a given text is 'decidable' or 'determinate' in meaning, that is, 'readable' according to a common definition of readability. If this is a case of ' "a" and "not a," ' it is a sepcial case, namely the reflexive case that undermines the law which would subsume it. This moment, when analysis turns back on itself to pull the carpet, figured or not, out from under itself, is a crucial one in demonstrative criticism, as, for example, the moment in Jacques Derrida's 'La Mythologie blanche' (1972) when he speaks of the one inaugural metaphor too many which escapes the definition of metaphor since it was necessary to construct the definition of metaphor in the first place, or the moment in a more recent essay, 'La Loi du genre/The law of Genre' (1980), in which Derrida writes of the way the mark of generic belonging escapes the law of genre. If structuralism is an enterprise of mastery, deconstruction sees all analytical discourse as being invaded, contaminated, finally mastered by the illogic it would master.

Second point: Another important difference between my assumptions and those of Shlomith Rimmon-Kenan is signalled by her in passing: 'Miller replaces the narrow notion of ambiguity as a feature of some texts by the broad notion of unreadability as a characteristic of all texts'. As she says, 'one drawback of such a procedure is that it would ultimately do away with the *differentia specifica* of these texts I labelled ambiguous'. Precisely. Though much is at stake here and a full working out would take too much space, it can be said that this desire to limit the range of ambiguity and to make it a tool of differentiation is one of the features Shlomith Rimmon-Kenan's procedure shares with that of 'science'. There are certain works which are ambiguous, just as there are certain roses which are pink, or certain elementary particles which have a negative charge. If the concept of ambiguity may be formulated as ' "a" and "not a" ', the concept itself is developed to facilitate clear distinctions between ' "a" and "not a" '. Shlomith Rimmon-Kenan mentions

'James, Gogol, Robbe-Grillet, Sarraute, Pynchon' as writers of ambiguous texts in her sense, i.e., 'the "conjunction" of exclusive disjuncts'. It will be noted that all these writers are novelists and that all are 'modern'. Her study of James is supported by received notions of genre of a literary history which it does not on the whole challenge. This is one of the ways it belongs to that vast collective 'scientific' enterprise. The 'notion' or 'experience' of unreadability, on the other hand, since it is a feature in one way or another of all literary works, tends to break down such generic and historical distinctions. If it does not make literary history impossible, it requires a redefinition of what is meant by 'genres', 'periods', 'tradition', 'influences', 'history', 'literature' itself – all the *differentia specifica* of 'traditional' 'literary' 'history' (all three of these words must be separately put in quotation marks).

Third and final point: Shlomith Rimmon-Kenan identifies or exemplifies well enough the comic see-saw whereby each method of interpretation attempts to encompass its antagonists by defining them as special or incomplete versions of its own procedures. If I saw her notion of ambiguity as a flawed version of 'indecidability', in her comment on my essay she tries to demonstrate that I was showing that James's story is ambiguous in her sense, i.e. governed by binary oppositions which must both be true, on the evidence of the text, though they are logically incompatible. Something curious happens, however, as her comment continues, something already signaled in her title, which was presumably added after the reply was written. From the straightforward claim that I was doing the same thing she was doing (the binary opposite of my claim that she was [imperfectly] a deconstructionist), she moves on toward seeing an oscillation in 'infinite regress' between structuralism and deconstruction: 'Just as in The Figure in the Carpet' the figurative and the literal are like figure and ground reversing constantly (Miller, 1980:111, 112), so ambiguity and undecidability incessantly change positions.' Precisely. The necessary inherence of one position in the other, as opposed to their side-by-side presentation, is one of the distinctions I make in my essay between what 'deconstruction' finds in contradictions and what 'ambiguity' finds. The 'canniness' of the first part of Shlomith Rimmon-Kenan's reply becomes, as the comment continues, contaminated by the 'uncanny' she is trying to encompass. She ends up sounding more more like a deconstructionist here than she does in her book on James. The last part of her reply has considerable eloquence and power, but it is eloquence of a deconstructive sort. It is now no longer, 'She is doing it again', but that she starts doing, to some degree at least, what I was doing: 'She [He] is [are] doing it again'.

This is a striking case of the way scientific rationality in literary criticism cannot avoid being invaded by the 'alogical' in the literary texts it seeks to reduce. This would suggest that the language of literature cannot be seen as one more object among others for 'scientific' language to master, but is something dangerous to the whole enterprise of science. It is not only masterable. It also tends to subvert the language of the would-be master. It might be safest for science to leave literature alone, if it wishes to remain itself. Shlomith Rimmon-Kenan's reply, on the other hand, shows that what she is doing is not logical literary analysis but, for the moment at least, deconstruction. To borrow again the figure she borrows from my 'The Critic as Host' (1979), I welcome her as a guest in that house.

References

Derrida, Jacques, 1972, "La Mythologie blanche", in *Marges* (Paris: Les Éditions de Minuit), 247–324.

1980 "La Loi du genre/The Law of Genre", *Glyph* 7, 176–229.

Rimmon-Kenan, Shlomith, 1977. *The Concept of Ambiguity: The Example of James* (Chicago UP).

Miller, J. Hillis, 1969. "The Critic as Host", in Harold Bloom et al., *Deconstruction and Criticism* (New York: The Seabury Press), 217–253.

1980 "The Figure in the Carpet," *Poetics Today* 1:3, 107–118.

SECTION THREE

DISCOURSE AND THE SOCIAL

Broadly speaking the formative writings in this trajectory can be seen as, on the one hand, Michel Foucault's work on discourse and power, and, on the other, Volosinov/Bahktin's work on discourse as concrete, socio-ideological communication. These form key points on the conceptual map of this aspect of post-structuralism. In common with the deconstructive tendency, and in contradistinction to structuralism, this trajectory acknowledges that meaning is not fixed and stable, and that there can be no single, final and true inter-pretation. However, unlike deconstruction, Volosinov/Bahktin sees, in the social conditions of language use, a variety of temporal, provi-sional and contested fixings of meaning, while Foucault sees, in the configuration of discourse, power and knowledge the production and surveillance of the social itself. In this model the relations between language and socio-cultural practice often seem to emphasize discourse as control and repression, but this function is frequently set against a fascination for forms and writings which escape or transgress social/official rationality.

The work of Volosinov/Bahktin first emerged alongside Russian Formalism in the 1920s and though Volosinov's concern was pri-marily with linguistics and Bahktin's with literature, their work exhibits a number of common features which, along with other evi-dence, suggests that they were one and the same person, forced by circumstance in Stalin's Russia to publish under two names. In recent years the work undertaken by Volosinov/Bahktin has proved fertile ground for literary theorists for though aspects of the work mark it as 'of its time', it also contains some remarkably post-structural themes.

In *Marxism and the Philosophy of Language* (1929) Volosinov undertakes a powerful critique of the 'abstract objectivism' of Saus-sure's theory of language. The basis of his critique is the recognition that language is a social *process*; language is utterance, emerging from concrete social communication not from any abstract, objective system of langue. When viewed in its social contexts language appears not as a closed system of 'self-identical forms' (that is, the one-to-one correspondence of a signifier to a signified) but as a generative and continuous process, as utterances which respond to and anticipate other utterances. These utterances, existing in and as social interchange, form the arena of struggle between different social groups who inflect the same sign-forms with different 'evaluative accents' to produce different 'ideological themes' or meanings for their utterances. So, whilst acknowledging that the sign is not stable or fixed, Volosinov adds that 'multiplicity of meaning' has to be seen in relation to what he calls 'multi-accentuality' – that is, its openness to different evaluative orientations.

Bahktin develops this view, seeing language not as singular and monolithic, but as plural and multiple; languages inscribed with various evaluative accents become socio-ideological languages intimately bound up with material and social conditions and with the contexts of their production – i.e. their 'heteroglossia'. Bahktin applies this to the novel, the form which is exemplary in its ability to represent a dialogic interanimation of socio-ideological languages. The dialogic nature of the novel can be either open or closed; the author can either let the interplay of languages speak for itself or can impose a privileged authorial metalanguage. In Bahktin the dialogic is closely linked to his notion of carnivalization – to popular forms that disrupt and relativize meaning in opposition to the 'official' discourse and its attempt to close down the polysemy of language. (Bahktin 1966; White and Stallybrass 1986).

Bahktin's theory of the text can be seen as oriented towards literary production in that the novel is emphasized as a form which juxtaposes the various meaning-systems of socio-ideological languages. In the essay by Bennett, reprinted here, the inter-animation of discourses and discursive practices – different meaning systems – is used to develop a model that is oriented toward consumption/reading, one that acknowledges the indeterminacy of the text but places it more firmly in social practice and discursive context.

For Michel Foucault the 'social' is produced in the network of discourses and discursive practices through which we seem to acquire knowledge about the world. Broadly, Foucault's argument is that it is the modalities of discourses and discursive practices that actually produce both that knowledge and the social itself, and the modalities function differently in different historical 'epistemes'. (An episteme is an historical period that is unified by the rules and procedures – the modalities – for producing knowledge.) The history of epistemes is not a matter of progression or continuity, but of discontinuity. In his earlier work Foucault attempts to uncover the concealed modalities of discourse which govern and produce various 'knowledges'. In *Birth of the Clinic* (1963) and *The Order of Things* (1966) he investigated the 'discursive formations' of medicine and the human sciences, noting how these 'discourses' delimited a field of objects, defined legitimate practices and positions for 'subjects' to adopt, and fixed the norms for producing concepts and theories.

Foucault's work has been concerned primarily with the configuration of discourse, knowledge and power, and it is through these three key notions that he elaborates a complex theory. In his earlier work, he emphasizes discourse; in his later work the emphasis shifts to power. 'The Order of Discourse' is balanced between this shift in emphasis. Where, in earlier work, he had sought to delineate the principles of regularity by which knowledge was produced, here he outlines the forces and technologies of power by which the production of discourse and knowledge is surveyed and controlled; however, if power here appears to be simply repressive, account should be taken of his later writings where he is careful to point out that power is productive – power *produces* discourse, as well as setting its boundaries.

Though Foucault's name appears less often in literary studies than Derrida's or Lacan's, his work provides a way of investigating the relation between text/discourse and power/practice that is becoming increasingly important. Homi BhaBha's essay reprinted here deploys a Foucauldian method, though it also resonates with other post-structuralist theory. His analysis of a particular colonial subject, interesting in its own right, is also valuable as an illustration of post-structuralism in action.

Foucault's work has brought to the fore the operation of discursive practices within institutions and the terms of his analysis seem readily applicable to the study of the discursive formation of literary studies. Ian Hunter takes a less obvious line of approach, subjecting the notion of character and the ways character has been read to a mode of investigation suggested by Foucault's later work.

While Edward Said's article seems not to be mobilizing any specific post-structuralist theory his language and style are clearly conditioned by his theoretical knowledge. We have included this piece because it raises, directly and polemically, important issues about the function and relation of both educational institutions and the discourse of literary studies to the social world; issues that can easily disappear in the theoretical enterprise.

22 M.M. Bahktin,

From 'Discourse in the Novel', *The Dialogic Imagination*, ed
M. Holquist

p269–273; 295–296; 301–305

The novel is an artistic genre. Novelistic discourse is poetic discourse, but one that does not fit within the frame provided by the concept of poetic discourse as it now exists. This concept has certain underlying presuppositions that limit it. The very concept – in the course of its historical formulation from Aristotle to the present day – has been oriented toward the specific 'official' genres and connected with specific historical tendencies in verbal ideological life. Thus a whole series of phenomena remained beyond its conceptual horizon.

Philosophy of language, linguistics and stylistic (i.e., such as they have come down to us) have all postulated a simple and unmediated relation of speaker to his unitary and singular 'own' language, and have postulated as well as simple realization of this language in the monologic utterance of the individual. Such disciplines actually know only two poles in the life of language, between which are located all the linguistic and stylistic phenomena they know: on the one hand, the system of a *unitary language*, and on the other the *individual* speaking in this language.

Various schools of thought in the philosophy of language, in linguistics and stylistics have, in different periods (and always in close connection with the diverse concrete poetic and ideological styles of a given epoch), introduced into such concepts as 'system of language', 'monologic utterance', 'the speaking *individuum*', various differing nuances of meaning, but their basic content remains unchanged. This basic content is conditioned by the specific sociohistorical destinies of European languages and by the destinies of ideological discourse, and by those particular historical tasks that ideological discourse has fulfilled in specific social spheres and at specific stages in its own historical development.

These tasks and destinies of discourse conditioned specific verbal-ideological movements, as well as various specific genres of ideological discourse, and ultimately the specific philosophical concept of discourse itself – in particular, the concept of poetic discourse, which has been at the heart of all concepts of style.

The strength and at the same time the limitations of such basic stylistic categories become apparent when such categories are seen as conditioned by specific historical destinies and by the task that an ideological discourse assumes. These categories arose from and were shaped by the historically *aktuell* forces at work in the verbal-ideological evolution of specific social groups; they comprised the theoretical expression of actualizing forces that were in the process of creating a life for language.

These forces are the *forces that serve to unify and centralize the verbal-ideological world*.

Unitary language constitutes the theoretical expression of the historical processes of linguistic unification and centralization, an expression of the centripetal forces of language. A unitary language is not something given [*dan*] but is always in essence posited [*zadan*] – and at every moment of its linguistic life it is opposed to the realities of heteroglossia. But at the same time it makes its real presence felt as a force for overcoming this heteroglossia, imposing specific limits to it, guaranteeing a certain maximum of mutual understanding and crystalizing into a real, although still relative, unity – the unity of the reigning conversational (everyday) and literary language, 'correct language'.

A common unitary language is a system of linguistic norms. But these norms do not constitute an abstract imperative; they are rather the generative forces of linguistic life, forces that struggle to overcome the heteroglossia of language, forces that unite and centralize verbal-ideological thought, creating within a heteroglot national language the firm, stable linguistic nucleus of an officially recognized literary language, or else defending an already formed language from the pressure of growing heteroglossia.

What we have in mind here is not an abstract linguistic minimum of a common language, in the sense of a system of elementary forms (linguistic symbols) guaranteeing a *minimum* level of comprehension in practical communication. We are taking language not as a system of abstract grammatical categories, but rather language conceived as ideologically saturated, language as a world view, even as a concrete opinion, insuring a *maximum* of mutual understanding in all spheres of ideological life. Thus a unitary language gives expression to forces working toward concrete verbal and ideological unification and centralization, which develop in vital connection with the processes of sociopolitical and cultural centralization.

Aristotelian poetics, the poetics of Augustine, the poetics of the medieval church, of 'the one language of truth', the Cartesian poetics of neoclassicism, the abstract grammatical universalism of Leibniz (the idea of a 'universal grammar'), Humboldt's insistence on the concrete – all these, whatever their differences in nuance, give expression to the same centripetal forces in socio-linguistic and ideological life; they serve one and the same project of centralizing and unifying the European languages. The victory of one reigning language (dialect) over the others, the supplanting of languages, their enslavement, the process of illuminating them with the True Word, the incorporation of barbarians and lower social strata into a unitary language of culture and truth, the canonization of ideological systems, philology with its methods of studying and teaching dead languages, languages that were by that very fact 'unities', Indo-European linguistics with its focus of attention, directed away from language plurality to a single proto-language – all this determined the content and power of the category of 'unitary language' in linguistic and stylistic thought, and determined its creative, style-shaping role in the majority of the poetic genres that coalesced in the channel formed by those same centripetal forces of verbal-ideological life.

But the centripetal forces of the life of language, embodied in a 'unitary language', operate in the midst of heteroglossia. At any given moment of its evolution, language is stratified not only into linguistic dialects in the strict sense of the word (according to formal linguistic markers, especially phonetic), but also – and for us this is the essential point – into languages that are socio-ideological: languages of social groups, 'professional' and 'generic' languages, languages of generations and so forth. From this point of view, literary language itself is only one of these heteroglot languages – and in its turn is also stratified into languages (generic, period-bound and others). And this stratification and heteroglossia, once realized, is not only a static invariant of linguistic life, but also what insures its dynamics: stratification and heteroglossia widen and deepen as long as language is alive and developing. Alongside the centripetal forces, the centrifugal forces of language carry on their uninterrupted work; alongside verbal-ideological centralization and unification, the uninterrupted processes of decentralization and disunification go forward.

Every concrete utterance of a speaking subject serves as a point where centrifugal as well as centripetal forces are brought to bear. The processes of centralization and decentralization, of unification and disunification, intersect in the utterance; the utterance not only answers the requirements of its own language as an individualized embodiment of a speech act, but it answers the requirements of heteroglossia as well; it is in fact an active participant in such speech diversity. And this active participation of every utterance in living heteroglossia determines the linguistic profile and style of the utterance to no less a degree than its inclusion in any normative-centralizing system of a unitary language.

Every utterance participates in the 'unitary language' (in its centripetal forces and tendencies) and at the same time partakes of social and historical heteroglossia (the centrifugal, stratifying forces).

Such is the fleeting language of a day, of an epoch, a social group, a genre, a school and so forth. It is possible to give a concrete and detailed analysis of any utterance, once having exposed it as a contradiction-ridden, tension-filled unity of two embattled tendencies in the life of language.

The authentic environment of an utterance, the environment in which it lives and takes shape, is dialogized heteroglossia, anonymous and social as language, but simultaneously concrete, filled with specific content and accented as an individual utterance.

At the time when major divisions of the poetic genres were developing under the influence of the unifying centralizing, centripetal forces of verbal-ideological life, the novel – and those artistic-prose genres that gravitate toward it – was being historically shaped by the current of decentralizing, centrifugal forces. At the time when poetry was accomplishing the task of cultural, national and political centralization of the verbal-ideological world in the higher official socio-ideological levels, on the lower levels, on the stages of local fairs and at buffoon spectacles, the heteroglossia of the clown sounded forth, ridiculing all 'languages' and dialects; there developed the literature of the *fabliaux* and *Schwänke* of street songs, folksayings, anecdotes, where there was no language-center at all, where there was to be found a lively play with the 'languages' of poets, scholars, monks, knights and others, where all 'languages' were masks and where no language could claim to be an authentic, incontestable face.

Heteroglossia, as organized in these low genres, was not merely heteroglossia vis-à-vis the accepted literary language (in all its various generic expressions), that is, vis-à-vis the linguistic center of the verbal-ideological life of the nation and the epoch, but was a heteroglossia consciously opposed to this literary language. It was parodic, and aimed sharply and polemically against the official languages of its given time. It was heteroglossia that had been dialogized.

. . . .

Concrete socio-ideological language consciousness, as it becomes creative – that is, as it becomes active as literature – discovers itself already surrounded by heteroglossia and not at all a single, unitary language, inviolable and indisputable. The actively literary linguistic consciousness at all times and everywhere (that is, in all epochs of literature historically available to us) comes upon 'languages' and not language. Consciousness finds itself inevitably facing the necessity of *having to choose a language.* With each literary-verbal performance, consciousness must actively orient itself amidst heteroglossia, it must move in and occupy a position for itself within it, it chooses, in other words, a 'language'. Only by remaining in a closed environment, one without writing or thought, completely off the maps of socio-ideological becoming, could a man fail to sense this activity of selecting a language and rest assured in the inviolability of his own language, the conviction that his language is predetermined.

Even such a man, however, deals not in fact with a single language, but with languages – except that the place occupied by each of these languages is fixed and indisputable, the movement from one to the other is predetermined and not a thought process; it is as if these languages were in different chambers. They do not collide with each other in his consciousness, there is no attempt to coordinate them, to look at one of these languages through the eyes of another language.

Thus an illiterate peasant, miles away from any urban center, naively immersed in an unmoving and for him unshakable everyday world, nevertheless lived in several language systems: he prayed to God in one language (Church Slavonic), sang songs in another, spoke to his family in a third and, when he began to dictate petitions to the local authorities through a scribe, he tried speaking yet a fourth language (the official-literate language, 'paper' language). All these are *different languages*, even from the point of view of abstract socio-dialectological markers. But these languages were not dialogically coordinated in the linguistic consciousness of the peasant; he passed from one to the other without thinking, automatically: each was indisputably in its own place, and the place of each was indisputable. He was not yet able to regard one language (and the verbal world corresponding to it) through the eyes of another language (that is, the language of everyday life and the everyday world with the language of prayer or song, or vice versa).[1]

As soon as a critical interanimation of languages began to occur in the consciousness of our peasant, as soon as it became clear that these were not only various different languages but even internally variegated languages, that the ideological systems and approaches to the world that were indissolubly connected with these languages contradicted each other and in no way could live in peace and quiet with one another – then the inviolability and predetermined quality of these languages came to an end, and the necessity of actively choosing one's orientation among them began.

The language and world of prayer, the language and world of song, the language and world of labor and everyday life, the specific language and world of local authorities, the new language and world of the workers freshly immigrated to the city – all these languages and worlds sooner or later emerged from a state of peaceful and moribund equilibrium and revealed the speech diversity in each.

Of course the actively literary linguistic consciousness comes upon an even more varied and profound heteroglossia within literary language itself, as well as outside it. Any fundamental study of the stylistic life of the word must begin with this basic fact. The nature of the heteroglossia encountered and the means by which one orients oneself in it determine the concrete stylistic life that the word will lead.

. . . .

[1] We are of course deliberately simplifying: the real life peasant could and did do this to a certain extent.

The compositional forms for appropriating and organizing hetero-glossia in the novel, worked out during the long course of the genre's historical development, are extremely heterogeneous in their variety of genetic types. Each such compositional form is connected with parti-cular stylistic possibilities, and demands particular forms for the artistic treatment of the heteroglot 'languages' introduced into it. We will pause here only on the most basic forms that are typical for the majority of novel types.

The so-called comic novel makes available a form for appropriating and organizing heteroglossia that is both externally very vivid and at the same time historically profound; its classic representatives in England were Fielding, Smollett, Sterne, Dickens, Thackeray and others, and in Germany Hippel and Jean Paul.

In the English comic novel we find a comic-parodic re-processing of almost all the levels of literary language, both conversational and written, that were current at the time. Almost every novel we mentioned above as being a classic representative of this generic type is an encyclopedia of all strata and forms of literary language: depending on the subject being represented, the story-line parodically reproduces first the forms of parliamentary eloquence, then the eloquence of the court, or particular forms of parliamentary protocol, or court protocol, or forms used by reporters in newspaper articles, or the dry business language of the City, or the dealings of speculators, or the pedantic speech of scholars, or the high epic style, or Biblical style, or the style of the hypocritical moral sermon or finally the way one or another concrete and socially determined personality, the subject of the story, happens to speak.

This usually parodic stylization of generic, professional and other strata of language is sometimes interrupted by the direct authorial word (usually as an expression of pathos, of Sentimental or idyllic sensibility), which directly embodies (without any refracting) semantic and axio-logical intentions of the author. But the primary source of language usage in the comic novel is a highly specific treatment of 'common language'. This 'common language' – usually the average norm of spoken and written language for a given social group – is taken by the author precisely as the *common view*, as the verbal approach to people and things normal for a given sphere of society, as the *going point of view* and the going *value*. To one degree or another, the author distances himself from this common language, he steps back and objectifies it, forcing his own intentions to refract and diffuse themselves through the medium of this common view that has become embodied in language (a view that is always superficial and frequently hypocritical).

The relationship of the author to a language conceived as the common view is not static – it is always found in a state of movement and oscilla-tion that is more or less alive (this sometimes is a rhythmic oscillation):

the author exaggerates, now strongly, now weakly, one or another aspect of the 'common language', sometimes abruptly exposing its inadequacy to its object and sometimes, on the contrary, becoming one with it, maintaining an almost imperceptible distance, sometimes even directly forcing it to reverberate with his own 'truth', which occurs when the author completely merges his own voice with the common view. As a consequence of such a merger, the aspects of common language, which in the given situation had been parodically exaggerated or had been treated as mere things, undergo change. The comic style demands of the author a lively to-and-fro movement in his relation to language, it demands a continual shifting of the distance between author and language, so that first some, then other aspects of language are thrown into relief. If such were not the case, the style would be monotonous or would require a greater individualization of the narrator – would, in any case, require a quite different means for introducing and organizing heteroglossia.

Against this same backdrop of the 'common language', of the impersonal, going opinion, one can also isolate in the comic novel those parodic stylizations of generic, professional and other languages we have mentioned, as well as compact masses of direct authorial discourse – pathos-filled, moral-didactic, sentimental-elegiac or idyllic. In the comic novel the direct authorial word is thus realized in direct, unqualified stylizations of poetic genres (idyllic, elegiac, etc.) or stylizations of rhetorical genres (the pathetic, the moral-didactic). Shifts from common language to parodying of generic and other languages and shifts to the direct authorial word may be gradual, or may be on the contrary quite abrupt. Thus does the system of language work in the comic novel.

We will pause for analysis on several examples from Dickens, from his novel *Little Dorrit*.

(1) The conference was held at four or five o'clock in the afternoon, when all the region of Harley Street, Cavendish Square, was resonant of carriage-wheels and double-knocks. It had reached this point when Mr. Merdle came home *from his daily occupation of causing the British name to be more and more respected in all parts of the civilized globe capable of appreciation of wholewide commercial enterprise and gigantic combinations of skill and capital.* For, though nobody knew with the last precision what Mr. Merdle's business was, except that it was to coin money, these were the terms in which everybody defined it on all ceremonious occasions, and which it was the last new polite reading of the parable of the camel and the needle's eye to accept without inquiry. (book 1, ch. 33)

The italicized portion represents a parodic stylization of the language of ceremonial speeches (in parliaments and at banquets). The shift into this style is prepared for by the sentence's construction, which from the very beginning is kept within bounds by a somewhat ceremonious epic tone. Further on – and already in the language of the author (and consequently in a different style) – the parodic meaning of the ceremoniousness of Merdle's labors becomes apparent: such a characterization turns out to be 'another's speech', to be taken only in quotation marks 'these were the terms in which everybody defined it on all ceremonious occasions').

Thus the speech of another is introduced into the author's discourse (the story) in *concealed form*, that is, without any of the *formal* markers usually accompanying such speech, whether direct or indirect. But this is not just another's speech in the same 'language' – it is another's utterance in a language that is itself 'other' to the author as well, in the archaicized language of oratorical genres associated with hypocritical official celebrations.

> (2) In a day or two it was announced to all the town, that Edmund Sparkler, Esquire, son-in-law of the eminent Mr. Merdle of worldwide renown, was made one of the Lords of the Circumlocution Office; and proclamation was issued, to all true believers, that this admirable *appointment was to be hailed as a graceful and gracious mark of homage, rendered by the graceful and gracious Decimus, to that commercial interest which must ever in a great commercial country – and all the rest of it, with blast of trumpet.* So, bolstered by this mark of Government homage, the *wonderful* Bank and all the other *wonderful* undertakings went on and went up; and gapers came to Harley Street, Cavendish Square, only to look at the house where the golden-wonder lived. (book 2, ch. 12)

Here, in the italicized portion, another's speech in another's (official-ceremonial) language is openly introduced as indirect discourse. But it is surrounded by the hidden, diffused speech of another (in the same official-ceremonial language) that clears the way for the introduction of a form more easily perceived *as* another's speech and that can reverberate more fully as such. The clearing of the way comes with the word 'Esquire', characteristic of official speech, added to Sparkler's name; the final confirmation that this is another's speech comes with the epithet 'wonderful'. This epithet does not of course belong to the author but to that same 'general opinion' that had created the commotion around Merdle's inflated enterprises.

> (3) It was a dinner to provoke an appetite, though he had not had one. The rarest dishes, sumptuously cooked and sumptuously served; the choicest fruits, the most exquisite wines; marvels of workmanship in gold and silver, china and glass; innumerable things delicious to the senses of taste, smell, and sight, were insinuated into its composition. *O, what a wonderful man this Merdle, what a great man, what a master man, how blessedly and enviably endowed – in one word*, what a rich man! (book 2, ch. 12)

The beginning is a parodic stylization of high epic style. What follows is an enthusiastic glorification of Merdle, a chorus of his admirers in the form of the concealed speech of another (the italicized portion). The whole point here is to expose the real basis for such glorification which is to unmask the chorus' hypocrisy: 'wonderful', 'great', 'master', 'endowed' can all be replaced by the single word 'rich'. This act of authorial unmasking, which is openly accomplished within the boundaries of a single simple sentence, merges with the unmasking of another's speech. The ceremonial emphasis on glorification is complicated by a second emphasis that is indignant, ironic, and this is the one that ultimately predominates in the final unmasking words of the sentence.

We have before us a typical double-accented, double-styled *hybrid construction*.

What we are calling a hybrid construction is an utterance that belongs, by its grammatical (syntactic) and compositional markers, to a single speaker, but that actually contains mixed within it two utterances, two speech manners, two styles, two 'languages', two semantic and axiological belief systems. We repeat, there is no formal – compositional and syntactic – boundary between these utterances, styles, languages, belief systems, the division of voices and languages takes place within the limits of a single syntactic whole, often within the limits of a simple sentence. It frequently happens that even one and the same word will belong simultaneously to two languages, two belief systems that intersect in a hyrid construction – and, consequently, the word has two contradictory meanings, two accents (examples below). As we shall see, hybrid constructions are of enormous significance in novel style.[2]

(4) But Mr. Tite Barnacle was a buttoned-up man, and *consequently* a weighty one. (book 2, ch. 12)

The above sentence is an example of *pseudo-objective motivation*, one of the forms for concealing another's speech – in this example, the speech of 'current opinion'. If judged by the formal markers above, the logic motivating the sentence seems to belong to the author, i.e., he is formally at one with it; but in actual fact, the motivation lies within the subjective belief system of his characters, or of general opinion.

Pseudo-objective motivation is generally characteristic of novel style,[3] since it is one of the manifold forms for concealing another's speech in hybrid constructions. Subordinate conjunctions and link words ('thus', 'because', 'for the reason that', 'in spite of' and so forth), as well as words used to maintain a logical sequence ('therefore', 'consequently', etc.) lose their direct authorial intention, take on the flavour of someone else's language, become refracted or even completely reified.

---

[2] For more detail on hybrid constructions and their significance, see ch. 4 of the present essay.
[3] Such a device is unthinkable in the epic.

23 Tony Bennett,

'Texts, Readers, Reading Formations', *The Bulletin of the Midwest Modern Language Association*, vol 16;1 1983

p3–17

> The frontiers of a book are never clear-cut: beyond the title, the first line and the last full-stop, beyond its internal configuration, its autonomous form, it is caught up in a system of references to other books, other texts, other sentences: it is a node within a network. . . . The book is simply not the object that one holds in one's hands; and it cannot remain within the relative parallelepiped that contains it: its unity is variable and relative. As soon as one questions that unity it loses its self-evidence: it indicates itself, constructs itself, only on the basis of a complex field of discourse.
>
> Michel Foucault
> *The Archaeology of Knowledge*

I

By exploring the issues that Foucault raises here, I want to open up a set of questions concerning reading, especially popular reading, and the determinations within which it is produced. Although my primary concern is with the reading of written texts, especially fictions, I intend the term 'reading' in the more general sense of referring to the means and mechanisms whereby all texts – literary, filmic and televisual, fictional or otherwise – may be 'productively activated' during what is traditionally, and inadequately, thought of as the process of their consumption or reception. For reasons that I hope will become clear, I venture the concept of the 'productive activation' of texts as a means of displacing, rather than of substituting for, the concept of interpretation and the particular construction of relations between texts and readers that it implies.

I should also explain that I do not intend the term 'popular', in a narrow or exclusive sense, as having a singular class articulation. Rather, in speaking of 'popular readings', I have in mind what, from another perspective, might be classified as 'untutored readings', that is, readings produced outside the academy, at a considerable remove from, and relatively untouched by, the discourses of textual criticism that circulate within it. I prefer 'popular readings' to 'untutored reading', however, because of its more positive connotations; it implies readings that may be assessed as valid and productive on their own terms. By contrast, 'untutored readings' implies an absence or a lack. It is a negative definition entailing a negative judgment: readings that 'don't count' and whose only destiny, unless they are earmarked for preservation as curiosities, is to be 'corrected'.

So much for preliminaries. Before going further, let me give an example of what would count as a popular reading under my definition and, in doing so, outline what I mean by a 'reading formation'. The case I have in mind is that of Menocchio, the sixteenth-century miller whose reading habits constitute the subject of Carlo Ginzburg's *The Cheese and the Worms*.[1] Menocchio was twice hauled before the Inquisition, once in 1584 and again in 1599, to account for his belief that God and the angels were created from worms that emerged from a vast primordial cheese before the elements had separated.[2] At the level of his handling of the practical difficulties involved in unraveling the sources of this extraordinary cosmogeny, Ginzburg says all that needs to be said on the subject of 'texts, readers, and reading formations'. At another level, however, Ginzburg occludes the issue by using theoretical formulations that preserve intact the conventional view of texts as 'things' that have 'meanings' that readers may variously 'interpret'.

The problem which exercises Ginzburg concerns the roots of Menocchio's inspired cosmogeny, his 'fantastic opinions' (Ginzburg, *CW*, p. 32). Clearly at odds with the views of the Catholic Church, they also differed significantly from those of Lutheranism and Anabaptism, while sharing elements with both. Where, then, did they come from? Menocchio, when pressed on this point, answered: 'My opinions came out of my head' (Ginzburg, *CW*, p. 27). Ginzburg seeks to disclose what put these opinions in Menocchio's head by examining both the books he read and the way he read them, as well as by reconstructing the cultural sources that produced his, on the face of it, singularly aberrant readings. The key text at issue here, of course, was the Bible, which Menocchio had read in the vernacular, and especially Genesis; for, when his back was again to the wall, Menocchio would claim a textual warrant for his materialist account of creation by invoking the authority of the Biblical account itself.

In a later essay, Ginzburg theorizes the relationship between clues and scientific method within the human and social sciences by means of an analogy with the situation of a hunter who learns 'to construct the

[1] C. Ginzburg, *The Cheese and the Worms: The Cosmos of a Sixteenth-Century Miller* (London: Routledge & Kegan Paul, 1980).

[2] Menocchio provides a succinct summary of his cosmogeny as follows: 'I have said that, in my opinion, all was chaos, that is, earth, air, water, and fire were mixed together; and out of that bulk a mass formed – just as cheese is made out of milk – and worms appeared in it, and these were the angels. The most holy majesty decreed that these should be God and the angels, and among that number of angels, there was also God, he too having been created out of that mass at the same time, and he was made lord, with four captains, Lucifer, Michael, Gabriel, and Raphael. That Lucifer sought to make himself lord equal to the king, who was the majesty of God, and for this arrogance God ordered him driven out of heaven with all his host and his company; and this God later created Adam and Eve and people in great number to take the place of the angels who had been expelled' (Ginzburg, *CW*, pp. 5–6).

appearances and movements of an unseen quarry through its tracks'.[3] In the same essay, he likens the situation of the historian of ideas to Gaboriau's detective hero, Monsieur Lecocq, 'who felt he was crossing "an unknown territory, covered with snow", marked with the tracks of the criminal, like "a vast white page on which the people we are searching for have left not only footprints and traces of movements but also the prints of their innermost thoughts, the hopes and fears by which they are stirred" ' (Ginzburg, *CW*, p. 23). In *The Cheese and the Worms*, Ginzburg too is a hunter, with Menocchio's 'thoughts of his sentiments – fears, hopes, ironies, rages, despairs' as his quarry (Ginzburg, *CW*, p. xi). The clues from which Ginzburg works are those provided by the transcripts of Menocchio's trials. Hunting down the books Menocchio read – lives of the saints and the Virgin Mary, medieval chronicles, the *Travels* of Mandeville, Boccaccio's *Decameron*, and perhaps the *Koran* in Italian translation – he seeks the key to the way in which Menocchio read them by tracing the correspondences, the inversions, and mutated echoes of these texts in the text of Menocchio's testimony before the Inquisitors.

Ginzburg ultimately tracks his quarry down to the sphere of the intertextual. He finds the key to Menocchio's reading of the Bible in, on the one hand, the relations between the official Biblical culture of the Church and the fringes of the new intellectual humanism of the Renaissance, and, on the other, the interaction (in Menocchio's head) between these two written cultures and the orally transmitted underculture of the Italian peasantry. Placed in this context, Menocchio's fantastic cosmogeny is rendered intelligible: a materialist subversion of the Biblical myth of creation is effected by reading the relations between Genesis and Renaissance humanism through the filter of the belly materialism – the cheese and worms materialism – of peasant oral culture. This, then, is what I mean by a 'reading formation': a set of intersecting discourses that productively activate a given body of texts and the relations between them in a specific way. Menocchio's reading – his 'productive activation' of the Bible and of the texts of Renaissance humanism into a 'teeth-gritting harmony' – is the result of his installation within a network of intersecting but contradictory cultures, each with its own rules and procedures, and for which his native peasant culture serves as the dominant ingredient.

This reading formation, moreover, had its historical and material foundations in reading relations, or social relations of reading, of a particular kind:

> In Menocchio's talk we see emerging, as if out of a crevice in the earth, a deep-rooted cultural stratum so unusual as to appear almost incomprehensible. This case . . . involves not only a reaction filtered through the written

[3] C. Ginzburg, 'Clues and Scientific Method', *History Workshop Journal, 9 (Spring* 1980), 12.

page, but also an irredicible residue of oral culture. The Reformation and the diffusion of printing had been necessary to permit this *different* culture to come to light. Because of the first, a simple miller had dared to think of *speaking out*, of voicing his own opinions about the Church and the world. Thanks to the second, *words* were at his disposal to express the obscure, inarticulate vision of the world that fermented with him.

(Ginzburg, CW, pp. 58–59)

Indeed, Ginzburg ventures a more precise social location for the reading formation to which Menocchio's fantastic cosmogeny bears witness. Considering the case of another miller, Pellegrino Baroni, whose heresies suggested an abrasive relation among Biblical culture, Renaissance humanism and the oral culture of the peasantry similar to the one that organized Menocchio's reading, Ginzburg notes that the social situation of millers rendered them uniquely exposed to the contradictory crosscurrents of the culture of the period. In close contact with the peasants who daily brought their grain to the mill, yet also distanced from the peasantry by virtue of the mistrust that traditionally characterized the peasant's attitude toward the miller, millers were also economically tied to the feudal nobility, who retained possession over the milling privilege. Accordingly, they were often involved in quasi-familiar forms of social interaction with the local nobility – and hence, indirectly, with the secular intellectual culture of the period – in ways that would have been inconceivable for the vast mass of the peasantry.

Menocchio, however, is not Ginzburg's only quarry in *The Cheese and the Worms*. He also hunts down, although in a different way, two other adversaries. The first is the view that readings, and especially popular readings, can be inferred from the analysis of popular texts. In his 'Preface', he takes issue with Robert Mandrou's analysis of the literature of *colportage*, especially the view that its constituent texts can be defined as the 'instruments of a victorious process of acculturation, "the reflection . . . of a world view" of the popular classes of the *Ancien Régime*' (Ginzburg, *CW*, p. xv). This implies, Ginzburg argues, that popular reading is a process characterized by a 'complete cultural passivity' and rests on a 'hypodermic syringe' model of the relations between texts and readers, as well as of the relations between dominant and subordinate cultures (Ginzburg, *CW*, p. xv). Consequently, Ginzburg's second adversary is the view, variously attributable, that the traffic between the official (or high) culture and the popular culture of a society is all one way, exclusively from the former to the latter. Against this position, Ginzburg appeals to the authority of Bakhtin's *Rabelais and His World* insofar as it demonstrates the degree to which the intellectual culture of Renaissance humanism was fuelled by the popular, materialist belly of carnival.[4] Indeed, *Rabelais and His World* is the master text of *The*

---

[4] Mikhail Bakhtin, *Rabelais and His World* (Cambridge, Mass.: The MIT Press, 1968).

Cheese and the Worms, the text that productively activates Ginzburg's own reading of the way Menocchio read the texts that he read. As Bakhtin listens for the echoes of carnival in Rabelais's *Gargantua and Pantagruel*, so Ginzburg, in listening to the evidence of Menocchio's testimony, interrogates the relations between his materialist cosmogony and the humanist writings of the period. Ginzburg hears in the former, not the diluted versions of the latter, but an independent voice, vigorously materialist and humanistically tolerant, a voice 'from below' that actively influences the intellectual culture of the period and which, in some respects, shows itself to be considerably in advance of that culture. A secularly inclined, humanistic utopianism; a tendentially scientific account of the spontaneous generation of life from inanimate matter; a universal tolerance of the diversity of faiths; a tendential reduction of religion to morality – Ginzburg finds aspects of all of these in Menocchio's testimony, not as handed-down versions of intellectual humanism, but as more vigorously materialistic extensions of it. In short, as concerns their philosophical if not their literal sense, Menocchio's 'heresies' were destined to become orthodoxies – orthodoxies, moreover, that would claim their warrant in the very texts that Menocchio seemed to have traduced so violently.

It is surprising, therefore, that Ginzburg sometimes, but not always, speaks of Menocchio's relation to his texts as one of misrepresentation.

> The almanacs, the songsters, the books of piety, the lives of saints, the entire pamphlet literature that constituted the bulk of the book trade, today appear static, inert, and unchanging to us. But how were they read by the public of the day? To what extent did the prevalently oral culture of those readers interject itself in the use of the text, modifying it, reworking it, perhaps to the point of changing its very essence? Menocchio's accounts of his readings provide us with a striking example of a relationship to the text that is totally different from that of today's educated reader. They permit us to measure, at last, the discrepancy that . . . existed between the texts of 'popular' literature and the light in which they appeared to peasants and artisans. . . . As far as the quantitative history of ideas is concerned, only knowledge of the historical and social variability of the person of the reader will really lay the foundations for a history of ideas that is also qualitatively different.
>
> (Ginzburg, *CW*, p. xii)

It may be no more than a quibble, but it is the notion of 'essence' that I balk at here. Who said that texts had 'essences''? And how can an essence be 'changed'? And why should the relationship between popular texts and their readers be conceived of as a 'discrepancy'?

Or again:

> Any attempt to consider these books as 'sources' in the mechanical sense of the term collapses before the aggressive originality of Menocchio's reading. More than the text, then, what is important is the key to his reading, a screen that he unconsciously placed between himself and the printed page: a filter

that emphasized certain words while obscuring others, that stretched the meaning of a word, taking it out of its context, that acted on Menocchio's memory and distorted the very words of the text.

(Ginzburg, *CW*, p. 33)

The problem that Ginzburg confronts here is clearly the problem of *difference*; of the *difference* between the 'aggressive originality' of Menocchio's readings and more established readings. And he clearly wants to theorize this difference non-hierarchically, to place Menocchio's readings on an equal footing with those of the Church and those of contemporary humanists, to restore the grid of intelligibility to Menocchio's apparently demented discourse so as to bring him 'very close to us: a man like ourselves, one of us' (Ginzburg, *CW*, p. xi). Yet, from time to time, this relation of *difference* is theorized as one of *misrepresentation* or *distortion*, as a difference, not between Menocchio's readings and other readings, but between Menocchio's readings and the 'texts themselves'. Although everything else that Ginzburg has to say works against it, it is through such formulations that there occasionally obtrudes the view that texts are *things* that *have* meanings that may be *traduced*.

It is this view that I want to dispute – and indeed, which must be disputed – if Ginzburg's project of a qualitatively different history of ideas that results from taking account of 'the historical and social variability of the person of the reader' is to be realized. Meaning is a transitive phenomenon. It is not a *thing* that texts can *have*, but is something that can only be produced, and always differently, within the reading formations that regulate the encounters between texts and readers. To be sure, some readings regularly carry more cultural weight than others; and some, like Menocchio's, may never settle to provide the framework for an enduring pattern of 'response'. Yet meanings are meanings; and marginalized, subordinate, quirky, fantastic, or quixotic ones are just as real, just as ontologically secure, just as much wrapped up in the living social destinies of texts as are dominant ones.

Although the problem remains generally applicable to the analysis of all texts, it has a particular pertinence to the study of popular fictions. In the case of canonized texts, there is a considerable degree of coincidence between the discourses of academic criticism and the reading formations that productively activate such texts. Inasmuch as, for most readers, some form of acquaintance with those discourses constitutes a necessary apprenticeship for reading, this coincidence constitutes the means by which readers are socialized into the literary community. In the case of popular fictions, however, no such coincidence exists. Academic criticisms of all varieties have dissected popular texts, analyzed their internal relations, and made suppositions about their effects on readers. Yet all this has taken place without interrogating the necessary disparity that exists between the discourses of criticism and the reading formations that circulate outside the academy and effectively organize popular reading.

II

This, then, is the area that I want to explore: the determinations that bear on the formation of popular reading. Before fully coming to these, I should like to give my concerns a more general theoretical location by relating the problem of the relations between texts and readers to some contemporary problems in linguistics. For it is linguistics that has provided the master code for the various ways in which the question of such relations has been addressed within literary theory.

Broadly speaking, there have been two lines of approach to the subject. First, there are those approaches that concern themselves with the production within the text of a position for reading, with what has been described variously as the implied reader, the model reader, or the preferred reader.[5] Such approaches operate at the syntactical level of textual analysis: their concern is to determine how a place (or places) for reading is constructed within the system of sign relations that constitute the mode of address of a text. While remaining a necessary level of analysis, this approach also remains insufficient when confronted with the real variability of reader response. Stephen Heath puts the objection succinctly:

> It is possible with regard to a film or group of films to analyse a discursive organization, a system of address, a placing – a construction – of the spectator. . . . This is not to say, however, that any and every spectator – and, for instance, man or woman, of this class or that – will be completely and equally in the given construction, completely and equally there in the film; and nor then is it to say that the discursive organization and its production can exhaust – be taken as equivalent to – the effectivity, the potential effects, of a film.[6]

Something eventuates in the interaction between text and reader that cannot be deduced from the construction of the reader that is effected in the organization by the text of the process of its own reading. The second approach, however, which aims to confront empirical readers and the historical variability of their readings, is also couched within the terms of a linguistic paradigm, insofar as the relationship of readings to texts is construed as analogous to the Saussurean distinction between *parole* and *langue*. Here the semiotics of reading stands in relation to the semiotics

---

[5] See, for example, W. Iser, *The Act of Reading: A Theory of Aesthetic Response* (London: Routledge & Kegan Paul, 1978); W.J. Slatoff, *With Respect to Readers: Dimensions of Literary Response* (Ithaca and London: Cornell Univ. Press, 1970); D. Morley. 'Texts, readers, subjects' and S. Hall, 'Encoding/decoding', in Hall, Hobson, Lowe, and Willis, eds., *Culture, Media, Language* (London: Hutchinson, 1980).

[6] S. Heath, 'Difference', *Screen*, 19, 3 (Autumn 1978), 105–6.

of texts much as the study of *parole* stands in relation to the study of *langue*. It is a question *first* of analyzing the structure of the text, and *then* of disclosing the ways in which that structure is variably realized in consequence of the different determinations that are brought to bear on it by reading subjects in the act of reading. To the text, as to Saussure's *langue*, there belong all those systemic properties of structure; the text supplies the objective datum within the analysis, the object to be read. In its objectivity, moreover, the text is also the realm of necessity, the realm in which hold sway those laws and structures that *necessarily* constrain the act of reading (although they may not *entirely* determine it). By contrast, the study of reading and of the reader, as with Saussure's *parole*, is the study of the realm of the subjective and contingent, of the random and chance determinations that animate the text by way of the person of the reader.

In short, the study of reading occupies the same relation to the study of the text as, in linguistics, pragmatics occupies in relation to syntactics. It is the area in which the reign of the subject, excluded from the analysis of textual structures just as much as from the study of *langue*, is triumphantly reinstalled. The theoretical terms posited here construct a terrain in which subject (the reader) encounters object (the text) – a paradigm in which at issue remains the use of the text, its interpretation, or its decoding by the subject. No matter what the particular terminology and no matter how sociological the analysis of the determinations that mold the activity of the reader, this approach construes the text as an object, a structure, a system of necessary relations – call it what you will – that is pregiven to the reader. Readings may vary but, when all is said and done, they are all readings of the same thing: 'the text' as a set of necessary and objective relations conceived of as existing in some pure and limiting condition of 'in-itselfness' that is independent from the reading relations that regulate its productive activation in different moments of its history. (This condition of 'in-itselfness', it should be added, is not *of* the text, but rather, is a space produced *for* it by the specific terms of theorization employed). Such an approach cannot help but be normative, it inevitably ranks and assigns readings their place according to their degree of conformity with the reading that analysis of the 'text itself' confirms as most correct, most meaningful, most valid, or most appropriate.

Let me give an example. Umberto Eco concludes his discussion of Eugène Sue's *Les Mystères de Paris* as follows:

> The whole of the foregoing examination represents a method of study employed by one particular reader relying on the 'cultivated' codes that were supposedly shared by the author and his contemporary critics. We know perfectly well that other readers in Sue's day did not use this key to decipher the book. They did not grasp its reformist implications, and from the total message only certain more obvious meanings filtered through to them (the

dramatic situation of the working classes, the depravity of some of those in power, the necessity for change of no matter what kind, and so on). Hence the influence, which seems proved, of *Les Mystères* on the popular uprising of 1848. . . . For this reason we must keep in mind a principle characteristic of any examination of mass communication media . . .: the message which has been evolved by an educated elite . . . is expressed at the outset in terms of a fixed code, but it is caught by diverse groups of receivers and deciphered on the basis of other codes. The sense of the message often undergoes a kind of filtration or distortion in the process, which completely alters its 'pragmatic' function.[7]

That seems eminently fair and reasonable, a model of openness. Yet it is caught within precisely the system of polarities I have been describing: *first* the analysis of the text and its 'fixed code', *then* the analysis of its differing pragmatic functions. The difficulty here is that what is presented as the 'fixed code' turns out, on Eco's own admission, to be a *relational code* located, not in the text of *Les Mystères de Paris* itself, but in its relations to the 'cultivated' codes supposedly shared by the author and his contemporary critics. Why start there, however, especially in analyzing a popular novel that, again on Eco's own admission, had its most significant impact within reading relations of a different kind? Further, those other readings, produced outside the cultivated codes that circulated between writer and critics, are conceived of as a lack. They are viewed as the product of a 'filtration' that produces a 'distortion' of the 'fixed code' of the text, as a reading that is marked by an incomprehension, a failure to grasp the reformist implications of the text, as a result of abstracting only 'the most obvious meanings' from the 'total message'. The domain of pragmatics, it turns out, is entered onesidedly: there are uses of the text that are uses of the 'text itself' – not really 'uses', in fact, but functions dictated by its 'fixed code' – and then there are those uses, properly speaking, that are not uses of the 'text itself', but uses of the selectively filtered, distorted, and inadequately understood text.

Hence, the question arises: what if Eco had started from the other direction, using popular rather than 'cultivated' codes as the 'key' with which to 'decipher the book'? Would not the 'fixed codes' of *Les Mystères de Paris* thus look different as a result of their having been inscribed analytically within a different network of signifying relations? The point of asking this question is not to recommend such a simple strategy of reversal. Rather, it is to challenge the procedure both in which the relations between different readings of a text are conceived of as differences between more or less appropriate responses and in which criteria of validity or appropriateness are supplied by the critic's own construction of the 'text itself'.

[7] U. Eco, *The Role of the Reader: Explorations in the Semiotics of Texts* (London: Hutchinson, 1981), pp. 140–41.

III

In order to suggest an alternative to the question of reading, and to indicate why an alternative is needed, let me return to Saussure. In his *Language, Semantics and Ideology,* Michel Pêcheux characterizes Saussure's notion of *parole* as 'the "weakest link" of the scientific apparatus set up in the form of the concept of *langue*'; Saussure's *parole,* he argues, is 'the very type of anti-concept, i.e., a pure ideological excipient "complementing" in its evidentness the concept of *langue*, i.e., a stop-gap, a plug to close the "gap" opened up by the scientific definition of *langue* as systematicity in operation'.[8] Pêcheux argues that the couples langue/parole, system/speaking subject, as well as other such implicit antinomies as object/subject and necessity/contingency, describe an ideological circle in which each term begets an opposite that it then requires as a condition of its own existence, intelligibility, and functioning. *Parole* requires *langue* as the system against which it manifests itself as a creative departure. *Langue*, in turn, requires *parole* as the creativity that prevents the total closure of the system of rules that comprises it. By means of this circular exchange, *langue* preserves its own status as a closed system yet prevents the total closure of that system. It does so by opening itself up through *parole* to the impact of a residue of determinations not given within *langue* itself, but which operate on it by way of speaking subjects and their concrete situations. In this way, simply by pointing to it, Saussure's theory accounts for that for which it cannot account, namely, the full range and variability of language in use.

In like manner, the relations between the semiotics of texts and the semiotics of reading have been developed along the path of a mutually numbing symbiosis. Within this construction, readers require the 'text itself' as that against which their readings can be registered as a creative departure: a use or interpretation that is in no way preordained. The subject triumphs: contingency overrules necessity; the subject conquers the object; Man has his day. On the other side of this exchange, the 'text itself' requires such a reader as the means of affirming its own objectivity and necessity – misunderstood, maybe, but still intact and indissoluble into the acts of reading which, in Robert Escarpit's terms, it is 'creatively betrayed'.[9] The text and its readings, meanings and their different interpretations, the 'fixed code' and its variant 'decodings' – these terms are retained in their separateness, although never without threatening to dissolve into one another.

It is precisely such a dissolution that I wish to recommend: *not* the

---

[8] M. Pêcheux, *Language, Semantics and Ideology: Stating the Obvious* (London: Macmillan, 1982), p. 174.
[9] See R. Escarpit, 'Creative Treason as a Key in Literature', *Yearbook of Comparative and General Literature,* 10 (1961).

dissolution of the 'text itself' into the million and one readings of individual subjects, however, but rather its dissolution into reading relations and, within those, reading formations that concretely and historically structure the interaction between texts and readers. As a result of such a dissolution, the interaction between text and reader no longer would be conceived of as an interaction between, on the one hand, the 'text itself', as a pure entity uncontaminated by any exterior determinations and, on the other, the 'subject', whether conceived as 'raw' and unacculturated, or as situationally formed. Rather, such interaction would be conceived of as occurring between the *culturally activated* text and the *culturally activated* reader, and interaction structured by the material, social, ideological, and institutional relationships in which *both* text and readers are inescapably inscribed.

To develop my argument here, I want to take another leaf out of Pêcheux's book. In an earlier critique of Saussure's concept of *langue*, Vološinov observes that the constitution of *langue* as a system of objective and universal rules ignores the struggle over meaning that takes place within language as a result of the opposition between 'differently orientated social interests within one and the same sign community'.[10] Pêcheux argues that the unity of *langue*, although real (he rejects the notion that there are separate, class-based languages within a given sign community), is only *tendential*. Not merely at the level of practice or use, but at that of structure as well, this tendential unity is riven by the contradictions and antagonisms between different *discursive formations* that initiate, in relation to *langue*, different *discursive processes* that result in 'contrasting' "vocabulary-syntaxes" and "arguments" which lead, *sometimes with the same words,* in different directions depending on the nature of the ideological interests at stake' (Pêcheux, p. 9). *Langue*, then, constitutes the basis – a definite set of phonological, morphological, and syntactic structures – in relation to which there form antagonistic discursive processes. Pêcheux goes to some pains to stress that what he has in mind here is not another variant of *parole*. A discursive process, he writes, 'is not a "concrete" individual way of inhabiting the "abstraction" of the *langue'* (Pêcheux, p. 58). A discursive process is rather the putting to use, on the basis of *langue*, of a discursive formation rooted in a specific ideological class relationship. Individual speech acts, or, if the term is to be retained, the events of *parole*, are not the product of individual and subjective uses of *langue*, but instead are located in the intersections among class-based discursive processes that traverse *langue* and which, in so doing, make its unity only tendential rather than actual.

What I am interested in here are the implications of his position for the analysis of meaning. Pêcheux summarizes these as follows:

[10] V.N. Vološinov, *Marxism and the Philosophy of Language* (New York: Seminar Press, 1973), p. 23.

The first consists of the proposition that the meaning of a word, expression, proposition, etc., does not exist 'in itself' (i.e., in its transparent relation to the literal character of the signifier), but is determined by the ideological positions brought into play in the socio-historical process in which words, expressions and propositions are produced (i.e., reproduced). This thesis could be summed up in the statement: *words, expressions, propositions, etc., change their meaning according to the positions held by those who use them*, which signifies that they find their meaning by reference to those positions, i.e., by reference to the *ideological formations . . .* in which those positions are inscribed.

(Pêcheux, p. 111)

Again, Pêcheux goes to some lengths to make it clear that what he has in mind is not another version of polysemanticity, or what Volosinov calls the 'multi-accentuality of the sign'. The concept of polysemanticity implies either that a word may have several possible meanings before it has *a* meaning or that it has *a* meaning which may be variously interpreted. Pêcheux contests this assumption. He endorses Lacan's argument concerning the primacy of the signifier over the sign and over meaning, and hence, the view that meaning is produced within the relations of substitutability between signifiers. Meaning is an effect of the ceaselessly mobile relations between signifiers rather than a property of signifiers as such. It follows that 'meaning does not exist anywhere except in the metaphorical relationships (realized in substitution effects, paraphrases, synonym formations) which happen to be more or less provisionally located historically in a given discursive formation: words, expressions and propositions get their meaning from the discursive formation to which they belong' (Pêcheux, p. 189).

Put another way, because the same signifier may function differently within different discursive formations, it is impossible to locate a linguistic space within which the signifier may be said to have *a* meaning in relation to which other uses of it can then be conceived of as distortions. The only 'possibility' of doing so is in fact by privileging the linguistic values at work within one discursive formation over those in evidence elsewhere. Yet, as we have seen, this is precisely the means whereby the linguistic values of dominant social groups become reified as properties of *langue* itself rather than as properties of a specific mode of social accentuation. In short, 'a meaning effect does not pre-exist the discursive formation in which it is constituted' (Pêcheux, p. 187).

And so I want to argue that a 'reading effect' similarly does not pre-exist the 'reading formation' in which it is constituted. The analogy, of course, is not a strict one. It is clear that a text would count as an instance of what Pêcheux characterizes as a discursive formation. So too would what I have called a 'reading formation', although I think it is useful to retain this concept as a separate term that designates a region of discourse that is specifically concerned with the production of readings, with the operation of a hermeneutic. While it is true, however, that texts always effect a certain embedding of meanings within a discursive formation – they consist not just of signifiers but of definite orders of relations between signifiers – those meanings can always be dis-embedded and re-embedded in alternative discursive formations through the ways in which texts are productively activated within different reading formations. These reading formations, moreover, are themselves put to work within reading relations of different kinds, as texts, in the course of their histories, are constantly *re-written* into a variety of material, social, institutional, and ideological contexts. It is for this reason that I prefer the concept 'productive activation' to that of 'interpretation'. To speak of interpretation is to permit variability to enter the process of reading only through the person of the reader. In speaking of the 'productive activation' of texts, I mean to imply a process in which texts, readers, and the relations between them are *all* subject to variable determinations.

IV

What are the practical consequences of this? To be honest, I'm not altogther sure. My concern has been less to provide answers than to raise awkward questions. For the most part, these concern the status that a text is to be conceived of as having within a given critical or theoretical enterprise. This question is troubling since, once the seductive facticity of the 'text itself' is challenged, there seems to be nothing to stop the total dissolution of the text into a potentially infinite series of different readings – in which case there seems to be nothing left for criticism to get hold of or to address. The only solution to this dilemma is for criticism to realize that what it has got hold of is different from the object that it has traditionally supposed was given to it, and to modify its practice accordingly. This is precisely the step that Fredric Jameson recommends in *The Political Unconscious*. Constructing criticism as an enterprise that 'takes place within a Homeric battlefield, on which a host of interpretive options are either openly or implicitly in conflict', he disclaims any concern with 'the criteria by which a given interpretation may be faulted or accredited' and addresses himself instead to the question of the relations between readings.[11] His book 'presupposes, as its organizational fiction, that we never really confront a text, immediately, in all its freshness as a thing-in-itself', a supposition that 'dictates the use of a method . . . according to which our object of study is less the text itself than the interpretations through which we attempt to confront and to appropriate it' (Jameson, pp. 9–10).

[11] F. Jameson, *The Political Unconscious: Narrative as a Socially Symbolic Act* (Ithaca and London: Cornell Univ. Press, 1981), p. 13.

The method of the 'metacommentary', which Jameson here proposes, is one in which a criticism seeks validity – for its own time and circumstances – by virtue of its ability to net other interpretations and locate them within its own discourse, rather than by virtue of its appeal to the authority of the 'text itself'. Criticism thus recognizes its own specificity as a productive activation of the text, as the product of a reading formation (in this case, Marxism) put to work within reading relations of a particular kind. It equally recognizes, as a condition of effective political intervention within the battleground of readings, a need to make space for itself by producing its own relation to contending readings. An attempt to warrant specific readings and to discredit others through appeal to the authority of the 'text itself', therefore, must be recognized for what it is: a political strategy for reading in which the critic's own construction of the 'text itself' is mobilized in order to bully other interpretations off the field.

If, moreover, one's concern is with the analysis of the social destinies of texts – with the real and varied history of their productive activations – such attribution of any authority to the 'text itself' has the effect, not just of bullying other readings off the field, but of bullying them out of existence altogether. It becomes the means whereby readings are dismissed as distortions or misunderstandings; as 'untutored' readings, they are located as part of a history of incomprehension, rather than as readings that, like Menocchio's, deserve to be understood on their own terms. As it has been developed so far, the study of reading has been characterized by a marked onesidedness. It has placed the reader into the melting pot of variability while retaining the text as a fixed pole of analytical reference. It is high time that the text be placed into the melting pot of variability; it is necessary to recognize that the history of reading is not one in which different readers encounter 'the same text' but one in which the text that readers encounter is already 'overworked', 'overcoded', productively activated as a result of its particular inscription within the social, material, ideological, and institutional relationships that distinguish specific reading relations. The text has no meaning effects that can be constituted outside of such reading relationships. It has no meanings that can be traduced.

As I've already indicated, I think these considerations apply with particular force to the study of popular texts. These texts are usually studied, and not infrequently condemned, for their effects on 'other people' without making any real attempt to take account of the specific determinations that mold and structure popular reading, that is, readings produced outside the academy and at a considerable remove from the critical discourses that circulate within it. Jameson writes that texts come before us as 'the always-already-read', apprehended through the sedimented reading habits and categories developed within inherited interpretive traditions (Jameson, p. 9). That is true insofar as one is concerned with the canonized tradition, for which the most consequential activations of the relations between texts and readers consist of precisely those forms of critical commentary that circulate within cultural apparatuses (critical journals, educational institutions, publishing houses) that have a primary investment in the institution of Literature. Yet what about the popular reading of popular texts? What are the orders of intertextuality within which such reading is located? What are the discursive forms and institutional apparatuses through which popular reading is superintended? No one knows, at least not in a detailed way. One might point to the operation of the star system, and to the social production of popular heroes, as instances of the superintendence of popular reading; these indeed constitute hermeneutic systems that pin down the meaning of popular texts in particular ways, thus fixing the ideological coordinates within which they are to be read. One might also point to the similar function of interviews with actors, actresses, writers and directors; which appear in publications that impinge directly on the social organization of popular reading: film reviews, fan magazines, and the like. Yet we scarcely have an adequate knowledge of the workings of such hermeneutic activators of popular texts, and we know even less about the cultural resources that may be mobilized against such 'triggers' of reading. It is not an exaggeration to say that, in the absence of an adequate knowledge and theorization of these matters, any attempt to make a political intervention within the sphere of popular reading runs the risk of being radically inappropriate.

To put the point simply, the problem is that the text that critics have on the desk before them may not be the same as the text that is culturally active in the relations of popular reading. Accordingly, analysis must start with the determinations that organize the social relations of popular reading, if we are to understand the nature of the cultural business that is conducted around, through, and by means of popular texts in the real history of their productive activation. Rather than taking the text as a given, it is necessary to introduce a radical hesitancy into analysis, a hesitancy such that the text will be *the last thing* one speaks of, and even then, only in regard to the historical reading relations in which the text has been located analytically. Only in this way, moreover, can the study of the 'living life' of written texts advance beyond the empty-headed gesture of stating that there are texts with 'fixed properties' that may, *of course*, be variously 'interpreted'. While this assertion displays a fine openmindedness – 'anything is possible' – it also singularly fails to broach the real issue: namely, accounting for such *real* variations in the social destinies of texts as *have actually* taken place.

The Open University
Milton Keynes, England

24 Michel Foucault,

From 'The Order of Discourse', *Untying the Text,* **ed R. Young**

p52–64

II

Here is the hypothesis which I would like to put forward tonight in order
to fix the terrain – or perhaps the very provisional theatre – of the work
I am doing: that in every society the production of discourse is at once
controlled, selected, organised and redistributed by a certain number of
procedures whose role is to ward off its powers and dangers, to gain
mastery over its chance events, to evade its ponderous, formidable
materiality.

In a society like ours, the procedures of exclusion are well known. The
most obvious and familiar is the prohibition. We know quite well that we
do not have the right to say everything, that we cannot speak of just
anything in any circumstances whatever, and that not everyone has the
right to speak of anything whatever. In the taboo on the object of speech,
and the ritual of the circumstances of speech, and the privileged or exclusive right of the speaking subject, we have the play of three types of prohibition which intersect, reinforce or compensate for each other,
forming a complex grid which changes constantly. I will merely note that
at the present time the regions where the grid is tightest, where the black
squares are most numerous, are those of sexuality and politics; as if discourse, far from being that transparent or neutral element in which
sexuality is disarmed and politics pacified, is in fact one of the places
where sexuality and politics exercise in a privileged way some of their
most formidable powers. It does not matter that discourse appears to be
of little account, because the prohibitions that surround it very soon
reveal its link with desire and with power. There is nothing surprising
about that, since, as psychoanalysis has shown, discourse is not simply
that which manifests (or hides) desire – it is also the object of desire; and
since, as history constantly teaches us, discourse is not simply that which
translates struggles or systems of domination, but is the thing for which
and by which there is struggle, discourse is the power which is to be
seized.

There exists in our society another principle of exclusion, not another
prohibition but a division and a rejection. I refer to the opposition
between reason and madness. Since the depths of the Middle Ages, the
madman has been the one whose discourse cannot have the same currency as others. His word may be considered null and void, having

neither truth nor importance, worthless as evidence in law, inadmissible in the authentification of deeds or contracts, incapable even of bringing about the trans-substantiation of bread into body at Mass. On the other hand, strange powers not held by any other may be attributed to the madman's speech: the power of uttering a hidden truth, of telling the future, of seeing in all naivety what the others' wisdom cannot perceive. It is curious to note that for centuries in Europe the speech of the madman was either not heard at all or else taken for the word of truth. It either fell into the void, being rejected as soon as it was proffered, or else people deciphered in it a rationality, naive or crafty, which they regarded as more rational than that of the sane. In any event, whether excluded, or secretly invested with reason, the madman's speech, strictly, did not exist. It was through his words that his madness was recognised; they were the place where the division between reason and madness was exercised, but they were never recorded or listened to. No doctor before the end of the eighteenth century had ever thought of finding out what was said, or how and why it was said, in this speech which nonetheless determined the difference. This whole immense discourse of the madman was taken for mere noise, and he was only symbolically allowed to speak, in the theatre, where he would step forward, disarmed and reconciled, because there he played the role of truth in a mask.

You will tell me that all this is finished today or is coming to an end; that the madman's speech is no longer on the other side of the divide; that it is no longer null and void; and on the contrary, it puts us on the alert; that we now look for a meaning in it, for the outline or the ruins of some oeuvre; and that we have even gone so far as to come across this speech of madness in what we articulate ourselves, in that slight stumbling by which we lose track of what we are saying. But all this attention to the speech of madness does not prove that the old division is no longer operative. You have only to think of the whole framework of knowledge through which we decipher that speech, and of the whole network of institutions which permit someone – a doctor or a psychoanalyst – to listen to it, and which at the same time permit the patient to bring along his poor words or, in desperation, to withhold them. You have only to think of all this to become suspicious that the division, far from being effaced, is working differently, along other lines, through new institutions, and with effects that are not at all the same. And even if the doctor's role were only that of lending an ear to a speech that is free at last, he still does this listening in the context of the same division. He is listening to a discourse which is invested with desire, and which – for its greater exaltation or its greater anguish – thinks it is loaded with terrible powers. If the silence of reason is required for the curing of monsters, it is enough for that silence to be on the alert, and it is in this that the division remains.

It is perhaps risky to consider the opposition between true and false as a third system of exclusion, along with those just mentioned. How could one reasonably compare the constraint of truth with divisions like those, which are arbitrary to start with or which at least are organised around historical contingencies; which are not only modifiable but in perpetual displacement; which are supported by a whole system of institutions which impose them and renew them; and which act in a constraining and sometimes violent way?

Certainly, when viewed from the level of a proposition, on the inside of a discourse, the division between true and false is neither arbitrary nor modifiable nor institutional nor violent. But when we view things on a different scale, when we ask the question of what this will to truth has been and constantly is, across our discourses, this will to truth which has crossed so many centuries of our history; what is, in its very general form, the type of division which governs our will to know (notre volonté de savoir), then what we see taking shape is perhaps something like a system of exclusion, a historical, modifiable, and institutionally constraining system.

There is no doubt that this division is historically constituted. For the Greek poets of the sixth century BC, the true discourse (in the strong and valorised sense of the word), the discourse which inspired respect and terror, and to which one had to submit because it ruled, was the one pronounced by men who spoke as of right and according to the required ritual; the discourse which dispensed justice and gave everyone his share; the discourse which in prophesying the future not only announced what was going to happen but helped to make it happen, carrying men's minds along with it and thus weaving itself into the fabric of destiny. Yet already a century later the highest truth no longer resided in what discourse was or did, but in what it said: a day came when truth was displaced from the ritualised, efficacious and just act of enunciation, towards the utterance itself, its meaning, its form, its object, its relation to its reference. Between Hesiod and Plato a certain division was established, separating true discourse from false discourse: a new division because henceforth the true discourse is no longer precious and desirable, since it is no longer the one linked to the exercise of power. The sophist is banished.

This historical division probably gave our will to know its general form. However, it has never stopped shifting: sometimes the great mutations in scientific thought can perhaps be read as the consequences of a discovery, but they can also be read as the appearance of new forms in the will to truth. There is doubtless a will to truth in the nineteenth century which differs from the will to know characteristic of Classical culture in the forms it deploys, in the domains of objects to which it addresses itself, and in the techniques on which it is based. To go back a little further: at the turn of the sixteenth century (and particularly in England), there appeared a will to know which, anticipating its actual contents, sketched out schemas of possible, observable, measurable, classifiable objects; a will to know which imposed on the knowing subject, and in some sense prior to all experience, a certain position, a certain gaze and a certain function (to see rather than to read, to verify rather than to make commentaries on); a will to know which was prescribed (but in a more general manner than by any specific instrument) by the technical level where knowledges had to be invested in order to be verifiable and useful. It was just as if, starting from the great Platonic division, the will to truth had its own history, which is not that of constraining truths: the history of the range of objects to be known, of the functions and positions of the knowing subject, of the material, technical, and instrumental investments of knowledge.

This will to truth, like the other systems of exclusion, rests on an institutional support: it is both reinforced and renewed by whole strata of practices, such as pedagogy, of course; and the system of books, publishing, libraries; learned societies in the past and laboratories now. But it is also renewed, no doubt more profoundly, by the way in which knowledge is put to work, valorised, distributed, and in a sense attributed, in a society. Let us recall at this point, and only symbolically, the old Greek principle: though arithmetic may well be the concern of democratic cities, because it teaches about the relations of equality, geometry alone must be taught in oligarchies, since it demonstrates the proportions within inequality.

Finally, I believe that this will to truth – leaning in this way on a support and an institutional distribution – tends to exert a sort of pressure and something like a power of constraint (I am still speaking of our own society) on other discourses. I am thinking of the way in which for centuries Western literature sought to ground itself on the natural, the 'vraisemblable', on sincerity, on science as well – in short, on 'true' discourse. I am thinking likewise of the manner in which economic practices, codified as precepts or recipes and ultimately as morality, have sought since the sixteenth century to ground themselves, rationalise themselves, and justify themselves in a theory of wealth and production. I am also thinking of the way in which a body as prescriptive as the penal system sought its bases or its justification, at first of course in a theory of justice, then, since the nineteenth century, in a sociological, psychological, medical, and psychiatric knowledge: it is as if even the word of the law could no longer be authorised, in our society, except by a discourse of truth.

Of the three great systems of exclusion which forge discourse – the forbidden speech, the division of madness and the will to truth, I have spoken of the third at greatest length. The fact is that it is towards this third system that the other two have been drifting constantly for centuries. The third system increasingly attempts to assimilate the others, both in order to modify them and to provide them with a founda-

[margin handwritten note: – Systems of exclusion rest on institutional support]

tion. The first two are constantly becoming more fragile and more uncertain, to the extent that they are now invaded by the will to truth, which for its part constantly grows stronger, deeper, and more implacable.

And yet we speak of the will to truth no doubt least of all. It is as if, for us, the will to truth and its vicissitudes were masked by truth itself in its necessary unfolding. The reason is perhaps this: although since the Greeks 'true' discourse is no longer the discourse that answers to the demands of desire, or the discourse which exercises power, what is at stake in the will to truth, in the will to utter this 'true' discourse, if not desire and power? 'True' discourse, freed from desire and power by the necessity of its form, cannot recognise the will to truth which pervades it; and the will to truth, having imposed itself on us for a very long time, is such that the truth it wants cannot fail to mask it.

Thus all that appears to our eyes is a truth conceived as a richness, a fecundity, a gentle and insidiously universal force, and in contrast we are unaware of the will to truth, that prodigious machinery designed to exclude. All those who, from time to time in our history, have tried to dodge this will to truth and to put it into question against truth, at the very point where truth undertakes to justify the prohibition and to define madness, all of them, from Nietzsche to Artaud and Bataille, must now serve as the (no doubt lofty) signs for our daily work.

III

There are, of course, many other procedures for controlling and delimiting discourse. Those of which I have spoken up to now operate in a sense from the exterior. They function as systems of exclusion. They have to do with the part of discourse which puts power and desire at stake.

I believe we can isolate another group: internal procedures, since discourses themselves exercise their own control; procedures which function rather as principles of classification, of ordering, of distribution, as if this time another dimension of discourse had to be mastered: that of events and chance.

In the first place, commentary. I suppose – but without being very certain – that there is scarcely a society without its major narratives, which are recounted, repeated, and varied; formulae, texts, and ritualised sets of discourses which are recited in well-defined circumstances; things said once and preserved because it is suspected that behind them there is a secret or a treasure. In short, we may suspect that there is in all societies, with great consistency, a kind of gradation among discourses: those which are said in the ordinary course of days and exchanges, and which vanish as soon as they have been pronounced; and those which give rise to a certain number of new speech-acts which take them up, transform them or speak of them, in short, those discourses which, over and above their formulation, are said indefinitely, remain said, and are to be said again. We know them in our own cultural system: they are religious or juridical texts, but also those texts (curious ones, when we consider their status) which are called 'literary'; and to a certain extent, scientific texts.

This differentiation is certainly neither stable, nor constant, nor absolute. There is not, on the one side, the category of fundamental or creative discourses, given for all time, and on the other, the mass of discourses which repeat, gloss, and comment. Plenty of major texts become blurred and disappear, and sometimes commentaries move into the primary position. But though its points of application may change, the function remains; and the principle of a differentiation is continuously put back in play. The radical effacement of this gradation can only ever be play, utopia, or anguish. The Borges-style play of a commentary which is nothing but the solemn and expected reappearance word for word of the text that is commented on; or the play of a criticism that would speak forever of a work which does not exist. The lyrical dream of a discourse which is reborn absolutely new and innocent at every point, and which reappears constantly in all freshness, derived from things, feelings or thoughts. The anguish of that patient of Janet's for whom the least utterance was gospel truth, concealing inexhaustible treasures of meaning and worthy to be repeated, re-commenced, and commented on indefinitely: 'When I think,' he would say when reading or listening, 'when I think of this sentence which like the others will go off into eternity, and which I have perhaps not yet fully understood.'

But who can fail to see that this would be to annul one of the terms of the relation each time, and not to do away with the relation itself? It is a relation which is constantly changing with time; which takes multiple and divergent forms in a given epoch. The juridical exegesis is very different from the religious commentary (and this has been the case for a very long time). One and the same literary work can give rise simultaneously to very distinct types of discourse: the 'Odyssey' as a primary text is repeated, in the same period, in the translation by Bérard, and in the endless 'explications de texte', and in Joyce's 'Ulysses'.

For the moment I want to do no more than indicate that, in what is broadly called commentary, the hierarchy between primary and secondary text plays two roles which are in solidarity with each other. On the one hand it allows the (endless) construction of new discourses: the dominance of the primary text, its permanence, its status as a discourse which can always be re-actualised, the multiple or hidden meaning with which it is credited, the essential reticence and richness which is attributed to it, all this is the basis for an open possibility of speaking. But on the other hand the commentary's only role, whatever the techniques used, is to say at last what was silently articulated 'beyond', in the text.

By a paradox which it always displaces but never escapes, the commentary must say for the first time what had, nonetheless, already been said, and must tirelessly repeat what had, however, never been said. The infinite rippling of commentaries is worked from the inside by the dream of a repetition in disguise: at its horizon there is perhaps nothing but what was at its point of departure – mere recitation. Commentary exorcises the chance element of discourse by giving it its due; it allows us to say something other than the text itself, but on condition that it is this text itself which is said, and in a sense completed. The open multiplicity, the element of chance, are transferred, by the principle of commentary, from what might risk being said, on to the number, the form, the mask, and the circumstances of the repetition. The new thing here lies not in what is said but in the event of its return.

I believe there exists another principle of rarefaction of a discourse, complementary to the first, to a certain extent: the author. Not, of course, in the sense of the speaking individual who pronounced or wrote a text, but in the sense of a principle of grouping of discourses, conceived as the unity and origin of their meanings, as the focus of their coherence. This principle is not everywhere at work, nor in a constant manner: there exist all around us plenty of discourses which circulate without deriving their meaning or their efficacity from an author to whom they could be attributed: everyday remarks, which are effaced immediately; decrees or contracts which require signatories but no author; technical instructions which are transmitted anonymously. But in the domains where it is the rule to attribute things to an author – literature, philosophy, science – it is quite evident that this attribution does not always play the same role. In the order of scientific discourse, it was indispensable; during the Middle Ages, that a text should be attributed to an author, since this was an index of truthfulness. A proposition was considered as drawing even its scientific value from its author. Since the seventeenth century, this function has steadily been eroded in scientific discourse: it now functions only to give a name to a theorem, an effect, an example, a syndrome. On the other hand, in the order of literary discourse, starting from the same epoch, the function of the author has steadily grown stronger: all those tales, poems, dramas or comedies which were allowed to circulate in the Middle Ages in at least a relative anonymity are now asked (and obliged to say) where they come from, who wrote them. The author is asked to account for the unity of the texts which are placed under his name. He is asked to reveal or at least carry authentification of the hidden meaning which traverses them. He is asked to connect them to his lived experiences, to the real history which saw their birth. The author is what gives the disturbing language of fiction its unities, its nodes of coherence, its insertion in the real.

I know that I will be told: 'But you are speaking there of the author as he is reinvented after the event by criticism, after he is dead and there is nothing left except for a tangled mass of scribblings; in those circumstances a little order surely has to be introduced into all that, by imagining a project, a coherence, a thematic structure that is demanded of the consciousness or the life of an author who is indeed perhaps a trifle fictitious. But that does not mean he did not exist, this real author, who bursts into the midst of all these worn-out words, bringing to them his genius or his disorder.

It would of course, be absurd to deny the existence of the individual who writes and invents. But I believe that – at least since a certain epoch – the individual who sets out to write a text on the horizon of which a possible oeuvre is prowling, takes upon himself the function of the author: what he writes and what does not write, what he sketches out, even by way of provisional drafts, as an outline of the oeuvre, and what he lets fall by way of commonplace remarks – this whole play of differences is prescribed by the author-function, as he receives it from his epoch, or as he modifies it in his turn. He may well overturn the traditional image of the author; nevertheless, it is from some new author-position that he will cut out, from everything he could say and from all that he does say every day at any moment, the still trembling outline of his oeuvre.

The commentary-principle limits the chance-element in discourse by the play of an identity which would take the form of repetition and sameness. The author-principle limits this same element of chance by the play of an identity which has the form of individuality and the self.

We must also recognise another principle of limitation in what is called, not sciences but 'disciplines': a principle which is itself relative and mobile; which permits construction, but within narrow confines.

The organisation of disciplines is just as much opposed to the principle of commentary as to that of the author. It is opposed to the principle of the author because a discipline is defined by a domain of objects, a set of methods, a corpus of propositions considered to be true, a play of rules and definitions, of techniques and instruments: all this constitutes a sort of anonymous system at the disposal of anyone who wants to or is able to use it, without their meaning or validity being linked to the one who happened to be their inventor. But the principle of a discipline is also opposed to that of commentary: in a discipline, unlike a commentary, what is supposed at the outset is not a meaning which has to be rediscovered, nor an identity which has to be repeated, but the requisites for the construction of new statements. For there to be a discipline, there must be a possibility of formulating new propositions, ad infinitum.

But there is more; there is more, no doubt, in order for there to be less: a discipline is not the sum of all that can be truthfully said about something; it is not even the set of all that can be accepted about the same data in virtue of some principle of coherence or systematicity. Medicine is not constituted by the total of what can be truthfully said about illness;

botany cannot be defined by the sum of all the truths concerning plants. There are two reasons for this: first of all, botany and medicine are made up of errors as well as truths, like any other discipline – errors which are not residues or foreign bodies but which have positive functions, a historical efficacity, and a role that is often indissociable from that of the truths. And besides, for a proposition to belong to botany or pathology, it has to fulfil certain conditions, in a sense stricter and more complex than pure and simple truth: but in any case, other conditions. It must address itself to a determinate plane of objects: from the end of the seventeenth century, for example, for a proposition to be 'botanical' it had to deal with the visible structure of the plant, the system of its close and distant resemblances or the mechanism of its fluids; it could no longer retain its symbolic value, as was the case in the sixteenth century, nor the set of virtues and properties which were accorded to it in antiquity. But without belonging to a discipline, a proposition must use conceptual or technical instruments of a well-defined type; from the nineteenth century, a proposition was no longer medical – it fell 'outside medicine' and acquired the status of an individual phantasm or popular imagery – if it used notions that were at the same time metaphorical, qualitative, and substantial (like those of engorgement, of overheated liquids or of dried-out solids). In contrast it could and had to make use of notions that were equally metaphorical but based on another model, a functional and physiological one (that of the irritation, inflammation, or degeneration of the tissues). Still further: in order to be part of a discipline, a proposition has to be able to be inscribed on a certain type of theoretical horizon: suffice it to recall that the search for the primitive language, which was a perfectly acceptable theme up to the eighteenth century, was sufficient, in the second half of the nineteenth century, to make any discourse fall into – I hesitate to say error – chimera and reverie, into pure and simple linguistic monstrosity.

Within its own limits, each discipline recognises true and false propositions; but it pushes back a whole teratology of knowledge beyond its margins. The exterior of a science is both more and less populated than is often believed: there is of course immediate experience, the imaginary themes which endlessly carry and renew immemorial beliefs; but perhaps there are no errors in the strict sense, for error can only arise and be decided inside a definite practice; on the other hand, there are monsters on the prowl whose form changes with the history of knowledge. In short, a proposition must fulfil complex and heavy requirements to be able to belong to the grouping of a discipline; before it can be called true or false, it must be 'in the true', as Canguilhem would say.

People have often wondered how the botanists or biologists of the nineteenth century managed not to see that what Mendel was saying was true. But it was because Mendel was speaking of objects, applying methods, and placing himself on a theoretical horizon which were alien to the biology of his time. Naudin, before him, had of course posited the thesis that hereditary traits are discrete; yet, no matter how new or strange this principle was it was able to fit into the discourse of biology, at least as an enigma. What Mendel did was to constitute the hereditary trait as an absolutely new biological object, thanks to a kind of filtering which had never been used before: he detached the trait from the species, and from the sex which transmits it; the field in which he observed it being the infinitely open series of the generations, where it appears and disappears according to statistical regularities. This was a new object which called for new conceptual instruments and new theoretical foundations. Mendel spoke the truth, but he was not 'within the true' of the biological discourse of his time: it was not according to such rules that biological objects and concepts were formed. It needed a complete change of scale, the deployment of a whole new range of objects in biology for Mendel to enter into the true and for his propositions to appear (in large measure) correct. Mendel was a true monster, which meant that science could not speak of him; whereas about thirty years earlier, at the height of the nineteenth century, Scheiden, for example, who denied plant sexuality, but in accordance with the rules of biological discourse, was merely formulating a disciplined error.

It is always possible that one might speak the truth in the space of a wild exteriority, but one is 'in the true' only by obeying the rules of a discursive 'policing' which one has to reactivate in each of one's discourses.

The discipline is a principle of control over the production of discourse. The discipline fixes limits for discourse by the action of an identity which takes the form of a permanent re-actuation of the rules.

We are accustomed to see in an author's fecundity, in the multiplicity of the commentaries, and in the development of a discipline so many infinite resources for the creation of discourses. Perhaps so, but they are nonetheless principles of constraint; it is very likely impossible to account for their positive and multiplicatory role if we do not take into consideration their restrictive and constraining function.

IV

There is, I believe, a third group of procedures which permit the control of discourses. This time it is not a matter of mastering their powers or averting the unpredictability of their appearance, but of determining the condition of their application, of imposing a certain number of rules on the individuals who hold them, and thus of not permitting everyone to have access to them. There is a rarefaction, this time, of the speaking subjects; none shall enter the order of discourse if he does not satisfy certain requirements or if he is not, from the outset, qualified to do so. To be more precise: not all the regions of discourse are equally open and penetrable; some of them are largely forbidden (they are differentiated and differentiating), while others seems to be almost open to all winds and put at the disposal of every speaking subject, without prior restrictions.

In this regard I should like to recount an anecdote which is so beautiful that one trembles at the thought that it might be true. It gathers into a single figure all the constraints of discourse: those which limit its powers, those which master its aleatory appearances, those which carry out the selection among speaking subjects. At the beginning of the seventeenth century, the Shogun heard tell that the Europeans' superiority in matters of navigation, commerce, politics, and military skill was due to their knowledge of mathematics. He desired to get hold of so precious a knowledge. As he had been told of an English sailor who possessed the secret of these miraculous discourses, he summoned him to his palace and kept him there. Alone with him, he took lessons. He learned mathematics. He retained power, and lived to a great old age. It was not until the nineteenth century that there were Japanese mathematicians. But the anecdote does not stop there: it has its European side too. The story has it that this English sailor, Will Adams, was an autodidact, a carpenter who had learnt geometry in the course of working in a shipyard. Should we see this story as the expression of one of the great myths of European culture? The universal communication of knowledge and the infinite free exchange of discourses in Europe, against the monopolised and secret knowledge of Oriental tyranny?

This idea, of course, does not stand up to examination. Exchange and communication are positive figures working inside complex systems of restriction, and probably would not be able to function independently of them. The most superficial and visible of these systems of restriction is constituted by what can be gathered under the name of ritual. Ritual defines the qualification which must be possessed by individuals who speak (and who must occupy such-and-such a position and formulate such-and-such a type of statement, in the play of a dialogue, of interrogation or recitation); it defines the gestures, behaviour, circumstances, and the whole set of signs which must accompany discourse; finally, it fixes the supposed or imposed efficacity of the words, their effect on those to whom they are addressed, and the limits of their constraining value. Religious, judicial, therapeutic, and in large measure also political discourses can scarcely be dissociated from this deployment of a ritual which determines both the particular properties and the stipulated roles of the speaking subjects.

A somewhat different way of functioning is that of the 'societies of discourse', which function to preserve or produce discourses, but in order to make them circulate in a closed space, distributing them only according to strict rules, and without the holders being dispossessed by this distribution. An archaic model for this is provided by the groups of rhapsodists who possessed the knowledge of the poems to be recited or potentially to be varied and transformed. But though the object of this knowledge was after all a ritual recitation, the knowledge was protected, defended and preserved within a definite group by the often very complex exercises of memory which it implied. To pass an apprenticeship in it allowed one to enter both a group and a secret which the act of recitation showed but did not divulge; the roles of speaker and listener were not interchangeable.

There are hardly any such 'societies of discourse' now, with their ambiguous play of the secret and its divulgation. But this should not deceive us: even in the order of 'true' discourse, even in the order of discourse that is published and free from all ritual, there are still forms of appropriation of secrets, and non-interchangeable roles. It may well be that the act of writing as it is institutionalised today, in the book, the publishing-system and the person of the writer, takes place in a 'society of discourse', which though diffuse is certainly constraining. The difference between the writer and any other speaking or writing subject (a difference constantly stressed by the writer himself), the intransitive nature (according to him) of his discourse, the fundamental singularity which he has been ascribing for so long to 'writing', the dissymmetry that is asserted between 'creation' and any use of the linguistic system – all this shows the existence of a certain 'society of discourse', and tends moreover to bring back its play of practices. But there are many others still, functioning according to entirely different schemas of exclusivity and disclosure: e.g., technical or scientific secrets, or the forms of diffusion and circulation of medical discourse, or those who have appropriated the discourse of politics or economics.

At first glance, the 'doctrines' (religious, political, philosophical) seem to constitute the reverse of a 'society of discourse', in which the number of speaking individuals tended to be limited even if it was not fixed; between those individuals, the discourse could circulate and be transmitted. Doctrine, on the contrary, tends to be diffused, and it is by the holding in common of one and the same discursive ensemble that individuals (as many as one cares to imagine) define their reciprocal allegiance. In appearance, the only prerequisite is the recognition of the same truths and the acceptance of a certain rule of (more or less flexible) conformity with the validated discourses. If doctrines were nothing more than this, they would not be so very different from scientific disciplines, and the discursive control would apply only to the form or the content of the statement, not to the speaking subject. But doctrinal allegiance puts in question both the statement and the speaking subject, the one by the other. It puts the speaking subject in question through and on the basis of the statement, as is proved by the procedures of exclusion and the mechanisms of rejection which come into action when a speaking subject has formulated one or several unassimilable statements; heresy and orthodoxy do not derive from a fanatical exaggeration of the doctrinal mechanisms, but rather belong fundamentally to them. And conversely the doctrine puts the statements in question on the basis of the speaking subjects, to the extent that the doctrine always stands as the sign, manifestation and instrument of a prior adherence to a class, a social status, a race, a nationality, an interest, a revolt, a resistance or an acceptance. Doctrine binds individuals to certain types of enunciation and consequently forbids them all others; but it uses, in return, certain types of enunciation to bind individuals amongst themselves, and to differentiate them by that very fact from all others. Doctrine brings about a double subjection: of the speaking subjects to discourses, and of discourses to the (at least virtual) group of speaking individuals.

On a much broader scale, we are obliged to recognise large cleavages in what might be called the social appropriation of discourses. Although education may well be, by right, the instrument thanks to which any individual in a society like ours can have access to any kind of discourse whatever, this does not prevent it from following, as is well known, in its distribution, in what it allows and what it prevents, the lines marked out by social distances, oppositions and struggles. Any system of education is a political way of maintaining or modifying the appropriation of discourses, along with the knowledges and powers which they carry.

I am well aware that it is very abstract to separate speech-rituals, societies of discourse, doctrinal groups and social appropriations, as I have just done. Most of the time, they are linked to each other and constitute kinds of great edifices which ensure the distribution of speaking subjects into the different types of discourse and the appropriation of discourses to certain categories of subject. Let us say, in a word, that those are the major procedures of subjection used by discourse. What, after all, is an education system, other than a ritualisation of speech, a qualification and a fixing of the roles for speaking subjects, the constitution of a doctrinal group, however diffuse, a distribution and an appropriation of discourse with its powers and knowledges? What is 'écriture' (the writing of the 'writers') other than a similar system of subjection, which perhaps takes slightly different forms, but forms whose main rhythms are analogous? Does not the judicial system, does not the institutional system of medicine likewise constitute, in some of their aspects at least, similar systems of subjection of and by discourse?

25 Homi BhaBha,

'Of Mimicry and Man: The Ambivalence of Colonial Discourse', *October*, no 28, Spring 1984*

p125 – 133

Mimicry reveals something in so far as it is distinct from what might be called an itself that is behind. The effect of mimicry is camouflage. . . . It is not a question of harmonizing with the background, but against a mottled background, of becoming mottled – exactly like the technique of camouflage practised in human warfare.

– Jacques Lacan,
'The Line and Light', *Of the Gaze.*

It is out of season to question at this time of day, the original policy of conferring on every colony of the British Empire a mimic representation of the British Constitution. But if the creature so endowed has sometimes forgotten its real insignificance and under the fancied importance of speakers and maces, and all the paraphernalia and ceremonies of the imperial legislature, has dared to defy the mother country, she has to thank herself for the folly of conferring such privileges on a condition of society that has no earthly claim to so exalted a position. A fundamental principle appears to have been forgotten or overlooked in our system of colonial policy – that of colonial dependence. To give to a colony the forms of independence is a mockery; she would not be a colony for a single hour if she could maintain an independent station.

– Sir Edward Cust,
'Reflections on West African Affairs . . . addressed to the Colonial
Office',
Hatchard, London 1839.

The discourse of post-Enlightenment English colonialism often speaks in a tongue that is forked, not false. If colonialism takes power in the name of history, it repeatedly exercises its authority through the figures of farce. For the epic intention of the civilizing mission, 'human and not wholly human' in the famous words of Lord Rosebery, 'writ by the finger of the Divine'[1] often produces a text rich in the traditions of *trompe l'oeil*, irony, mimicry, and repetition. In this comic turn from the high ideals of the colonial imagination to its low mimetic literary effects, mimicry emerges as one of the most elusive and effective strategies of

* This paper was first presented as a contribution to a panel of 'Colonialist and Post-Colonialist Discourse', organized by Gayatri Chakravorty Spivak for the Modern Language Association Convention in New York, December 1983. I would like to thank Professor Spivak for inviting me to participate on the panel and Dr. Stephen Feuchtwang for his advice in the preparation of the paper.
[1] Cited in Eric Stokes, *The Political Ideas of English Imperialism*, Oxford, Oxford University Press, 1960, pp. 17–18.

colonial power and knowledge.

Within that conflictual economy of colonial discourse which Edward Said[2] describes as the tension between the synchronic panoptical vision of domination – the demand for identity, stasis – and the counterpressure of the diachrony of history – change, difference – mimicry represents an *ironic* compromise. If I may adapt Samuel Weber's formulation of the marginalizing vision of castration,[3] then colonial mimicry is the desire for a reformed, recognizable Other, as *a subject of a difference that is almost the same, but not quite.* Which is to say, that the discourse of mimicry is constructed around an *ambivalence*; in order to be effective, mimicry must continually produce its slippage, its excess, its difference. The authority of that mode of colonial discourse that I have called mimicry is therefore stricken by an indeterminacy: mimicry emerges as the representation of a difference that is itself a process of disavowal. Mimicry is, thus, the sign of a double articulation; a complex strategy of reform, regulation, and discipline, which 'appropriates' the Other as it visualizes power. Mimicry is also the sign of the inappropriate, however, a difference or recalcitrance which coheres the dominant strategic function of colonial power, intensifies surveillance, and poses an immanent threat to both 'normalized' knowledges and disciplinary powers.

The effect of mimicry on the authority of colonial discourse is profound and disturbing. For in 'normalizing' the colonial state or subject, the dream of post-Enlightenment civility alienates its own language of liberty and produces another knowledge of its norms. The ambivalence which thus informs this strategy is discernible, for example, in Locke's Second Treatise which *splits* to reveal the limitations of liberty in his double use of the word 'slave': first simply, descriptively as the locus of a legitimate form of ownership, then as the trope for an intolerable, illegitimate exercise of power. What is articulated in that distance between the two uses is the absolute, imagined difference between the 'Colonial' State of Carolina and the Original State of Nature.

It is from this area between mimicry and mockery, where the reforming, civilizing mission is threatened by the displacing gaze of its disciplinary double, that my instances of colonial imitation come. What they all share is a discursive process by which the excess or slippage produced by the *ambivalence* of mimicry (almost the same, *but not quite*) does not merely 'rupture' the discourse, but becomes transformed into an uncertainty which fixes the colonial subject as a 'partial' presence. By 'partial' I mean both 'incomplete' and 'virtual'. It is as if the very emergence of the 'colonial' is dependent for its representation upon some strategic limitation or prohibition *within* the authoritative

---

[2] Edward Said, *Orientalism*, New York, Pantheon Books, 1978, p. 240.

[3] Samuel Weber: 'The Sideshow, Or: Remarks on a Canny Moment', *Modern Language Notes*, vol. 88, no. 6 (1973), p. 1112.

discourse itself. The success of colonial appropriation depends on a proliferation of inappropriate objects that ensure its strategic failure, so that
mimicry is at once resemblance and menace.

A classic text of such partiality is Charles Grant's 'Observations on the
State of Society among the Asiatic Subjects of Great Britain' (1792)[4]
which was only superseded by James Mills's *History of India* as the most
influential early nineteenth-century account of Indian manners and
morals. Grant's dream of an evangelical system of mission education
conducted uncompromisingly in English was partly a belief in political
reform along Christian lines and partly an awareness that the expansion
of company rule in India required a system of 'interpellation' – a reform
of manners, as Grant put it, that would provide the colonial with 'a sense
of personal identity as we know it.' Caught between the desire for religious reform and the fear that the Indians might become turbulent for
liberty, Grant implies that it is, in fact the 'partial' diffusion of Christianity, and the 'partial' influence of moral improvements which will
construct a particularly appropriate form of colonial subjectivity. What
is suggested is a process of reform through which Christian doctrines
might collude with divisive caste practices to prevent dangerous political
alliances. Inadvertently, Grant produces a knowledge of Christianity as
a form of social control which conflicts with the enunciatory assumptions which authorize his discourse. In suggesting, finally, that 'partial
reform' will produce an empty form of 'the *imitation* of English manners
which will induce them [the colonial subjects] to remain under our protection,'[5] Grant mocks his moral project and violates the Evidences of
Christianity – a central missionary tenet – which forbade any tolerance
of heathen faiths.

The absurd extravagance of Macaulay's *Infamous Minute*
(1835) – deeply influenced by Charles Grant's *Observations* – makes a
mockery of Oriental learning until faced with the challenge of conceiving
of a 'reformed' colonial subject. Then the great tradition of European
humanism seems capable only of ironizing itself. At the intersection of
European learning and colonial power, Macaulay can conceive of
nothing other than 'a class of interpreters between us and the millions
whom we govern – a class of persons Indian in blood and colour, but
English in tastes, in opinions, in morals and in intellect'[6] – in other
words a mimic man raised 'through our English School', as a missionary
educationist wrote in 1819, 'to form a corps of translators and be
employed in different departments of Labour'.[7] The line of descent of

[4] Charles Grant, 'Observations on the State of Society among the Asiatic Subjects of Great
Britain', *Sessional Papers 1812–13*, X (282), East India Company.

[5] *Ibid.*, chap. 4, p. 104.

[6] T.B. Macaulay, 'Minute on Education,' in *Sources of Indian Tradition*, vol. II, ed. William
Theodore de Bary, New York, Columbia University Press, 1958, p. 49.

[7] Mr Thomason's communication to the Church Missionary Society, September 5, 1819, in *The
Missionary Register*, 1821, pp. 54–55.

the mimic man can be traced through the works of Kipling, Forester, Orwell, Naipaul, and to his emergence, most recently, in Benedict Anderson's excellent essay on nationalism, as the anomalous Bipin Chandra Pal.[8] He is the effect of a flawed colonial mimesis, in which to be Anglicized, is *emphatically* not to be English.

The figure of mimicry is locatable within what Anderson describes as 'the inner incompatibility of empire and nation.'[9] It problematizes the signs of racial and cultural priority, so that the 'national' is no longer naturalizable. What emerges between mimesis and mimicry is a *writing*, a mode of representation, that marginalizes the monumentality of history, quite simply mocks its power to be a model, that power which supposedly makes it imitable. Mimicry *repeats* rather than *re-presents* and in that diminishing perspective emerges Decoud's displaced European vision of Sulaco as

> the endlessness of civil strife where folly seemed even harder to bear than its ignominy . . . the lawlessness of a populace of all colours and races, barbarism, irremediable tyranny. . . . America is ungovernable.[10]

Or Ralph Singh's apostasy in Naipaul's *The Mimic Men*:

> We pretended to be real, to be learning, to be preparing ourselves for life, we mimic men of the New World, one unknown corner of it, with all its reminders of the corruption that came so quickly to the new.[11]

Both Decoud and Singh, and in their different ways Grant and Macaulay, are the parodists of history. Despite their intentions and invocations they inscribe the colonial text erratically, eccentrically across a body politic that refuses to be representative, in a narrative that refuses to be representational. The desire to emerge as 'authentic' through mimicry – through a process of writing and repetition – is the final irony of partial representation.

What I have called mimicry is not the familiar exercise of *dependent* colonial relations through narcissistic identification so that, as Fanon has observed,[12] the black man stops being an actional person for only the white man can represent his self-esteem. Mimicry conceals no presence or identity behind its mask: it is not what Césaire describes as 'colonization-thingification'[13] behind which there stands the essence of the *présence Africaine*. The *menace* of mimicry is its *double* vision which in disclosing the ambivalence of colonial discourse also disrupts its authority. And it is a double-vision that is a result of what I've described as the partial representation/recognition of the colonial object. Grant's

---

8 Benedict Anderson, *Imagined Communities*, London, Verso, 1983, p. 88.
9 *Ibid.*, pp. 88–89.
10 Joseph Conrad, *Nostromo*, London, Penguin, 1979, p. 161.
11 V.S. Naipaul, *The Mimic Men*, London, Penguin, 1967, p. 146.
12 Frantz Fanon, *Black Skin, White Masks*, London, Paladin, 1970, p. 109.
13 Aimé Césaire, *Discourse on Colonialism*, New York, Monthly Review Press, 1972, p. 21.

colonial as partial imitator, Macaulay's translator, Naipaul's colonial politician as playactor, Decoud as the scene setter of the *opéra bouffe* of the New World, these are the appropriate objects of a colonialist chain of command, authorized versions of otherness. But they are also, as I have shown, the figures of a doubling, the part-objects of a metonymy of colonial desire which alienates the modality and normality of those dominant discourses in which they emerge as 'inappropriate' colonial subjects. A desire that, through the repetition of *partial presence*, which is the basis of mimicry, articulates those disturbances of cultural, racial, and historical difference that menace the narcissistic demand of colonial authority. It is a desire that reverses 'in part' the colonial appropriation by now producing a partial vision of the colonizer's presence. A gaze of otherness, that shares the acuity of the genealogical gaze which, as Foucault describes it, liberates marginal elements and shatters the unity of man's being through which he extends his sovereignty.[14]

I want to turn to this process by which the look of surveillance returns as the displacing gaze of the disciplined, where the observer becomes the observed and 'partial' representation rearticulates the whole notion of *identity* and alienates it from essence. But not before observing that even an exemplary history like Eric Stokes's *The English Utilitarians in India* acknowledges the anomalous gaze of otherness but finally disavows it in a contradictory utterance:

> Certainly India played *no* central part in fashioning the distinctive qualities of English civilisation. In many ways it acted as a disturbing force, a magnetic power placed at the periphery tending to distort the natural development of Britain's character. . . .[15]

What is the nature of the hidden threat of the partial gaze? How does mimicry emerge as the subject of the scopic drive and the object of colonial surveillance? How is desire disciplined, authority displaced?

If we turn to a Freudian figure to address these issues of colonial textuality, that form of difference that is mimicry – *almost the same but not quite* – will become clear. Writing of the partial nature of fantasy, caught *inappropriately*, between the unconscious and the preconscious, making problematic, like mimicry, the very notion of 'origins', Freud has this to say:

> Their mixed and split origin is what decides their fate. We may compare them with individuals of mixed race who taken all round resemble white men but who betray their coloured descent by some striking feature or other and on that account are excluded from society and enjoy none of the privileges.[16]

Almost the same but not white: the visibility of mimicry is always pro-

---

[14] Michel Foucault, 'Nietzche, Genealogy, History', in *Language, Counter-Memory, Practice*, trans. Donald F. Bouchard and Sherry Simon, Ithaca, Cornell University Press, p. 153.

[15] Eric Stokes, *The English Utilitarians and India*, Oxford, Oxford University Press, 1959, p. xi.

[16] Sigmund Freud, 'The Unconscious' (1915), *SE*, XIV, pp. 190–191.

duced at the site of interdiction. It is a form of colonial discourse that is uttered *inter dicta*: a discourse at the crossroads of what is known and permissible and that which though known must be kept concealed; a discourse uttered between the lines and as such both against the rules and within them. The question of the representation of difference is therefore always also a problem of authority. The 'desire' of mimicry, which is Freud's *striking feature* that reveals so little but makes such a big difference, is not merely that impossibility of the Other which repeatedly resists signification. The desire of colonial mimicry – an interdictory desire – may not have an object, but it has strategic objectives which I shall call the *metonymy of presence*.

Those inappropriate signifiers of colonial discourse – the difference between being English and being Anglicized; the identity between stereotypes which, through repetition, also become different; the discriminatory identities constructed across traditional cultural norms and classifications, the Simian Black, the Lying Asiatic – all these are metonymies of presence. They are strategies of desire in discourse that make the anomalous representation of the colonized something other than a process of 'the return of the repressed', what Fanon unsatisfactorily characterized as collective catharsis.[17] These instances of metonymy are the nonrepressive productions of contradictory and multiple belief. They cross the boundaries of the culture of enunciation through a strategic confusion of the metaphoric and metonymic axes of the cultural production of meaning. For each of these instances of 'a difference that is almost the same but not quite' inadvertently creates a crisis for the cultural priority given to the *metaphoric* as the process of repression and substitution which negotiates the difference between paradigmatic systems and classifications. In mimicry, the representation of identity and meaning is rearticulated along the axis of metonymy. As Lacan reminds us, mimicry is like camouflage, not a harmonization or repression of difference, but a form of resemblance that differs/defends presence by displaying it in part, metonymically. Its threat, I would add, comes from the prodigious and strategic production of conflictual, fantastic, discriminatory 'identity effects' in the play of a power that is elusive because it hides no essence, no 'itself'. And that form of *resemblance* is the most terrifying thing to behold, as Edward Long testifies in his *History of Jamaica* (1774). At the end of a tortured, negrophobic passage, that shifts anxiously between piety, prevarication, and perversion, the text finally confronts its fear; nothing other than the repetition of its resemblance 'in part':

> (Negroes) are represented by all authors as the vilest of human kind, to which they have little more pretension of resemblance *than what arises from their exterior forms* (my italics).[18]

[17] Fanon, p. 103.
[18] Edward Long, *A History of Jamaica*, 1774, vol. II, p. 353.

From such a colonial encounter between the white presence and its black semblance, there emerges the question of the ambivalence of mimicry as a problematic of colonial subjection. For if Sade's scandalous theatricalization of language repeatedly reminds us that discourse can claim 'no priority', then the work of Edward Said will not let us forget that the 'ethnocentric and erratic will to power from which texts can spring'[19] is itself a theater of war. Mimicry, as the metonymy of presence is, indeed, such an erratic, eccentric strategy of authority in colonial discourse. Mimicry does not merely destroy narcissistic authority through the repetitious slippage of difference and desire. It is the process of the *fixation* of the colonial as a form of cross-classificatory, discriminatory knowledge in the defiles of an interdictory discourse, and therefore necessarily raises the question of the *authorization* of colonial representations. A question of authority that goes beyond the subject's lack of priority (castration) to a historical crisis in the conceptuality of colonial man as an *object* of regulatory power, as the subject of racial, cultural, national representation.

'This culture . . . fixed in its colonial status', Fanon suggests, '(is) both present and mummified, it testified against its members. It defines them in fact without appeal.'[20] The ambivalence of mimicry – almost but not quite – suggests that the fetishized colonial culture is potentially and strategically an insurgent counter-appeal. What I have called its 'identity-effects', are always crucially *split*. Under cover of camouflage, mimicry, like the fetish, is a part-object that radically revalues the normative knowledges of the priority of race, writing, history. For the fetish mimes the forms of authority at the point at which it deauthorizes them. Similarly, mimicry rearticulates presence in terms of its 'otherness', that which it disavows. There is a crucial difference between this *colonial* articulation of man and his doubles and that which Foucault describes as 'thinking the unthought'[21] which, for nineteenth-century Europe, is the ending of man's alienation by reconciling him with his essence. The colonial discourse that articulates an *interdictory* 'otherness' is precisely the 'other scene' of this nineteenth-century European desire for an authentic historical consciousness.

The 'unthought' across which colonial man is articulated is that process of classificatory confusion that I have described as the metonymy of the substitutive chain of ethical and cultural discourse. This results in the *splitting* of colonial discourse so that two attitudes towards external reality persist; one takes reality into consideration while the other disavows it and replaces it by a product of desire that repeats,

[19] Edward Said, 'The Text, the World, the Critic,' in *Textual Strategies*, ed. J.V. Harari, Ithaca, Cornell University Press, 1979, p. 184.
[20] Frantz Fanon, 'Racism and Culture,' in *Toward the African Revolution*, London, Pelican, 1967, p. 44.
[21] Michel Foucault, *The Order of Things*, New York, Pantheon, 1970, part II, chap. 9.

rearticulates 'reality' as mimicry.

So Edward Long can say with authority, quoting variously, Hume, Eastwick, and Bishop Warburton in his support, that:

Ludicrous as the opinion may seem I do not think that an orangutang husband would be any dishonour to a Hottentot female.[22]

Such contradictory articulations of reality and desire – seen in racist stereotypes, statements, jokes, myths – are not caught in the doubtful circle of the return of the repressed. They are the effects of a disavowal that denies the differences of the other but produces in its stead forms of authority and multiple belief that alienate the assumptions of 'civil' discourse. If, for a while, the ruse of desire is calculable for the uses of discipline soon the repetition of guilt, justification, pseudoscientific theories, superstition, spurious authorities, and classifications can be seen as the desperate effort to 'normalize' *formally* the disturbance of a discourse of splitting that violates the rational, enlightened claims of its enunciatory modality. The ambivalence of colonial authority repeatedly turns from *mimicry* – a difference that is almost nothing but not quite – to *menace* – a difference that is almost total but not quite. And in that other scene of colonial power, where history turns to farce and presence to 'a part', can be seen the twin figures of narcissism and paranoia that repeat furiously, uncontrollably.

In the ambivalent world of the 'not quite/not white', on the margins of metropolitan desire, the *founding objects* of the Western world become the eratic, eccentric, accidental *objets trouvés* of the colonial discourse – the part-objects of presence. It is then that the body and the book loose their representational authority. Black skin splits under the racist gaze, displaced into signs of bestiality, genitalia, grostesquerie, which reveal the phobic myth of the undifferentiated whole white body. And the holiest of books – the Bible – bearing both the standard of the cross and the standard of empire finds itself strangely dismembered. In May 1817 a missionary wrote from Bengal:

Still everyone would gladly receive a Bible. And why? – that he may lay it up as a curiosity for a few pice; or use it for waste paper. Such it is well known has been the common fate of these copies of the Bible. . . . Some have been bartered in the markets, others have been thrown in snuff shops and used as wrapping paper.[23]

[22] Long, p. 364.
[23] *The Missionary Register*, May 1817, p. 186.

26 Ian Hunter,

From 'Reading Character', *Southern Review*, vol 16;2, 1983

p228–233

In what follows I will suggest that literature or culture has no (such) general form. Instead, grouped under the term we find a heterogeneous set of texts, discourses, practices and institutional relations which possess no common core. The representations that emerge from this field are quite diverse and are not defined by a single general relation to 'real determinations', functional or transcendental. So my object in indicating the contours of a small part of this field – nineteenth-century readings of character – is not to answer the question, 'What is character?' by discovering something that underlies character and explains it. Rather, it is to describe a set of practical circumstances. These exist at the same level as character and form a surface on which it emerges, possessing neither a function nor an essence but a duration, effects and an intelligibility governed by our practical familiarity with the circumstances themselves.

Consider, then, the difference between what counts as a reading of character in the middle of the eighteenth century, and what we still recognise as one today. First, George Stubbes, writing in 1736:

> We are now come to a Scene which I have always much admired. I cannot think it possible that such an Incident could have been managed better, nor more conformably to Reason and Nature. The Prince, conscious of his own good Intentions and the Justness of the Cause he undertakes to plead, speaks with that Force and Assurance which Virtue always gives; and yet manages his Expressions so as not to treat his Mother in a disrespectful Manner. . . . And his inforcing the Heinousness of his Mother's Crime with so much Vehemence, and her guilty Confessions of her Wickedness . . . are all Strokes from the Hand of a great Master in the Imitation of Nature. . . .
>
> The Ghost's not being seen by the Queen was very proper; for we could hardly suppose that a Woman . . . could be able to bear so terrible a Sight . . .[1]

Next, A.C. Bradley, writing in 1904:

> The Queen was not a bad-hearted woman, not at all the woman to think little of murder. But she had a soft animal nature, and was very dull and very

These remarks began life as a lecture given in the Forms of Communication area at Griffith University, Australia in 1979–80. I have not attempted to erase the signs of this origin by revising the paper, which is therefore best read as an introductory reformulation of the concept of character.

[1] George Stubbes, in *Shakespeare: The Critical Heritage*, ed. Brian Vickers, III (London: Routledge and Kegan Paul, 1975), 59–60.

shallow. She loved to be happy, like a sheep in the sun. . . . She never saw that drunkenness is disgusting till Hamlet told her so; and, though she knew that he considered her marriage 'o'er-hasty,' . . . she was untroubled by any shame at the feelings which had led to it. It was pleasant to sit upon her throne and see smiling faces round her, and foolish and unkind in Hamlet to persist in grieving for his father instead of marrying Ophelia and making everything comfortable. . . . The belief at the bottom of her heart was that the world is a place constructed simply that people may be happy in it in a good-humoured sensual fashion.[2]

Now it should be fairly clear even from a first reading of the two examples that they indicate the operation of quite different techniques and operations of reading. Although both passages are concerned with the characters of Hamlet and the Queen, they are not concerned with character in the same way. In particular, the eighteenth-century critic treats character as above all an element of the scene, which is in turn treated as an organisational unit of the play. Character here is to be classified and judged according to a set of primarily rhetorical rules and norms for the proper construction of a dramatic representation. Character is not linked immediately (as it is in the second example) to the portrayal of an apparently real personality governed by universal moral norms. In the Stubbes passage, the reading of character is the effect of the operation of a definite set of norms and rules that determine what is to count as a plausible and appropriate characterisation. The most obvious manifestation of these norms and rules in this passage is the statement of how proper it is that the Queen doesn't see the ghost of her dead husband when it appears quite near to her. This is appropriate because the eighteenth-century rules governing characterisation specify certain things which female characters should not see, say or do. Equally there are norms and rules that determine what it is appropriate and inappropriate for male characters (particularly those of a certain social rank) to say and do. So we find Stubbes a little later in the same essay criticising the fact that Hamlet makes jokes over the corpse of someone he has just killed. This is thought to be quite inappropriate and implausible as a representation of a prince, because a jocular speech of this type in this situation is not in keeping with the rules governing the diction of a notable. Now the central point to be kept in mind is that it is not the characters of the Queen and Hamlet that are good or bad here, but rather their characterisation. That is, it is their dramatic representation, judged against certain rules and norms which are not in the first instance (or not solely) moral rules or norms applied to personality, but are instead rhetorical rules or norms governing dramatic representation.

In order to understand the function of the rules and norms governing eighteenth-century readings of character, it is necessary to see them in

[2] A.C. Bradley, *Shakespearean Tragedy* (London: Macmillan, 1904), p. 167.

the context of those applied to dramatic representation as such at this time. Rather than provide an exhaustive list I will simply mention the following: rules and norms governing characterisation, and in particular the appropriate modes of speech and action for different character types; neoclassical norms governing that which can be represented directly on stage (for example, Stubbes criticises Shakespeare for attempting to stage battles instead of having them described by minor figures, as was the case in classical drama); and finally the famous unities of time and action. So it can be said that the norms of characterisation – the rules determining unity of time and action, and the criteria for what could be represented on stage (and for how long) – are examples of techniques and operations of reading. They are not simply techniques for staging plays but are techniques for reading and judging plays. That is, the eighteenth-century rules and norms of dramatic representation form what might be called a grid of classification and judgement. This grid determines the plausibility of a dramatic representation, and determines what (to use our terms) will count as realistic. It is from this grid that the contours of the text emerge. The grid establishes a particular form of relation to the text, such that one can say that the rules and norms of dramatic representation determine what sorts of object the text and its components are. Or equivalently, they establish in what sort of discursive space the text and its components can appear in a reading. Obviously, a philological reading of the same scene would be quite unlike Stubbes's or Bradley's, and the sort of reading one might find in the high period of *Scrutiny* would differ again from these three.[3] What is being suggested is that these differences in reading do not index differences in subjectivities, but rather differences in operations of reading, differences in the historical surfaces on which the content of a text can appear. It is these concepts which are indicated by a phrase such as 'discursive space'. Reading here is simply another name for the activation of the rhetorical rules and norms of dramatic representation. In particular (and this is the point of the comparison) characters are read not by comparing them with so-called real personalities, but by applying the norms and rules of characterisation current at this time. Character is thus primarily a rhetorical object rather than a moral one, and appears in a space opened by a rhetoric of dramatic representation. This would seem to suggest that to read character in this manner is a historically relative and socially attributed capacity, and this fact becomes even clearer when considering the second example, with which we are much more familiar.

---

[3] In this practice of reading, represented by L.C. Knights's "How Many Children Had Lady Macbeth?" (*Explorations* [London: Chatto and Windus, 1946], pp. 1–39), we find the intelligibility of characters emerging from a poetic analysis of the language of their speeches. This constitutes an apparatus in which the character appears in the same space of judgement as the author of a poem, in so far as his sincerity, lack of commitment, and so on, are read off from a grid which locates these qualities in the originators of the texts. So a character as the originator of a speech is put in the same place as the authorial originator of a poem or play.

Bradley has been chosen to exaggerate as much as possible the differences between the two readings of character. I'm not denying that a piece from, say, Johnson on Shakespeare would diminish the contrast: nonetheless, the contrast as it stands has its point.

If character in the eighteenth-century reading is primarily a rhetorical object emerging from the iteration of a set of rules/norms determining what counts as an appropriate or plausible representation, then it is possible to say that character in the nineteenth-century practice of reading is primarily a moral object. Which is to say that character in this second example appears in a space opened by a set of techniques and practices whose object is not 'character as an element of a dramatic representation' but rather 'character as a projection or correlate of the reader's moral self and personality'. And it is this emergence of fictional character as a projection or correlate of the reader's own moral interiority that marks the key difference here. It is possible then to repeat our earlier question: what are the techniques and practices that permit this quite different formation of the object, character? And again, a very partial list can be provided.

First, there is a particularly interesting practice of supplementing the text with a moral discourse on character-type, and this is a peculiarly nineteenth-century discourse. So we have phrases such as 'soft animal nature', the simile, 'like a sheep in the sun', and the assertion, 'the belief at the bottom of her heart was that the world is a place constructed simply that people may be happy in it in a good-humoured sensual fashion'. Diverging slightly, it needs to be remembered that the idea of women's 'soft natures' has a very precise set of connotations in nineteenth-century moral psychology (which theorised women's bodies very definitely). For example, the analysis of hysteria and the treatment of hysteria in asylums were constructed in terms of the softness, the pliability, and the labile quality of the female body, which was believed to transmit sensations (particularly moral sensations) much more quickly than the male body. It was a much more ductile body in which the reason was much more quickly overwhelmed, and in which the passions were in a different relation to the will.[4] Further, nineteenth-century moral psychology also constructs a typology of animals, a bestiary which ranges animals in relation to moral types. What Bradley exhibits is a capacity to draw on this set of collateral knowledges, in which character is emerging as it were parallel to literature, in another field, another set of institutions, and under another set of treatments, but still very closely connected and drawing closer together all the time. So here, 'soft animal nature' constitutes a new supplementary discourse which is quite clearly different from anything to be found in Stubbes.

---

[4] See Michel Foucault, *Madness and Civilization: A History of Insanity in the Age of Reason*, trans. Richard Howard (New York: Pantheon, 1964), Ch. 5.

Secondly, we find a technique for deriving moral imperatives from the text, resulting in a common moral space for reader and character. Hence the present tense in the phrase, 'she never saw that drunkenness is disgusting'. Not 'was', nor 'was in the world of the play'; it simply *is* disgusting according to norms of conduct whose activation is part of what we call reading here. The imperative is a universal applying to the reader as well as to the Queen.

Thirdly, we have a set of operations for constructing the characters' point of view that forms part of a technique of reader-identification with the character. The point-of-view statements are of course things not found in Shakespeare's text: 'It was pleasant to sit upon her throne and see smiling faces round her'. This is a novelistic statement brought to the reading of the play, a way of projecting the interiority of the Queen on to an introspective surface constructed in the reader. For us it goes along with what we would now call 'character appreciation', and the surface of introspection is organised by the deployment of statements in the practice of writing 'character appreciations'.

What I'm indicating here is that character, under these circumstances, emerges in a quite new field and as a new object. It now appears in the space of moral interrogation and moral training. Character appears as a moral object common to the play and the reader; and I think the key change here is the emergence of nineteenth-century moral psychology, and its widespread deployment as a means of diagnosing and treating madness via an interrogation of moral character. Its appearance provides what Foucault terms an 'adjacent field' opening on to the domain of the literary and providing it with models, devices, and techniques of analysis that form part of the new surface on which character appears. It should now be clear that this reading of literary character is in fact a practice of writing, for to speak of reading here is to speak of a definite set of techniques and operations performed on the text. What we have to come to terms with is that to read a character in late nineteenth-century criticism means to be able to go through a series of practical operations and to employ a definite set of techniques, such as: the practice of supplementing the text with elements of a moral discourse; techniques for activating moral norms common to reader and character; and the operations by which readers construct the characters' point of view as part of a technique of identification.

Now it is as a result of the practical employment of these operations that character is read as a projection or correlate of this thing I've been calling 'the reader's moral self'. But equally one could say that 'the reader's moral self' appears in this relation as a projection or correlate of the fictional character. The two things are not happening independently of one another but occur in a dual relationship. These operations and techniques, of course, are quite radically different from the iteration of the rhetorical rules and norms which constitutes Stubbe's reading of the

Queen's character. The problem then becomes: how are we to understand this change in the apparatus of reading? Are we dealing with a
change in the practice of reading character that is equivalent to, say, a
change in the reader's point of view? Or are we confronted with a change
in the practical operations and techniques whose attribution to readers
changes the whole public structure of what is to count as a reading?
These questions can be reformulated in the following way. Is it simply
the eighteenth-century critic's point of view which prevents him from
reading character as a projection/correlate of moral self or personality?
That is, if the critic had looked a little more deeply into the text and read
the soliloquies more closely, could this reading have become visible? The
answer, I think, must be no. It is not that the eighteenth-century critic
fails to see through the rhetorical analysis of characterisation to a moral
reading of character. Rather, it is that the techniques and operations
which link rhetorical and moral readings are not available to the
eighteenth-century critic. This is to suggest that rhetorical and moral
analyses of character are both going on in the eighteenth century, but
they are not linked in the same way as they are in nineteenth-century
cultural institutions. In other words, it is not that the eighteenth-century
critic fails to see the moral reading of character; rather it is that the social
apparatus which constitutes this form of looking has not yet emerged.
Now if this remark is correct, then what we are dealing with is not a
change in the reader's consciousness of the object 'character'. Instead,
we are dealing with a change in the practical deployment of a public
apparatus of reading, in which what is to count as character is determined. The question we have to answer, then, does not pertain to the
cirtic's consciousness or point of view. It's not as if we could deal with
these problems by saying that René Wellek or Jacques Derrida came
along later and solved everything by giving us the absolute, definitive
account of reading. Nor do I think we could say that an aggregate of all
these readings would produce *Hamlet* as it existed in Shakespeare's
mind. Rather, it has to do with changes in historical conditions of
reading. In particular we have to ask how it became possible to treat
dramatic characterisation as a systematic projection or correlate of the
audience's or the reader's moral character.

Crudely speaking, in the early eighteenth century the judging of
dramatic characterisation and the constitution and interrogation of a
personal moral self are carried out in quite different social institutions.
The former is carried out by the apparatus of neoclassical criticism
embodied in the academy, and more importantly in the salons; whereas
the latter is overwhelmingly organised by the churches, and these two
things are quite distinct. During the seventeenth and early eighteenth
centuries, then, the techniques of interrogation and confession which
construct a moral self are still closely connected to church ritual and are
not an important factor in drama criticism. In *The History of Sexuality*

Foucault describes a process of secularisation of techniques of moral interrogation and confession.[5] He argues that these techniques are freed from their singular attachment to the church and to church ritual, and start to appear in a very wide variety of apparatuses and institutions: in the keeping of diaries; in the apparatus of self-interrogation and the formation of conscience characteristic of puritanism; in the first modern forms of biography and autobiography; and in secular practices of counselling and interviewing, found increasingly in the secular domain, and in educational institutions in particular. I'm suggesting that we can begin to see the way in which rhetorical analysis and the formation of moral selves begin to form a common field, if we follow the detachment of the forms of production of moral interiorities from the church and their re-emergence in a range of new apparatuses – including moral psychology and literary analysis – whose object is the production of knowledge via disciplinary individuation. It is in this context that I want to suggest that the emergence of an apparatus of popular education in the nineteenth century is what finally establishes the technical connection between the rhetorical analysis of characterisation and the machinery for the construction of moral selves or good personal character.

[5] Foucault, *The History of Sexuality*, trans. Robert Hurley (London: Allen Lane, 1978), I, 18–23, 58–70.

---

27 Edward Said,

From 'Opponents, Audiences, Constituencies and Community', *Postmodern Culture*, ed Hal Foster

p135–141; 153–156

Who writes? For whom is the writing being done? In what circumstances? These, it seems to me, are the questions whose answers provide us with the ingredients making for a politics of interpretation. But if one does not wish to ask and answer the questions in a dishonest and abstract way, some attempt must be made to show why they are questions of some relevance to the present time. What needs to be said at the beginning is that the single most impressive aspect of the present time – at least for the 'humanist', a description for which I have contradictory feelings of affection and revulsion – is that it is manifestly the Age of Ronald Reagan. And it is in this age as a context and setting that the politics of interpretation and the politics of culture are enacted.

I do not want to be misunderstood as saying that the cultural situation

I describe here caused Reagan, or that it typifies Reaganism, or that everything about it can be ascribed or referred back to the personality of Ronald Reagan. What I argue is that a particular situation within the field we call 'criticism' is not merely related to but is an integral part of the currents of thought and practice that play a role within the Reagan era. Moreover, I think, 'criticism' and the traditional academic humanities have gone through a series of developments over time whose beneficiary and culmination is Reaganism. Those are the gross claims that I make for my argument.

A number of miscellaneous points need to be made here. I am fully aware that any effort to characterize the present cultural moment is very likely to seem quixotic at best, unprofessional at worst. But that, I submit, is an aspect of the present cultural moment, in which the social and historical setting of critical activity is a totality felt to be benign (free, apolitical, serious), uncharaterizable as a whole (it is too complex to be described in general and tendentious terms) and somehow outside history. Thus it seems to me that one thing to be tried – out of sheer critical obstinacy – is precisely *that* kind of generalization, *that* kind of political portrayal, *that* kind of overview condemned by the present dominant culture to appear inappropriate and doomed from the start.

It is my conviction that culture works very effectively to make invisible and even 'impossible' the actual *affiliations* that exist between the world of ideas and scholarship, on the one hand, and the world of brute politics, corporate and state power, and military force, on the other. The cult of expertise and professionalism, for example, has so restricted our scope of vision that a positive (as opposed to an implicit or passive) doctrine of non-interference among fields has set in. This doctrine has it that the general public is best left ignorant, and the most crucial policy questions affecting human existence are best left to 'experts', specialists who talk about their specialty only, and – to use the word first given social approbation by Walter Lippmann in *Public Opinion* and *The Phantom Public* – 'insiders', people (usually men) who are endowed with the special privilege of knowing how things really work and, more important, of being close to power.[1]

Humanistic culture in general has acted in tacit compliance with this antidemocratic view, the more regrettably since, both in their formulation and in the politics they have given rise to, so-called policy issues can hardly be said to enhance human community. In a world of increasing interdependence and political consciousness, it seems both violent and wasteful to accept the notion, for example, that countries ought to be classified simply as pro-Soviet or pro-American. Yet this classification – and with it the reappearance of a whole range of cold war motifs and symptoms (discussed by Noam Chomsky in *Towards a New*

---

[1] See Ronald Steel, *Walter Lippmann and the American Century* (Boston: Little, Brown & Co., 1980), pp. 180–85 and 212–16.

Cold War) – dominates thinking about foreign policy. There is little in humanistic culture that is an effective antidote to it, just as it is true that few humanists have very much to say about the problems starkly dramatized by the 1980 Report of the Independent Commission on International Development Issues, *North-South: A Programme for Survival*. Our political discourse is now choked with enormous, thought-stopping abstractions, from terrorism, Communism, Islamic fundamentalism, and instability, to moderation, freedom, stability and strategic alliances, all of them as unclear as they are both potent and unrefined in their appeal. It is next to impossible to think about human society either in a global way (as Richard Flak eloquently does in *A Global Approach to National Policy* [1975]) or at the level of everyday life. As Philip Green shows in *The Pursuit of Inequality*, notions like equality and welfare have simply been chased off the intellectual landscape. Instead a brutal Darwinian picture of self-help and self-promotion is proposed by Reaganism, both domestically and internationally, as an image of the world ruled by what is being called 'productivity' or 'free enterprise'.

Add to this the fact that liberalism and the Left are in a state of intellectual disarray and fairly dismal perspectives emerge. The challenge posed by these perspectives is not how to cultivate one's garden despite them but how to understand cultural work occurring within them. What I propose here, then, is a rudimentary attempt to do just that, notwithstanding a good deal of inevitable incompleteness, overstatement, generalization, and crude characterization. . . .

My use of 'constituency', 'audience', 'opponents' and 'community' serves as a reminder that no one writes simply for oneself. There is always an Other; and this Other willy-nilly turns interpretation into a social activity, albeit with unforseen consequences, audiences, constituencies and so on. And, I would add, interpretation is the work of intellectuals, a class badly in need today of moral rehabilitation and social redefinition. The one issue that urgently requires study is, for the humanist no less than for the social scientist, the status of *information* as a component of knowledge: its sociopolitical status, its comtemporary fate, its economy (a subject treated recently by Herbert Schiller in *Who Knows: Information in the Age of the Fortune 500*). We all think we know what it means, for example, to *have* information and to write and interpret texts containing information. Yet we live in an age which places unprecedented emphasis on the production of knowledge and information, as Fritz Machlup's *Production and Distribution of Knowledge in the United States* dramatizes clearly. What happens to information and knowledge, then, when IBM and AT&T – two of the world's largest corporations – claim that what they do is put 'knowledge' to work 'for the people'? What is the role of humanistic knowledge and information if they are not to be unknowing (many ironies there) partners in commodity production and marketing, so much so that what humanists do may in the end turn out to be a quasi-religious concealment of this peculiarly unhumanistic process? A true secular politics of interpretation sidesteps this question at its peril.

At a recent MLA convention, I stopped by the exhibit of a major university press and remarked to the amiable sales representative on duty that there seemed to be no limit to the number of highly specialized books of advanced literary criticism his press put out. 'Who reads these books?' I asked, implying of course that however brilliant and important most of them were they were difficult to read and therefore could not have a wide audience – or at least an audience wide enough to justify regular publication during a time of economic crisis. The answer I received made sense, assuming I was told the truth. People who write specialized, advanced (i.e., New New) criticism faithfully read each other's books. Thus each such book could be assured of, but wasn't necessarily always getting, sales of around three thousand copies, 'all other things being equal'. The last qualification struck me as ambiguous at best, but it needn't detain us here. The point was that a nice little audience had been built and could be routinely mined by this press; certainly, on a much larger scale, publishers of cookbooks and exercise manuals apply a related principle as they churn out what may seem like a very long series of unnecessary books, even if an expanding crowd of avid food and exercise aficionados is not quite the same thing as a steadily attentive and earnest crowd of three thousand critics reading each other.

What I find peculiarly interesting about the real or mythical three thousand is that whether they derive ultimately from the Anglo-American New Criticism (as formulated by I.A. Richards, William Empson, John Crowe Ransom, Cleanth Brooks, Allen Tate, and company, beginning in the 1920s and continuing for several decades thereafter) or from the so-called New New Criticism (Roland Barthes, Jacques Derrida, *et al.*, during the 1960s), they vindicate, rather than undermine, the notion that intellectual labor ought to be divided into progressively narrower niches. Consider very quickly the irony of this. New Criticism claimed to view the verbal object as in itself it really was, free from the distractions of biography, social message, even paraphrase. Matthew Arnold's critical program was thereby to be advanced not by jumping directly from the text to the whole of culture but by using a highly concentrated verbal analysis to comprehend cultural values available only through a finely wrought literary structure finely understood.

Charges made against the American New Criticism that its ethos was clubby, gentlemanly or Episcopalian are, I think, correct only if it is added that in practice New Criticism, for all its elitism, was strangely populist in intention. The idea behind the pedagogy, and of course the

preaching, of Brooks and Robert Penn Warren was that everyone
properly instructed could feel, perhaps even act, like an educated gentleman. In its sheer projection this was by no means a trivial ambition. No
amount of snide mocking at their gentility can conceal the fact that, in
order to accomplish the conversion, the New Critics aimed at nothing
less than the removal of *all* of what they considered the specialized
rubbish – put there, they presumed, by professors of literature –
standing between the reader of a poem and the poem. Leaving aside the
questionable value of the New Criticism's ultimate social and moral
message, we must concede that the school deliberately and perhaps
incongruously tried to create a wide community of responsive readers
out of a very large, potentially unlimited, constituency of students and
teachers of literature.

In its early days, the French *nouvelle critique*, with Barthes as its chief
apologist, attempted the same kind of thing. Once again the guild of pro-
fesional literary scholars was characterized as impeding responsiveness
to literature. Once again the antidote was what seemed to be a specialized
reading technique based on a near jargon of linguistic, psychoanalytic
and Marxist terms, all of which proposed a new freedom for writers and
literate readers alike. The philosophy of *écriture* promised wider
horizons and a less restricted community, once an initial (and as it turned
out painless) surrender to structuralist activity had been made. For
despite structuralist prose, there was no impulse among the principal
structuralists to exclude readers; quite the contrary, as Barthes's often
abusive attacks on Raymond Picard show, the main purpose of critical
reading was to create new readers of the classics who might otherwise
have been frightened off by their lack of professional literary
accreditation.

For about four decades, then, in both France and the United States,
the schools of 'new' critics were committed to prying literature and
writing loose from confining institutions. However much it was to
depend upon carefully learned technical skills, reading was in very large
measure to become an act of public depossession. Texts were to be
unlocked or decoded, then handed on to anyone who was interested. The
resources of symbolic language were placed at the disposal of readers
who it was assumed suffered the debilitations of either irrelevant 'professional' information or the accumulated habits of lazy inattention.

Thus French and American New Criticism were, I believe, competitors
for authority within mass culture, not other-worldly alternatives to it.
Because of what became of them, we have tended to forget the original
missionary aims the two schools set for themselves. They belong to precisely the same moment that produced Jean-Paul Sartre's ideas about an
engaged literature and a commited writer. Literature was about the
world, readers were in the world; the question was not *whether* to be but
how to be, and this was best answered by carefully analyzing language's

symbolic enactments of the various existential possibilities available to human beings. What the Franco-American critics shared was the notion that verbal discipline could be self-sufficient once you learned to think pertinently about language stripped of unnecessary scaffolding; in other words, you did not need to be a professor to benefit from Donne's metaphors or Saussure's liberating distinction between *langue* and *parole*. And so the New Criticism's precious and cliquish aspect was mitigated by its radically anti-institutional bias, which manifested itself in the enthusiastic therapeutic optimism to be observed in both France and the United States. Join humankind against the schools: this was a message a great many people could appreciate.

How strangely perverse, then, that the legacy of both types of New Criticism is the private-clique consciousness embodied in a kind of critical writing that has virtually abandoned any attempt at reaching a large, if not a mass, audience. My belief is that both in the United States and in France the tendency toward formalism in New Criticism was accentuated by the academy. For the fact is that a disciplined attention to language can only thrive in the rarefied atmosphere of the classroom. Linguistics and literary analysis are features of the modern school, not of the marketplace. Purifying the language of the tribe – whether as a project subsumed within modernism or as a hope kept alive by embattled New Criticisms surrounded by mass culture – always moved further from the really big existing tribes and closer toward emerging new ones, comprised of the acolytes of a reforming or even revolutionary creed who in the end seemed to care more about turning the new creed into an intensely separatist orthodoxy than about forming a large community of readers.

To its unending credit, the university protects such wishes and shelters them under the umbrella of academic freedom. Yet advocacy of *close reading* or of *écriture* can quite naturally entail hostility to outsiders who fail to grasp the salutary powers of verbal analysis; moreover, persuasion too often has turned out to be less important than purity of intention and execution. In time the guild adversarial sense grew as the elaborate techniques multiplied, and an interest in expanding the constituency lost out to a wish for abstract correctness and methodological rigor within a quasi-monastic order. Critics read each other and cared about little else.

The parallels between the fate of a New Criticism reduced to abandoning universal literacy entirely and that of the school of F.R. Leavis are sobering. As Francis Mulhern reminds us in *The Moment of Scrutiny*, Leavis was not a formalist himself and began his career in the context of generally Left politics. Leavis argued that great literature was fundamentally opposed to a class society and to the dictates of a coterie. In his view, English studies ought to become the cornerstone of a new, fundamentally democratic outlook. But largely because the Leavisites concentrated their work both in and for the university, what began as a healthy oppositional participation in modern industrial society changed into a shrill withdrawal from it. English studies became narrower and narrower, in my opinion, and critical reading degenerated into decisions about what should or should not be allowed into the great tradition.

I do not want to be misunderstood as saying that there is something inherently pernicious about the modern university that produces the changes I have been describing. Certainly there is a great deal to be said in favour of a university manifestly not influenced or controlled by coarse partisan politics. But one thing in particular about the university – and here I speak about the modern university without distinguishing between European, American, or Third World and socia- list universities – does appear to exercise an almost totally unrestrained influence: the principle that knowledge ought to exist, be sought after and disseminated in a very divided form. Whatever the social, political, economic and ideological reasons underlying this principle, it has not long gone without its challengers. Indeed, it may not be too much of an exaggeration to say that one of the most interesting motifs in modern world culture has been the debate between proponents of the belief that knowledge can exist in a synthetic universal form and, on the other hand, those who believe that knowledge is inevitably produced and nurtured in specialized compartments. Georg Lukács's attack on reification and his advocacy of 'totality', in my opinion, very tantalizingly resemble the wide-ranging discussions that have been taking place in the Islamic world since the late nineteenth century on the need for mediating between the claims of a totalizing Islamic vision and modern specialized science. These epistemological controversies are therefore centrally important to the workplace of knowledge production, the university, in which *what* knowledge is and how it ought to be discovered are the very lifeblood of its being.

. . . .

The organized study of literature – *en soi* and *pour soi* – is premised on the constitutively primary act of literary (that is, artistic) repre- sentation, which in turn absorbs and incorporates other realms, other representations, secondary to it. But all this institutional weight has pre- cluded a sustained, systematic examination of the coexistence of and the interrelationship between the literary and the social, which is where representation – from journalism, to political struggle, to economic production and power – plays an extraordinarily important role. Con- fined to the study of one representational complex, literary critics accept and paradoxically ignore the lines drawn around what they do.

This is depoliticization with a vengeance, and it must, I think, be understood as an integral part of the historical moment presided over by

Reaganism. The division of intellectual labor I spoke of earlier can now be seen as assuming a *thematic* importance in the contemporary culture as a whole. For if the study of literature is 'only' about literary representation, then it must be the case that literary representations and literary activities (writing, reading, producing the 'humanities', and arts and letters) are essentially ornamental, possessing at most secondary ideological characteristics. The consequence is that to deal with literature as well as the broadly defined 'humanities' is to deal with the non-political, although quite evidently the political realm is presumed to lie just beyond (and beyond the reach of) literary, and hence *literate*, concern.

A perfect recent embodiment of this state of affairs is the 30 September 1981 issue of *The New Republic*. The lead editorial analyzes the United States's policy toward South Africa and ends up supporting this policy, which even the most 'moderate' of Black African states interpret (correctly, as even the United States explicitly confesses) as a policy supporting the South African settler-colonial regime. The last article of the issue includes a mean personal attack on me as 'an intellectual in the thrall of Soviet totalitarianism', a claim that is as disgustingly McCarthyite as it is intellectually fraudulent. Now at the very center of this issue of the magazine – a fairly typical issue by the way – is a long and decently earnest book review by Christopher Hill, a leading Marxist historian. What boggles the mind is not the mere coincidence of apologies for apartheid rubbing shoulders with good Marxist sense but how the one antipode includes (without any reference at all) what the other, the Marxist pole, performs unknowingly.

There are two very impressive points of reference for this discussion of what can be called the national culture as a nexus of relationship between 'fields,' many of them employing representation as their technique of distribution and production. (It will be obvious here that I exclude the creative arts and the natural sciences.) One is Perry Anderson's 'Components of the National Culture' (1969);[2] the other is Regis Debray's study of the French intelligentsia, *Teachers, Writers, Celebrities* (1980). Anderson's argument is that an absent intellectual center in traditional British thought about society was vulnerable to a 'white' (anti-revolutionary, conservative) immigration into Britain from Europe. This in turn produced a blockage of sociology, a technicalization of philosophy, an idea-free empiricism in history and an idealist aesthetics. Together these and other disciplines form 'something like a closed system', in which subversive discourses like Marxism and psychoanalysis were for a time quarantined; now, however, they too have

[2] See Perry Anderson, "Components of the National Culture," in *Student Power*, ed. Alexander Cockburn and Robin Blackburn (London: Harmondsworth, Penguin; NLR, 1969).

been incorporated. The French case, according to Debray, exhibits a series of three hegemonic conquests in time. First there was the era of the secular universities, which ended with World War I. That was succeeded by the era of the publishing houses, a time between the wars when Galimard-NRF – agglomerates of gifted writers and essayists that included Jacques Rivière, André Gide, Marcel Proust and Paul Valéry – replaced the social and intellectual authority of the somewhat overproductive, masspopulated universities. Finally, during the 1960s, intellectual life was absorbed into the structure of the mass media: worth, merit, attention and visibility slipped from the pages of books to be estimated by frequency of appearance on the television screen. At this point, then, a new hierarchy, what Debray calls a mediocracy, emerges, and it rules the schools and the book industry.

There are certain similarities between Debray's France and Anderson's England, on the one hand, and Reagan's America, on the other. They are interesting, but I cannot spend time talking about them. The differences are, however, more instructive. Unlike France, high culture in America is assumed to be above politics as a matter of unanimous convention. And unlike England, the intellectual center here is filled not by European imports (although they play a considerable role) but by an unquestioned ethic of objectivity and realism, based essentially on an epistemology of separation and difference. Thus each field is separate from the others because the subject matter is separate. Each separation corresponds immediately to a separation in function, institution, history and purpose. Each discourse 'represents' the field, which in turn is supported by its own constituency and the specialized audience to which it appeals. The mark of true professionalism is accuracy of representation of society, vindicated in the case of sociology, for instance, by a direct correlation between representation of society and corporate and/or governmental interests, a role in social policymaking, access to political authority. Literary studies, conversely, are realistically *not* about society but about masterpieces in need of periodic adulation and appreciation. Such correlations make possible the use of words like 'objectivity', 'realism' and 'moderation' when used in sociology or in literary criticism. And these notions in turn assure their own confirmation by careful selectivity of evidence, the incorporation and subsequent neutralization of dissent (also known as pluralism) and networks of insiders, experts whose presence is due to their conformity, not to any rigorous judgment of their past performance (the good team player always turns up).

But I must press on, even though there are numerous qualifications and refinements to be added at this point (e.g., the organized relationship between clearly affiliated fields such as political science and sociology versus the use by one field of another unrelated one for the purposes of national policy issues; the network of patronage and the insider/outsider dichotomy; the strange cultural encouragement of theories stressing such 'components' of the structure of power as chance, morality, American innocence, decentralized egos, etc.). The particular mission of the humanities is, in the aggregate, to represent *non-interference* in the affairs of the everyday world. As we have seen, there has been a historical erosion in the role of letters since the New Criticism, and I have suggested that the conjuncture of a narrowly based university environment for technical language and literature studies with the self-policing, self-purifying communities erected even by Marxist, as well as other disciplinary, discourses, produced a very small but definite function for the humanities: to represent humane marginality, which is also to preserve and if possible to conceal the hierarchy of powers that occupy the center, define the social terrain, and fix the limits of use functions, fields, marginality and so on. Some of the corollaries of this role for the humanities generally and literary criticism in particular are that the institutional presence of humanities guarantees a space for the deployment of free-floating abstractions (scholarship, taste, tact, humanism) that are defined in advance as indefinable; that when it is not easily domesticated, 'theory' is employable as a discourse of occultation and legitimation; that self-regulation is the ethos behind which the institutional humanities allow and in a sense encourage the unrestrained operation of market forces that were traditionally thought of as subject to ethical and philosophical review.

Very broadly stated, then, noninterference for the humanist means laissez-faire; 'they' can run the country, we will explicate Wordsworth and Schlegel.

. . . .

This is not the place, nor is there time, to advance a fully articulated program of interference. I can only suggest in conclusion that we need to think about breaking out of the disciplinary ghettos in which as intellectuals we have been confined, to reopen the blocked social processes ceding objective representation (hence power) of the world to a small coterie of experts and their clients, to consider that the audience for literacy is not a closed circle of three thousand professional critics but the community of human beings living in society, and to regard social reality in a secular rather than a mystical mode, despite all the protestations about realism and objectivity.

Two concrete tasks – again adumbrated by Berger – strike me as particularly useful. One is to use the visual faculty (which also happens to be dominated by visual media such as televison, news photography and commercial film, all of them fundamentally immediate, "objective" and ahistorical) to restore the nonsequential energy of lived historical memory and subjectivity as fundamental components of meaning in representation. Berger calls this an alternative use of photography: using photomontage to tell other stories than the offical sequential or ideological ones produced by institutions of power. (Superb examples are Sarah Graham-Brown's photoessay *The Palestinians and Their Society* and Susan Meisalas's *Nicaragua*.) Second is opening the culture to experiences of the Other which have remained "outside" (and have been repressed or framed in a context of confrontational hostility) the norms manufactured by "insiders." An excellent example is Malek Alloula's *Le Harem colonial*, a study of early twentieth-century post-cards and photographs of Algerian harem women. The pictorial capture of colonized people by colonizer, which signifies power, is reenacted by a young Algerian sociologist, Alloula, who sees his own fragmented history in the pictures, then reinscribes this history in his text as the result of understanding and making that intimate experience intelligible for an audience of modern European readers.

In both instances, finally, we have the recovery of a history hitherto either misrepresented or rendered invisible. Stereotypes of the Other have always been connected to political actualities of one sort or another, just as the truth of lived communal (or personal) experience has often been totally sublimated in official narratives, institutions and ideo-logies. But in having attempted – and perhaps even successfully accompli-shing – this recovery, there is the crucial next phase: connecting these more politically vigilant forms of interpretation to an ongoing political and social praxis. Short of making that connection, even the best-inten-tioned and the cleverest interpretive activity is bound to sink back into the murmur of mere prose. For to move from interpretation to its politics is in large measure to go from undoing to doing, and this, given the cur-rently accepted divisions between criticism and art, is risking all the dis-comfort of a great unsettlement in ways of seeing and doing. One must refuse to believe, however, that the comforts of specialized habits can be so seductive as to keep us all in our assigned places.

SECTION FOUR
NEW HISTORICISM

According to one of its leading proponents, Stephen Greenblatt, New Historicism is not so much a theory or doctrine of literary criticism as a textual practice. It is, however, a method of reading informed by and arising out of the theoretical ferment of the seventies, so that its concern to examine the textual traces of the past is premised on the notion that the past is available to us only in the form of a textuality which is also embedded in that of the present. Old 'historicism', with its Hegelian idealist sense of history as a developing totality or its evolutionary notion of teleology, had produced such classic literary critical accounts of history as Tillyard's *The Elizabethan World Picture* (1943). For New Historicists, however, there can be no such seamless, overarching unity, but only the shifting and contradictory representations of numerous 'histories'. History can only be a narrative construction involving a dialectical relationship of past and present concerns. Thus the critic is neither a transcendent commentator nor an objective chronicler because he/she is always implicated in the discourses which help to construct the object of knowledge. Hypothetical grand narratives such as the 'Elizabethan World Picture' are ideological projections based on the exclusivity of sameness. The New Historicist is more concerned to focus attention on the multiple and contradictory material practices which embed each historical event or expressive act as contexts of production and reception.

These material practices do not, however, constitute historical 'givens'. Eroding the distinction between text and context, the new historicist views social contexts in themselves as narrative constructions produced through the discursive management of relations of power. There is no 'background' and no absolute and autonomous literary text: literariness as well as cultural value are terms opened to contestation and reconstruction.

The practice of New Historicism is mainly associated with two groups of critics, one arising within studies of Romanticism (Marilyn Butler, Marjorie Levinson, Jerome McGann and David Simpson) and the other within Renaissance Studies (Jonathan Goldberg, Stephen Greenblatt and Louis Montrose). The first have been concerned to offer a critique of Romanticism's own self-presentation as aesthetic transcendence, egotistical sublime or poetic autonomy. The second group have used colonialism and theatricality both as political concepts and as looser metaphors to examine strategies of subversion and containment in Renaissance texts.

Stephen Greenblatt named the New Historicism in 1988, but the practice had been developing throughout the eighties, particularly in the pages of the journal *Representations*. In 1987 Marilyn Butler had called for a New Historicist practice in her Cambridge lecture 'Repossessing the Past : The Case for an Open Literary History'. In this, she called also for the study of actual literary communities as they function within larger communities in time and in particular places. Butler and Greenblatt emphasize that political and social needs shape literary production and reception and argue that criticism must therefore examine the ways in which traces of social circulation are effaced to produce the illusion of the 'autonomous' literary work : the Ideal Poem.

New Historicism follows a trajectory out of American formalist criticism with its close reading practices, through a hybrid mix of seventies theory, in order to return to history. Influences include Bakhtin, Althusser, Hayden White, Gadamer, Raymond Williams, Clifford Geertz and Foucault. Specific theoretical insights are derived from : Althusser's notion of ideology as contradictory and lived and his concept of the *relative* autonomy of the text and the interpellation of subjects in history; Gadamer's hermeneutic understanding of the past as ever constructed in relation to a present which is also a development out of that past; Hayden White's view of history as narrative construction or 'stories' and Bakhtin's articulation of all human utterances (including literary texts) as social acts which are multiaccentual and available for divergent uses.

Probably the most pervasive influence on New Historicist practice, however, is the work of Foucault. His writings have consistently shown how so-called objective historical accounts are always products of a will to power enacted through formations of knowledge within specific institutions. His own 'histories' resist the allure of 'total theories 'which offer overarching narratives and instead focus attention on the 'other' excluded by and constructed through such accounts. His view of power as omniscient though not omnipotent has been taken up by Greenblatt, but also by British 'cultural materialists' such as Jonathan Dollimore who also draw on Raymond Williams' later work on ideology. Greenblatt remains pessimistic, however, about the possibilities of subversion, viewing resistance as ultimately always contained. Cultural materialists tend to be more politically optimistic, tracing the potential for radical appropriation of dominant cultural meanings and values.

The two essays included here mark the beginnings of a move away from formalist concerns or the pursuit of totally coherent theoretical paradigms. Each advocates a more historically oriented and particularized engagement with the text. Weimann's essay arises more obviously out of Marxist thought and is less open than McGann's piece to the accusation sometimes levelled against New Historicism that it is simply a neo-pragmatist reaction against high theory. He presents a hermeneutic account of the relation of past and present, drawing loosely on E.D. Hirsch's concepts of meaning and significance and firmly rejecting the idea of the autonomy of the text. McGann's essay argues for the recognition of poetry as a social act and distinguishes between the text which is 'complete' and the poem which is ever open. His focus is on the circulation and reception of texts, arguing against the Kantian sense of the poem as Idea and viewing the critical failure to engage with the materiality of a text as necessarily leading to the blindness of literary critics to the time-bound nature of their own discourses.

---

28 Robert Weimann

Past Significance and Present Meaning in Literary History, *Structure and Society in Literary History*, 1976

With the decline of the New Criticism, an exploration of the idea of literary history is the most urgent task confronting the student of literature today. But it is a difficult task, and it involves problems whose solution is directly and indirectly linked with an awareness of crisis in both criticism and society. If, in England and the United States, the historical study of literature is to achieve a new sense of direction and purpose, it must first be prepared to face (with all that this implies) the full extent of the crisis of its discipline. This crisis is in many ways a symptom of the larger crisis of Western society, in which the revolutionary idea of change, organic and dialectical concepts of evolution, and the liberal and humanist traditions of progress are all, in various degrees, affected. Following the academic rebellion of the sixties, the consciousness of this wider background of crisis seems once more to be gaining ground; perhaps one may hazard the conjecture that a new interest in historical method can only benefit from an awareness of its present background. In fact, such awareness has already facilitated the first steps toward reopening, in the realm of literary history, the question of method and purpose from an angle that points, at least in several important aspects, beyond the assumptions of formalist criticism.

Contradictions beyond Formalism

The need for theory and method is usually felt most acutely when, in a time of rapid changes, the object of theoretical inquiry no longer functions in its traditional context. It seems significant, therefore, that there has recently developed a new consciousness of the need for historical theory, historiography, and hermeneutics which, in England and North America, was formerly an almost unheard-of phenomenon. This consciousness, as expressed in the work of Stanley Fish, Geoffrey Hartman, E. D. Hirsch, Jr., Paul de Man, Hayden White, and others, has provided some new and welcome perspectives on the current discussion of the aims and methods of literary criticism – perspectives which, at least by implication, point beyond the ahistorical orientation of the New Criticism. But for all their advances beyond some of the programmatic ideas of the intrinsic school of criticism, the outcome and the overall results of these new departures seem strangely tentative, incoherent, and, finally, disappointing. The reason is not primarily that some of the most basic questions, such as the relationship of text and context or that of literary structure and social function, have been left vague or have not been systematically explored. Nor can it be said that some of the new positions are not solidly developed and admirably argued. In fact, most of these new departures are, each in its own direction, profoundly searching, and they certainly constitute highly intelligent reflections of a transitional situation in American literary criticism and theory. However, taken together, they fail to provide a new paradigm consistent and coherent enough to supersede the ahistorical orientation of the formalist school of criticism.

The charge of failure, inconsistency, and incoherence is, of course, a grave one and needs to be substantiated. Let us, therefore, briefly refer to some of the new positions that, over the last eight or ten years, have emerged in varying contexts. There is (to begin with what may well be the most sustained theoretical contribution) the renewed emphasis on the author as an element in the relationship between the meaning of a text and that 'person', or 'conception', or 'situation' to which that meaning is (in historical criticism and judgment) related. In this sense there has been established a methodological difference 'between the meaning of a text (which does not change) and the meaning of a text to us today (which changes)'.[1] From a vastly different position, the reader, who in formalist criticism was excluded by legislation, has been

[1] E.D. Hirsch, Jr., *Validity in Interpretation* (New Haven, 1967), pp. 8, 255.

reconsidered 'as an actively mediating presence.' Along these lines, the 'meaning of an utterance' has been redefined as, simply, 'its experience': the sentence or the utterance 'is no longer an object, a thing-in-itself, but an *event*, something that *happens* to, and with the participation of, the reader.'[2] More generally, there is the search for 'a larger conception of literary form' that attempts to go beyond 'formalism, structuralism, and myth criticism' because 'the structuralist science of myth does not allow us to cross over from its theory of form to a descriptive or critical account of the artist's historical consciousness.'[3] Among the attempts to work out a 'theory linking the form of the medium to the form of the artist's historical consciousness,' attention has been drawn to the artist's struggle with his vocation as 'a version of a universal human struggle: of genius with Genius, and of genius with the *genius loci*.'[4] Thus, the new interest in method has led to a call for a new 'metahistory' by which 'the explanatory and the interpretative aspects of the narrative tend to be run together' in such a way that the distinction between 'proper history' and 'metahistory' has no longer any 'adequate theoretical justification.'[5] Such a broad perspective is finally corroborated when the expressed 'need to revise the foundations of literary history' is seen in connection with the 'disquieting' assumption that 'literary history could in fact be paradigmatic for history in general.'[6]

This brief and purely descriptive (and highly selective) summary of some of the new departures must here suffice to convey an idea of the various directions from which recent scholars and critics have developed suggestions toward a new historical perspective in criticism. But this perspective remains fragmentary, spontaneous, and unstable because none of these contributions has developed a comprehensive consciousness, let alone a methodology, of the full correlative connections between literature and history. For although the author has been reconsidered as against the formalist theory of authorial irrelevance and although the reader has been vindicated as against the intrinsic assumption of the affective fallacy, the theoretical and practical framework of these extensions—and, above all, the methodological connections between author and reader, structure and function—have not been developed historically. But the failure to connect these most basic points of reference reflects more than some necessary (and provisional) division of interest and labor among scholars. Even the most systematically elaborated positions reveal a deliberate abstention

[2]Stanley Fish, "Literature in the Reader: Affective Stylistics," *New Literary History*, 2 (1970/71), 123, 160, 125.

[3]Geoffrey Hartman, "Toward Literary History," *Daedalus*, 99 (Spring 1970), 357, 362.

[4]Ibid., pp. 364, 369.

[5]Hayden White, "Interpretation in History," *New Literary History*, 4 (1973/74), 282, 309.

[6]Paul de Man, "Literary History and Literary Modernity," *Daedalus*, 99 (Spring 1970), 403.

from, or lack of awareness of, the need for a more sustained and coherent methodology for historical criticism.

To illustrate, I can here refer only in passing to the assertion of 'the timelessness of understanding' that is a major premise even in the most impressive recent American contribution to hermeneutics.[7] To 'disregard the historicity of understanding,' however, raises some fundamental methodological questions as to the validity of historical generalizations at large. For instance, do the differences among individual perspectives on art and society, from the point of view of historiography, have priority as against the differences between the social perspectives associated with changing historical eras? Can literary history be based on the assumption that 'the real ontological gap' is 'the one that subsists between persons, not the one that subsists between historical eras'?[8] From a position like this the rationale for an approach to the changes and temporal complications in literary writing and reading might more easily be found in psychology and anthropology than in sociology and history. Thus, even the most cogent hermeneutical refutation of the theory of semantic autonomy does not by itself help to constitute the basis on which a new methodological perspective in literary history can be reestablished.

The recent approach to 'the reader as an actively mediating presence' in literature presents similar problems. It is of course true that a study of the reader in *Paradise Lost*, for instance, may be profoundly rewarding in terms of an understanding of the experience (and the structure of the response) that literature can actually provoke.[9] But as soon as this approach tends to limit itself to a study of 'the developing responses of the reader in relation to the words as they succeed one another in time,'[10] it has surrendered the full field of *Wirkungsgeschichte* to a much more narrowly conceived 'Affective Stylistics.' Again, stylistics can provide a very meaningful 'bridging of life and art' in the sense that it establishes not only 'the continuing presence of the author in the work' but also that of the reader 'as created and creating power in the poem.'[11] But as long as the reader's responses are studied intrinsically (exclusively 'in relation to the words'), the reader himself can hardly be defined historically, as a changing *ensemble* of social and aesthetic values, attitudes, and forms of consciousness. Instead, the reader is defined as 'a construct, an ideal or idealized reader,' and the structure of his response is viewed primarily in terms of 'linguistic experiences.'

[7]Hirsch, *Validity*, p. 137.
[8]Ibid., pp. 256, 258.
[9]Stanley Fish, *Surprised by Sin: The Reader in Paradise Lost* (New York, 1967).
[10]Fish, "Literature in the Reader," p. 139.
[11]Joan Webber, "Stylistics: A Bridging of Life and Art in Seventeenth-Century Studies," *New Literary History*, 2 (1970/71), 294.

On what grounds, then, can it be said of this type of stylistics that the 'method will obviously be radically historical'?[12] Such a claim, if it does not remain completely unjustified, amounts to an unconscious apology for the unhelpful relativism ('The meaning of an utterance . . . is its experience') in accordance with which criteria of critical evaluation as well as standards in aesthetics are *expressis verbis* rejected. (This 'method allows for no such aesthetic and no such fixings of value: In fact it is oriented *away* from evaluation. . . ')[13] But to dismiss 'the objectivity of the text' as 'an illusion' is as problematic as it seems unnecessary from a position which, for all its concern with 'language as an experience,' still approaches the text (as a perceptive commentator remarks) 'as an autonomous structure of internal relationships.'[14] In the last resort it is this lingering hermetic conception of literary structure that leads the new stylistics (if not to the idea of 'the timelessness of understanding') to the postulate of the timelessness reading and an ahistorical conception of the reader and his responses. For it is precisely the implied timelessness of reading that makes it difficult to conceive of the activity of the reader as some form of social and historical activity involving the changing nature and the reciprocal quality of the relationship between the past world of the art work and the present world and mode of its reception.

If, judged by the requirements of historical method, the most important contributions to the rehabilitation of both the author and the reader prove vulnerable, it is perhaps not surprising that the more general recent reorientations 'toward literary history' also leave a number of questions unanswered. It is certainly noteworthy when (writing under that title) a distinguished American scholar-critic urges the 'importance' of literary history and deplores 'the absence of methodological thinking in that area'. It is indeed interesting to read that in reference to a phrase used by Werner Krauss literary history is understood as 'our "historical duty" because it alone can provide today a sorely needed defense of art'.[15] Here the implied emphasis on a larger historical conception of literary form is related to a new sense of the public function of art. But in contrast to Werner Krauss's concept of *geschichtlicher Auftrag*, the expressed need for a defense of art is

[12]Fish, "Literature in the Reader," pp. 145, 159, 146. Michael Riffaterre ("The Stylistic Approach to Literary History," *New Literary History*, 2 [1970/71], 39–55) betrays a comparable lack of awareness of the degree to which the concept of "the reader" is an abstraction from cultural activities in history, as when he completely ignores the changing social and ideological contexts and functions of reading (see, e.g., pp. 46 f.). Based on such premises, the "contribution of stylistics to diachronic analysis" (p. 52) amounts to no more than a reaffirmation of the principle of verbal autonomy: "Literary history should therefore be a history of words" (p. 55).

[13]Fish, "Literature in the Reader," p. 146.

[14]Hayden White, "Literary History: The Point of It All," *New Literary History*, 2 (1970/71), 177.

[15]Hartman, "Toward Literary History," p. 356.

conceived as pragmatic rather than historical: the postulate seems divorced from the more comprehensive process of history that links the past work of the artist and the present world of its historian.

It is true that there is no really satisfying English equivalent for the German term *Auftrag;* but the context in which *Auftrag* is rendered by 'historical duty' turns the implied consciousness of historical function almost into a postulate of self-defence. For the advocated 'defence of art' sounds more like a defence of art for its own sake than a defence of art in its relation to society. At this point to urge 'the formality of art ... as a central issue in any literary history' involves an emphasis that tends to predetermine the attempt 'to bring together the form of art and the form of its historical consciousness'. Again, it is true that the new conception of form is to be based on 'a theory of *literary* as well as *functional* form' and that, in this connection, the theory of literary vocation definitely points beyond the hermetic conception of function as an order of internal relationships. Yet can the repeated emphasis on the vocational crisis of the poet and his rite of passage serve to integrate the new concept of function in a more comprehensive perspective on history? Does this provide a frame of reference large enough for both the genesis and the impact of literature? The question is at least an open one, since it is the individual poet's literary self-consciousness and self-objectification that are taken to furnish criteria for the identification of, or conflict between, 'genius' and 'Genius', or 'genius' and '*genius loci*'.[16]

Although such categories and such a relationship do point to important manifestations of the growth in, and crisis of, historical consciousness, they still reflect the same preoccupation with *literaturnost'* ('literariness') that is revealed in the work of another well-known critic and scholar when, in order to underline the essential unity of history and literary history, he postulates 'that the bases for historical knowledge are . . . written texts, even if these texts masquerade in the guise of wars or revolutions'.[17] To view literary history as a paradigm for 'history in general' points to an altogether larger dimension of methodology. But the question that has to be asked is, Can the nature of the *sources* of history and literary history be made to provide a basis for the paradigmatic quality of the latter? Here, to point to written texts as presumably the only, or major, source for historical knowledge seems to disvalue the practical experience of living in society (in a society that reflects and promulgates the very outcome of wars and revolutions) as the crucial impulse and criterion of knowledge and insight. The written

---

[16]Ibid., pp. 356, 361, 364, 365 ff.

[17]De Man, p. 403. The original version of the text has (wrongly, I suppose) "wars or evolutions." I have corrected this after consulting the reprinted version of the essay in de Man's *Blindness and Insight: Essays in the Rhetoric of Contemporary Criticism* (New York, 1971), p. 165.

texts are taken to be both source and message, the actual process of history providing a mere guise, or costume.

This takes us very close to that metaphorical terminology according to which historical events are defined in terms of 'scenario', 'act', and 'stage'. The underlying ambiguities in the implied relationship between art and history seem significant. The function of art is not described and criticized in terms of the language of history; the function of history is described in terms of the language of art criticism. The resulting metaphors dramatize and formalize the modes of correlation between art and history (and in that they reflect some changing patterns of perception and expression that developed in the sixties). But as a basis for a methodology of literary history, let alone for one that could in fact be paradigmatic for history in general,[18] this provides a questionable frame of reference.

Although these new departures in historical criticism are too serious to be reduced to the level of a fashionable phraseology, the trend toward an *Ästhetisierung der Historie*, instead of a *Historisierung der Ästhetik*, seems to affect even the most carefully developed theoretical contributions to a new sense of historical method. Small wonder. For even the two most prestigious critics and theoreticians writing in the West at the present time, Claude Lévi-Strauss and Northrop Frye, have tended to view the modes and principles of interpretation in history not as historical but as mythical. It may seem highly tempting to many who now begin to grapple with problems of historical method and interpretation to take up these cues. We will take up only one (but the most brilliant) example.

It is possible to argue that 'interpretation in history consists of the provisions of a plot-structure for a sequence of events so that their nature as a comprehensible process is revealed by their figuration as a *story of a particular kind*'. The suggested differentiation between story and plot and the resulting 'Modes of Employment (Romance, Comedy, Tragedy, Satire), together with corresponding Modes of Explanation and Ideological Implication', amount to a triangle of quaternary forms that is as ingenious as, and possibly more fearful than, Northrop Frye's patterns of symmetry. And although the achieved complexity in the interconnections of the three basic modes of reference (aesthetic, epistemological, and moral) is certainly impressive, the final, though still tentative, definition of 'interpretation' in historical thought leads the modes of conceptualization away from its objects in reality. For if historical interpretation is said to consist of the 'formalization of the phenomenal field originally constituted by language itself on the basis of a dominant tropological wager', the present activity of the interpreter of past works and events finds itself at two removes from the historical

[18]De Man, "Literary History and Literary Modernity," p.403.

process.[19] Consequently, the analysis of the modalities of historical interpretation becomes purely *geistesgeschichtlich* and breaks away from what that interpretation is all about. The present methods of historiography and the past objects of history seem so unrelated that the process of historiography itself can only be defined logically and poetically, but never historically. Thus, the modes of historiography are being established spatially, in an almost autonomous manner that ignores or contradicts (and is ignored or contradicted by) the mode of existence of its own object and content. Again, the reciprocal quality of the relationship between 'past significance' and 'present meaning', between historical structures and modern functions, seems to escape.

As this brief and highly selective survey of some of the new departures in literary theory and history indicates, there have emerged a number of fresh and genuinely stimulating perspectives on historical criticism, but a more comprehensive functional attitude toward both the objects and the interpretations of literary history has, in practice, failed to develop. For all the increased consciousness of the need to revise the foundations of literary history, such revision is slow to move beyond the limitations of formalism. If the formulated task is considered, again in the words of Paul de Man, 'a desperately vast undertaking,'[20] then the task seems so formidable partly because there has not developed a unifying methodological perspective in accordance with which the various aspects of the history of both reading and writing might be organized and interrelated under an integrating idea and method of history and criticism. Such a view of the whole is sorely needed; without it, the limitations of formalism (and the more recent contradictions beyond formalism) cannot be overcome. So long as some of the most distinguished critics of formalism are still haunted by an increasingly blurred and ambivalent concept of autonomy, the process of literary history is still, historically and categorically, dissociated from the worlds of both its creation and reception.

It is true, at this date, that the concept of autonomy is hardly used any more in the sterile sense of the intrinsic school of criticism, but it still involves some of the old ambiguities and it already reflects new uncertainties. How do we view 'literature in history without denying its autonomy'? is the sort of question asked by even the most historical-minded of the newer critics.[21] But is this not a question that recalls the old, sterile dualism of the intrinsic and the extrinsic, as well as the older postulate of a literary or inside history of literature? What exactly is the meaning of autonomy in a context like this? Has it simply come to stand as a synonym for a (justified) demand that we observe the specific

---

[19]White, "Interpretation in History," pp. 291, 307, 312.
[20]De Man, p. 403.
[21]Hartman, "Toward Literary History," p. 356.

nature and function of poetry? This seems to be contradicted by the general trend toward an *Ästhetisierung der Historie*, which I have observed above.[22]

The paradox of the situation is perhaps best expressed by Geoffrey Hartman when he in an essay with the programmatic title 'Beyond Formalism' writes: 'To go beyond formalism is as yet too hard for us; and may even be . . . against the nature of understanding'.[23] Indeed, the heritage of the New Criticism is a burden for critics still. This holds good more or less for most of these counterproposals, be they hermeneutical or stylistic, on the relation of form and consciousness or on that of history and literary history, or, finally, on the modes of historiography itself. Wherever we look there is some remnant, however hidden, of some of the ahistorical ideas and concepts of formalism. Perhaps it is not saying too much to suggest that it is the lingering impact of the formalist aesthetic which, more than anything else, stands in the way of a more functional and comprehensive integration of the new perspectives on the author and the reader. Thus, genesis and impact, the approaches to the structure of, and the response to, style remain fundamentally dissociated.

What, then, accounts for the hold that the intrinsic school of criticism has even over its critics? To answer this question historically is to inquire into the function of ideology as it affects the needs and perspectives of literary criticism as a social and academic institution in the United States today. Although since the fifties the function and status of the university has been involved in struggle, controversy, and recession, there is an

[22]On the other hand, if this "characteristic autonomy of literature" is understood as the " 'capacity of art-forms to outlast the destined hour' " (ibid.), then it must be pointed out that the very process of survival witnesses the historical *functioning* (which is highly specific) of the art work, i.e., a continued mode of social, not autonomous, existence. It is curious to find that, at this late date, Hartman and scholar-critics like Paul de Man persist in an increasingly vague conception of "the autonomous domain of literature" (de Man, p. 401). But in the same book in which de Man still writes in seeming approval of this concept (*Blindness and Insight*, p. 162) he can already demand "a long overdue re-examination of the assumptions on which the position of autonomy was founded" (p. 22); indeed, he does so himself mainly (and in a characteristically limited manner) by questioning the new critical "rejection of *intentionality*" (p. 25) and the related notion "that literature is a privileged *Language*" (p. 12; again my italics). Thus, there results the ambivalent charge that formalist ideas of autonomy "may very well have been founded on preconceptions that were themselves derived from non-literary models" and that (consequently, one assumes) the concept of autonomy "has to be redefined" (p. 22; but see p. 21). In a totally different context, where the concept is redefined (James S. Ackerman, "Toward a New Social Theory of Art," *New Literary History*, 4 [1972/73], 330) "autonomous" merely seems to emphasize an objective mode of existence, as when it is said that "a work of art has an autonomous existence (since, whether or not it communicates, it is still there)." But is not communication (function) an implicit condition and a constituting (structuring) factor of "existence" (genesis)? It would be easy to trace several more versions of autonomy, but the conceptual content of this semantic confusion seems to reflect at least some of the contradicitons in current attempts to move beyond formalism.

[23]Geoffrey Hartman, "Beyond Formalism," in *Issues in Contemporary Literary Criticism*, ed. Polletta, p. 162.

obvious element of continuity. And even though it can be said that the academic rebellion in the sixties witnessed significant and, indeed, radical changes in the social role and class alignment of many students and professors, the social and cultural context and, together with it, some of the most basic problems that challenge literary study and the literary profession have largely remained the same. As some recent radical critics of society have observed, these problems (which arise from the roles culture and its bearers have played in bourgeois society) persistently affect not only the study of literature but the most general assumptions about the practical uses of literature as an agent of social change and consciousness. Criticism reflects this situation by skepticism and retreat; it no longer fulfills the cultural needs and expectations of society: it has become related to the institutional procedures of education rather than to the education of a social class. In other words, so much academic criticism is written to fulfill professional require-ments that it is possible to say that the primary function of writing literary criticism has . . . become certifying college and university teachers of literature.[24] If this seems an exaggerated statement, it does point to a social and ideological context which is radically different from that of the past, in which criticism was more intimately bound up with the whole business of living in the present. But whereas critics like Johnson, Diderot, Lessing, or Belinski made a point of relating literature not to the professional specialists but, rather, to the intellec-tual and practical needs of the whole of their readers' lives, Western academic critics have largely abandoned this broadly civilizing function of criticism.

In a subsequent chapter I shall return to the narrowing scope of the function of criticism (and discuss at greater length the consequences for the modern ahistorical conception of tradition). Here it must suffice to suggest that the rise and success (and the survival) of the intrinsic idea of the autonomy of literature is, at least indirectly, connected with the social and cultural dilemma of a society where the professionalized use of criticism is alienated from the practical concerns and the culture of the majority of the people. As a matter of course, the institutional function of criticism (as against its civilizing role in society at large) tends to encourage the approach to literature as a formal discipline. As a mere body of formalized knowledge, the object of study and the purpose to which it can be put become more and more unrelated. The correlation between knowledge and education becomes precarious. There is a dissociation between the self-contained needs and standards of the discipline (and the corresponding emphasis on formality, autonomy, on internal relationships and demonstrably written texts),

[24]*The Politics of Literature: Dissenting Essays on the Teaching of English*, ed. Louis Kampf and Paul Lauter (New York, Vintage Books, 1972), pp. 7, 18 f.

on the one hand, and the role that the discipline (and the use of its results) can play in the lives and the society of those who practice it, on the other. And since the objects of the discipline are usually taken from the literature of the past, the dissociation tends to disturb, or leave undeveloped, the reciprocal quality of the most basic historical relationship between the past significance of the work and the present meaning of its revitalized use and interpretation.

The methodological dilemma of the new historical criticism, then, is also, and perhaps even primarily, a cultural one. This is not to say that the outcome of the recent methodological debate is predetermined by the type of social relationships that it, among other things, reflects. (If this were so, any discussion of method and principle would, in this context, be a futile waste of time.) But if the prolonged influence and the lingering impact of the intrinsic approach to literature as an autonomous object of formal knowledge is to be understood, this social background must be taken into account. Here, finally, are the cultural conditions which, through schools and publishing houses, have been instrumental in creating a situation in which the reading of literature and the understanding of history are not self-evident (and mutually intertwined) modes of social activity for the majority of citizens. It is a situation in which 'people are not participants in a cultural enterprise but spectators at a performance'.[25] The achievement of the literature of the past and the participation in, and control of, the civilization in the present appear (to the ordinary reader) as unrelated as the world of beauty and the world of labor or (for the formal critic) past aesthetic structure and present social function.

The ultimate contradictions, then, are to be found in the relationship between work and leisure, social facts and artifacts. In the last analysis, they cannot be resolved without a reconsideration of that larger question of the relationship of social history and cultural (or aesthetic) value that I have raised in the Introduction. The reader does not have to accept my own position in order to understand that a theoretical challenge (not to say solution) of the problem is possible not on the basis of some partial revision or some single specific counter-suggestion but only in the full context of a new literary theory and history that attempts to recover a sense of the unity of man's activities in society, of which writing and reading form a part. So long as the specific modes of art and criticism are conceived as categorically and historically unrelated to the process of the more basic and ordinary civilizing activities of man, the burden of formalism is likely to remain heavy, and the methodological alienation of art from the history of society cannot finally be overcome.

[25]Ibid., p. 46.

New Criticism and Historical Philology

If, under these circumstances, the intrinsic approach to literature is still 'the most powerful programmatic idea' in American criticism, the relationship between the New Criticism and the traditional modes of literary history needs to be reconsidered more closely. The ahistorical orientation of formalism is well known; but while it is impossible not to reject this orientation, the New Critics' objections to traditional literary history did raise a number of very important questions. There is no need to oversimplify their critique or to reject it out of hand. Now that the New Criticism has itself become part of the history of criticism, the neohumanist and formalist revolt against positivism, as well as its consequences, can more nearly be seen in perspective. At this date there is no need to go back to the nineteenth-century tradition of historical philology. To criticize the New Criticism involves no apology for the uncritical study of sources, influences, and biographical data as an end in itself. To ignore the fact that the formalist critique of literary history involved areas of strength and consistency as well as limitations is not helpful; to do so does not allow us to focus on and confront the complexity of those premises, both theoretical and practical, on which the historical approach to literature was bound for crisis.

This is not the place for a full survey of the theoretical positions from which the New Criticism challenged the methods of traditional literary history, but perhaps a few illustrations will suffice to bring out its main direction and emphasis. Even when, with some effort, the New Critics would retain a grudging modicum of respect for the 'intense and precise labors of the Victorian philologists in the service of authenticity and other forms of factuality', their rejection of historical antiquarianism was as consistent as it was complete. If this had entailed a formulated alternative in historical method, there might have been more to be said for their polemics, especially for their attacks on the academic accumulation of unrelated historical facts, and even their scarcely concealed scorn for those mechanistic 'exercises relating literature to various kinds of influence—social, political, economic, climatic, national, regional, traditional, psychological, and genealogical'.[26] Such polemics, of course, were almost as vigorous in Britain and Europe, as in F. R. Leavis's protests against the usual compilation . . .—names, titles, dates, "facts about," irrelevancies, superficial comments, and labour-saving descriptions.[27]

These attacks (which were also aimed at the 'verbose inanities of tendencies', zeitgeist, and the like and which were echoed by a good

---

[26]William K. Wimsatt, Jr., and Cleanth Brooks, *Literary Criticism: A Short History* (New York, 1957), pp. 537, 543.

[27]"Criticism and Literary History," *The Importance of Scrutiny*, ed. Eric Bentley (New York, 1964), p. 12.

many liberal critics) are too well known to call for further documenta-
tion. They were all more or less explicitly based on certain theoretical
assumptions which, reduced to their common denominator, can
perhaps best be phrased negatively: they saw 'the great mistake of the
scientific-historical scholarship' in the fact that it 'had allied itself with
the physical sciences of the nineteenth century'. The most disreputable
symptoms of such mesalliance were diagnosed in 'the whole underlying
assumption that literature should be explained by the methods of the
natural sciences, by causality, by such external determining forces as . . .
race, *milieu*, *moment*'. Such 'scientism', it was argued, was behind both
the 'study of causal antecedents and origins' and the use of 'quantitative
methods of science: statistics, charts, and graphs'.[28]

Again, this is not the place to open the vast question of the relation of
historical scholarship and natural science, and in any case an answer to
this question would have to show, as many scholars and critics have
done, that literary criticism is not an exact science. But even though the
early battle in 'the revolt against positivism' was in many ways justified,
later new critical polemics tended toward complacency and ingenuous-
ness. Even when the enemy was routed, the attacks continued to be
directed at a straw man who supposedly still believed in the methodological identity of history and mechanical physics. Although positivism was dead, its specter was not allowed to find rest. These polemics,
which served as a comfortable *alibi* to the antihistorical bias of the New
Criticism, were questionable in several respects.

In the first place, the attack against the mechanistic aspects of
nineteenth-century literary scholarship never paused to consider that
the tradition of historical inquiry was much older than, and never solely
identical with, the pseudoscientific pose of some latter-day philologists.
The rise of historical criticism can roughly be traced in the decline of the
social and theorectical presuppositions of natural law, and dates from,
say, Vico's *La Scienza Nuova* (1725), the work of Leibniz, Shaftesbury,
the French Enlightenment, and, in its fully developed form, from
Herger's *Ideenzur Philosophie der Geschichte der Menschheit* (1784–
91). It finds its mature expression in Goethe's own 'sense of the past and
the present as one', for him a 'powerful and overwhelming feeling',
which could hardly 'be expressed wonderfully enough'. (Ein Gefühl
aber, das bei mir gewaltig überhand nahm und sich nicht wundersam
genug äußern konnte, war die Empfindung der Vergangenheit und
Gegenwart in Eins. . .) This is a poet's statement that corresponds to
Schiller's attempt, in his theory of *Universaleschichte*, 'to connect the
past with the present' ('das Vergangene mit dem Gegenwärtigen zu

---

[28]Lionel Trilling, "The Sense of the Past," *The Liberal Imagination* (London, Mercury
Books, 1961), p. 182; René Wellek, "The Revolt against Positivism in Recent European Literary
Scholoarship," *Concepts of Criticism*, ed. Stephen G. Nichols, Jr. (New Haven, 1963), pp. 256,
257.

verknüpfen'). From here, through Hegel, this tradition of historical thought branched off in two directions. On the one hand there was the *geisteswissenschaftliche* idealism of Dilthey and the later historians of *Historismus*, Ernst Troeltsch and Friedrich Meinecke, whose philosophy of history certainly contained elements of irrationalism, but not of mechanism. On the other hand it was, in the context of revolutionary materialism, carried on by Engels and especially Marx, who in his well-known comment on classical Greek art argued that certain great works of art can only arise at an early or undeveloped stage of social development and that 'the charm of their art for us' is not opposed to their historical origins; so that the true 'difficulty' of the historian's task lies not in the fact that 'the Greek epic and Greek art are connected with certain social forms of development' but rather that these works of art 'still offer aesthetic pleasure to us and in some respect serve as norm and unattainable standard'. ('Aber die Schwierigkeit liegt nicht darin, zu verstehn, daß griechische Kunst und Epos an gewisse gesellschaftliche Entwicklungsformen geknüpft sind. Die Schwierigkeit ist, daß sie für uns noch Kunstgenuß, gewähren und in gewisser Beziehung als Norm und unerreichbare Muster gelten'.)[29]

It was an illusion, therefore, to assume that the indictment of philological positivism could refute the tradition of historical inquiry at large. At the time when Hippolyte Taine was developing his determinism in terms of the *moment*, the *race*, and the *milieu* (1863), the more dialectical concepts of historical criticism were perhaps overshadowed by what Nietzsche contemptuously called the reign of 'that blind force of facts' (jene blinde Macht der Fakta),[30] but they certainly had not ceased to be available. There was, from the point of view of method, a tradition in which the past and the present could be considered as one and in which the present charm (and meaning) of great art, its norm and standard, might well be reconciled with a thorough understanding of its past genesis.

If it was undiscriminating to charge the historical approach with the abuse of 'the methods of the natural sciences', then it was no less questionable, in the fourth decade of the twentieth century, to conceive of these methods solely or mainly in terms of nineteenth-century ideas of causality and such mechanistic assumptions as 'that the world was reflected' with perfect literalness in the will-less mind of the observer'.[31] Again and again the literary historian was warned to keep away from the methods of science—but of a science that was hopelessly out of date.

[29] J. W. Goethe, *Dichtung und Wahrheit*, *Goethes Sämltche Werke* (Jubiläums-Ausgabe), XXIV, 213; Friedrich Schiller, *Was heißt und zu welchem Ende studiert man Unversalgeschichte?* 2d ed. (1790; rpt. 1953, ed. F. Schneider), p. 36; Karl Marx, "Einleitung zur Kritik der politischen Ökonomie," Marx and Engels, *Werke* (Dietz Verlag), XIII, 641.

[30] Friedrich Nietzsche, *Vom Nutzen und Nachteil der Historie für das Leben* (Leipzig, Kröners Pocket Edition [1933]), p. 70.

[31] Trilling, *The Liberal Imagination, p. 182.*

Nor was there, on the side of the critics, any curiosity as to whether the method of historiography itself had not (like that of modern science) developed considerably. By now to condemn the writing of history on the charge that it adopts the methods of the natural sciences (*which* 'natural sciences'?) has become meaningless, if not downright complacent. At any rate (and this is not the place to say more), it ignores a great deal in modern physics; for instance the tendency among physicists in recent years to speak of their science in terms which (as a distinguished historian notes) suggest an 'identity of aim between scientists and historians' and even 'more striking analogies between the physical universe and the world of the historian'.[32] It may be that in the light of such statements and recent insights into the nature of 'the two cultures' (and how dangerous it is 'to have two cultures which can't or don't communicate'),[33] the responsible literary critic will have to be more and more wary of stressing the irreconcilability of the two disciplines.

To say this is not to minimize the basic differences in method, and is emphatically no apology for positivism, but it may help us to recover a more sober perspective, from which the nineteenth century's 'serene unification of scientific conscience' can be viewed with less ambiguity (than Cleanth Brooks betrays in the context of this phrase). Whatever its shortcomings, historical philology was intellectually the most coherent movement in nineteenth-century scholarship, and it is with some feeling of respect that one would wish to see *the necessary criticism* be based on more facts and less arrogance. It would take more detailed investigation into the method and practice of nineteenth-century literary history to assess the degree to which the attempts at historical syntheses were actually thwarted by the pseudoscientific pose. Not that the 'blind power of facts' can ever be admired again, but on the basis of a recent study of traditional literary history in America, one is inclined to think that the really important works are less seriously affected by the mechanism of uncritical research than is commonly assumed by the critics of positivism.[34] A sober reassessment of these works (some of which, by the way, are eminently readable) would, among other things,

---

[32]E. H. Carr, *What Is History* (London, 1962), pp. 80, 66. Contrasting modern and nineteenth-century assumptions of method, Carr writes: "Nowadays both scientists and historians entertain the more modest hope of advancing progressively from one fragmentary hypothesis to another, isolating their facts through the medium of their interpretations, and testing their interpretations by the facts; and ways in which they go about it do not seem to me essentially different" (pp. 77-78).

[33]C. P. Snow, *The Two Cultures: And a Second Look* (New York, Mentor Books, 1964), p. 90. Snow raises a vast question which has been asked, independently, in the distinguished work of Jacob Bronowski (see, e.g., *Science and Human Values* [London, 1961], p. 50, et passim).

[34]See my comments on the work of Moses Coit Tyler, pp. 99-100.

reveal a startling contrast to the much more analytical and experimental prose of the New Criticism.[35]

If the new critical attitude toward historical scholarship was somewhat ambiguous, it was also, of course, not uniform. The various critics reacted rather differently, and there were quite a number of protests (some of them undoubtedly sincere) 'that the literary historian and the critic need to work together' and that both functions should, ideally, be united in one and the same man.[36] But, as the main works in the tradition of historical inquiry were generally treated with more condescension than knowledge and as their results were, in the practical business of criticism, usually ignored, such protests often rang hollow. So whereas the critics did not offer any theoretical alternative, there developed and spread a climate of critical opinion in which historical scholarship per se seemed hostile to critical evaluation; likewise, the genetic approach per se seemed to be an expression of relativism; the study of the writer's background and biography per se seemed to be a symptom of the 'intentional fallacy'. As the New Criticism reaped its academic triumphs in the forties and early fifties and one scholarly journal after the other thinned the volume of its historical contributions, it must have appeared to many that the study of literary genesis could only detract from, and never add to, the critical approach to literature as a serious art form. Small wonder, when even the most thoughtful observers approached the relations of history and criticism as 'something unavoidably problematic, part of a troublesome opposition which runs through all our experience'.[37] Such an opposition was in many quarters not merely taken for granted; it was justified by, and elaborated into, the theory of 'absolute' criteria of evaluation. It was an 'absolutism' by which the (undouted) relativism of the traditional literary historian was, unfortunately, not overcome but relegated to a series of opposites, among which change and value, development and order, history and aesthetics, past significance and present meaning appeared more irreconcilable than ever before.

Criticism and Present Meaning

However, it would be a gross oversimplification to imply that the new

[35]Ironically it "was precisely this scientific pose, conscious or unconscious, that constituted one of the main strengths of the New Criticism" (J H. Raleigh, "The New Criticism as an Historical Phenomenon," *Comparative Literature*, 11 [1959/60], 23). The irony of it was noticed by at least one critic who—finding in Allen Tate's work "a rage, so deep a hatred of science and positivism, not to say democracy"—saw "a certain irony in his position, since the very textual analysis he defended was an aping of scientific method and rigor" (Alfred Kazin, *On Native Grounds* [New York, Overseas ed., 1942], p. 361).

[36]Cleanth Brooks, "A Note on the Limits of 'History' and the Limits of 'Criticism,' " *Sewanee Review*, 61(1953), 132.

[37]W. K. Wimsatt, Jr., "History and Criticism: A Problematic Relationship," *The Verbal Icon: Studies in the Meaning of Poetry* (Lexington, Ky., 1954), p. 253.

critical view of traditional literary history was entirely based on a series of formalist fallacies. Nor would one wish to minimize the extent to which the virtue of close textual analysis can survive the decline of the dogma of the autonomy of literature, thereby making a very consider-able contribution to the more recent rapprochement of literary criticism and historical scholarship. And in the work of critics such as F. R. Leavis, Yvor Winters, and Kenneth Burke, these possibilities reach as far back as the thirties and forties. For whatever the degree of the failure of the New Criticism in the field of literary history, even in its heyday it raised a number of serious issues and asked several very penetrating questions that a new approach would not wish easily to dismiss.

Among them, the question of relevance was foremost. Inspiring the attack on historical antiquarianism, it asserted the need for a new consciousness of 'the relation between antique fact and poetic value'. The simplest and the most straightforward form in which the problem was posed was one in which the purpose of literary history was defined from the angle of the present. A history of English literature, F. R. Leavis wrote, 'will be undertaken because the works of certain poets are judged to be of lasting value – of value in the present'. From this position, which may be said to stress one aspect of one basic truth, the need for evaluation was articulated with a new sense of urgency: if the criteria for a history of literature somehow correspond to a living system of values, then an awareness of these values would indeed seem to be *one* prerequisite for historical studies. F. R. Leavis (without bothering much about the emphasis carried by my cautious italics) put this quite bluntly: 'Such a history, then, could be accomplished only by a writer interested in, and intelligent about, the present. It would, for one thing, be an attempt to establish a perspective, to determine what of English poetry of the past is, or ought to be, alive for us now'.[38]

The strength of this position consisted in the fact *that* (not in the method *how*) the literature of the past was related to what was felt to be 'alive' in the present. When the interests of contemporary literature can find an echo in the literature of the past, then there must exist some community of poetic values (and, we should add, of historical moments). Even when this community was defined solely in terms of 'modern' values, it comprised, and had to be defined in terms of, a sense of tradition. But then, again, 'tradition' was taken as a mode of relating (rather than *correlating*) past poetry to present practice. F. R. Leavis and most of the New Critics still behaved as if their literary history virtually had the choice between past significance and present meaning – *their* choice being, of course, in favour of the latter.

---

[38]Wimsatt and Brooks, *Literary Criticism*, p. 537; Leavis, "Criticism and Literary History," pp. 13, 14.

The result, even though it satisfied current aesthetic assumptions, was not very helpful in establishing criteria by which a new approach to literary history might have prospered. F. R. Leavis's *The Great Tradition* (1948) and Cleanth Brooks's *Modern Poetry and the Tradition* (1947) yielded the proof that by and large the historical community of values had been defined solely in terms of 'modern' meaning. Here were two accomplished critics, both of them certainly interested in, and intelligent about, the present and both venturing into literary history, but with a result that somehow defeated the very aims and functions of this discipline. To be sure, neither critic had intended to write anything like a history of the English novel or a history of English poetry – as they are, 'or ought to be, alive for us now'. But the historical elements of tradition that they recommended were so much at odds with the history of English literature as an actual process of possibilities (a process, that is, of both developments *and* values) that not even the rudiments for a future synthesis of history and aesthetics were laid. (In this, Leavis and Brooks followed the critical theory and practice of T. S. Eliot, who, however – interestingly enough – had defined the idea of tradition more generally and less exclusively when he said that tradition involves the 'historical sense' with its 'perception not only of the pastness of the past, but of its presence'.)[39]

To take up only one example, the criteria by which Leavis defined the great tradition of the English novel were not merely narrow and exclusive, but also confusing. To dismiss, usually in the form of a footnote, Defoe (without mentioning *Robinson Crusoe*) as well as Thackeray, Scott, and Hardy may perhaps be legitimate for one who wishes to bring out the undoubted greatness of George Eliot, Henry James, and Joseph Conrad. But in this context to introduce such concepts as 'historical importance' or the 'important lines of English literary history' is entirely to beg the question, not merely of literary history, but of a workable synthesis of criticism and history. If Leavis states his 'reason for not including Dickens in the line of great novelists' and then proceeds to assure us that he is 'a great genius and is permanently among the classics', if he gives a mere 'note' to Emily Brontë 'because [her] astonishing work seems to me a kind of sport' and then continues to say that 'out of her a minor tradition comes . . .'; if Fielding is rejected as 'simple' and then is said to have 'made Jane Austen possible by opening the central tradition of English fiction'— then there must be something wrong with a criticism that conceives of tradition not historically, not as a process of both developments and values, but in terms of three or four major modern novelists. Again, the complex relationship between past significance and present meaning is

---

[39]T. S Eliot, "Tradition and the Individual Talent," *Selected Essays: 1917–1932* (London, 1932), p. 14. But see my critique of Eliot's definition in the following chapter.

overlooked. It is ignored or replaced by a concept of tradition which can conceive of no unity and of no living interplay between the past world of the English novel and its present reception, but which judges everything in terms of 'the significant few' major novelists. (Leavis touches on the real problem, which he prefers not to go into, when he says: 'To be important historically is not, of course, to be necessarily one of the significant few'.)[40]

But to raise these objections is not to dispute the relevance of a concept of value, which (for Leavis) is seen 'in terms of that human awareness . . . of the possibilities of life'.[41] Nor can such a concept of value be anything but critical. That is to say that it will evaluate the literature of the past not 'as a record of past customs, past habits, past manners, past fashions in taste',[42] or anything that is in the nature of a museum. If, as the New Criticism was perfectly justified to insist, literature is properly understood as literature and not as a medium of sociological reference and exemplification, then indeed the poetic value of a work of literature is not to be easily abstracted from its ideological or biographical significance. To elucidate the latter is not in itself identical with an awareness of the former. And to achieve this awareness, it is certainly not enough to assume 'that the specific problem of reading and judging literature is completely met in the process of learning the meaning of words, the political and philosophical allusions, the mental climate in which the poem originated, etc. etc'.[43]

The most valuable contribution of the New Criticism, then, was to raise (if not to answer) the question as to the function and the criteria of literary history. To stress the need for evaluation involved an awareness of both, the necessity of selection and the importance of achieving a point of view from which to select and hence to evaluate. In the words of W. K. Wimsatt: 'We are bound to have a point of view in literary criticism, and that point of view, though it may have been shaped by tradition, is bound to be our own. . . . Our judgments of the past cannot be discontinuous with our experience or insulated from it'. The realization of one's own point of view as both distinct from, and shaped by the past, finally called for a recognition that the object of evaluation was (just like its 'subject', its ego) part of a more comprehensive process

[40]*The Great Tradition* (Harmondsworth, Penguin Books, 1962), pp 29, 38, 11. There seems to be a similar contradiction, of which Cleanth Brooks is probably unaware, when he says "that we need to revise drastically our conventional *estimate* of the *course* of English poetry" ("Criticism, History, and Critical Relativism," *The Well Wrought Urn: Studies in the Structure of Poetry* [New York, Harvest Books, 1947], p. 224; my italics). At any rate, this is too facile a way of correlating value ("estimate") and development ("course").

[41]Leavis, *The Great Tradition*, p. 10.

[42]Cleanth Brooks, "The Quick and the Dead: A Comment on Humanistic Studies," in *The Humanities: An Appraisal*, ed. Julian Harris (Madison, Wis., 1950), p. 5.

[43]Cleanth Brooks, "Literary History vs. Criticism," *Kenyon Review*, 2 (1940), 407.

of tradition and experience. Such an approach could conceive of history not only 'in its several antecedent or causal relations to the writing of literature' but it could also raise the question 'whether antecedents themselves, if viewed in a certain light, do not become meanings'.[44]

But to answer this question already involved a break with the formalist dogma of the autonomy of the work of art. This paved the way toward the more recent synthesis between literary criticism and historical scholarship that reveals the extent to which the virtues of close textual analysis can survive the decline of formalism. In subsequent chapters I shall return to the inevitable compromises so characteristic of the late fifties and the sixties. For obviously there were plenty of ways and means through which historical concepts such as, say, the author as 'the necessary stylist' (Mark Spilka) could be reintroduced, and the whole question of rhetoric be used to overcome the frustrations of the formalist approach to the novel. Once the 'implied author' was conceived as a 'core of norms and choices', a 'choosing, evaluating person' who attempts 'consciously or unconsciously to impose his fictional world upon the reader', the 'strategy of point of view' (Percy Lubbock) could no longer be entirely divorced from the world of history and sociology. This was a far cry from the formalist ghost of 'the affective fallacy'; and even though *The Rhetoric of Fiction* still neglected the 'social and psychological forces that affect authors and readers',[45] it again pointed to what is potentially the historical meaning in the narrative structure of point of view. Similar tendencies have for some time been noticed in the interpretation of imagery, another domain of formalist interpretation, where we shall note a tendency to widen the scope of the term *image* and to stress its subject matter, or 'tenor', as opposed to its 'vehicle' – the real subject of the discourse as opposed to the adventitious and imported image.[46] It surely was a sign of the times when a critic like W. K. Wimsatt produced a historical monograph on the portraits of Alexander Pope or when Cleanth Brooks, former explicator of paradox and irony, began to write at great length on the geographical theme and background of Yoknapatawpha County. To recognize 'that a writer's choice of a subject is an aesthetic decision' prepared the way for a deeper understanding of history as part of the literary theme.[47] The renewed interest in thematics, like that in poetic personality and rhetoric, was an indication of far-reaching transitions and changes in critical doctrine. By reopening the neglected dimensions of change and society, the work of these critics began to move toward,

[44]Wimsatt, "History and Criticism," pp. 258, 254.

[45]Wayne C. Booth, *The Rhetoric of Fiction* (Chicago, 1961), pp. 74, [ix]. See also Mark Spilka, "The Necessary Stylist: A New Critical Revision," *Modern Fiction Studies*, 6 (1960/61), 285.

[46]See chapter 5, "Metaphor and Historical Criticism: Shakespeare's Imagery Revisited" in *Structure and Society in Literary History* by Robert Waxman.

[47]Harry Levin, "Thematics and Criticism," in *The Discipline of Criticism*, ed. Peter Demetz et al. (New Haven, 1968), p. 145.

and raise, those authorial, functional, and metahistorical contexts that, as I have noted above, the literary criticism and theory of the late sixties and early seventies has begun to discuss in what is still a somewhat fragmentary, spontaneous, and, finally, ahistorical manner.

Toward a Dialectic of Genesis and Function

A dialectical approach, which is conscious of its own social function, will wish to consider the problem of literary history from an angle where literature *is* history, and history is an element of literary structure and aesthetic experience. What is needed is not simply an act of combination between the literary historian's approach ('A is derived from X') and that of the critic ('A is better than Y'). It is not good enough to have in F. W. Bateson's sense – a 'more intimate co-operation' of their efforts or anything less than an integration in method and purpose. To say that the historian is concerned with a task like 'A is derived from X' is in itself a somewhat superficial formula; but even if this is read as a symbol of the genetic approach, it will not do merely to combine or to *link* the study of genesis with the critical evaluation of the art work. One has to be contained in the other, and the historical sense of the critic needs to be quite indistinguishable from the critical sense of the historian.

A postulate like this may sound presumptuous and, perhaps, overoptimistic, but the object and the function of literary history can demand no less. Let us for a moment ask the question, What *is* the object of the literary historian as critic? Is it the work of art as it is experienced today? Or is it the work of art in *statu nascendi*, in the contemporary context of its genesis and original audience? To ask the question is to draw attention to both the unity and the contradiction of the past world of the art work and the present world of its reception; or, in other words, to suggest that the historian's task (and the pastness of the work) cannot be separated from the critic's task (and the work of art as a present experience). Obviously, we cannot afford to isolate these two necessary aspects: merely to do the former is to fall back into some kind of antiquarianism; merely to do the latter is to run all the risks of misunderstanding and distortion that the New Criticism was guilty of so often. The one alternative will finally reduce literary history to a study of origins and influences, a mere *Entstehungsgeschichte*; the other reduces the discipline to a series of modern appreciations, a mere *Wirkungsgeschichte*. Neither is (as an alternative) acceptable: in the last resort, for literary history to study past significance makes no sense without an awareness of present meaning, and an awareness of present meaning is incoherent without the study of past significance.

Thus the object of the literary historian as critic is necessarily complex. It involves both genesis and value, development and order, the work of art as a product of the past and the work of art as an experience in the present. To stress these two dimensions of the art work in terms of their interrelationships is to argue for more than just expediency (in the sense that an awareness of history might prevent us from making a mistake or overlooking an anachronism in interpretation). The point that has to be made is not that the historian (or the critic) had better do his job thoroughly. The point is that these two dimensions are *inherent* in the work of art and that the study of genesis and the pursuit of evaluation find an equivalent in the similar relationship, which is a historical *and* an aesthetic one, between the mimesis and the morality of the work of art itself. Or, to make this point from a somewhat different angle, one might refer to two basic functions of literature; on the one hand, the work of art as a product of its time, a mirror of its age, a historical reflection of the society to which both the author and original audience belonged. On the other hand, it is surely no idealism to assume that the work of art is not merely a product, but a producer of its age; not merely a mirror of the past, but a lamp to the future. Incidentally, it was Karl Marx who pointed out that art is one of the 'besondere Weisen der Produktion'—one of the special forms of production—for instance, in the sense that the work of art can produce its audience and influence their attitudes and values.[48]

In order to distinguish these two basic functions of literature one might call them, although this is to oversimplify, the mimetic and the 'moral'. (The oversimplification does not reveal that each is, indeed, correlated with the other: the moral element is implicit in mimesis as representation, just as the sensuous nature of representation points to the only process through which morality can be translated into art.) But if, for the present purpose, we accept this provisional distinction of terms, it may be said that the mimetic function results from the artist's holding 'a mirror up to nature'. The world that is reflected in the mirror is, inevitably, the contemporary world: the past world at the time of the composition. In this sense the mimetic function of *Tom Jones* is related to an eighteenth-century world, just as the mimetic dimension of *Hard Times* reflects nineteenth-century society. But whereas the study of mimesis points back to origins and genesis, the interpretation of 'moral' and artistic meanings (while it cannot disregard the mimetic dimension) is concerned with the art work as a living presence, its ever-changing impact on the reader and society. Critical value judgments as to the literary quality and, of course, the 'morality' of the work of art cannot be conceived in disregard of the present world in which these aesthetic and 'moral' qualities are judged and experienced. So if for the moment we ignore the oversimplification involved in so schematic a distinction, it may be said that some of the basic functions of literature itself call for

[48]Marx and Engels, *Werke*, Ergänzungsband, I, 53 f.

the twofold activity of the historian as critic and of the critic as historian. Once the work of art is seen as both imitation and creation, it must be conceived as not merely a product of the past but also as a 'producer' of the future. And while the former function is involved in the genesis (and is rooted in the past world of the art work), the latter function is realized in both the past world and the present world of its reception: it is rooted in a creative capacity for 'production' which transcends the very time and age that are the object of the mimesis. Thus, the 'mimetic' (the historical) and the 'moral' (the ever-present) functions interact: the literary historian as critic approaches an object in which *Zeitlichkeit* and '*Überzeitlichkeit*', discontinuity and continuity, can be fused into one.

This is the very stuff that literary history is made of. The past significance of the work of art, its background and origins, is ultimately indivisible from its present meaning and its survival into the future. The literary historian is confronted with more than the coexistence of these aspects: he has to face both their contradiction and unity. But to say this is not to make a new and particularly sophisticated demand on the historian of literature. Eventually, this is the same problem that, some three hundred fifty years ago, Ben Jonson faced when he paid his highly complex tribute to his dead rival's work as 'a Moniment, without a tombe'; Shakespeare's work, he said, was 'for all time', but at the same time (or even before this) he also remarked that Shakespeare was the 'Soule of the Age'.[49] Jonson's epitaph can hardly be said to anticipate the systematic approach of a modern literary history, but the basic problem, which is a dialectical one, is there quite clearly. It is the problem of origin and survival or, in a different light, of a great work as the product of its age and the 'producer' of its future. For the modern literary historian to grasp the dialectics of *Zeitlichkeit* und *Überzeitlichkeit* calls for an awareness of the art work as having both a past and a present dimension (as well as a present and a future existence). And it calls for a perception from this awareness that, as an object of literary history, these dimensions are simultaneous in their interaction and tension.

The task of the literary historian, consequently, cannot be abstracted from either the genetic or the functional aspects of literature. For the historical study of origins helps to assess the continuity of, or the degree of change in, its social functions; while the study of its present functions can, in its turn, help us to appreciate the potential richness of the conditions presiding at its origin. In this sense history can be studied as meaning: the structure of the work of art is potentially inherent in its genesis, but in society it becomes functional only through its effect in terms of a human and social experience. Structure is intimately linked

---

[49]I use the text in E. K. Chambers, *William Shakespeare: A Study of Facts and Problems* (Oxford, 1930), II, 208 f.

up with, though not determined by, either its genesis or its affective relations. It is correlated to both its past genesis and its present functioning; for the critic to understand the full measure of this correlation is to become conscious of the necessary complexity of structure as history.

Past and Present Correlated: The Case of Shakespeare Criticism

To discuss this correlation in terms of history and aesthetics yields only very general results, which do not by themselves suggest a more practical application of theory. In order to illustrate some of the issues involved, I propose to raise the problem in the more practical context of the historical, critical, and theatrical interpretation of Shakespearean drama. Although here the gulf that separates the critical and the historical approaches has in recent years been considerably narrowed, there still exist an astonishing number of conflicting assumptions as to the aims and methods of literary inquiry into a great work of the past. Among these, the unresolved tension between past genesis and present function looms large, although as a problem of method it has hardly been perceived or discussed.

At the risk of repetition, the basic problem may perhaps again be phrased in terms of the question asked above: What is the object of a historical and critical approach to Shakespeare? What does the literary historian as critic mean when he refers to *Hamlet*? Presumably the answer would still be quite different according to whether the person in question would wish to stress the importance of historical research or the priority of critical judgment. On the one hand (in terms of historical research), the answer would preferably be 'the Renaissance play'. Hamlet, according to this approach, will be a historical figure, the play's message an Elizabethan one in the sense that its past significance is to be explored without implicit reference to its modern meaning. On the other hand (and this would be the more critical approach), the answer would involve a different object, one primarily related not to the Elizabethan theatre or even the Elizabethan text but to the modern sensibility that it is meant to evoke. From this angle an interpretation (or a theatrical production) would be authentic so long as it achieves the tone and tenor of our own age: Hamlet will be a modern symbol and the play's message a contemporary one in the sense that in the last resort its present meaning has priority over its past significance.

Actually, the two points of reference may not be so diametrically opposed, but the contradiction involved is an objective one. No matter what the approach is, there remains a historical text for modern readers (or actors). On the one hand, there is the Elizabethan context and meaning, on the other, the modern understanding and interpretation.

There is no getting away from this inevitable tension between the historical and the modern points of view, and no one-sided solution is feasible. The most learned and historical-minded scholar cannot physically become an Elizabethan; he cannot recreate the Globe or visualize the original production. Even if he conceived of Shakespeare's drama as being enacted in the theatre, he would still be influenced by his own experience of the modern stage, its twentieth-century audience and actors and their social relationships, which are quite different from those that, in Shakespeare's Globe, then constituted part of the play's meaning.

The underlying contradiction is not an academic one, and the more we think of it in terms of practical interpretation (including the theatrical interpretation of Shakespeare on the modern stage) the clearer the theoretical implications will emerge. Since today it is just as impossible to understand Shakespeare without a modern interpretation as it is to have an interpretation without Shakespeare, we cannot proceed from either a genuine Elizabethan production (and this already contained an interpretation of the text) or from one that makes us believe that *Hamlet* is a modern play. Today *any* Shakespeare interpretation has to come to terms with the tension between historical values and modern evaluations. But this contradiction is not necessarily frustrating, and the way it is solved constitutes the most essential decision of both historical criticism and serious theatrical interpretation. Viewed from the angle of the drama as a work of the theatre, this contradiction involves an inevitable tension between the mimetic (or expressive) and the affective aspects, between the significance of what Shakespeare's work reflected (or expressed) in plot and character and the changing impact of this on the contemporary spectator. To recreate the mimetic and the expressive dimensions is impossible without reference to Shakespeare's world and his intentions; to reassess their affective and moral effects is impossible without reference to our audience and our world.

For the literary historian and critic the question, then, is not *whether* to accept both worlds as points of reference, but rather *how* to relate them so as to obtain their maximum dimensions. To put it like this may appear provocatively superficial, but to resolve the contradiction one cannot minimize the conflicting elements when each is – in its different world – so inevitable and necessary. The 'maximum dimensions' then, can mean no more and no less than this: to have as much of the historical significance and as much of the contemporary meaning merged into a new unity. Of course there is no easy formula as to how this synthesis of historical values and modern evaluations can be achieved. But in order to grasp its dialectic, it is well to remember that it is not entirely a case of opposites. On the contrary, it would be a grave mistake to overlook those many points of contact and identity, where, say, Shakespeare's

Renaissance values can today be considered valid. This area of identity or interaction, however, is not simply given; it will be enlarged from a contemporary point of view that can conceive its own social direction as historical in the sense that it affirms both the revulsions and the links of contact between the past and the future. In the end this relationship involves a social and a methodological position from which both the change and the continuity can be accepted as part of a meaningful movement in history. In the present interpretation of Renaissance drama, therefore, the area of identity will radically differ between, say, a Marxist interpretation and one based on the premises of Jacques Maritain's neoscholasticism. Where the Renaissance heritage is not repudiated, there is bound to be a wide range of living contact, in which the 'historical' element can be viewed as part of a wider configuration in which the present reproduction of past art is one way of bringing about a meaningful future.

Thus, the 'area of identity' between past significance and present meaning is a complex and changing one. Yet it has a certain amount of permanence which, among other things, has to do with man's anthropological status. (That is only one of the reasons why it is not confined to the Renaissance tradition.) We are all – the great dramatists of the past, their contemporary producers and critics – characters in history; our own points of reference are, like our predecessors', products of history. In this, our present values emerge from the same historical process that is both reflected in, and accelerated by, Shakespeare's contribution. This is quite obvious in the history of literature, which can only be written in reference to a scheme of values that (among other things) has to be abstracted from its great objects, including Shakespeare's dramas. Their greatness has been confirmed by the very contribution they have made in furnishing us with criteria by which to judge, and to judge not only modern plays but also the history of the drama as a whole.

Since such area of identity may be accepted as given, the relationship between Shakespeare's vision and its modern perspectives cannot simply be described as one of conflict or opposition. The difference between his world and ours is obvious enough, but it does not exclude some kind of concurrence. As Arnold Kettle has remarked, 'The best way to emphasize the value of Shakespeare in *our* changing world is to see him in *his*, recognizing that the two worlds, though very different, are at the same time a unity'.[50] This unity is at the basis of all our veneration for Shakespeare; without it, the impact of his work would not be possible. At the same, this unity does not preclude a contradiction that is at the basis of all our conflicting interpretations. In very much oversimplified terms: the unity creates the need of our interpretations of *Shakespeare*; the contradiction accounts for the need of our

---

[50]*Shakespeare in a Changing World*, ed. Arnold Kettle (London, 1964), p. 10.

interpretations of Shakespeare. But actually each is contained in the other, and the interpretation as a whole can only succeed when these two aspects are inextricably welded into one. (By himself the modern historian can, as we have seen, either enhance or reduce the sphere of unity or the area of contradiction, but he can never entirely annihilate either.)

Once this relationship (although here still oversimplified) is understood more deeply, the historical study of literature has gained at least two negative standards of evaluation. These may have some practical use for judging not only the literary but also the theatrical interpretation of the great drama of the past. For in the theatre as elsewhere, the modernized classic is no more acceptable than the museum version. This may not be saying anything new, but perhaps it helps to recover certain assumptions that might prove practicable to both the theatre director and the historical scholar. If the rift between them could thus be narrowed, the present theatrical interpretation of Shakespeare need be neither academic nor irresponsible. In modern Shakespearean productions, then, Hamlet need not become a hippy in order to convince, nor would it be necessary, as Martin Walser thinks it is, to produce the 'old play' in order 'to show us what things were like formerly' ('um uns zu sagen, wie es früher war'). If the past can be conceived, neither in its identity with, nor in its isolation from, the present, a historical perspective could evolve that might be both theatrically effective and convincing to the scholar. No topical effects are wanted, but a sense of history that can discover permanence in change but also change in seeming permanence; the past in the present but also the present in the past. Hence the 'timeless' would result through a sense of time and history. It is in this sense that Shakespeare is 'for all time' precisely because he was the 'Soule of the Age'. In this view, a historical vision can be made to yield a contemporary meaning. Its past significance was achieved because, at the time, it was contemporary and *then* incorporated the experience of the present. The meaning of literary history today can best be discovered through this past present, or that part of it which – although past – is still present and meaningful in a contemporary frame of reference. Thus, past significance and present meaning engage in a relationship which, in its interdependence, may illuminate either – the past work as against its present reception, and the contemporary interpretation against the historical significance of the work of art.

The Concept of Tradition Reconsidered

ONCE the relationship of past significance and present meaning is viewed as one involving both social function and literary structure, the links between past writing and present reading (and new writing) need to be considered more closely. Obviously, such links, if they are sought for on historical and aesthetic planes, must be conceived in the complex terms of literature as an aesthetic mode of social activity involving individual sensibilities as well as social attitudes, craftsmanship and ideology, originality and 'influence'. The study of these interrelations is a more comprehensive task than can be summed up by any one critical term or postulate; but a reconsideration of the concept of 'tradition' may help provide us with some idea, or even a paradigm, of the nature of the links between past writing, present reading, and new writing. For a dialectical theory of literary history to ignore the *process* that sustains and informs these links is not possible. If this process is seen as a historical one, the concept of tradition, which I propose to use in this connection, will have to be redefined. The reason is obvious; the most widely shared and well-known definition of tradition in English and American criticism, that of T. S. Eliot, provides us with a singularly unhelpful category for historical criticism. Judged by the needs and perspectives of literary history, this definition has failed to come to terms with tradition as the temporal and functional process of handing down, through writing, reading, and new writing, ideas and literary values in history.

Again, as in the case of 'genesis', any counterproposal worth making must be prepared to challenge a close context of terminology and methodology. In Anglo-American criticism the contexts of its origins and its later historical development is to free the reader from the ignorance of his presentness, to alienate him from himself and make him a pilgrim, if not *of* eternity, then at least *with* all 'the noble living and the noble dead'.

Shall these bones live? Surely if they do not – surely if we neglect the dynamic relation which exists between past and present – the dead will bury the dead. There can be no present or future, in life or in art, if the past is not a living reality *in its pastness*. Editors, bibliographers, textual critics, and pedants of all sorts hold the keys in their hands, the keys to the kingdom not merely of literature, but of all human culture.

(1980)

29 Jerome J. McGann,
The Text, the Poem, and the Problem of Historical Method,
The Beauty of Inflections, 1985

p111–32

I

At this point in academic time, the problem of historical method emerges most dramatically at the elementary levels of textual interpretation. The problem appears in two typical forms which are inversely related to each other. On the one hand, intrinsic critics cannot see that historical studies go to the heart of literary objects. Since the latter appear to address problems (and people) which are not historically limited, the 'problem' with historical studies is that they continue to be pursued at all. Why should works which transcend their originary moment require historical analysis and commentary?

On the other hand, historical method is also a problem for scholars and critics who work in any of the areas of extrinsic criticism: in bibliography and textual criticism, in philology, in biography and literary history, and so forth. In this case, the difficulty is that the scholar's work so often does seem irrelevant to the understanding and appreciation of poetry. What is most disturbing about this situation is that so few scholars even acknowledge that their methods require a theoretical grounding in hermeneutics.

These brief remarks will come as news to no one. We are all aware of the situation. Before I try to suggest how we might try to deal with these issues, however, permit me another brief essay into familiar territory. For I believe that we can best come to grips with these problems of historical method if we see more clearly how they came to assume their present form.

It is well known that the most advanced literary studies in the nineteenth century were those which developed and modified the enormous advances in theory and method made in classical and biblical philology and textual criticism. Wolf and Eichhorn are only the most familiar names among that group of brilliant, predominantly German, critics of the late eighteenth century who made the initial breakthrough in transforming literary studies into a modern scientific discipline. These are the scholars who created both the Lower (or textual) Criticism and the Higher (or philological) Criticism. Historical philology in the nineteenth century brought analytic techniques to bear upon previously synthesized material in order to see more clearly the strokes of the tulip and the parts of the rainbow. The most advanced of such critics – in England, men like Coleridge and Arnold hoped to enlist these analytic techniques in the service of a new and higher synthesis: to adapt Coleridge's famous declaration, by dissolving, diffusing, and dissipating, 'to recreate . . . to idealize and to unify'.

In the twentieth century, however, the historical methods of the Lower and Higher Criticism gave way before the advance of several sorts of form criticism and structural analysis. As we know, the principal impetus behind these critical movements came from language study and especially from linguistics. What Wolf, Lachmann, and Strauss were to nineteenth-century literary criticism, Saussure and Hjelmslev have been to the twentieth century. Hjelmslev's lucid *Prolegomena to a Theory of Language* (1943) accurately describes the shift which took place as a deliberate effort to break free of the descriptive, atomistic, and empirical approaches which flourished in the nineteenth century. 'The study of literature and the study of art', Hjelmslev says, had been carried out under 'historically descriptive rather than systematizing disciplines', and his project, which explicitly follows Saussure, proposes a systematic rather than an empirical analytic of humanistic phenomena. *A priori* it would seem to be a generally valid thesis that for every *process* there is a corresponding *system*, by which the process can be analyzed and described by means of a limited number of premises. It must be assumed that any process can be analyzed into a limited number of elements recurring in various combinations.'[1] In this passage Hjelmslev prepares the ground for a systematic linguistics, but his words clearly underwrite any number of other twentieth century programmes of a formal or structural sort (Bultmann in biblical criticism, Lévi-Strauss in anthropology, Propp, Greimas, and many others in literary studies). These new semiological methods can be applied in all humanistic disciplines, as Hjelmslev well knew.

The shift from an empirical to a structural analytic has deeply influenced twentieth-century approaches to literary works, with far-reaching consequences. Before I turn to them, however, and thus reconnect with my initial two-handed 'problem of historical method', let me point out an interesting peripheral remark in Hjelmslev's book. When he attacks the empirical methods of the nineteenth century, its anti-systematic bias, he also explains the particular aesthetic position which underlies that

> humanistic tradition which, in various dress, has till now predominated . . . According to this view, humanistic, as opposed to natural, phenomena, are non-recurrent and for that very reason cannot, like natural phenomena, be subjected to exact and generalizing treatment. In the field of the humanities, consequently, there would have to be a different method – namely, mere description,

[1]Louis Hjelmslev, *Prolegomena to a Theory of Language*, trans. Francis J. Whitfield, Madison, 1961, p. 9.

which would be nearer to poetry than to exact science – or, at any event, a method that restricts itself to a discursive form of presentation, in which the phenomena pass by, one by one, without being interpreted through a system (pp. 8-9).

As far as the appreciation of poetry is concerned, the nineteenth-century's 'humanistic' methods sought to preserve and illuminate the uniqueness of the poetic object. We would do well to remember this fact about nineteenth-century philology, for in the modern period – as we survey those prelapsarian Germanic tomes of dryasdust scholarship – we do not always recall (indeed, their authors do not always recall) the aesthetic phenomena those critical procedures were designed to illuminate. Our preoccupation with the minute particularities of poetical works emerged from the philological traditions which gave us 'textual criticism'. The contemporary vulgarization of this philological term eloquently demonstrates the position that modern literary studies takes in relation to its immediate forebears.

The structural and semiological approaches to language and, in particular, to literature provided modern critics with operational procedures for analysing literature in a Kantian mode. In the *Critique of Judgement*, Kant offered a novel philosophy of art grounded in the notion that aesthetic works were integral phenomena whose finality was exhausted in the individual's experience of the work. The modern concept of 'the poem itself' as a self-referential linguistic system is fundamentally Kantian, though twentieth-century developments in linguistics provided this Kantian approach with its basic procedural rules for an actual critical practice.

These procedural rules operated under one fundamental premise: that literary works are special sorts of linguistic 'texts', that every poem is coextensive with its linguistic structure. Twentieth-century literary criticism contains a rich variety of schools and methods – analytical, structural, rhetorical, stylistic – but for all their important differences, they tend to share the conviction that poems are self-subsistent linguistic systems. The function of criticism is to illuminate the operations of those linguistic structures which we now like to call 'texts'. According to the classic formulation of Roman Jakobson: 'Poetics deals with problems of verbal structure . . . Since linguistics is the global science of verbal structure, poetics may be regarded as an integral part of linguistics.'[2]

This idea of the poem as verbal object is so commonplace in modern criticism that we may seem perverse to question it. Still we must do so,

[2] Roman Jakobson, 'Linguistics and Poetics', in *Style in Language*, ed. T.A. Sebeok, Cambridge, Mass., 1960, p. 350. In the latest, post-structural phase of these traditions the models are more generically semiological than linguistic. The shift in emphasis – from specific 'text' to the process of 'textuality' – marks the increased self-consciousness in this tradition, but not a departure from its fundamental premises.

for the 'problem of historical method' – whether we approach it from an 'intrinsic' or an 'extrinsic' point of view – will never be opened to solutions until we see one of the signal failures of modern criticism: its inability to distinguish clearly between a concept of the *poem* and a concept of the *text*. Indeed, when we recover this essential analytic distinction, we will begin to reacquire some other, equally crucial distinctions which have fallen into disuse: for example, the distinction between concepts of *poem* and of *poetical work*. For the present I will concentrate on the first of these distinctions, and my analysis will proceed through a series of illustative examples.[3]

II

When Byron sent the manuscript of *Don Juan* Cantos I and II to his publisher John Murray late in 1818, the poet was not only, with Goethe, the most famous writer in the Western world, his works were the most saleable products on the English literary market. He was not an author Murray wanted to lose. But this new work set Murray back on his heels. He was filled with wonder at its genius and with loathing at its immorality – at its obscenity, its blasphemy, its libellous attacks upon the poet laureate, and its seditious attitude toward the English government's policies at home and abroad.[4]

In the struggle that ensued, Murray and his London circle (which included some of Byron's best and oldest friends) pressed the poet either to withdraw the poem altogether or to revise it drastically and remove its objectionable parts. Byron agreed to some revisions, but his final line of retreat still seemed a fearful one to his publisher. When

---

[3]Literary criticism in general would benefit if certain clear distinctions were preserved when using words (and concepts) like *text, poem*, and *poetical work*. In the present essay, the word *text* is used as a purely bibliographical concept which means to deal with the material of poetry in a purely physical or impersonal frame of reference. The term deliberately abstracts away the critic's or the reader's immediate (social) point of view. Poetry is a social phenomenon, but the concept of *text* withholds from consideration all matters that relate to the involvement of reader or audience in the reproduction of the work. It does so, of course, for analytic purposes, and *only provisionally*. I propose that we use the term *text* when we deal with poems as they are part of a productive (or reproductive) process, but when we are withholding from consideration all matters that relate to the process of consumption. *Poem*, on the other hand, is the term I will use to refer to the work as it is the locus of a specific process of production (or reproduction) and consumption. *Poetical work* is my term for the global history of some particular work's process of production/reproduction and consumption. I use the term *poetry* to refer generically to imaginative literary works without respect to any specific social or historical factors. The terms *text* and *Ideal Text* also appear in this essay, and these refer to various (non-historical and non-sociological) twentieth-century critical concepts.

I hope it is clear that these distinctions mean to counter the semiological approach to the concepts of *text* and *textuality*. A paradigm example of the latter approach will be found in Roland Barthes's famous essay 'From Work to Text': see above, pp. 91-93.

[4]See *Don Juan: A Variorum Edition*, ed. T.G. Steffan and W. W. Pratt, Austin, 1957, i. 11-32 and iv. 293-308.

Byron threatened to take his poem elsewhere, Murray agreed to publish; he did not, however, tell his celebrated author precisely *how* he would publish.

For Murray, the problem was how to issue this inflammatory work without provoking a legal action against himself either by the government directly or by the notorious Society for the Suppression of Vice. His plan of action was ingenious but, in the end, self-defeating. Murray decided to issue a short run (1,500 copies) of the poem in a sumptuous quarto edition and to print it without either Byron's name as author or even his own as publisher. The price – £1 11s. 6d. – was set high in order to ensure a circulation limited alike in numbers and in social class.

The immediate effect of this manoeuvre was successful, for *Don Juan* stole into the world without provoking any moral outcry. The earliest reviewers were generally quite favourable, even from entrenched conservative quarters like *The Literary Gazette*.

But Murray's plan for avoiding the censors failed, in the end, because it was, in the words of Hugh J. Luke, Jr., 'a contradictory one'.[5] Murray avoided prosecution for issuing *Don Juan*, but his method of publication ensured a widespread piratical printing of the poem in the radical press. Thousands of copies of *Don Juan* were issued in cheap pirated editions, and as the work received wider celebrity and distribution, so the moral outcry against it was raised, and spread.

The significance which this story holds for my present purposes – i.e. for my aim to elucidate the problematics of the 'text' – is neatly explained by an anonymous article (possibly by Southey) printed in the conservative *Quarterly Review* in April 1822. In its quarto form, the reviewer notes, *Don Juan*

> would have been confined by its price to a class of readers with whom its faults might have been somewhat compensated by its merits; with whom the ridicule, which it endeavors to throw upon virtue, might have been partially balanced by that with which it covers vice, particularly the vice to which the class of readers to whom we are alluding are most subject – that which pleads romantic sensibility, or ungovernable passion; to readers, in short, who would have turned with disgust from its indecencies, and remembered only its poetry and its wit.[6]

But the poem was issued in numerous cheap piracies and therein lay the mischief, 'some publishing it with obscene engravings, others in weekly numbers, and all in a shape that brought it within the reach of purchasers on whom its poison would operate without mitigation – who would search its pages for images to pamper a depraved imagination and for a sanction for the insensibility to the sufferings of others, which is often one of the most unhappy results of their own'. In short as the reviewer says so well: 'Don Juan in quarto and on hot-pressed paper

[5]'The Publishing of *Don Juan*', *PMLA* lxxx (June 1965), p. 200.
[6]For the *Quarterly Review* quotations see ibid., p. 202.

would have been almost innocent – in a whity-brown duodecimo it was one of the worst of the mischievous publications that have made the press a snare'.

Several important conclusions follow from this eventful narrative. In this first place, the example illustrates how different texts, in the bibliographical sense, embody different poems (in the aesthetic sense) despite the fact that both are linguistically identical. In the second place, the example also suggests that the method of printing or publishing a literary work carries with it enormous cultural and aesthetic significance for the work itself. Finally, we can begin to see, through this example, that the essential character of a work of art is not determined *sui generis* but is, rather, the result of a process involving the actions and interactions of a specific and socially integrated group of people.[7]

The contemporary fashion of calling literary works 'texts' carries at least one unhappy critical result: it suggests that poems and works of fiction possess their integrity *as poems and works of fiction* totally aside from the events and materials describable in their bibliographies. In this usage we are dealing with 'texts' which transcend their concrete and actual textualities. This usage of the word *text* does not mean anything written or printed in an actual physical state; rather, it means the opposite: it points to an *Ur*-poem or meta-work whose existence is the Idea that can be abstracted out of all concrete and written texts which have ever existed or which ever will exist.[8] All these different texts are what can be called – Ideally – 'The Text'.

This Ideal Text is the object of almost all the critical scrutiny produced in the New Critical and post-New Critical traditions, whether formal, stylistic, or structural.[9] To arrive at such a Text, however, the critic normally obligates himself to make certain that his physical text is 'correct', which is to say that it corresponds, linguistically, to the

[7]Cf. Levin Schüking, *The Sociology of Literary Taste*, London, 1966.

[8]Post-structural critiques of their own (formalist) tradition have been widespread during the past ten years and have contributed to the break-up of the academic consensus which developed between 1935 and 1965. See John Fekete, *The Critical Twilight*, London, 1978. The attacks upon the New Criticism have tended to accuse it of an arrogant and technocratic empiricism, with its insistence upon taking the poem as *sui generis*. These attacks – see Richard Palmer, *Hermeneutics* (Evanston, 1969), for example – charge the New Criticism with a crude theory of the poem as 'object' or 'thing'. This sort of attack is deeply misguided and misses entirely the fundamental Idealism of both the New Criticism in particular and its later formalist context in general. A revisionist commentator like Gerald Graff has been able to see the mistake in such critiques and to suggest what is in fact the case: that New Criticism and its academic inheritors (including many of its recent antagonists) are part of a single tradition (*Literature Against Itself*, Chicago, 1979, chap. 5). As Graff notes, New Criticism was marked throughout by contradictions along an Ideal/Empirical fault-line; nor could it have been otherwise with a fundamentally Idealist theory which was seeking to establish its authority in a scientific, rational, and technological world. Graff's views have been anticipated by a number of trenchant critiques put out from relatively orthodox Marxist writers: see, e.g. Robert Weimann, 'Past Significance and Present Meaning in Literary History', in *New Directions in Literary History*, ed. Ralph Cohen, Baltimore, 1974, esp. pp. 43–50.

[9]That an Ideal Text is the object of contemporary 'textual' interpreters is patent; see also Tony Bennett, *Formalism and Marxism*, London, 1979, pp. 70-1.

author's final intentions about what editors call his work's substantive and accidental features. By meeting this obligation the critic pays his dues to the philological traditions of the last three hundred years. At the same time, the critic places himself in a position from which he can treat the literary work as if it were a timeless object, unconnected with history. The Text is viewed *sub specie aeternitatis*, and modern criticism approaches it much as the pre-critical scholar of Sacred Scripture approached the Word of God.

But in fact not even a linguistic uniformity sanctioned by philology can deliver over to us a final, definitive Text which will be the timeless object of critical interpretation and analysis. The example from Byron suggests this, clearly, but that case is merely paradigmatic. No literary work is definable purely in linguistic terms, and the illustration from Byron could easily be replaced by examples from any writer one might choose. It would not be very difficult to show, from the works of William Blake, that linguistic uniformity will hardly serve to establish a definitive Text. Of course everyone knows that Blake's *words* do not comprehend Blake's 'poetical works', so that (Ideally) critics recognize the necessity of 'reading' Blake in facsimile editions; and, in fact, facsimile editions do deliver more of Blake's work to the reader. But a Blake text comprising both words and illustrative matter still falls short of delivering this artist's work to an audience today.

Since Blake's work operates in an integrated verbal and visual medium, we are forced to see that the 'linguistic level' of this work corresponds to the entire mixed medium and not merely to the verbal one. But that Blake's 'poetical works' are not finished and complete in some Ideal mixed-medium Text is apparent if we simply recall the character of Blake's original methods of 'publication'. He is probably the most private and individualistic artist ever to emerge from England, and each of his engraved works was a unique publication by itself. It was part of Blake's artistic project that each of his works *be* unique, and he in fact achieved his purpose – most notoriously, I suppose, in his masterwork *Jerusalem*. Fewer than ten original copies of this work survive, and each is quite distinct. To speak of the Text of *Jerusalem*, then, as if that term comprehended some particular concrete reality rather than a heuristic idea, is manifestly to talk nonsense. One might as well try to speak of the Text of Emily Dickinson's verse. In reality, there is no such Text; there are only texts, of various kinds, prepared by various people (some by the author), at various periods, for particular and various purposes.

Yet the example of Blake carries a moral which takes us beyond the insight that an artist's work is not equivalent to an Ideal Text, nor even to some particular text or edition (say, an especially meticulous one prepared by a skilled editor). For every work of art is the product of an interaction between the artist, on the one hand, and a variety of social determinants on the other. Even the simplest textual problem – establishing a work's *linguistic* correctness – can involve other problems that are, quite literally, insoluble. Keats, we recall, wrote two distinct and finished versions of 'La Belle Dame Sans Merci'.[10] But even if one were to set aside these special problems and assume that we can establish 'the author's final intentions' toward the language or even the entire format of a work we would still have, as readers, merely one text of the work, or – as scholars – the means for producing a number of possible editions, or texts.

The fact is that the works of an artist are produced, at various times and places, and by many different sorts of people, in a variety of different textual constitutions (some better than others). Each of these texts is the locus of a process of artistic production and consumption involving the originary author, other people (his audience[s], his publisher, etc.), and certain social institutions. Blake's special way of creating his works emphasizes the presence of these impinging social factors precisely because Blake strove so resolutely, even so obsessively, to produce work that was wholly his own. Each original copy of *Jerusalem* is unique, and in them Blake has achieved an extraordinary degree of artistic freedom. Had his work been reproduced through the procedures maintained by the ordinary publishing institutions of his day, it would have been a very different product altogether (it would have been reviewed, for example, and it would have fallen into many people's hands).[11] Nor are these differences merely accidental, and unimportant for the 'meaning' of Blake's work. Certainly to Blake they seemed immensely consequential; indeed – and he was quite right – they seemed definitive of the difference between one sort of art (free, creative) and another (commonplace, generalized).

In his own day Blake insisted upon having his artistic freedom, and the proper measure of his success in this aim – ironic though it seems – lies in his contemporary artistic anonymity. Yet the social life of an artist transcends his particular historical moment, and so Blake, lost to his own age, was 'discovered' by the Pre-Raphaelites, who initiated the process of full social integration which his work has since achieved. Blake's unique works, in consequence, would become mass-produced, and his fierce individuality would itself become deeply integrated into various ideologies and social institutions. We may well see an irony in this event. Even more, however, should we see how it illustrates a

[10] For a more thorough discussion see chap. 1 of Keats and the Historical Method in Literary Criticism, pp. 15–67, by McGann in the same book *The Beauty of Inflections*.

[11] As is well known, Blake purchased his artistic freedom at a fearful personal cost, for his conscious artistic policies ensured his contemporary isolation. Appealing to what Byron called 'the Avenger, Time', Blake's work had to wait for the justice of history. Cf. the discussion in J.W. Saunders, *The Profession of Letters*, London, 1964, pp. 146–73 *passim* and, on Blake particularly, pp. 164–6; see also Jerome J. McGann, *A Critique of Modern Textual Criticism*, Chicago, 1983, pp. 44–7.

fundamental fact about all art: that it is a social product with various, and changing, social functions to perform.

The initial example from Byron and the general case of Blake illustrate very clearly, I think, that a work of art – a poem, in this case – is no more the isolate creation of an artist than 'the poem itself' is defined either by some particular text on the one hand, or by the Ideal Text on the other. Poems are artistic works produced, and maintained, under specific socialized conditions. It is the business of analytic criticism to isolate and categorize the various social factors which meet and interact in various works of art, and finally, to explain those interactions.

In attempting to show how different poetical works have acquired different textual constitutions, I have drawn attention to certain physical characteristics of some texts of *Don Juan* and *Jerusalem*. The physical differences between the several texts stand as signs of a productive process which is different in each case, and which, consequently, produces several different artistic works. The first two cantos of *Don Juan*, as issued by Murray, are not the same work as the first two cantos as issued by the pirates. The fact that Byron's *Don Juan* should have called out these two sorts of edition is one sign of its creative power, just as the poem's long and complex bibliographical history has testified to its trans-historical character and relevance.

Let there be no confusion in this matter, however: when we see that an author's work exists in many different textual constitutions, we do not mean to suggest that, for example, there are as many poems called *Jerusalem* as there are texts or editions. We must resist the modern fashion of referring to poems as 'texts' precisely because this vulgar usage confuses the fundamental difference between a poem's *text* – which is one thing – and a poem – which is quite another. Preserving this distinction is crucial for purposes of critical method, since the distinction facilitates a clear view of a poem's changing life in human society. Speaking of poems as 'texts' implicitly affirms an idea of literary works which involves two contradictory propositions: (1) that a poem is equivalent to its linguistic constitution and (2) that the textual differences in a poem's bibliographical history have no necessary relation to issues of literary criticism as such. The poem-as-text, then, is a critical idea which at once reduces poetry to a verbal construct and inflates it to the level of an immaterial, non-particular pure Idea (the poem as Ideal Text). This result seems paradoxical, but in fact it is the necessary consequence of a view of literary works which is founded on a contradiction.

The example of *Don Juan* must not be taken to suggest, however, that a poetical work is the product of a social engagement entered into, voluntarily or otherwise, by author, printer, and publisher alone. Rather, the local publishing relationship among these three persons is itself a sign needing critical analysis. The fact that Blake deliberately avoided any involvement in this, the normal publishing relationship of his day, is of immense critical significance for his work and especially for a late work like *Jerusalem*. To know the publishing options taken (and refused) by Chaucer, or Donne, or Pope, or Blake, or Byron enables the critic to explain the often less visible, but more fundamental, social engagements which meet in and generate the work in question.

The illustration from Byron is especially illuminating because it brings to our attention another crucial productive figure (anterior to the audience of consumers) who participates in the artistic process initiated by the artist. I mean, of course, the reviewer (or critic), who is the final mediating force between author and audience. It is the function of the (contemporary) reviewer and (subsequent) critic to make explicit the lines of interpretation which exist *in potentia* in their respective audiences. Critics and reviewers – to adapt a phrase from Shelley – imagine what students and audiences already know about the works they are to read.

III

At this point in the analysis, though we have, I believe, established the generic functional usefulness of preserving distinctions among texts, poems, and poetical works, the specific value of such distinctions for literary criticism is still unclear. Are these the sort of distinctions which, in the end, make no difference?

In the example which follows I mean to illustrate two related points: first (on the negative side), that the failure to maintain these distinctions creates a procedural error which necessarily threatens any subsequent practical criticism with disaster; and second (on the positive side), that the pursuit and elucidation of such distinctions sharply increases our understanding of poetry and poems in both the theoretical and the practical spheres. This second aspect of the demonstration will return us to the 'problem of historical method' which was raised at the outset. By framing these historically self-conscious demonstrations along the traditional 'intrinsic' lines of formal and thematic analysis, I propose to show: (1) that poems are, by the nature of the case (or, as Kant might say, 'transcendentally'), time- and place-specific; (2) that historical analysis is, therefore, a necessary and essential function of any advanced practical criticism.

The case I propose to consider is Allen Tate's famous interpretation of Emily Dickinson's poem 'Because I could not Stop for Death'.[12] His

[12]This is poem no. 172 in *The Poems of Emily Dickinson*, ed. Thomas H. Johnson, Cambridge, Mass., 1955, ii. 546-7. For Tate's discussion, see his 'New England Culture and Emily Dickinson', in *The Recognition of Emily Dickinson*, ed. C.E. Blake and C.F. Wells, Ann Arbor, 1968, pp. 153-67, esp. pp. 160-2, from which the quotations below are taken.

discussion raises, once again, the whole range of unresolved problems which lie in wait for any critical method which cannot make serious distinctions between texts and poems.

Tate begins by quoting the poem in full and declaring it to be 'one of the greatest in the English language' and 'one of the perfect poems in English'. His argument for these judgements rests upon T. S. Eliot's famous discussion of the 'dissociation of sensibility'. Dickinson's poem is 'perfect' because it displays a perfect 'fusion of sensibility and thought': 'The framework of the poem is, in fact, the two abstractions, mortality and eternity, which are made to associate in equality with images: she sees the ideas, and thinks the perceptions. She did, of course, nothing of the sort; but we must use the logical distinctions, even to the extent of paradox, if we are to form any notion of this rare quality of mind' (p. 161). Tate argues for this general position by instancing what he sees as the poem's precision and tight structure of rhythm, image, and theme. The poem has nothing to excess; it is marked throughout by 'a restraint that keeps the poet from carrying' her dramatic images too far. As for the poem's ideas, they are something altogether different from 'the feeble poetry of moral ideals that flourished in New England in the eighties':

> The terror of death is objectified through this figure of the genteel driver, who is made ironically to serve the end of Immortality. This is the heart of the poem: she has presented a typical Christian theme in its final irresolution, without making any final statements about it. There is no solution to the problem; there can be only a presentation of it in the full context of intellect and feeling. A construction of the human will, elaborated with all the abstracting powers of the mind, is put to the concrete test of experience: the idea of immortality is confronted with the fact of physical disintegration. We are not told what to think; we are told to look at the situation. (p. 161)

In evaluating this criticism we begin with the text quoted by Tate. When he calls the poem 'The Chariot', as he does at the beginning of his discussion, he tells us what his text shows: Tate is reading the work printed in 1890 by Todd and Higginson. But of course, 'The Chariot' is not what Dickinson wrote, at any time; rather, it is a text which her first editors produced when they carefully worked over the (untitled) text written by the author. Among other, less significant changes, an entire stanza was removed (the fourth) and several lines underwent major alteration.[13] Since Tate's argument for the greatness of the poem depends heavily upon his view of its linguistic perfection, we are faced with a rather awkward situation. Under the circumstances, one would not find it very difficult to embarrass Tate's reading by subjecting it to an ironical inquisition on the subject of textual criticism.

---

[13]See *Poems by Emily Dickinson*, ed. Mabel Loomis Todd and Thomas W. Higginson, Boston, 1890. Also see Johnson's edition, where the textual issues are succinctly presented.

Of course, Tate had no access to the text Dickinson actually wrote. Nevertheless, his critical judgement ought to have been warned that textual problems existed since he did have available to him another – and, as it happens, more accurate – text of Dickinson's work. This text appeared in Martha Dickinson Bianchi's 1924 edition of *The Complete Poems*, and it is the one cited by Yvor Winters in the critique of Tate's essay first published by Winters in *Maule's Curse*.[14] But Tate's critical method could not prepare him to deal with problems in textual criticism. Indeed, he could not even *see* such problems, much less analyse their critical relevance. In this case, the impoverished historical sense of his general critical method appears as an inability to make critical judgements about poetic texts, to make distinctions between poems and their texts, and to relate those judgements and distinctions to the final business of literary criticism.

We have no call, nor any desire, to ridicule Tate's essay on this matter. Nevertheless, the issue must be faced squarely, for the problems raised by Tate's lack of textual scrupulousness appear at other points, and in other forms, in his discussion, and his example typifies the sorts of problem that remain widespread in Western modes of formal, stylistic, structural, and post-structural procedures. We may observe the congruence of his critical practice – the symmetry between his lack of interest in textual matters and his general interpretive approach – by examining his remarks on the poem's thematic concerns. We shall notice two matters here: first, a tendency to overread the poem at the linguistic level; and second, a reluctance to take seriously, or even notice, either the fact or the importance of the poem's ideological attitudes. In each case we are dealing with something fundamental to Tate's literary criticism and to twentieth-century interpretive approaches generally: their attempt to lift the poem out of its original historical context and to erase the distance between that original context and the immediate context of the critical act.

In this next phase of my analysis, then, I am proposing to extend the discussion from its specific interest in 'the problem of the text' to the more general issue which that problem localizes. Critics who do not or cannot distinguish between the different concrete texts which a poem assumes in its historical passage are equally disinclined to study the aesthetic significance of a poem's topical dimensions, or its didactic, ethical, or ideological materials. Poems that have no textual histories have, at the thematic level, only those meanings and references which 'transcend' the particulars of time and place. The poetry of poems, in this view, is a function not of specific ideology or topical matters but of 'universal' themes and references – and the *most* universal of these universals are a poem's formal, stylistic, or structural excellences. The

[14]Winters' essay is reprinted in *The Recognition of Emily Dickinson*; see esp. pp. 192-3.

ultimate consequence of such approaches is that the present critic loses altogether his awareness that his own criticism is historically limited and time-bound in very specific ways. Losing a critical sense of the past, the interpreter necessarily loses his ability to see his own work in a critical light.

Let me return to Tate's analysis and the Dickinson poem, however, where we can study these problems as they emerge in concrete forms. When Tate says, for example, that the poem presents 'the problems of immortality . . . confronted with the fact of physical disintegration', we observe a critical move characteristic of twentieth-century criticism: that is, the habit of dealing with poetry's substantive concerns at the most abstract and generalized thematic levels. I will have more to say about this sort of critical abstraction in a moment. For now we want most to query Tate's interpretation of the thematic aspects of the Dickinson poem. When he argues, for example, that the poem does not treat 'moral ideas', and that it takes a non-committal ('unresolved') stance toward a serious intellectual problem, we are surely justified in demurring. The civil kindliness of Death is of course ironically presented, but the irony operates at the expense of those who – foolishly, the poem implies – regard Death as a fearful thing and who give all their attention to their mortal affairs ('My labor, and my leisure too') either because of their fear or as a consequence of it. Like the poem's speaker before Death 'stopped' for her, the readers of the poem are assumed to be fearful of Death and too busy with the affairs of their lives to 'stop' for him.[15] The poem does indeed have a 'a moral', and it appears in an unmistakable form in the final stanza:

> Since then – 'tis Centuries – and yet
> Feels shorter than the Day
> I first surmised the Horses Heads
> Were toward Eternity –

'We are not told what to think' by the poem, Tate asserts, but his position is only technically correct. Of course the poem does not *tell* us what to think, but its message about the benevolence of Death is plain enough. This message, however, like the poem which carries it, is no simple-minded pronouncement; the message is rich and affecting because it is delivered in human rather than abstract space. Dickinson's poem locates a set of relationships in which Dickinson, her fictive speaker, and her invited readers engage with each other in various emotional and intellectual ways.[16] The focus of these engagements is

[15]This motif is an ancient one in the tradition of Christian art and poetry. For its biblical sources see Matt. 24:43 and 1 Thess. 5:2-4. An excellent contemporary example is to be found in Alan Dugan's 'Tribute to Kafka for Someone Taken'.

[16]See V. N. Volosinov (i.e. M. M. Bakhtin), 'Discourse in Life and Discourse in Art', in *Freudianism, A Marxist Critique*, trans. I.R. Titunik, New York, 1976, where Bakhtin distinguishes among the author, the reader, and the figure he calls 'the hero' or the 'third participant'.

the poem's commonplace Christian theme: that people who are too busily involved with their worldly affairs give little serious thought to Death and the Afterlife. Criticizing such thoughtlessness, the poem encourages its readers to ponder Death and the Afterlife in a positive way. Its procedure for doing so involves the assumption of another thematic commonplace – that people fear to think about Death – and then undermining its force by a play of wit.

The wit appears most plainly in the rhetorical structure of the poem, which pretends to be spoken by a person already dead. Like some Christian Blessed Damozel from New England, Dickinson's speaker addresses this world from the other side, as it were, and lets us know that Death leads us not to oblivion but to 'Eternity' and 'Immortality'.[17] But the wit goes deeper, for Dickinson does not present her fiction as anything *but* fiction. The playfulness of the poem – which is especially evident in the final stanza, whose quiet good humour has been remarked upon frequently – is the work's most persuasive argument that Death can be contemplated not merely without fear but – more positively – with feelings of civilized affection. The kindliness and civility of the carriage driver are qualities we recognize in the *voice* of the poem's speaker and in the *wit* of its maker.

When we speak of the poem's wit, however, we should not lose ourselves in a hypnotic fascination with its verbal reality alone. The wit is at least as much a function of Dickinson's perspicuous observations of, and comments upon, social reality as it is of her facility with language. We may see this more clearly if we recall the standard critical idea that the figure of Death in this poem is – in the words of a recent critic – a 'gentlemanly suitor'.[18] Tate seems to have initiated this reading when he spoke of the driver as 'a gentleman taking a lady out for a drive', and when he proceeded to notice the 'erotic motive' associated with 'this figure of the genteel driver'. His commentary shows an acute awareness of one of the poem's subtlest and least explicit aspects, but it also displays a failure to see a more obvious but no less important fact about the driver.

This man is not a suitor but an undertaker, as we see quite clearly in the penultimate line's reference to 'Horses Heads'.[19] This small matter of fact has considerable importance for anyone wishing to develop an accurate critical account of the poem. It forces us to see, for example, that the journey being presented is not some unspecified drive in the country, but a funeral ride which is located quite specifically in relation

---

[17] In adopting this rhetorical model, Dickinson was following a literary practice that had grown extremely popular in the nineteenth century. See Ann Douglas, 'Heaven Our Home: Consolation Literature in the Northern United States 1830-1880', in *Death in America*, ed. Daniel Stannard, Philadelphia, 1974; see esp. pp. 58-9, 61-2. But the procedure is deeply traditional: see also Rosemary Woolf, *English Religious Lyric in the Middle Ages*, Oxford, 1963, chap. 9 *passim*.

[18] Robert Weisbuch, *Emily Dickinson's Poetry*, Chicago, 1972, p. 114.

[19] That is to say, a suitor's carriage would have had only one horse.

to Emily Dickinson and her Amherst world. The hearse in the poem is on its way out from Pleasant Street, past Emily Dickinson's house, to the cemetery located at the northern edge of the town just beyond the Dickinson homestead.[20] Of course, these details are not verbalized into the Dickinson poem as explicit description. They are only present implicitly, as an originally evoked context which we – at our historical remove – can (and must) reconstitute if we wish to focus and explain the special emotional character of the work.

Consider once again, for example, the undertaker who appears in the poem. The behaviour of this man – his correctness, his rather stiff but kindly formality, his manner of driving the carriage – defines a character-type well-known in nineteenth-century culture, and a favourite one with contemporary caricaturists.[21] Behind the civility and kindly formal behaviour of Emily Dickinson's undertaker lies a tradition which saw in this man a figure of grotesque obsequiousness, as we know from Mark Twain's memorable scene in *Huckleberry Finn*. Indeed, I do not see how one could fully appreciate the finesse of what Tate calls the 'erotic motive' without also seeing just how the poem plays with it, and how Dickinson's poetic style both *re*presents and quietly modifies the contemporary stereotype of this important social functionary so well known to the inhabitants of towns like Amherst. The poem's general ideology, as a work of Christian consolation, would be merely religious claptrap without these 'poetic'[22] elements; and such elements can only escape the critical method which does not seek to grasp the poem at a level more comprehensive than a merely linguistic one.

The power of the poem, then, rests in its ability to show us not merely the thoughts and feelings of Dickinson and her fictive speaker, but the

[20]The hearse's journey to the Amherst cemetery – one of the new, so-called rural cemeteries – must have been appallingly familiar to Emily Dickinson. The mortality rate in Amherst was high, and Emily Dickinson's room overlooked the cemetery route. See Millicent Todd Bingham, *Emily Dickinson's Home*, New York, 1955, the map facing p. 62 and pp. 179-80; also Jay Leyda, *The Years and Hours of Emily Dickinson*, New Haven, 1960, ii. 2-3. Emily Dickinson's bedroom was the best vantage in the house for observing the stately procession of the funeral hearse as it moved out from Pleasant Street to the cemetery. The special location of the Dickinson house meant that the funeral hearse would always pass by, no matter where the deceased person had lived in town. One should also note that the poem's references to the 'School' and the 'Fields of Gazing Grain' are precise. In point of fact, 'Because I could not Stop for Death' narrates the imagined (non imaginary) journey of the hearse from somewhere in the central part of Amherst out along Pleasant Street, past the schoolhouse on the left, and out to the beginning of the 'Fields of Gazing Grain', at which point the undertaker would have turned to the right and driven past more fields to the gravesite. For a general discussion of the rural cemetery see Neil Harris, 'The Cemetery Beautiful', in *Passing: The Vision of Death in America*, ed. Charles O. Jackson, Westport, 1977, pp. 103-11.

[21]See Alfred Scott Warthen, 'The Period of Caricature' and 'The Modern Dance of Death', in *The Physician of the Dance of Death*, New York, 1934. Twain was fond of presenting the undertaker from a comic point of view. See *Huckleberry Finn*, chap. 27, and his essay 'The Undertaker's Chat'.

[22]What makes them 'poetic' is their ability to dramatize the relationships which exist between specific social realities and a complex set of related – and often antagonistic – ideological attitudes and formations.

attitudes of her implied readers as well. For all her notorious privacy, Emily Dickinson is, like every poet, a creator of those structures of social energy which we call poems. 'Because I could not Stop for Death' locates not merely an expressive lyrical act, but a significant relationship between the poet and her readers which we, as still later readers, are meant to recognize, enter into, and (finally) extend. Our sympathy with the poem may not be the same as that felt by a Christian reader, whether contemporary with the poem or not; nevertheless, it is *continuous* with the sympathy of such readers (who are consciously and explicitly assumed by the poem) because it takes those readers as seriously as it takes Emily Dickinson and her fictive speaker. Indeed, it must do this, for all are part of the poem in question. Later readers may not share the ideologies of the people represented by this poem, but they cannot read it without recognizing and respecting those ideologies – without, in fact, perpetuating them in a critical human memory whose sympathetic powers are drawn from a historical consciousness.

Having discussed the 'ideological set' of this poem – its poetically rendered 'message' – let us return to Allen Tate's essay, where an absence of ideological commitments is imputed to Dickinson's work. We return to ask why Tate should insist upon 'misreading' the poem as he has done.

The reason emerges when we ponder carefully Tate's use of T. S. Eliot. Tate's interpretation shows that he shares Eliot's ideas about how moral concepts should appear in verse (not 'didactically' but dramatically); that he prizes Eliot's views on Metaphysical verse and its excellences; and that he is anxious to deliver his praise of Dickinson's poem in critical terms that will draw her into the company of those poets who illustrate Eliot's standards. In short, Tate reads Emily Dickinson in the same spirit that Eliot read Donne and the Metaphysicals. *Why* Tate, and Eliot before him, should have taken such a position toward the moral aspects of poetry – and especially of Christian poetry in its various forms – is beyond the scope of this analysis, though scholars recognize that the answer lies in the historical factors which generated modernism and its various ideologies.[23]

I have not dwelt upon Tate's discussion in order to debunk it, but rather in order to show the consonance between his interpretation of the Dickinson poem and his ignorance of its textual problems. Tate's eye is no more focused upon Dickinson's poem than it is on the 1890 text of 'The Chariot'. Rather, Tate has 'taken "The Chariot" for his text', as we might say of one who delivers a sermon or a moral lesson. 'The Chariot' is the occasion for his ideological polemic on behalf of certain aesthetic criteria.

[23]See Richard Ohmann, 'Studying Literature at the End of Ideology' in *The Politics of Literature*, ed. Louis Kampf and Paul Lauter, New York, 1973, esp. pp. 134-59; Renato Poggioli, *The Theory of the Avant-Garde*, trans, Gerald Fitzgerald, New York, 1971; and see nn. 3 and 8 above, and below chap. IV.2 ('The Religious Poetry of Christina Rossetti').

One important lesson to be drawn from this investigation of Tate's essay is that literary criticism – and even the analysis of poems – is not fundamentally a study of verbal structure *per se*. The very existence of Tate's influential and justly admired essay demonstrates that fact. Literary criticism must study poetic texts – the 'verbal structures' of poems – but the analysis of these verbal structures does not comprehend a poetic analysis. This paradox of critical method emerges forcibly in Tate's essay, which dramatizes, in its very limitations, the distinction between text and poem – a distinction, indeed, which Tate's analysis is incapable of making. Yet the distinction must be made – and textual criticism, in the traditional sense, must be revived among literary critics – if our received works of literature are to regain their full human resources – that is to say, if the entire history of poetry and all the potential of specific poems are to be made known and available to each new generation. Poetry and poems are, in this sense, trans-historical, but they acquire this perpetuity by virtue of the particular historical adventures which their texts undergo from their first appearance before their author's eyes through all their subsequent constitutions.

The textual histories of poems, in other words, are paradigm instances of the historically specific character of all poetry. By clarifying the distinction between a poem and its various texts, the examples from Byron and Blake illustrate the need for a systematic theory and method of historical criticism. On the other hand, the example from Dickinson argues, at the level of practical criticism, the specific critical powers inherent in a historical method. These powers appear as a special capacity for elucidating, in a systematic way, whatever in a poem is most concrete, local, and particular to it. Criticism cannot analyse poems, or reveal their special characteristics and values, if it abstracts away from their so-called accidental features. Attending merely to the formal or linguistic phenomena of poems constitutes an initial and massive act of abstraction from what are some of the most crucial particulars of all poems.

Facing the poem and its texts, then, historical criticism tries to define what is most peculiar and distinctive in specific poetical works. Moreover, in specifying these unique features and sets of relationships, it transcends the concept of the-poem-as-verbal-object to reveal the poem as a special sort of communication event. This new understanding of poems takes place precisely because the critical act, occurring in a self-conscious present, can turn to look upon poems created in the past not as fixed objects but as the locus of certain past human experiences. Some of these are dramatized *in* the poems, while others are preserved *through* the poetical works, which embody various human experiences *with* the poems, beginning with the author's own experiences. In this way does a historical criticism define poetry not as a formal structure or immediate event but as a continuing human process. That *act* of definition is the fundamental *fact* of literary criticism.

The new fact about *historical* criticism, however, is that it systematically opposes its own reification. Being first of all an *act* of definition rather than a *set* of definitions, historical criticism calls attention to the time-specific and heuristic character of its abstractions. Like the poetry it studies, criticism is always tendentious because it always seeks to define and preserve human values. One of the special values of historical criticism, to my view at any rate, lies in its eagerness to specify and examine its polemical positions. This self-critical aspect of an historical approach seems to be a direct function of its basic method, for in attempting to specify historical distinctions, we set a gulf between our past and our present. It is this gulf which enables us to judge and criticize the past, but it is equally this gulf which enables the past – so rich in its achievements – to judge and criticize us. Thus in our differences do we learn about, and create, a community.

(1980-1)

SECTION FIVE
POSTMODERNISM

For the American novelist John Barth, commenting on the term in 1980, postmodernism was essentially a continuation but modification of cultural modernism , a way of 'telling stories'. By 1990, although the term has spilled out of the boundaries of literary critical debate, it still carries with it this earlier sense, but the stories are now indistinguishable from what was once assumed to be knowledge: scientific truth, ethics, law, history. Somewhere in the 1980s, the term shifted from functioning primarily as a description of a range of aesthetic practices involving irony, parody, self-consciousness, fragmentation, playful self-reflexivity and parataxis, to a use encompassing a more general shift of thought and registering a pervasive loss of faith in the progressivist and rationalist discourses of Enlightened modernity . It is now used variously as a term to describe the cultural epoch through which we are living (often apocalyptically, sometimes as the logic of Late Capitalism); an aesthetic practice (viewed as co-extensive with the commodified surfaces of this culture or as a disruption of its assumptions from within through a 'micropolitics' or 'politics of desire') or as a critique of the foundationalist assumptions of Enlightened political and philosophical thought. Lyotard's *The Postmodern Condition* (1979), marked the point where the specifically literary critical debate began to be dissolved into the larger theoretical and cultural one, though post-structuralists had already undermined the concept of grand and metanarratives, the unity and autonomy of the subject and the ability of discourses to stabilise and contain cultural meanings.

Postmodernism is a 'mood' expressed theoretically across a diverse range of theoretical discourses and involving: a focus on the collapse of grand narratives into local incommensurable language games or 'little narratives'; a Foucauldian emphasis on the discontinuity and plurality of history as discursively produced and formulated, and a tendency to view the discourses of Enlightenment reason as complicit with the instrumental rationalisation of modern life. The historian Arnold Toynbee first used the term in 1947 to describe the current, fourth and final, phase of Western history, dominated by anxiety and irrationalism. In the contemporary version, there is no longer a transcendent space from which to offer a critique of this culture: only disruption from within, micropolitics, language games, parody and fragmentation. Postmodernism wages war on totality. Postmodernists claim the exhaustion of all metanarratives which claim to legitimate foundations for truth, though some surreptitiously import new foundationalisms (the body, the aesthetic, desire). History becomes a plurality of islands of discourse arising out of the institutionally produced languages which we bring to bear on it. Or it is a network of agonistic language games where surface phenomena can no longer be 'explained' as the manifestations of deeper underlying truths. Absolute systems of knowledge give way to contingencies and ironies, aesthetic fictionality displaces philosophical certainty.

Whether influenced by post-Heideggerian hermeneutics, Nietzschean perspectivism or Wittgensteinian language games, postmodernists such as Lyotard, Baudrillard and Rorty see knowledge of the world as indissociable from being-in-the-world: knowledge and experience are inextricably bound to each other and always culturally situated. There can be no transcendental 'view from nowhere', no position from outside culture from which to offer a criticism of it. Implication is all. We live in a pluralized culture surrounded by a multiplicity of styles, knowledges, stories that we tell ourselves about the world. To attempt to impose an overarching narrative on such experience is to perpetuate the violences of modernity with their exclusions and terrors. The relativisation of styles which is postmodernism, throws into doubt the claims of any one discourse or story to be offering the 'truth' about the world or an authoritative version of the real. Issues of ethics, law, equality and authority become deeply problematic in such a context: how is one to legitimate knowledge and where to locate value?

Jameson's essay reprinted here locates the postmodern as a condition arising out of the development in the sixties of a late, consumer phase of capitalism. It is characterised by the proliferation of depthless surface and the penetration of capital into all areas of social and cultural experience. Jameson seems to suggest our inevitable implication in the fragmentariness of the postmodern, but he does underpin his argument with a 'totalizing' economic theory derived from Mandel's book *Late Capitalism* (1978). The essay on feminism and postmodernism examines the implications for political movements such as feminism of the postmodern dismantling of foundationalist arguments and of the concepts of universal justice, unity and liberation.

30 Fredric Jameson

Periodizing the 60s, *The Sixties Without Apology*, 1984

p178-218

Nostalgic commemoration of the glories of the 60s and abject public confession of the decade's many failures and missed opportunities are two errors that cannot be avoided by some middle path that threads its way in between. The following sketch starts from the position that History is Necessity, that the 60s had to happen the way it did, and that its opportunities and failures were inextricably intertwined, marked by the objective constraints and openings of a determinate historical situation, of which I thus wish to offer a tentative and provisional model.

To speak of the 'situation' of the 60s, however, is necessarily to think in terms of historical periods and to work with models of historical periodization, which are at the present moment theoretically unfashionable, to say the least. Leave aside the existential fact that the veterans of the decade, who have seen so many things change dramatically from year to year think more historically than their predecessors; the classification by generations has become as meaningful for us as it was for the Russians of the late nineteenth century, who sorted character types out with reference to specific decades. And intellectuals of a certain age now find it normal to justify their current positions by way of a historical narrative ('then the limits of Althusserianism began to be evident', etc.). Now, this is not the place for a theoretical justification of periodization in the writing of history, but to those who think that cultural periodization implies some massive kinship and homogeneity or identity within a given period, it may quickly be replied that it is surely only against a certain conception of what is historically dominant or hegemonic that the full value of the exceptional – what Raymond Williams calls the 'residual' or 'emergent' – can be assessed. Here, in any case, the period in question is understood not as some omnipresent and uniform shared style or way of thinking and acting, but rather as the sharing of an objective situation, to which a whole range of varied responses and creative innovations is then possible, but always within that situation's structural limits.

Yet a whole range of rather different theoretical objections will also bear on the selectiveness of such a historical narrative: if the critique of periodization questions the possibilities of diachrony, these involve the problems of synchrony and in particular of the relationship to be established between the various 'levels' of historical change singled out for attention. Indeed, the present narrative will claim to say something meaningful about the 60s by way of brief sketches of but four of those levels: the history of philosophy, revolutionary political theory and practice, cultural production, and economic cycles (and this in a context limited essentially to the United States, France, and the Third World). Such selectiveness seems not merely to give equal historical weight to base and superstructure indifferently, but also to raise the spectre of a practice of homologies – the kind of analogical parallelism in which the poetic production of Wallace Stevens is somehow 'the same' as the political practice of Che Guevara – which have been thought abusive at least as far back as Spengler.

There is of course no reason why specialized and elite phenomena, such as the writing of poetry, cannot reveal historical trends and tendencies as vividly as 'real life' – or perhaps even more visibly, in their isolation and semi-autonomy which approximates a laboratory situation. In any case, there is a fundamental difference between the present narrative and those of an older organic history that sought 'expressive' unification through analogies and homologies between widely distinct levels of social life. Where the latter proposed identities between the forms on such various levels, what will be argued here is a series of significant homologies between the *breaks* in those forms and their development. What is at stake, then, is not some proposition about the organic unity of the 60s on all its levels, but rather a hypothesis about the rhythm and dynamics of the fundamental situation in which those very different levels develop according to their own internal laws.

At that point, what looked like a weakness in this historical or narrative procedure turns out to be an unexpected strength, particularly in allowing for some sort of 'verification' of the separate strands of the narrative. One sometimes believes – especially in the area of culture and cultural histories and critiques – that an infinite number of narrative interpretations of history are possible, limited only by the ingenuity of the practitioners whose claim to originality depends on the novelty of the new theory of history they bring to market. It is more reassuring, then, to find the regularities hypothetically proposed for one field of activity (e.g., the cognitive, or the aesthetic, or the revolutionary) dramatically and surprisingly 'confirmed' by the reappearance of just such regularities in a widely different and seemingly unrelated field, as will be the case with the economic in the present context.

At any rate, it will already have become clear that nothing like a history of the 60s in the traditional, narrative sense will be offered here. But historical representation is just as surely in crisis as its distant cousin, the linear novel, and for much the same reasons. The most intelligent 'solution' to such a crisis does not consist in abandoning historiography altogether, as an impossible aim and an ideological category all at once, but rather – as in the modernist aesthetic itself – in reorganizing its traditional procedures on a different level. Althusser's proposal seems the wisest in this situation: as old-fashioned narrative or 'realistic' historiography became problematical, the historian should reformulate her vocation – not any longer to produce some vivid representation of History 'as it really happened', but rather to produce the *concept* of history. Such will at least be the gamble of the following pages.

1 Third World Beginnings

It does not seem particularly controversial to mark the beginnings of what will come to be called the 60s in the Third World with the great movement of decolonization in British and French Africa. It can be argued that the most characteristic expressions of a properly First World 60s are all later than this, whether they are understood in countercultural terms – drugs and rock – or in the political terms of a student New Left and a mass antiwar movement. Indeed, politically, a First World 60s owed much to Third-Worldism in terms of politicocultural models, as in a symbolic Maoism, and, moreover, found its mission in resistance to wars aimed precisely at stemming the new revolutionary forces in the Third World. Belden Fields has indeed suggested that the two First World nations in which the most powerful student mass movements emerged – the United States and France – became privileged political spaces precisely *because* these were two countries involved in colonial wars, although the French New Left appears after the resolution of the Algerian conflict. The one significant exception to all this is in many ways the most important First World political movement of all – the new black politics and the civil rights movement, which must be dated, not from the Supreme Court decision of 1954, but rather from the first sit-ins in Greensboro, North Carolina, in February of 1960. Yet it might be argued that this was also a movement of decolonization, and in any case the constant exchange and mutual influences between the American black movements and the various African and Caribbean ones are continuous and incalculable throughout this period.

The independence of Ghana (1957), the agony of the Congo (Lumumba was murdered in January 1961), the independence of France's sub-Saharan colonies following the Gaullist referendum of 1959, finally the Algerian Revolution (which might plausibly mark our schema here with its internal high point, the Battle of Algiers, in January–March 1957, as with its diplomatic resolution in 1962) – all of these signal the convulsive birth of what will come in time to be known as the 60s:

> Not so very long ago, the earth numbered two thousand million inhabitants: five hundred million *men* and one thousand five hundred million *natives*. The former

had the Word; the others merely had use of it.[1]

The 60s was, then, the period when all these 'natives' became human beings, and this internally as well as externally: those inner colonized of the First World – 'minorities', marginals, and women – fully as much as its external subjects and official 'natives'. The process can and has been described in a number of ways, each one of which implies a certain 'vision of History' and a certain uniquely thematized reading of the 60s proper: it can be seen as a decisive and global chapter in Croce's conception of history as the history of human freedom; as a more classically Hegelian process of the coming to self-consciousness of subject peoples; as some post-Lukácsean or more Marcusean, New Left conception of the emergence of new 'subjects of history' of a nonclass type (blacks, students, Third World peoples); or as some poststructuralist, Foucaultean notion (significantly anticipated by Sartre in the passage just quoted) of the conquest of the right to speak in a new collective voice, never before heard on the world stage – and of the concomitant dismissal of the intermediaries (liberals, First World intellectuals) who had hitherto claimed to talk in your name; not forgetting the more properly political rhetoric of self-determination or independence, or the more psychological and cultural rhetoric of new collective 'identities'.

It is, however, important to situate the emergence of these new collective 'identities' or 'subjects of history' in the historical situation which made that emergence possible, and in particular to relate the emergence of these new social and political categories (the colonized, race, marginality, gender, and the like) to something like a crisis in the more universal category that had hitherto seemed to subsume all the varieties of social resistance, namely the classical conception of social class. This is to be understood, however, not in some intellectual but rather in an institutional sense; it would be idealistic to suppose the deficiencies in the abstract idea of social class, and in particular in the Marxian conception of class struggle, can have been responsible for the emergence of what seem to be new nonclass forces. What can be noted, rather, is a crisis in the institutions through which a real class politics has however imperfectly been able to express itself. In this respect, the merge of the AFL and the CIO in 1955 can be seen as a fundamental 'condition of possibility' for the unleashing of the new social and political dynamics of the 60s: that merger, a triumph of McCarthyism, secured the expulsion of the Communists from the American labour movement, consolidated the new antipolitical 'social contract' between American business and the American labour unions, and created a situation in which the privileges of a white male labour force take

[1]J.P. Sartre, "Preface" to Frantz Fanon, *The Wretched of the Earth*, trans. Constance Farrington (New York, 1965).

precedence over the demands of black and women workers and other minorities. These last have therefore no place in the classical institutions of an older working-class politics. They will thus be 'liberated' from social class, in the charged and ambivalent sense that Marxism gives to that word (in the context of enclosure, for instance); they are separated from the older institutions and thus 'released' to find new modes of social and political expression.

The virtual disappearance of the American Communist Party as a small but significant political force in American society in 1956 suggests another dimension to this general situation: the crisis of the American party is 'overdetermined' by its repression under McCarthyism and by the 'revolution' in the Soviet bloc unleashed by Khrushchev's de-Stalinization campaign, which will have analogous but distinct and specific equivalents for the European Communist parties. In France, in particular, after the brief moment of a Communist 'humanism', developed essentially by philosophers in the eastern countries, and with the fall of Khrushchev himself and the definitive failure of his various experiments in 1964, an unparalleled situation emerges in which, virtually for the first time since the Congress of Tours in 1919, it becomes possible for radical intellectuals to conceive of revolutionary work outside and independent of the French Communist Party. (The older attitudes – 'we know all about it, we don't like it much, but nothing is to be done politically without the CP' – are classically expressed in Sartre's own political journalism, in particular in *Les Communistes et la paix*. Now Trotskyism gets a new lease on life, and the new Maoist forms, followed by a whole explosion of extraparliamentary formations of all ideological complexions, the so-called groupuscules, offer the promise of a new kind of politics equally 'liberated' from the traditional class categories.

Two further key events need to be noted here before we go on. For many of us, indeed, the crucial detonator – a new Year I, the palpable demonstration that revolution was not merely a historical concept and a museum piece but real and achievable – was furnished by a people whose imperialist subjugation had developed among North Americans a sympathy and a sense of fraternity we could never have for other Third World peoples in their struggle, except in an abstract and intellectual way. Yet by January 1, 1959, the Cuban Revolution remained symbolically ambiguous. It could be read as a Third World revolution of a type different from either the classical Leninist one or the Maoist experience, for it had a revolutionary strategy entirely its own, the *foco* theory, which we will discuss later. This great event also announces the impending 60s as a period of unexpected political innovation rather than as the confirmation of older social and conceptual schemes.

Meanwhile, personal testimony seems to make it clear that for many white American students – in particular for many of those later active in the New Left – the assassination of President Kennedy played a significant role in delegitimizing the state itself and in discrediting the parliamentary process, seeming to mark the decisive end of the well-known passing of the torch to a younger generation of leadership, as well as the dramatic defeat of some new spirit of public or civic idealism. As for the reality of the appearance, it does not much matter that, in hindsight, such a view of the Kennedy presidency may be wholly erroneous, considering his conservatism and anticommunism, the gruesome gamble of the 'missile crisis', and his responsibility for the American engagement in Vietnam itself. More significant, the legacy of the Kennedy regime to the development of a 60s politics may well have been the rhetoric of youth and of the 'generation gap' which he exploited, but which outlived him and dialectically offered itself as an expressive form through which the political discontent of American students and young people could articulate itself.

Such were some of the preconditions or 'conditions of possibility' – both in traditional working-class political institutions and in the arena of the legitimation of state power – for the 'new' social forces of the 60s to develop as they did. Returning to these new forces, there is a way in which their ultimate fate marks the close of the 60s as well: the end of 'Third-Worldism' in the U.S. and Europe largely predates the Chinese Thermidor, and coincides with the awareness of increasing institutional corruption in many of the newly independent states of Africa and the almost complete militarization of the Latin American regimes after the Chilean coup of 1973 (the later revolutionary truimphs in the former Portuguese colonies are henceforth felt to be 'Marxist' rather than 'Third-Worldist', whereas Vietnam vanishes from American consciousness as completely after the ultimate American withdrawal as did Algeria from French consciousness after the Evian accords of 1963). In the First World of the late 60s, there is certainly a return to a more internal politics, as the antiwar movement in the United States and May 68 in France testify. Yet the American movement remains organically linked to its Third World 'occasion' in the Vietnam War itself, as well as to the Maoist inspiration of the Progressive Labor-type groups which emerge from SDS, such that the movement as a whole will lose its momentum as the war winds down and the draft ceases. In France, the 'common program' of the left (1972) – in which the current Socialist government finds its origins – marks a new turn toward Gramscian models and a new kind of Eurocommunist spirit which owes very little to Third World antecedents of any kind. Finally, the black movement in the U.S. enters into a crisis at much the same time, as its dominant ideology – cultural nationalism, an ideology profoundly linked to Third World models – is exhausted. The women's movement also owed something to this kind of Third World inspiration, but it too, in the period 1972-74, will know an increasing articulation into relatively

distinct ideological positions ("Bourgeois" feminism, lesbian separatism, socialist feminism).

For reasons enumerated above, and others, it seems plausible to mark
the end of the 60s around 1972-74; the problem of this general 'break'
will be returned to at the end of this sketch. For the moment we must
complete our characterization of the overall dynamic of Third World
history during this period, particularly if it is granted that this dynamic
or 'narrative line' entertains some privileged relationship of influence
on the unfolding of a First World 60s (through direct intervention – wars
of national liberation – or through the prestige of exotic political models
– most obviously, the Maoist one – or finally, owing to some global
dynamic which both worlds share and respond to in relatively distinct
ways).

This is, of course, the moment to observe that the 'liberation' of new
forces in the Third World is as ambiguous as this term frequently tends
to be (freedom as separation from older systems); to put it more
sharply, it is the moment to recall the obvious, that decolonization
historically went hand in hand with neocolonialism, and that the
graceful, grudging, or violent end of an old-fashioned imperialism
certainly meant the end of one kind of domination but evidently also the
invention and construction of a new kind – symbolically, something like
the replacement of the British Empire by the International Monetary
Fund. This is, incidentally, why the currently fashionable rhetoric of
power and domination (Foucault is the most influential of these
rhetoricians, but the basic displacement from the economic to the
political is already made by Max Weber) is ultimately unsatisfactory; it
is of course politically important to 'contest' the various forms of power
and domination, but the latter cannot be understood unless their
functional relationships to economic exploitation are articulated – that
is, until the political is once again subsumed beneath the economic. (On
the other hand – particularly in the historicizing perspective of the
present essay – it will obviously be a significant historical and social
symptom that, in the mid-60s, people felt it necessary to express their
sense of the situation and their projected praxis in a reified political
language of power, domination, authority and antiauthoritarianism,
and so forth: here, Second and Third World developments – with their
conceptions of a 'primacy of the political' under socialism – offer an
interesting and curious cross-lighting.) Meanwhile, something similar
can be said of the conceptions of collective identity and in particular of
the poststructuralist slogan of the conquest of speech, of the right to
speak in your own voice, for yourself; but to articulate new demands, in
your own voice, is not necessarily to satisfy them, and to speak is not
necessarily to achieve a Hegelian recognition from the Other (or at least
then only in the more sombre and baleful sense that the Other now has
to take you into consideration in a new way and to invent new methods

for dealing with that new presence you have achieved). In hindsight, the 'materialist kernel' of this characteristic rhetoric or ideological vision of the 60s may be found in a more fundamental reflection on the nature of cultural revolution itself (now independent of its local and now historical Chinese manifestation).

The paradoxical, or dialectical, combination of decolonization and neo-colonialism can perhaps best be grasped in economic terms by a reflection on the nature of another process whose beginning coincides with the general beginnings we have suggested for this period as a whole. This is a process generally described in the neutral but obviously ideological language of a technological 'revolution' in agriculture: the so-called Green Revolution, with its new applications of chemical procedures to fertilization, its intensified strategies of mechanization, and its predictable celebration of progress and wonder-working technology, supposedly destined to free the world from hunger (the Green Revolution, incidentally, finds its Second World equivalent in Khrushchev's disastrous 'virgin lands' experiment). But these are far from neutral achievements; nor is their export – essentially pioneered by the Kennedys – a benevolent and altruistic activity. In the nineteenth and early twentieth centuries, capitalist penetration of the Third World did not necessarily mean a capitalist transformation of the latter's traditional modes of production. Rather, they were for the most part left intact, 'merely' exploited by a more political and military structure. The very enclave nature of these older agricultural modes – in combination with the violence of the occupier and that other violence, the introduction of money – established a sort of tributary relation that was beneficial to the imperialist metropolis for a considerable period. The Green Revolution carries this penetration and expansion of the 'logic of capital' into a new stage.

The older village structure and precapitalist forms of agriculture are now systematically destroyed, to be replaced by an industrial agriculture whose effects are fully as disastrous as, and analogous to, the moment of enclosure in the emergence of capital in what was to become the First World. The 'organic' social relations of village societies are now shattered, an enormous landless preproletariat produced, which migrates to the urban areas (as the tremendous growth of Mexico City can testify), while new, more proletarian, wage-working forms of agricultural labour replaced the older collective or traditional kinds. Such ambiguous 'liberation' needs to be described with all the dialectical ambivalence with which Marx and Engels celebrate the dynamism of capital itself in the *Manifesto* or the historical progress achieved by the British occupation of India.

The conception of the Third World 60s as a moment when all over the world chains and shackles of a classical imperialist kind were thrown off in a stirring wave of 'wars of national liberation' is an altogether mythical simplification. Such resistance is generated as much by the new penetration of the Green Revolution as it is by the ultimate impatience with the older imperialist structures, the latter itself overdetermined by the historical spectacle of the supremacy of another former Third World entity, namely Japan, in its sweeping initial victories over the old imperial powers in World War II. Eric Wolf's indispensable *Peasant Wars of the Twentieth Century* (1969) underscores the relationship between possibilities of resistance, the development of a revolutionary ethos, and a certain constitutive distance from the more absolutely demoralizing social and economic logic of capital.

The final ambiguity with which we leave this topic is the following: the 60s, often imagined as a period when capital and First World power are in retreat all over the globe, can just as easily be conceptualized as a period when capital is in full dynamic and innovative expansion, equipped with a whole armature of fresh production techniques and new 'means of production'. It now remains to be seen whether this ambiguity, and the far greater specificity of the agricultural developments in the Third World, have any equivalent in the dynamics with which the 60s unfold in the advanced countries themselves.

2   The Politics of Otherness

If the history of philosophy is understood not as some sequence of timeless yet somehow finite positions in the eternal, but rather as the history of attempts to conceptualize a historical and social substance itself in constant dialectical transformation, whose aporias and contradictions mark all of those successive philosophies as determinate failures, yet failures from which we can read off something of the nature of the object on which they themselves came to grief – then it does not seem quite so farfetched to scan the more limited trajectory of that now highly specialized discipline for symptoms of the deeper rhythms of the 'real' or 'concrete' 60s itself.

As far as the history of philosophy during that period is concerned, one of the more influential versions of its story is told as follows: the gradual supersession of a hegemonic Sartrean existentialism (with its essentially phenomenological perspectives) by what is often loosely called 'structuralism', namely, by a variety of new theoretical attempts which share at least a single fundamental 'experience' – the discovery of the primacy of Language or the Symbolic (an area in which phenomenology and Sartrean existentialism remain relatively conventional or traditional). The moment of high structuralism – whose most influential monuments are seemingly not philosophical at all, but can be characterized, alongside the new linguistics itself, as linguistic transformations of anthropology and psychoanalysis by Claude Lévi-Strauss and Jacques Lacan respectively – is, however, inherently unstable and has the vocation of becoming a new type of universal mathesis, under pain of vanishing as one more intellectual fad. The breakdown products of that moment of high structuralism can then be seen, on the one hand, as the reduction to a kind of scientism, to sheer method and analytical technique (in *semiotics*); and, on the other hand, as the transformation of structuralist approaches into active ideologies in which ethical, political, and historical consequences are drawn from the hitherto more epistemological 'structuralist' positions; this last is of course the moment of what is now generally known as *poststructuralism*, associated with familiar names like those of Foucault, Deleuze, Derrida, and so forth. That the paradigm, although obviously French in its references, is not merely local can be judged from an analogous mutation of the classical Frankfurt School via problems of communication, in the work of Habermas; or by the current revival of pragmatism in the work of Richard Rorty, which has a home-grown American 'poststructuralist' feeling to it (Pierce after all having largely preceded and outclassed Saussure).

The crisis of the philosophical institution and the gradual extinction of the philosopher's classic political vocation, of which Sartre was for our time the supreme embodiment, can in some ways be said to be about the so-called death of the subject: the individual ego or personality, but also the supreme philosophical Subject, the cogito but also the *auteur* of the great philosophical *system*. It is certainly possible to see Sartre as one of the last great system builders of traditional philosophy (but then at least one dimension of classical existentialism must also be seen as an ideology or a metaphysic: that of the heroic pathos of existential choice and freedom in the void, and that of the 'absurd', more particularly in Camus). Some of us also came to *Marxism* through dialectical elements in the early Sartre (he himself then turning to follow up this avenue in his own later, more Marxian work, such as the *Critique of Dialectical Reason* [1960]). But on balance the component of his work that underwent the richest practical elaboration at other people's hands as well as his own was his theory of interpersonal relations, his stunning rewrite of Hegel's Master/Slave chapter, his conception of the Look as the most concrete mode in which I relate to other subjects and struggle with them, the dimension of my alienation in my 'being-for-other-people', in which each of us vainly attempts, by looking at the other, to turn the tables and transform the baleful alienating gaze of the Other into an object for my equally alienating gaze. Sartre will go on, in the *Critique*, to try to erect a more positive and political theory of group dynamics on this seemingly sterile territory; the struggle between two people now becoming dialectically transformed into the struggle between groups themselves. The *Critique* was an anticipatory work, however, whose import and significance would not finally be recognized until May 68 and beyond, whose rich consequences indeed have not even fully been drawn to this day. Suffice it to say, in the present context, that the *Critique* fails to reach its appointed terminus, and to complete the projected highway that was to have led from the individual subject of existential experience all the way to fully constituted social classes. It breaks down at the point of the constitution of small groups and is ultimately usable principally for ideologies of small guerilla bands (in a later moment of the 60s) and of microgroups (at the period's end). The significance of this trajectory will soon be clear.

However, at the dawn of the 60s, the Sartrean paradigm of the Look and the struggle for recognition between individual subjects will also be appropriated dramatically for a very different model of political struggle, in Frantz Fanon's enormously influential vision (*The Wretched of the Earth* [1961]) of the struggle between Colonizer and Colonized, where the objectifying reversal of the Look is apocalyptically rewritten as the act of redemptive violence of Slave against Master, the moment when, in fear and the anxiety of death, the hierarchical positions of Self and Other, Centre and Margin, are forcibly reversed, and when the subservient consciousness of the Colonized achieves collective identity and self-affirmation in the face of coloniziers in abject fight.

What is at once significant is the way in which what had been a technical philosophical subject (the 'problem' of solipsism, the nature of relationships between individual subjects or 'cogitos') has fallen into the world and become an explosive and scandalous political ideology: a piece of the old-fashioned technical philosophical system of high existentialism breaking off and migrating outside philosophy departments altogether, into a more frightening landscape of praxis and terror. Fanon's great myth could be read at the time, by those it appalled equally well as by those it energized, as an irresponsible call to mindless violence. In retrospect, and in the light of Fanon's other, clinical work (he was a psychiatrist working with victims of colonization and of the torture and terror of the Algerian war), it can more appropriately be read as a significant contribution to a whole theory of cultural revolution as the collective reeducation (or even collective psychoanalysis) of oppressed peoples or unrevolutionary working classes. Cultural revolution as a strategy for breaking the immemorial habits of subalternity and obedience which have become internalized as a kind of second nature in all the laborious and exploited classes in human history – such is the vaster problematic to which, today, Gramsci and Wilhelm Reich, Fanon and Rudolf Bahro, can be seen as contributing as richly as the more official practices of Maoism.

3 Digression on Maoism

But with this new and fateful reference, and awkward but unavoidable parenthetical digression is in order: Maoism, richest of all the great new ideologies of the 60s, will be a shadowy but central presence throughout this essay, yet owing to its very polyvalence it cannot be neatly inserted at any point or exhaustively confronted on its own. One understands, of course, why Left militants here and abroad, fatigued by Maoist dogmatisms, must have heaved a collective sigh of relief when the Chinese turn consigned 'Maoism' itself to the ashcan of history. Theories, however, are often liberated on their own terms when they are thus radically disjoined from the practical interests of state power. Meanwhile, as I have suggested above, the symbolic terrain of the present debate is fully as much chosen and dictated by the Right as by Left survivors; and the current propaganda campaign, everywhere in the world, to Stalinize and discredit Maoism and the experience of the Chinese cultural revolution – now rewritten as yet another Gulag to the East – all of this, make no mistake about it, is part and parcel of the larger attempt to trash the 60s generally. It would not be prudent to abandon rapidly and without thoughtful reconsideration any of this terrain to the 'other side'.

As for the more ludicrous features of Western Third-Worldism generally – a kind of modern exotic or orientalist version of Marx's revolutionaries of 1848, who 'anxiously conjure up the spirits of the Great Revolution of 1789 to their service and borrow from them names, battle cries and costumes'[2] – these are now widely understood in a more cynical light, as in Régis Debray's remark: 'In France, the Columbuses of political modernity thought that following Godards's *La Chinoise* they were discovering China in Paris, when in fact they were landing in California'.[3]

Most paradoxical and fascinating of all, however, is the unexpected and unpredictable sequel to the Sino-Soviet split itself: the new Chinese rhetoric, intent on castigating the Soviet bureaucracy as revisionistic and 'bourgeois', will have the curious effect of evacuating the class content of these slogans. There is then an inevitable terminological slippage and displacement: the new binary opposite to the term 'bourgeois' will no longer be 'proletarian' but rather 'revolutionary', and the new qualifications for political judgments of this kind are no longer made in terms of class or party affiliation but rather in terms of personal life – your relationship to special privileges, to middle-class luxuries and dachas and managerial incomes and other perks – Mao Zedong's own monthly 'salary', we are told, was something in the neighbourhood of a hundred American dollars. As with all forms of anticommunism, this rhetoric can of course be appropriated by the anti-Marxist thematics of 'bureaucracy', of the end of ideology and social

---

[2]Karl Marx, *The Eighteenth Brumaire of Louis Bonaparte* (New York, 1969), p. 15.
[3]Régis Debray, "A Modest Contribution," *New Literary Review*, 115 (May-June 1979), p. 58.

class, and so forth. But it is important to understand how for Western militants what began to emerge from this at first merely tactical and rhetorical shift was a whole new political space, a space which will come to be articulated by the slogan 'the personal is the political', and into which – in one of the most stunning and unforeseeable of historical turns – the women's movement will triumphantly move at the end of the decade, building a Yenan of a new and unpredictable kind which is still impregnable at the present moment.

4 The Withering Away of Philosophy

The limit as well as the strength of the stark Fanonian model of struggle was set by the relative simplicity of the colonial situation; this can be shown in two ways, first of all in the sequel to the 'war of national independence'. For with the Slave's symbolic and literal victory over the (now former) Master, the 'politics of otherness' touches its limit as well; the rhetoric of a conquest of collective identity has then nowhere else to go but into a kind of secessionary logic of which black cultural nationalism and (later on) lesbian separatism are the most dramatic examples (the dialectic of cultural and linguistic independence in Quebec province would be yet another instructive one). But this result is also contradictory, insofar as the newly constituted group (we here pick up Sartre's account in the *Critique*) *needs* outside enemies to survive as a group, to produce and perpetuate a sense of collective cohesion and identity. Ultimately, in the absence of the clear-cut Manichean situation of the older imperialist period, this hard-won collective self-definition of a first moment of resistance will break up into the smaller and more comfortable unities of face-to-face micro-groups (of which the official political sects are only one example).

The gradual waning of the Fanonian model can also be described from the perspective of what will shortly become its 'structuralist' critique. On this view, it is still a model based on a conception of individual subjects, albeit mythical and collective ones. It is thereby both anthropomorphic and transparent, in the sense in which nothing intervenes between the great collective adversaries, between the Master and the Slave, between the Colonizer and the Colonized. Yet even in Hegel, there was always a third term, namely matter itself, the raw materials on which the Slave is made to labour and to work out a long and anonymous salvation through the rest of history. The 'third term' of the 60s is, however, rather different from this. It was as though the protracted experiences of the earlier part of the decade gradually burned into the minds of the participants a specific lesson. In the United States, it was the experience of the interminable Vietnam War itself; in France, it was the astonishing and apparently invincible technocratic dynamism, and the seemingly unshakable inertia and resistance to de-Stalinization of the French Communist party; and everywhere, it was the tremendous expansion of the media apparatus and the culture of consumerism. This lesson might well be described as the discovery, within a hitherto antagonistic and 'transparent' political praxis, of the opacity of the Institution itself as the radically transindividual, with its own inner dynamic and laws, which are not those of individual human action or intention, something which Sartre theorized in the *Critique* as the 'pactico-inert', and which will take the definitive form, in competing structuralism, of 'structure' or 'synchronic system', a realm of impersonal logic in terms of which human consciousness is itself little more than an "effect of structure."

On this reading, then, the new philosophical turn will be interpreted less in the idealistic perspective of some discovery of a new scientific truth (the Symbolic) than as the symptom of an essentially protopolitical and social experience, the shock of some new, hard, unconceptualized, resistant object which the older conceptuality cannot process and which thus gradually generates a whole new problematic. The conceptualization of this new problematic in the coding of linguistics or information theory may then be attributed to the unexpected explosion of information and messages of all kinds in the media revolution, which will be discussed in more detail in the following section. Suffice it to remark at this point that there is some historical irony in the way in which this moment, essentially the Third Technological Revolution in the West (electronics, nuclear energy) – in other words, a whole new step in the conquest of nature by human praxis – is philosophically greeted and conceptually expressed in a kind of thought officially designated as 'antihumanist' and concerned to think what transcends or escapes human consciousness and intention. Similarly, the Second Technological Revolution of the late nineteenth century – an unparalleled quantum leap in human power over nature – was the moment of expression of a whole range of nihilisms associated with 'modernity' or with high modernism in culture.

In the present context, the Althusserian experiment of the mid- to late 60s is the most revealing and suggestive of the various 'structuralisms', since it was the only one to be explicitly political and indeed to have very wide-ranging political effects in Europe and Latin America. The story of Althusserianism can be told only schematically here: its initial thrust is twofold, against the unliquidated Stalinist tradition (strategically designated by the code words 'Hegel' and 'expressive causality' in Althusser's own texts), and against the 'transparence' of the Eastern attempts to reinvent a Marxist humanism on the basis of the theory of alienation in Marx's early manuscripts. That Althusserianism is essentially a meditation on the 'institutional' and on the opacity of the 'practico-inert' may be judged by the three successive formulations of this object by Althusser himself in the course of the 60s: that of a 'structure in dominance' or *structure à dominante* (in *For Marx*), that of 'structural causality' (in *Reading Capital*), and that of ideological state apparatuses (in the essay of that name). What is less often remembered, but what should be perfectly obvious from any rereading of *For Marx*, is the origin of this new problematic in Maoism itself, and particularly in Mao Zedong's essay 'On Contradiction', in which the notion of the complex, already-given *overdetermined* conjuncture of various kinds of antagonistic and nonantagonistic contradictions is mapped out.

The modification that will emerge from Althusser's 'process of theoretical production' as it works over its Maoist raw materials can be conveyed by the problem and slogan of the 'semi-autonomy' of the levels of social life (a problem already invoked in our opening pages). This formula will involve a struggle on two fronts: on the one hand, against the monism or 'expressive causality' of Stalinism, in which the 'levels' are identified, conflated, and brutally collapsed into one another (changes in economic production will be 'the same' as political and cultural changes), and, on the other, against bourgeois avant-garde philosophy, which finds just such a denunciation of organic concepts of totality most congenial, but draws from it the consequence of a post- or anti-Marxist celebration of Nietzschean heterogeneity. The notion of a semi-autonomy of the various levels or instances, most notably of the political instance and of the dynamics of state power, will have enormous resonance (outstandingly in the work of Nicos Poulantzas), since it seems to reflect, and to offer a way of theorizing, the enormous growth of the state bureaucracy since the war, the 'relative autonomy' of the state apparatus from any classical and reductive functionality in the service of big business, as well as the very active new terrain of political struggle presented by government or public sector workers. The theory could also be appealed to justify a semi-autonomy in the cultural sphere, as well, and especially a semi-autonomous cultural politics, of a variety that ranges from Godard's films and *situationisme* to the 'festival' of May 68 and the Yippie movement here (not excluding, perhaps, even those forms of so-called terrorism that aimed, not at any classical seizure of state power, but rather at essentially pedagogical or informational demonstrations, e.g., 'forcing the state to reveal its fundamentally fascist nature').

Nonetheless, the attempt to open up a semi-autonomy of the levels in one hand, while holding them altogether in the ultimate unity of some 'structural totality' (with its still classical Marxian ultimately determining instance of the economic), tends under its own momentum, in the centrifugal force of the critique of totality it had itself elaborated, to self-destruct (most dramatically so in the trajectory of Hindess and Hirst). What will emerge is not merely a heterogeneity of *levels* – henceforth, semi-autonomy will relax into autonomy *tout court*, and it will be conceivable that in the decentred and 'schizophrenic' world of late capitalism the various instances may really have no organic relationship to one another at all – but, more important, the idea will emerge that the struggles appropriate to each of these levels (purely political struggles, purely economic struggles, purely cultural struggles, purely 'theoretical' struggles) may have no necessary relationship to one another either. With this ultimate 'meltdown' of the Althusserian apparatus we are in the (still contemporary) world of microgroups and micropolitics – variously theorized as local or molecular politics, but clearly characterized, however different the various conceptions are, as a repudiation of old-fashioned class and party politics of a 'totalizing' kind, and most obviously epitomized by the challenge of the women's movement, whose unique new strategies and concerns cut across (or in some cases undermine and discredit altogether) many classical inherited forms of 'public' or 'official' political action, including the electoral kind. The repudiation of 'theory' itself as an essentially masculine enterprise of 'power through knowledge' in French feminism (see in particular the work of Luce Irigaray) may be taken as the final moment in this particular 'withering away of philosophy'.

Yet there is another way to read the density of Althusserianism, a way that will form the transition to our subsequent discussion of the transformation of the cultural sphere in the 60s; and this involves the significance of the slogan of 'theory' itself as it comes to replace the older term philosophy throughout this period. The 'discovery' of the Symbolic, the development of its linguistic-related thematics (as, e.g., in the notion of understanding as an essentially synchronic process, which influences the construction of relatively ahistorical 'structures', such as the Althusserian one described above), is now to be correlated with a modification of the practice of the symbolic, of language itself in the 'structuralist' texts, henceforth characterized as 'theory', rather than work in a particular traditional discipline. Two features of this evolution, or mutation, must be stressed. The first is a consequence of the crisis in, or the disappearance of, classical *canon* of philosophical writings which necessarily results from the contestation of philosophy as a discipline and an institution. Henceforth, the new 'philosophical' text will no longer draw its significance from an insertion into the issues and debates of the philosophical tradition, which means that its basic 'intertextual' references become random, an *ad hoc* constellation that forms and dissolves on the occasion of each new text. The new text must necessarily be a commentary on other texts (indeed, that dependence on a body of texts to be glossed, rewritten, interconnected in fresh ways will now intensify if anything), yet those texts, drawn from the most wildly distant disciplines (anthropology, psychiatry, literature, history of science), will be selected in a seemingly arbitrary fashion: Mumford side by side with Antonin Artaud, Kant with Sade, pre-Socratic

philosophy, President Schreber, a novel of Maurice Blanchot, Owen
Lattimore on Mongolia, and a host of obscure Latin medical treatises
from the eighteenth century. The vocation of what was formerly
'philosophy' is thereby restructured and displaced: since there is no
longer a tradition of philosophical problems in terms of which new
positions and new statements can meaningfully be proposed, such
works now tend toward what can be called metaphilosophy – the very
different work of coordinating a series of pregiven, already constituted
codes or systems of signifiers, of producing a discourse fashioned out of
the already fashioned discourse of the constellation of *ad hoc* reference
works. 'Philosophy' thereby becomes radically occasional; one would
want to call it disposable theory, the production of a *metabook*, to be
replaced by a different one next season, rather than the ambition to
express a proposition, a position, or a system with greater 'truth' value.
(The obvious analogy with the evolution of literary and cultural studies
today, with the crisis and disappearance of the latter's own canon of
great books – the last one having been augmented to include the once
recalcitrant 'masterpieces' of high modernism – will be taken for
granted in our next section.)

All of this can perhaps be grasped in a different way by tracing the
effects of another significant feature of contemporary theory, namely its
privileged theme in the so-called critique of representation. Traditional
philosophy will now be grasped in those terms, as a practice of
representation in which the philosophical text or system (misguidedly)
attempts to express something other than itself, namely truth or
meaning (which now stands as the 'signified' to the 'signifier' of the
system). If, however, the whole aesthetic of representation is metaphysical and ideological, philosophical discourse can no longer entertain this vocation, and it must stand as the mere addition of another text
to what is now conceived as an infinite chain of texts (not necessarily all
verbal – daily life is a text, clothing is a text, state power is a text, that
whole external world, about which 'meaning' or 'truth' were once
asserted and which is now contemptuously characterized as the illusion
of reference or the 'referent', is an indeterminate superposition of texts
of all kinds). Whence the significance of the currently fashionable
slogan of 'materialism', when sounded in the area of philosophy and
theory: materialism here means the dissolution of any belief in
'meaning' or in the 'signified' conceived as ideas or concepts that are
distinct from their linguistic expressions. However paradoxical a
'materialist' philosophy may be in this respect, a 'materialist theory of
language' will clearly transform the very function and operation of
'theory', since it opens up a dynamic in which it is no longer ideas, but
rather texts, material texts, which struggle with one another. Theory so
defined (and it will have become clear that the term now greatly
transcends what used to be called philosophy and its specialized

content) conceives of its vocation, not as the discovery of truth and the repudiation of error, but rather as a struggle about purely linguistic formulations, as the attempt to formulate verbal propositions (material language) in such a way that they are unable to imply unwanted or ideological consequences. Since this aim is evidently impossible to achieve, what emerges from the practice of theory – and this was most dramatic and visible during the high point of Althusserianism itself in 1967-68 – is a violent and obsessive return to ideological critique in the new form of a perpetual guerrilla war among the material signifiers of textual formulations. With the transformation of philosophy into a material practice, however, we touch on a development that cannot fully be appreciated until it is replaced in the context of a general mutation of culture throughout this period, a context in which 'theory' will come to be grasped as a specific (or semi-autonomous) form of what must be called postmodernism generally.

5   The Adventures of the Sign

Postmodernism is one significant framework in which to describe what happened to culture in the 60s, but a full discussion of this hotly contested concept is not possible here. Such a discussion would want to cover, among other things, the following features: that well-known poststructuralist theme, the 'death' of the subject (including the creative subject, the *auteur* or the 'genius'); the nature and function of a *culture of the simulacrum* (an idea developed out of Plato by Deleuze and Baudrillard to convey some specificity of a reproducible object world, not of copies or reproductions marked as such, but of a proliferation of trompe-l'oeil copies *without originals*); the relation of this last to media culture of the 'society of the spectacle' (Debord), under two heads: (1) the peculiar new status of the image, the 'material' or what might better be called the 'literal', signifier: a materiality or literality from which the older sensory richness of the medium has been abstracted (just as on the other side of the dialectical relationship, the old individuality of the subject and his/her 'brushstrokes' have equally been effaced); and (2) the emergence, in the work's temporality, of an aesthetic of *textuality* or what is often described as schizophrenic time; the eclipse, finally, of all depth, especially *historicity* itself, with the subsequent appearance of pastiche and nostalgia art (what the French call *la mode rétro*), and including the supersession of the accompanying models of depth-interpretation in philosophy (the various forms of hermeneutics, as well as the Freudian conception of 'repression', of manifest and latent levels).

What is generally objected to in characterizations of this kind is the empirical observation that all these features can be abundantly located in this or that variety of high modernism; indeed, one of the difficulties in specifying postmodernism lies in its symbiotic or parasitical relationship to the latter. In effect, with the canonization of a hitherto scandalous, ugly, disonant, amoral, antisocial, bohemian high modernism offensive to the middle classes, its promotion to the very figure of high culture generally, and perhaps most important, its enshrinement in the academic institution, postmodernism emerges as a way of making creative space for artists now oppressed by those henceforth hegemonic modernist categories of irony, complexity, ambiguity, dense temporality, and particularly, aesthetic and utopian monumentality. In some analogous way, it will be said, high modernism itself won its autonomy from the preceding hegemonic realism (the symbolic language or mode of representation of classical or market capitalism). But there is a difference in that realism itself underwent a significant mutation: it became *naturalism* and at once generated the representation forms of mass culture (the narrative apparatus of the contemporary best seller is an invention of naturalism and one of the most stunningly successful of French cultural exports). High modernism and mass culture then develop in dialectical opposition and interrelationship with one another. It is precisely the waning of their opposition, and some new conflation of the forms of high and mass culture, that characterizes postmodernism itself.

The historical specificity of postmodernism must therefore finally be argued in terms of the social functionality of culture itself. As stated above, high modernism, whatever its overt political content, was oppositional and marginal within a middle-class Victorian or philistine or gilded age culture. Although postmodernism is equally offensive in all the respects enumerated (think of punk rock or pornography), it is no longer at all oppositional in that sense; indeed, it constitutes the very dominant or hegemonic aesthetic of consumer society itself and significantly serves the latter's commodity production as a virtual laboratory of new forms and fashions. The argument for a conception of postmodernism as a periodizing category is thus based on the presupposition that, even if *all* the formal features enumerated above were already present in the older high modernism, the very significance of those features changes when they become a cultural *dominant*, with a precise socio-economic functionality.

At this point it may be well to shift the terms (or the 'code') of our description to the seemingly more traditional one of a cultural sphere, a conception developed by Herbert Marcuse in what is to my mind his single most important text, the great essay 'The Affirmative Character of Culture' (1937). (It should be added that the conception of a 'public sphere' generally is a very contemporary one in Germany in the works of Habermas and Negt and Kluge, where such a system of categories stands in interesting contrast to the code of 'levels' or 'instances' in

French poststructuralism.) Marcuse there rehearses the paradoxical dialectic of the classical (German) aesthetic, which projects as play and 'purposefulness without purpose' a Utopian realm of beauty and culture beyond the fallen empirical world of money and business activity, thereby winning a powerful critical and negative value through its capacity to condemn, by its own very existence, the totality of *what* is, at the same time forfeiting all ability to social or political intervention in what is, by virtue of its constitutive disjunction or autonomy from society and history.

The account therefore begins to coincide in a suggestive way with the problematic of autonomous or semi-autonomous levels developed in the preceding section. To historicize Marcuse's dialectic, however, would demand that we take into account the possibility that in our time this very autonomy of the cultural sphere (or level or instance) may be in the process of modification; and that we develop the means to furnish a description of the process whereby such modification might take place, as well as of the prior process whereby culture became 'autonomous' or 'semi-autonomous' in the first place.

This requires recourse to yet another (unrelated) analytic code, one more generally familiar to us today, since it involves the now classical structural concept of the *sign*, with its two components, the signifier (the material vehicle or image – sound or printed word) and the signified (the mental image, meaning, or 'conceptual' content), and a third component – the external object of the sign, its reference or 'referent' – henceforth expelled from the unity and yet haunting it as a ghostly residual aftereffect (illusion or ideology). The scientific value of this conception of the sign will be bracketed here since we are concerned, on the one hand, to historicize it, to interpret it as a conceptual symptom of developments in the period, and, on the other, to 'set it in motion', to see whether changes in its inner structure can offer some adequate small-scale emblem or electrocardiogram of changes and permutation in the cultural sphere generally throughout this period.

Such changes are already suggested by the fate of the 'referent' in the 'conditions of possibility' of the new structural concept of the sign (a significant ambiguity must be noted, however: theorists of the sign notoriously glide from a conception of reference as designating a 'real' object outside the unity of signifier and signified to a position in which the signified itself – or meaning, or the idea or the concept of a thing – becomes somehow identified with the referent and stigmatized along with it; we will return to this below). Saussure, at the dawn of the semiotic revolution, liked to describe the relationship of signifier to signified as that of the two sides, the recto and verso, of a sheet of paper. In what is then a logical sequel, and a text that naturally enough becomes equally canonical, Borges will push 'representation' to the point of imagining a map so rigorous and referential that it becomes coterminous with its object. The stage is then set for the structuralist emblem par excellence, the Moebius Strip, which succeeds in peeling itself off its referent altogether and thus achieves a free-floating closure in the void, a kind of absolute self-referentiality and autocirculatory from which all remaining traces of reference, or of any externality, have triumphantly been effaced.

To be even more eclectic about it, I will suggest that this process, seemingly internal to the sign itself, requires a supplementary explanatory code, that of the more universal process of reification and fragmentation at one with the logic of capital itself. Nonetheless, taken on its own terms, the inner convulsions of the sign is a useful initial figure of the process of transformation of culture generally, which must in some first moment (that described by Marcuse) separate itself from the 'referent' the existing social and historical world itself, only in a subsequent stage of the 60s, in what is here termed 'postmodernism', to develop further into some new and heightened, free-floating, self-referential 'autonomy'.

The problem now turns around this very term, 'autonomy', with its paradoxical Althusserian modification, the concept of 'semi-autonomy'. The paradox is that the sign, as an 'autonomous' unity in its own right as a realm divorced from the referent, can preserve that initial autonomy, and the unity and coherence demanded by it, only at the price of keeping a phantom of reference alive, as the ghostly reminder of its own outside or exterior, since this allows it closure, self-definition, and an essential boundary line. Marcuse's own tormented dialectic expresses this dramatically in the curious oscillation whereby his autonomous realm of beauty and culture returns upon some 'real world' to judge and negate it, at the same time separating itself so radically from that real world as to become a place of mere illusion and impotent 'ideals', the 'infinite' and so on.

The first moment in the adventures of the sign is perplexing enough as to demand more concrete, if schematic, illustration in the most characteristic cultural productions themselves. It might well be demonstrated in the classical French *nouveau roman* (in particular the novels of Robbe-Grillet himself), which established its new language in the early 1960s, using systematic variations of narrative segments to 'undermine' representation, yet in some sense confirming this last by teasing and stimulating an appetite for it.

Because an American illustration seems more appropriate, however, something similar may be seen in connection with the final and canonical form of high modernism in American poetry, namely the work of Wallace Stevens, which becomes, in the years following the poet's death in 1956, institutionalized in the university as a purer and more quintessential fulfillment of poetic language than the still impure (read: ideological and political) works of an Eliot or a Pound, and can therefore be numbered among the literary 'events' of the early 60s. As Frank Lentricchia has shown, in *After the New Criticism*,[4] the serviceability of Stevens' poetic production for this normative and hegemonic role depends in large measure on the increasing conflation, in that work of poetic practice and poetic theory:

> This endlessly elaborating poem
> Displays the theory of poetry
> As the life of poetry. . .

'Stevens' is therefore a locus and fulfillment of aesthetics and aesthetic theory fully as much as the latter's exemplar and privileged exegetical object; the theory or aesthetic ideology in question is very much an affirmation of the 'autonomy' of the cultural sphere in the sense developed above, a valorization of the supreme power of the poetic imagination over the 'reality' it produces. Stevens' work, therefore, offers an extraordinary laboratory situation in which to observe the autonomization of culture as a process: a detailed examination of his development (something for which we have no space here) would show how some initial 'set toward' or 'attention to' a kind of poetic *pensée sauvage*, the operation of great preconscious *stereotypes*, opens up a vast inner world in which little by little the images of things and their ideas begin to be substituted for the things themselves. Yet what distinguishes this experience in Stevens is the sense of a vast systematicity in all this, the operation of a whole set of cosmic oppositions far too complex to be reduced to the schemata of 'structuralist' binary oppositions, yet akin to those in spirit, and somehow pregiven in the Symbolic Order of the mind, discoverable to the passive exploration of the 'poetic imagination', that is, of some heightened and impersonal power of free association in the realm of 'objective spirit' or 'objective culture'. The examination would further show the strategic limitation of this process to landscape, the reduction of the ideas and images of things to the names for things, and finally to those irreducibles that are place names, among which the exotic has a privileged function (Key West, Oklahoma, Yucatan, Java). Here the poetic 'totality' begins to trace a ghostly mimesis or *analogon* of the totality of the imperialist world system itself, with Third World materials in a similarly strategic, marginal, yet essential place (much as Adorno showed how Schoenberg's twelve-tone system unconsciously produced a formal imitation of the 'total system' of capital). This very unconscious replication of the 'real' totality of the world system in the mind is then what allows culture to separate itself as a closed and self-sufficient 'system' in its own right: reduplication, and at the same time, floating above the real. It is an impulse shared by most of the great high modernisms, as has been

---

[4]Frank Lentricchia, *After the New Criticism* (Chicago, 1980), esp. pp. 31-35.

shown most dramatically in the recent critiques of architectural modernism, in particular of the international style, whose great monumental objects constitute themselves, by protecting a protopolitical and utopian spirit of transformation *against* a fallen city fabric all around them and, as Venturi has demonstrated, end up necessarily displaying and speaking of themselves alone. Now, this also accounts for what must puzzle any serious reader of Stevens' verse, namely the extraordinary combination of verbal richness and experimental hollowness or impoverishment in it (the latter being attributable as well to the impersonality of the poetic imagination in Stevens, and to the essentially contemplative and epistemological stance of the subject in it, over and against the static object world of his landscapes).

The essential point here, however, is that this characteristic movement of the high modernist impulse needs to justify itself by way of an ideology, an ideological supplement which can generally be described as that of 'existentialism' (the supreme fiction, the meaninglessness of a contingent object world unredeemed by the imagination, etc.). This is the most uninteresting and banal dimension of Stevens work, yet it betrays along with other existentialisms (e.g., Sartre's tree root in *Nausea*) that fatal seam or link that must be retained in order for the contingent, the 'outside world', the meaningless referent, to be just present enough dramatically to be overcome within the language. Nowhere is this ultimate point so clearly deduced, over and over again, as in Stevens, in the eye of the blackbird, the angels, or the Sun itself – that last residual vanishing point of reference as distant as a dwarf star upon the horizon, yet which cannot disappear altogether without the whole vocation of poetry and the poetic imagination being called back into question. Stevens thus exemplifies for us the fundamental paradox of the 'autonomy' of the cultural sphere: the sign can become autonomous only by remaining semi-autonomous, and the realm of culture can absolutize itself over against the real world only at the price of retaining a final tenuous sense of that exterior or external world of which it is the replication and the imaginary double.

All of this can also be demonstrated by showing what happens when, in a second moment, the perfectly logical conclusion is drawn that the referent is itself a myth and does not exist, a second moment hitherto described as postmodernism. Its trajectory can be seen as a movement from the older *Nouveau roman* to that of Sollers or of properly 'schizophrenic' writing, or from the primacy of Stevens to that of John Ashbery. This new moment is a radical break (which can be localized around 1967 for reasons to be given later), but it is important to grasp it as dialectical, that is, as a passage from quantity to quality in which the *same* force, reaching a certain threshold of excess, in its prolongation now produces qualitatively distinct effects and seems to generate a whole new system.

That force has been described as reification, but we can now also begin to make some connections with another figural language used earlier: in a first moment, reification 'liberated' the sign from its referent, but this is not a force to be released with impunity. Now, in a second moment, it continues its work of dissolution, penetrating the interior of the sign itself and liberating the signifier from the signified, or from meaning proper. This play, no longer of a realm of signs, but of pure or literal signifiers freed from the ballast of their signifieds, their former meanings, now generates a new kind of textuality in all the arts (and in philosophy as well, as we have seen above) and begins to project the mirage of some ultimate language of pure signifiers which is also frequently associated with schizophrenic discourse. (Indeed, the Lacanian theory of schizophrenia – a language disorder in which syntactical time breaks down and leaves a succession of empty signifiers, absolute moments of a perpetual present, behind itself – has offered one of the more influential explanations and ideological justifications for postmodernist textual practice.)

Such an account would have to be demonstrated in some detail by way of a concrete analysis of the postmodernist experience in all the arts today; but the present argument can be concluded by drawing the consequences of this second moment – the aculture of the signifier or of the simulacrum – for the whole problematic of some 'autonomy' of the cultural sphere which has concerned us here. For that autonomous realm is not itself spared by the intensified process by which the classical sign is dissolved; if its autonomy depended paradoxically on its possibility of remaining 'semi-autonomous' (in an Althusserian sense) and of preserving the last tenuous link with some ultimate referent (or, in Althusserian language, of preserving the ultimate unity of a properly 'structural totality'), then evidently in the new cultural moment culture will have ceased to be autonomous, and the realm of an autonomous play of signs becomes impossible, when that ultimate final referent to which the balloon of the mind was moored is now definitively cut. The break-up of the sign in mid-air determines a fall back into a now absolutely fragmented and anarchic social reality; the broken pieces of language (the pure signifiers) now fall again into the world, as so many more pieces of material junk among all the other rusting and superannuated apparatuses and buildings that litter the commodity landscape and that strew the 'collage city', the 'delirious New York' of a postmodernist late capitalism in full crisis.

But, returning to a Marcusean terminology, all of this can also be said in a different way: with the eclipse of culture as an autonomous space or sphere, culture itself falls into the world, and the result is not its disappearance but its prodigious expansion, to the point where culture becomes coterminous with social life in general; now all the levels become 'acculturated', and in the society of the spectacle, the image, or the simulacrum, everything has at length become cultural, from the superstructures down into the mechanisms of the infrastructure itself. If this development then places acutely on the agenda the neo-Gramscian problem of a new cultural politics today – in a social system in which the very status of both culture and politics have been profoundly, functionally, and structurally modified – it also renders problematic any further discussion of what used to be called 'culture' proper, whose artifacts have become the random experiences of daily life itself.

6   In the Sierra Maestra

The preceding section will, however, have been little more than a lengthy excursion into a very specialized (or 'elite') area, unless it can be shown that the dynamic therein visible, with something of the artificial simplification of the laboratory situation, finds striking analogies or homologies in very different and distant areas of social practice. It is precisely this replication of a common diachronic rhythm or 'genetic code' which we will not observe in the very different realities of revolutionary practice and theory in the course of the 60s in the Third World.

From the beginning, the Cuban experience affirmed itself as an original one, as a new revolutionary model, to be radically distinguished from more traditional forms of revolutionary practice. *Foco* theory, indeed, as it was associated with Che Guevara and theorized in Regis Debray's influential handbook, *Revolution in the Revolution*? (1967), asserted itself (as the title of the book suggests) both against a more traditional Leninist conception of party practice and against the experience of the Chinese revolution in its first essential stage of the conquest of power (what will later come to be designated as 'Maoism', China's own very different 'revolution in the revolution', or Great Proletarian Cultural Revolution, will not become visible to the outside world until the moment when the fate of the Cuban strategy has been sealed).

A reading of Debray's text shows that *foco* strategy, the strategy of the mobile guerrilla base or revolutionary *foyer*, is conceived as yet a third term, as something distinct from *either* the traditional model of class struggle (an essentially *urban* proletariat rising against a bourgeoisie or ruling class) *or* the Chinese experience of a mass peasant movement in the countryside (and also has little in common with a Fanonian struggle for recognition between Colonizer and Colonized). The *foco*, or guerrilla operation, is conceptualized as being neither 'in' nor 'of' either country or city; geographically, of course, it is positioned in the countryside, yet that location is not the permanently 'liberated' territory' of the Yenan region, well beyond the reach of the enemy forces of Chiang Kai-shek or of the Japanese occupier. It is not indeed located in the cultivated area of the peasant fields at all, but rather in that third or nonplace which is the wilderness of the Sierra Maestra, neither country nor city, but rather a whole new element in which the guerrilla band moves in perpetual displacement.

This peculiarity of the way in which the spatial coordinates of the Cuban strategy is conceived has, then, immediate consequences for the way in which the class elements of the revolutionary movement are theorized. Neither city nor country; by the same token, paradoxically, the guerrillas themselves are grasped as being neither workers nor peasants (still less, intellectuals), but rather something entirely new, for which the prerevolutionary class society has no categories: new revolutionary subjects, forged in the guerrilla struggle indifferently out of the social material of peasants, city workers, or intellectuals, yet now largely transcending those class categories (just as this moment of Cuban theory will claim largely to transcend the older revolutionary ideologies predicted on class categories, whether those of Trotskyist workerism, Maoist populism and peasant consciousness, or of Leninist vanguard intelletualism).

What becomes clear in a text like Debray's is that the guerrilla *foco* – so mobile as to be beyond geography in the static sense – is in and of itself a *figure* for the transformed, revolutionary society to come. Its revolutionary militants are not simply 'soldiers' to whose specialized role and function one would then have to 'add' supplementary roles in the revolutionary division of labour, such as political commissars and the political vanguard party itself, both explicitly rejected here. Rather, in them is abolished all such prerevolutionary divisions and categories. This conception of a newly emergent revolutionary 'space' – situated outside the 'real' political, social, and geographical world of country and city, and of the historical social classes, yet at one and the same time a figure or small-scale image and prefiguration of the revolutionary transformation of that real world – may be designated as a properly Utopian space, a Hegelian 'inverted world', an autonomous revolutionary sphere, in which the fallen real world over against it is itself set right and transformed into a new socialist society.

For all practical purposes, this powerful model is exhausted, even before Che's own tragic death in Bolivia in 1967, with the failure of the guerrilla movements in Peru and Venezuela in 1966; not uncoincidentally, that failure will be accompanied by something like a disinvestment of revolutionary libido and fascination on the part of a First World Left, the return (with some leavening of the newer Maoism) to its own current situation, in the American antiwar movement and May 68. In Latin America, however, the radical strategy that effectively replaces *foco* theory is that of the so-called urban guerrilla movement, pioneered in Uruguay by the Tupamaros; it will have become clear that this break-up of the utopian space of the older guerrilla *foco*, the fall of politics back into the world in the form of a very different style of political practice indeed – one that seeks to dramatize features of state power, rather than, as in traditional revolutionary movements, to build toward some ultimate encounter with it – will be interpreted here as something of a structural equivalent to the final stage of the sign as characterized above.

Several qualifications must be made, however. For one thing, it is clear that this new form of political activity will be endowed, by association, with something of the tragic prestige of the Palestinian liberation movement, which comes into being in its contemporary form as a result of the Israeli seizure of the West Bank and the Gaza Strip in 1967, and which will thereafter become one of the dominant worldwide symbols of revolutionary praxis in the late 60s. Equally clearly, however, the struggle of this desperate and victimized people cannot be made to bear responsibility for the excesses of this kind of strategy elsewhere in the world, whose universal results (whether in Latin America, or with Cointelpro in the United States, or, belatedly, in West Germany and Italy) have been to legitimize an intensification of the repressive apparatus of state power.

This objective coincidence between a misguided assessment of the social and political situation on the part of Left militants (for the most part students and intellectuals eager to force a revolutionary conjuncture by voluntaristic acts) and a willing exploitation by the state of precisely those provocations suggests that what is often loosely called 'terrorism' must be the object of complex and properly dialectical analysis. However rightly a responsible Left chooses to dissociate itself from such strategy (and the Marxian opposition to terrorism is an old and established tradition that goes back to the nineteenth century), it is important to remember that 'terrorism', as a 'concept', is also an ideologeme of the Right and must therefore be refused in that form. Along with the disaster films of the late 60s and early 70s, mass culture itself makes clear that 'terrorism' – the image of the 'terrorist' – is one of the privileged forms in which an ahistorical society imagines radical social change; meanwhile, an inspection of the content of the modern thriller or adventure story also makes it clear that the 'otherness' of so-called terrorism has begun to replace older images of criminal 'insanity' as an unexamined and seemingly 'natural' motivation in the construction of plots – yet another sign of the ideological nature of this particular pseudoconcept. Understood in this way, 'terrorism' is a collective obsession, a symptomatic fantasy of the American political unconscious, which demands decoding and analysis in its own right.

As for the thing itself, for all practical purposes it comes to an end with the Chilean coup in 1973 and the fall of virtually all the Latin American countries to various forms of military dictatorship. The belated reemergence of this kind of political activity in West Germany and in

Italy must surely at least in part be attributed to the fascist past of these two countries, to their failure to liquidate that past after the war, and to a violent moral revulsion against it on the part of a segment of the youth and intellectuals who grew up in the 60s.

7   Return of the 'Ultimately Determining Instance'

The two breaks that have emerged in the preceding section – one in the general area around 1967, the other in the immediate neighbourhood of 1973 – will not serve as the framework for a more general hypothesis about the periodization of the 60s in general. Beginning with the second of these, a whole series of other, seemingly unrelated events in the general area of 1972-74 suggests that this moment is not merely a decisive one on the relatively specialized level of Third World or Latin American radical politics, but signals the definitive end of what is called the 60s in a far more global way. In the First World, for example, the end of the draft and the withdrawal of American forces from Vietnam (in 1973) spell the end of the mass politics of the antiwar movement (the crisis of the New Left itself – which can be largely dated from the break-up of SDS in 1969 – would seem related to the other break mentioned, to which we will return below), while the signing of the Common Program between the Communist party and the new Socialist party in France (as well as the wider currency of slogans associated with 'Eurocommunism' at this time) would seem to mark a strategic turn away from the kinds of political activities associated with May 68 and its sequels. This is also the movement when as a result of the Yom Kippur war, the oil weapon emerges and administers a different kind of shock to the economies, the political strategies, and the daily life habits of the advanced countries. Concomitantly, on the more general cultural and ideological level, the intellectuals associated with the establishment itself (particularly in the United States) begin to recover from the fright and defensive posture that was theirs during the decade now ending, and again find their voices in a series of attacks on 60s culture and 60s politics, which, as was noted at the beginning, are not even yet at an end. One of the more influential documents was Lionel Trilling's *Sincerity and Authenticity* (1972), an Arnoldian call to reverse the tide of 60s' countercultural 'barbarism'. (This will, of course, be followed by the equally influential diagnosis of some 60s concept of 'authenticity' in terms of a 'culture of narcissism'.) Meanwhile, in July 1973, some rather different 'intellectuals', representing various concrete forms of political and economic power, will begin to rethink the failure in Vietnam in terms of a new global strategy for American and First World interests; their establishment of the Trilateral Commission will at least sym- bolically be a significant marker in the recovery of momentum by what must be called 'the ruling classes'. The emergence of a widely accepted new popular concept and term at this same time, the notion of the 'multinational corporation', is also another symptom, signifying, as the authors of *Global Reach* have suggested, the moment when private business finds itself obliged to emerge in public as a visible 'subject of history' and a visible actor on the world stage – think of the role of ITT in Chile – when the American government, having been badly burned by the failure of the Vietnam intervention, is generally reluctant to undertake further ventures of this kind.

For all these reasons it seems appropriate to mark the definitive end of the '60s' in the general area of 1972-74. But we have omitted until now the decisive element in any argument for a periodization or 'punctuation' of this kind, and this new kind of material will direct our attention to a 'level' or 'instance' which has hitherto significantly been absent from the present discussion, namely the economic itself. For 1973-74 is the moment of the onset of a worldwide economic crisis, whose dynamic is still with us today, and which put a decisive full stop to the economic expansion and prosperity characteristic of the postwar period generally and of the 60s in particular. When we add to this another key economic marker – the recession in West Germany in 1966 and that in the other advanced countries, in particular in the United States a year or so later – we may well thereby find ourselves in a better position more formally to conceptualize the sense of a secondary break around 1967-68 which has begun to surface on the philosophical, cultural, and political levels as they were analyzed or 'narrated' above.

Such confirmation by the economic 'level' itself of periodizing reading derived from other, sample levels or instances of social life during the 60s will now perhaps put us in a better position to answer the two theoretical issues raised at the beginning of this essay. The first had to do with the validity of Marxist analysis for a period whose active political categories no longer seemed to be those of social class, and in which in a more general way traditional forms of Marxist theory and practice seemed to have entered a 'crisis'. The second involved the problem of some 'unified field theory' in terms of which such seemingly distant realities as Third World peasant movements and First World mass culture (or indeed, more abstractly, intellectual or superstructural levels like philosophy and culture generally, and those of mass resistance and political practice) might conceptually be related in some coherent way.

A pathbreaking synthesis of Ernest Mandel, in his book *Late Capitalism*,[5] will suggest a hypothetical answer to both these questions at once. The book presents, among other things, an elaborate system of business cycles under capitalism, whose most familiar unit, the seven-to-ten-year alternation of boom, overproduction, recession, and

[5]Ernest Mandel, *Late Capitalism* (London, 1978).

economic recovery, adequately enough accounts for the midpoint break in the 60s suggested above.

Mandel's account of the worldwide crisis of 1974, however, draws on a far more controversial conception of vaster cycles of some thirty- to fifty-year periods each – cycles which are then obviously much more difficult to perceive experientially or 'phenomenologically' insofar as they transcend the rhythms and limits of the biological life of individuals. These 'Kondratiev waves' (named after the Soviet economist who hypothesized them) have, according to Mandel, been renewed four times since the eighteenth century, and are characterized by quantum leaps in the technology of production, which enable decisive increases in the rate of profit generally, until at length the advantages of the new production processes have been explored and exhausted and the cycle therewith comes to an end. The latest of these Kondratiev cycles is that marked by computer technology, nuclear energy, and the mechanization of agriculture (particularly in foodstuffs and also primary materials), which Mandel dates from 1940 in North America and the postwar period in the other imperialist countries; what is decisive in the present context is his notion that, with the worldwide recession of 1973-74, the dynamics of this latest 'long wave' are spent.

The hypothesis is attractive, however, not only because of its abstract usefulness in confirming our periodization schemes, but also because of the actual analysis of this latest wave of capitalist expansion, and of the properly Marxian version he gives of a whole range of developments that have generally been thought to demonstrate the end of the 'classical' capitalism theorized by Marx and to require this or that post-Marxist theory of social mutation (as in theories of consumer society, postindustrial society, and the like).

We have already described the way in which neocolonialism is characterized by the radically new technology (the so-called Green Revolution in agriculture: new machinery, new farming methods, and new types of chemical fertilizer and genetic experiments with hybrid plants and the like), with which capitalism transforms its relationship to its colonies from an old-fashioned imperialist control to market penetration, destroying the older village communities and creating a whole new wage-labour pool and lumpenproletariat. The militancy of the new social forces is at one and the same time a result of the 'liberation' of peasants from the older self-sustaining village communities, and a movement of self-defence, generally originating in the stabler yet more isolated areas of a given Third World country, against what is rightly perceived as a far more thoroughgoing form of penetration and colonization than the older colonial armies.

It is now in terms of this process of 'mechanization' that Mandel will make the link between the neocolonialist transformation of the Third World during the 60s and the emergence of that seemingly very different thing in the First World, variously termed consumer society, postindustrial society, media society, and the like:

> Far from representing a postindustrial society, late capitalism. . . constitutes *generalized universal industrialization* for the first time in history. Mechanization, standardization, overspecialization and parcellization of labor, which in the past determined only the realm of commodity production in actual industry, now penetrate into all sectors of social life. It is characteristic of late capitalism that agriculture is step by step becoming just as industrialized as industry, the sphere of circulation [e.g., credit cards and the like] just as much as the sphere of production, and recreation just as much as the organization of work. (p. 387)

With this last, Mandel touches on what he elsewhere calls the mechanization of the superstructure, or, in other words, the penetration of culture itself by what the Frankfurt School called the culture industry, and of which the growth of the media is only a part. We may thus generalize his description as follows: late capitalism in general (and the 60s in particular) constitute a process in which the last surviving internal and external zones of precapitalism – the last vestiges of noncommodified or traditional space within and outside the advanced world – are now ultimately penetrated and colonized in their turn. Late capitalism can therefore be described as the moment when the last vestiges of Nature which survived on into classical capitalism are at length eliminated: namely the Third World and the unconscious. The 60s will then have been the momentous transformational period when this systemic restructuring takes place on a global scale.

With such an account, our 'unified field theory' of the 60s is given: the discovery of a single process at work in First and Third Worlds, in global economy, and in consciousness and culture, a properly *dialectical* process, in which 'liberation' and domination are inextricably combined. We may now therefore proceed to a final characterization of the period as a whole.

The simplest yet most universal formulation surely remains the widely shared feeling that in the 60s, for a time, everything was possible; that this period, in other words, was a moment of a universal liberation, a global unbinding of energies. Mao Zedong's figure for this process is in this respect most revealing: 'Our nation', he cried, 'is like an atom. . . . When this atom's nucleus is smashed, the thermal energy released will have really tremendous power!'[6] The image evokes the emergence of a genuine mass democracy from the breakup of the older feudal and village structures, and from the therapeutic dissolution of the habits of those structures in cultural revolutions. Yet the effects of fission, the release of molecular energies, the unbinding of 'material signifiers', can be a properly terrifying spectacle; and we now know that Mao Zedong himself drew back from the ultimate consequences of the process he had

---

[6]Mao Zedong, *Chairman Mao Talks to the People*, ed. S. Schram (New York, 1974), pp. 92-93.

set in motion, when, at the supreme moment of the Cultural Revolution, that of the founding of the Shanghai Commune, he called a halt to the dissolution of the party apparatus and effectively reversed the direction of this collective experiment as a whole (with consequences only too obvious at the present time). In the West, also, the great explosions of the 60s have led, in the worldwide economic crisis, to powerful restorations of the social order and a renewal of the repressive power of the various state apparatuses.

Yet the forces these must now confront, contain, and control are new ones, on which the older methods do not necessarily work. We have described the 60s as a moment when the enlargement of capitalism on a global scale simultaneously produced an immense freeing or unbinding of social energies, a prodigious release of untheorized new forces: the ethnic forces of black and 'minority', or Third World, movements everywhere, regionalisms, the development of new and militant bearers of 'surplus consciousness' in the student and women's movements, as well as in a host of struggles of other kinds. Such newly released forces do not only not seem to compute in the dichotomous class model of traditional Marxism; they also seem to offer a realm of freedom and voluntarist possibility beyond the classical constraints of the economic infrastructure. Yet this sense of freedom and possibility – which is for the course of the 60s a momentarily objective reality, as well as (from the hindsight of the 80s) a historical illusion – can perhaps best be explained in terms of the superstructural movement and play enabled by the transition from one infrastructural or systemic stage of capitalism to another. The 60s were in that sense an immense and inflationary issuing of superstructural credit; a universal abandonment of the referential gold standard; an extraordinary printing up of ever more devalued signifiers. With the end of the 60s, with the world economic crisis, all the old infrastructural bills then slowly come due once more; and the 80s will be characterized by an effort, on a world scale, to proletarianize all those unbound social forces that gave the 60s their energy, by an extension of class struggle, in other words, into the farthest reaches of the globe as well as the most minute configurations of local institutions (such as the university system). The unifying force here is the new vocation of a henceforth global capitalism, which may also be expected to unify the unequal, fragmented, or local resistances to the process. And this is finally also the solution to the so-called crisis of Marxism and to the widely noted inapplicability of its forms of class analysis to the new social realities with which the 60s confronted us: 'traditional' Marxism, if 'untrue' during this period of a proliferation of new subjects of history, must necessarily become true again when the dreary realities of exploitation, extraction of surplus value, proletarianization, and the resistance to it in the form of class struggle, all slowly reassert themselves on a new and expanded world scale, as they seem currently in the process of doing.

31 Patricia Waugh,
Stalemates?: Feminists, Postmodernists and Unfinished Issues in Modern Aesthetics

George Eliot's Mr. Brooke could not have known as he reflected upon the perils of reading Adam Smith that his reservations about the benefits of a little theory would become central to many of the aesthetic debates of the late twentieth century: 'The fact is, human reason may carry you a little too far – over the hedge in fact. It carried me a good way at one time; but I saw it would not do. I pulled up; I pulled up in time. But not too hard'. Gentle deceleration is preferred, as he goes on to explain, because 'we must have Thought, else we shall be landed back in the dark ages' (*Middlemarch*, p.39).

However, reading much of the aesthetic theory arising out of the so-called 'Postmodern debate', it is difficult to avoid feeling that not only are we landed back in the dark ages but that it is the rationalisms of Enlightenment thought that have marooned us there in the first place.

Modernity, we are told, is coming to an end, strangled by its own contradictory logic, born astride of the grave which has become its own abyss. Just as Greek civilisation or the Feudal Age had come to an end and just as Nietzsche had announced the death of God a century earlier, so contemporary theorists like Foucault have announced the end of modern Western man, a face in the sand eroded by an ever encroaching sea. Yet while postmodernist thinkers (dare one say it – largely male) were proclaiming their own death (the end of humanism), feminists were in their most optimistic vein. For postmodernists, modernity might be exhausted, but for feminists it was clearly unfinished, needing to be renovated perhaps, but not abandoned.

Postmodernism was first used as a period term in the early fifties by Arnold Toynbee who announced that we were entering the fourth and final phase of Western history: one of irrationalism, anxiety and helplessness. If Modernism had tried to anchor in consciousness (that of the heroic, socially alienated artist) a centre which could no longer hold, Postmodernism had shown us an even darker side of modernity and the aporias of its aesthetic. It had shown that there is nothing for consciousness to be anchored to: no universal ground of truth, justice or reason, so that consciousness itself is thus 'decentred', no longer origin, author, location of intentional agency but a function through which impersonal forces pass and intersect – Dover beach displaced by an international airport lounge. In this context art seems to have no special role. In a world where truth is only the effect of power or rhetoric, where all interpretative models are provisional and contingent, neither the Romantic concept of poets as the unacknowledged legislators of mankind, nor the late Romantic (Freudian) concept of universal mind as a poeticising instrument, seem to carry any validity. Both concepts seemed to have been turned back on themselves in a bleak parody: if everything is fictional or textual then there can be no 'outside', no 'real', no way of saying that one act or text is better than another; no ethics, no aesthetics because existence is itself aestheticised and no ideology because no 'truth': at best provisional consensus, pragmatism, interpretative communities.

Such is the generally Apocalyptic vision of much postmodern thought. But, as Kermode had reminded us in the late sixties, if we do not have a sense of an ending, we invent one: concordances are reassuring, they produce the illusion of retrospective significance. Endings confer meaning and for all human beings, 'the End they imagine will reflect their irreducibly intermediary proccupations...we thrive on epochs' (Kermode, 1967, p.7). Could it be that Postmodernism is the Ending invented by its theorists searching for their own significance? Of what will that significance consist? Why have feminists on the whole, though registering the transitionality of the current epoch, not represented it through the same sense of an ending? Redemption through retrospective narrative significance is in itself, of course, also central to the modernist aesthetic. In that key text for Modernism, *Heart of Darkness*, when Marlow chooses to interpret Kurz's acknowledgement of 'the horror' as an heroic act,one can see in Marlow's eloquence a mirror of Kurz's own: it is the retrospective narrative rather than the experiential act which 'redeems'. But, despite the heroic adventure story quest form, redemption can, in the end, only be offered through the rhetorical structures of that same Enlightenment vocabulary which Conrad's text has exposed as corrupt and fraudulent. Nevertheless, to read this text is to feel that one remains in a state of hesitation about whether it is art or experience which redeems. Not so with postmodernism. Here , the sense of an ending has *continuously* to be revised through the endless deferral of repeated narrative reconstruction. There can be no experience outside text. History is narrative. The End is the insight that there can be no ending, no beginning, no ground and no telos. Again, however, in this world of hyperinflated discourse (Newman, 1985), one may begin to feel, indeed, that it is not the worst so long as we can say it is the worst, and thus to begin to question *whose* Apocalypse is being represented.

Which brings me to silence. And at last to feminism. Nietzsche's critique of Enlightenment modernity was basically that it had not been modern enough. He saw all its major institutions and categories of thought as redescriptions of Christianity: a slave mentality which could not confront the existence of the 'will to truth' as a form of the 'will to power' (1956, 1968). Postmodernism seems, in its renunciation of modernity, to have embraced an insistent secularism. It seems to me though that its rhetoric of Apocalypse is just as insistently religious as the modernist search for redemption through Art. Just as the narratives of Modernism search for their own self-grounded formal redemption, so too the narratives of postmodern theory seek a self-overcoming, though one outside the ultimately Aristotelian notion of form which underlies the modernist concept of formal autonomy. What alarms me as a feminist, however, is the pervasive redescription of this posibility of redemption, this space of the sacred beyond the linearity of Aristotelian form, as the space of the feminine. Kurz's Intended continues to be used as the justification for that necessary Lie which seems to offer us a Paradise regained outside the logic of modernity. Before this tendency is examined more closely, however, I wish to look briefly and more generally at the history of the relations between feminism and Postmodernism.

Modernity, Postmodernism and Feminism

Feminism as a discourse clearly arises out of modernity and its models of reason, justice and subjectivity. Feminism, however, has also been one of the discourses which has with similar clarity revealed some of the most entrenched and disguised contradictions and limitations of Enlightenment thought. To this extent, it can be seen as intrinsically post-modern, if problematically so. Yet, until very recently, the debates within Postmodernism have tended to ignore those taking place within feminist discourse, and vice versa. Things have begun to change. Feminist theory has developed a self-conscious awareness of its own hermeneutic perspectivism based on the recognition of a central contradiction in its attempts to define an epistemology: that women seek equality and valorisation for a gendered identity which has been constructed through the very culture and ideology that feminism seeks to challenge. In fact, one can see such contradictions manifesting themselves as early as 1971 in Kristeva's essay 'Women's Time'. The concept of a 'women's identity' functions in terms both of affirmation and negation, even within feminism itself. There can be no simple legitimation for feminists in throwing off a 'false consciousness' and revealing a true 'female self'. To embrace 'difference' in essentialist terms is to come dangerously close to reproducing that very patriarchal construction of gender which feminists have set out to contest.

Feminism of late, therefore, has developed a self-reflexive mode: questioning its own legitimating procedures in a manner which seems to bring it close to a Postmodernism which has absorbed the lessons of post-structuralism and consists at the most general level of a crisis of legitimation across culture, politics and aesthetic theory and practice. The slogan 'Let us wage war on totality', however, could be seen as Postmodernism's response to that earlier slogan of the feminist movement, 'The personal is the political'. But if the latter can be seen as a rallying cry, the former implies a hostile attitude towards its implicit ideals of collectivism and community. In fact the feminist cry situated its politics firmly within what Lyotard wishes to denounce and what Jürgen Habermas calls the 'project of modernity' (1987). It will be my argument that even if feminists have come to recognise in their own discourses some of the epistemological doubt and perspectivism that afflicts Postmodernism, feminism must still continue to define itself as an emancipatory movement broadly within the terms of the aforementioned project. Is it possible for feminists to draw on the aesthetics of Postmodernism as strategies for narrative disruption without embracing its nihilistic pragmatism? Surely to assume otherwise is in itself to embrace a naively reflectionist aesthetic which sees representation necessarily reflective of prior structures or ideologies. Can feminists occupy a position of hermeneutic perspectivism which questions epistemology without, therefore, relinquishing ethics in an embrace of hermeneutic anarchism where no discourse is seen as more valid than any other, simply more useful at a particular time or place? Can feminism remain opposed to Postmodernism's circular tendency to project itself onto the contemporary world and thus, not surprisingly, to find in that world an affirmation of its own theoretical presuppositions? Can it in other words continue to resist the implicitly religious terminology of the Postmodern sense of an Ending while recognising the force of its critique of epistemology?

One way of approaching these issues is to think about the implications of the various models of subjectivity with which feminists and postmodernists have worked. What the preceding discussion has suggested is that the epistemological and ethical contradictions now confronting both of them are fundamentally issues about identity and difference. Subjective transformation has been central to feminist agendas for political change. Similarly, over the last thirty years, the deconstruction of liberal individualism and the dissolution of traditional aesthetic conceptualisations of character have been central to postmodern art and theory. Like feminism, Postmodernism has been engaged in a re-examination of the Enlightenment concepts of subjectivity, truth and reason enshrined in the belief that human beings are collectively engaged in a progressive movement towards moral and intellectual self-realisation through the application to their situation of a universal rational faculty.

Personal freedom or autonomy in these terms has been defined as freedom from the irrational forces within and the social forces without. Freud's work has been seen as axiomatic for the former and the work of

Marx for the latter. The focus of much postmodern theory has been to dismantle the basic assumptions of their writing to lay bare an epistemology and methodology which, it is argued, is at one with an oppressive and authoritarian rationalism which has produced terror in place of emancipation and disguised its will to power as a disinterested 'scientific' desire for truth. The self-determining subject has had a similarly difficult time of it in postmodern fiction. Such fictions are often enactments of the frustration of attempting to find correspondences to their linguistic condition outside of language itself. In Robert Coover's 'Panel Game', he parodies the attempt to find an all-encompassing truth in language by showing the narrator caught up in a maze of the myriad possibilities of meaning, of *paroles* with no discoverable *langues*, while all the possible formal functions of language – emotive, referential, poetic, conative, phatic and finally, metalingual – whirl about him: 'So think. Stickleback. Freshwaterfish. Freshwaterfish: green seaman. Seaman: semen. Yes, but green : raw? spoiled? vigorous? Stickle: stubble. Or maybe scruple. Back: Bach: Bachus: Bachate: berry. Rawberry? Strawberry.' (1969, p.63). Through the emphasis on the arbitrary associations of sound, rhyme and image, attention is drawn to the formal organisation of language and away from its referential potential. The quotation could almost be an exercise in Jakobsonian linguistics as the internal operations of language produce that poetic equivalence which endlessly substitutes one arbitrary phoneme for another: Stickleback. Freshwaterfish (metonymic). Freshwaterfish : green seaman (metonymic/metaphoric) seaman : semen (metaphoric).

In Donald Barthelme's fictions abstract nouns and passive constructions almost entirely replace personal assertion or human agency. The story 'Brain Damage' (1971) begins: 'At the restaurant, sadness was expressed'; moods are reflexes of disembodied signifiers rather than of personal feeling. Endless lists, catalogues, insistent stylisation flaunt the materiality of writing as depthlessness, again seem to present a self-conscious articulation of the rules of selection and combination in grammar, an endless play of linguistic substitution for its own sake; metaphors proliferate, syntax continuously breaks down. The reader is offered sentences such as : 'The world is sagging, snagging, scaling, spalling, pulling, pinging, pitting, warping, checking, fading, chipping, cracking, yellowing, leaking, staling, shrinking and in dynamic unbalance' (1974, p.6). Certainly this sentence is, for as the material world shrinks, the linguistic one expands and it is the materiality of language again, what Jameson has characterized (1985) as the schizophrenic present of postmodernism, which is obsessively foregrounded.

Barthelme's sentence, of course, enacts entropy, another postmodern image of Apocalypse. I think Jameson is quite correct, however, in the essay mentioned above, to connect the 'schizophrenic' tendency in Postmodernism with a pervasive nostalgia. It is worth thinking about this in relation to feminism. It seems to me that much postmodernist writing is pervaded by a nihilism produced through nostalgia (Nietzsche is one of several thinkers who have connected these impulses). Often in such texts the possibility of humanist affirmation is destroyed by an insistent and excessive but familiar enough Romantic desire to rediscover a transcendent metaphysical truth, an essence of Being, whose impossible realization produces the urge to render absurd or to destroy altogether what can be: the human subject as an ethical, affective and effective historical agent.

In Pynchon's *V*, for example, V functions as both goal and negation of Stencil's quest for transcendent meaning and is pictured thus:

> skin radiant with the bloom of some new plastic; both eyes glass but now containing some photoelectric cells, connected by silver electrodes to optic nerves of purest copper wire leading to a brain exquisitely wrought as a diode matrix ever could be. Soleroid relays would be her ganglia, serio-actuators move her flawless nylon limbs, hydraulic fluid be sent by a platinum heart-pump through buthyrane veins and arteries. (1979, p.406)

For those who wish to equate 'totality' with totalitarianism (as Lyotard at times) or to conflate linguistic or textual with political subversion, then such postmodern strategies, which appear to dissolve humanist subjectivity into textual play, have been hailed as the only means of resisting the oppressive structures of global capitalism, of patriarchal surveillance and control of the pleasure principle. They are seen as part of the assault on the bondage of thought to regulative ideals such as 'truth' and 'goodness'. In response, one might point out some obvious difficulties here: why is V a woman, and surely it matters that Nietzsche insisted that such regulative ideals were tied to what he saw as phallic castration, an emasculation of the intellect he associated with all emancipatory movements, particularly feminism. The idea of truth as untruth has repeatedly been articulated through the image of the seductive woman, a Salome who is only her veils, whose adornments disguise a gaping absence. She continues to appear with monotonous frequency in the metaphorical femininity of postmodern writing. This grotesque version of the wearisome metaphor, for example, appears in Nietzsche's *My Sister and I*: 'Truth is still elusive. However, she is no longer a young girl but an old bitch with all her front teeth missing' (p.114). Before examining in more depth what such rhetoric means for actual women, whether, indeed, Pynchon's V assaults the oppressive structures of Late Capitalism for women, in particular, we need first to look at the historical and philosophical foundations of postmodernist and feminist aesthetics and to see whether it is indeed possible to move beyond the position of stalemate.

Founding Assumptions: Feminism and Postmodernism

Fredric Jameson has suggested that postmodernism's most radical insight may be seen as the view that the bourgeois individual subject is not only a thing of the past but also a myth. We have never possessed this sort of autonomy: 'Rather this construct is merely a philosophical and cultural mystification which sought to persuade people that they had individual subjects and possessed this unique personal identity' (1985, p.115). If the subject is a myth and if narrative as the reflection of the grand 'master plot' of history is a redundant illusion, why should I have the feeling, as I read much postmodernist writing, that its apocalyptic nihilism about the possibility of ethical and imaginative subjective existence is grounded in that very nostalgia of which I spoke earlier? A nostalgia for an ideal autonomous self. Nostalgia involves the projection of the self onto history through identification. It rewrites history in the terms of desire, for to see the past as past is to recognize one's own mortality and temporality, fundamentally to disturb one's sense of presence. Nostalgia is the desire to recover the past as Paradise, as a myth of origins. Identification, however, necessitates ideal images with which to identify. It seems to me that feminists are highly unlikely to bear this sort of relationship to history or to the ideal autonomous self central to the discourses of modernity. Those who have been excluded from the constitution of that so-called 'universal subject' – whether for reasons of gender, class, race, sexuality – are unlikely either to long nostalgically for what they have never experienced or possessed or to revel in the 'jouissance' of its disintegration. Never having experienced it as an ethical ideal which might be materially realized they are unlikely therefore to fall into nihilistic Apocalypticism at the recognition it may simply not be realizable at all in its pure or original form.

They will be more likely surely to want to occupy its position and to be able to offer a critique from both within and outside of it. In my view, the decentred and fragmented subject of much postmodernist writing is one whose existence is premised upon the disintegration of a pre-existing belief in the possibility of realizing the full autonomous subject of Enlightenment rhetoric, of German idealist philosophy and Kantian aesthetics. It is present at least as a structure of feeling if not fully articulated. It is clear from recent feminist scholarship that most women are unlikely to have experienced history in this way. Thus the goals of agency, autonomy and self-determination are not ones which feminists have taken for granted or glibly seen as exhausted. They are ideals which feminism has helped to reformulate, modify and challenge. Feminism needs a subject and it seems to me it has found a means of articulating it which both avoids the fetishization of Pure Reason as the locus of subjecthood and the irrationalism born out of the perceived failure of this ideal.

Alternative Histories

As part of our current experience, of the impossibility ultimately of separating knowledge from experience (which both Postmodernism and feminism have taught us), it is difficult to talk about 'origins' in relation to either. Postmodernism is a notoriously unstable concept, whether used in the more narrow aesthetic sense or the wider philosophical or sociological one. It entered American criticism in the fifties in Charles Olson's attempt to define the existence of a new non-anthropocentric poetry whose Heideggerian anti-humanism was directed at seeing 'man' as in the world, an object among objects. The same tendency can be detected at around the same time in the French New Novel and its theorization in the writings of Robbe-Grillet and in Susan Sontag's rejection of a hermeneutic depth/surface model of interpretation for a return to the sensual surface, an 'erotics' of literature. John Barth talked of abandoning the literature of exhaustion for the essentially parodic literature of replenishment, Leslie Fiedler of a new art which would bridge the gap between high and mass culture. For both Sontag and Ihab Hassan, in particular, postmodernism, an art of the surface, was the contemporary period's answer to Adorno's 'negative aesthetics' of Modernism: an art which in making itself opaque and difficult would refuse consumption even as it partook of a culture of consumption. By the early eighties, however, the term shifts from one used to describe a range of aesthetic practices involving playful irony, parody, self-consciousness, fragmentation, to one which encompasses a more general shift in thought and seems to register a pervasive cynicism about the progressivist ideals of modernity and a sense of a new cultural epoch in which distinctions between critical and functional knowledge break down and in which capitalism in its last and most insidious phase invades everything, leaving no oppositional space outside itself. Just as many novels of the seventies had displayed the hidden processes of artistic production, so too post-structuralist thought now proceeded by exposing the concealed rhetorical mechanisms which both produce and subvert conceptual meaning. Both undermine classical conceptions of representation in which truth precedes or determines the representations which either communicate it directly or mediate it indirectly. Potmodernism had gradually become a phrase describing a whole new 'episteme' of Western culture.

None of this says or said much about gender or feminism. In fact, as I mentioned earlier, although postmodern theory increasingly draws on a highly idealized and generalized notion of femininity as 'other' in its search for a space outside of the disintegrating logic of modernity, it rarely talks about (or to, one suspects) actual women or about feminism as a political practice. Yet there are obvious historical points of contact: both attacked the Romantic-Modernist cultivation of the Aesthetic as an autonomous realm, both assault Enlightenment discourses which universalize white, Western, middle-class male experience. Both recognize the need for a new ethics. Fundamentally each has offered critiques of foundationalist thinking to produce the recognition that gender is not a consequence of anatomy just as social institutions do not so much reflect universal truths as construct historical and provisional ones. Postmodernism is 'grounded' in the epistemological problematiz-ation of grounding itself, of the idea of identity as absolute or truth as essential. In terms of aesthetic practice, writers like Barth or Borges foreground epistemological and ontological questions about the con-struction of the 'real' and the 'self' by playing metafictionally on the textual paradox of the book as artefact and the book as world. Others, such as Rushdie, foreground the paradox of history as both a series of events which happened and also the imposition of a retrospective, paradigmatic and provisional linguistic structure which is itself the product of its own historical situation conceived of as an interplay of textual paradigms...ad infinitum. Postmodern writing may, indeed, proceed from this critique of foundationalism to social or political critique. In Salman Rushdie's *Shame*, for example, the intervention of alternative narrative voices is used as part of a critique of regimes of 'truth' as effects of power. As a strategy for dismantling oppressive concepts of truth, such narrative perspectivism is highly effective, but in a text where all positions are seen to be effects of rhetoric, the possibility of an oppositional space is also dismantled.

Feminism has also, of course, provided its own critique of essentialist and foundationalist assumptions. Arguably, though, however it draws upon postmodern narrative strategies, it cannot repudiate entirely the framework of Enlightened modernity without perhaps fatally under-mining itself as an emancipatory politics. In proceeding through the demands of political practice, feminism must posit some belief in the notion of effective human agency, the necessity for historical continuity in formulating identity and a belief in historical progress. Even if people are shaped by historical forces, they are not simply reflexive epi-phenomena of impersonal deep structures or of a global agonistics of circulating and competing language games. Feminism must believe in the possibility of a community of address situated in an oppositional space which can allow for the connection of the 'small personal voice' (Doris Lessing's term) of one feminist to another and to other liberationist movements. One writer producing personal confessional novels about 'women's identity' can then be seen to connect with the activity of another woman rewriting the history of slavery or one camped on the mud of Greenham Common, even as they accept and recognize each other's differences.

Glancing through the various postmodernisms, in fact, one can see how the range of conceptualizations of difference has entered feminist theory and aesthetic practice. An invigorating imaginative playfulness has appeared in recent feminist writing. Too often though political claims are made for avant-garde formal disruption which are difficult to justify. Ironically one can again see a reflectionist aesthetics at work here which sees one form of disruption simply reflecting another sort. Concepts are transferred unproblematically from the context of aesthetic to political practice with no analysis of the sort of problems mentioned above. Surely feminists should keep in mind the centrality to his work of Lyotard's assertion that emancipatory discourses are no longer possible because there can no longer be a belief in privileged metadiscourses which transcend local and contingent conditions in order to ground the 'truths' of all first order discourses (1984). According to this view, gender can only be seen as positional, shifting, and cannot be used cross-culturally to explain the practices of human societies. In one sense this is the state of affairs feminism is aiming for in the ideal society it imagines to be possible. It should not, however, mean that feminists should abandon their struggle against sexual oppression because 'gender' as a metanarrative is necessarily a repressive enactment of metaphysical authority. Lyotard unnecessarily conflates the concept of totality with that of totalitarianism. Feminists should remember that 'totalities', political unity, need not mean uniformity, that they can be enabling and liberating.

The postmodern concept of language games, dissensus and dispersal, developed by Lyotard's reading of Wittgenstein, has again often been naively appropriated by an avant-garde desire to conflate linguistic or textual disruption with political subversion and to claim a massive political significance for formally innovative writing, modernist and postmodernist. Feminists such as Kristeva have done as much as postmodernists like Lyotard to popularize this concept. It is here that the dangerous metaphor of 'femininity' as 'otherness' is most apparent in what seems to me to be the reproduction of a masculine space of the sacred which continues to be dependent upon concepts which deny the *material* existence of actual women. From Nietzsche through Hassan and Lacan, femininity has been used to signify an 'otherness' which has effectively been essentialized as the disruption of the legitimate (viewed as everything from the logic of the Law of the Father – the psychoanalytic version of God – to the Logocentric). This 'otherness' has itself been variously expressed as the repressed other, the hysterical body, the semiotic, the pre-oedipal, ecstatic, fluid, the maternal body. Women, however, have no privileged access to it, though several male avant-garde writers can speak it. In fact, as often as not this celebration of difference goes hand in hand with an amazing indifference to the material and psychological circumstances of actual women. The postmodern espousal of psychotextual 'decentring' as liberatory says little about women as beings in the world who continue to find themselves displaced and invisible even within a critique of epistemology which has supposedly, in deconstructing the centre, therefore done away with the margins. The idea of alterity as feminine can be seen as the attempt to name a space outside the rationalizing logic of modernity – a new space of the sacred? As in most religious discourses, it promises a non-linear space outside the sense of ending, a space of redemption beyond time, language, fixity. Within postmodern psychoanalytic theory it has been described as 'the body without organs' (the small boy's view of the mother?), 'becoming woman' (the male fantasy of plenitude) and the 'hysterical body' (the female object through which psychoanalysis first arrived at its definition of the implicitly masculine subject) (see Jardine 1985). It seems that as postmodernists obsessively register their sense of the collapsing legitimacy of the frameworks of Western knowledge, they are also registering unconsciously and metaphorically a fear specifically of the loss of the legitimacy of Western *patriarchal* grand narratives, a new form of fear of women, in effect. As always, appropriation becomes one of the means of dealing with this. Is it a coincidence that at the very historical moment when (male) postmodernists intensify their interest in (and master through their own discourses) a (religious) space described as the 'feminine' and nothing to do with actual women, feminists are establishing an (Enlightened modern) sense of their coherent identity as women through the very categories and discourses which postmodernists claim to have dismantled and done away with in the name of this 'femininity'. Surely this has an ominously familiar ring to it? Could one see the oppressed (women) returning in the form of the repressed (femininity) in postmodern discourse only to be worked through and mastered yet again in the language of theory?

If femininity has become, once more, a metaphor for a state beyond metaphysics, feminists should be certain that its tenor is not simply the contemporary theoretical counterpart to the Victorian parlour. If they have any suspicions then they should continue to hammer through its boundaries, those between public and private, in an assertion of their continued belief in their own capacity for agency and historical reconstruction. If Barthes writes a pseudo-autobiography to articulate the idea that 'to write an essay on oneself may seem a pretentious idea, but it is a simple idea, simple as the idea of suicide' (1977, p.56), feminists should remind themselves that the shelves of books by Barthes in libraries all over the world proclaims a confidence in his authorship even as he disclaims it. They should not be surprised then that so many women writers in the seventies articulated a desire to become 'authors of their own lives' at precisely the moment that Barthes was announcing the death of that concept. Whose death?

Jean Baudrillard's work, it seems to me, is even more problematic for feminism. For him postmodernity signifies the state of contemporary culture which exists as a simulacrum of signs where the information age has utterly dissolved identity through reflections to maskings, to complete absence. In this perspective all that literature can do is to play off 'alternative worlds' in a state of pluralistic anarchy where the subject is simply a simulating machine of commercial images, the mass a silent majority and the very idea of resistance, an absurdity. Simulation replaces imagination and human beings are left with no capacity to reshape their world even in their own heads. They act like the characters in Robert Coover's novel *Gerald's Party* (1986), as dense points of transmission for all the cop and thriller and porn movies which construct their desires and which churn out incessantly throughout this text in an orgy of hedonistic sensationalism. It may be that Coover is using the parodic mode of the postmodern to offer a critique of postmodernity from within its own codes, but again one is left with the claustrophobic sense that there can be no real opposition to it because there is no place outside. In most versions of the postmodern, in fact, any claim to a substantive reality outside representation, is discredited: if signs determine reality, there can be no opposition because no space which is not already reproduced.

One difficulty in discussing Postmodernism is that the apocalypticism of the theory may have unduly affected our response to the fictional artefacts (if I may be so old-fashioned as to hang onto such a distinction). It seems to me this is an important distinction to hang onto, because it is evident that many women writers are using postmodern aesthetic strategies of disruption to re-imagine the world in which we live, while resisting the nihilistic implications of the theory. Certainly one can see the writing of Angela Carter, Jeanette Winterson, Margaret Atwood, Maggie Gee, Fay Weldon, to name but a few, in this way. This is perhaps not so very surprising since women have always experienced themselves in a 'postmodern' fashion – decentred, lacking agency, defined through others. Which is why, it seems to me, they had to attempt to occupy the centre in the early seventies. It is why women began to seek a subjective sense of agency and collective identity within the terms of the discourses of modernity at precisely the moment when postmodernists were engaged in the repudiation of such discourses, proclaiming the 'death of the author' and the end of humanism. Much feminist fiction of this period, therefore, was either confessional or concerned with the idea of discovering an authentic identity. If its philosophical roots are clearly anywhere it is in existentialism rather than post-structuralism. It may now appear to be philosophically naive and formally unadventurous, espousing an uncontested aesthetics of expressive realism or a simple reversal of the romance quest plot which did little to problematize ideologies of romantic love or essential identity. I have argued that perhaps feminist writers needed to formulate a sense of identity , history and agency within these terms before they could begin to deconstruct them. However, feminist writers did not subsequently rush off to embrace the postmodern – indeed they have largely maintained a cautious distance, certainly from much of the theory . This is where I shall declare my own distance as a feminist in offering some 'grand and totalizing' narratives which allow us to think of subjectivity in ways which neither simply repeat the Enlightenment concept of modernity nor repudiate it in an embrace of anarchic dispersal.

Rethinking Subjectivity and Aesthetics: Alternative Feminist Positions

I want to suggest, somewhat tentatively, that despite differences in the theoretical construction of modernity and postmodernity, common to them both is the inheritance of a particular ideal of subjectivity defined in terms of transcendence and pure rationality. Postmodernism can be seen as a response to the perceived failure of this ideal. This notion of subjectivity, whether expressed through Descartes' rational 'I' and refined into Kant's categorical imperatives, or through Nietzsche's 'übermensch' or Lacan's phallogocentric symbolic order, has not only excluded women but has made their exclusion on the grounds of emotionality, failure of abstract intellect or whatever, the basis of its own identity. This position has been reproduced across philosophy, psychoanalysis and literature. In viewing this situation as fundamentally unchanged, I am, in effect, repudiating the postmodern notion that there are no longer any generally legitimated metanarratives. What I am saying is that patriarchal metanarratives function just as effectively within our so-called 'postmodern age' as in any other age and in its metaphorical play on notions of the feminine they continue insidiously to function powerfully within postmodern theory itself.

Jameson has diagnosed postmodernism as the schizophrenic condition of late capitalism, but I would argue that the autonomous transcendent self of German idealism, Enlightenment humanism, European Romanticism and realist aesthetics and the impersonally fragmented self of Postmodernism are a product of the same cultural tradition. Schizophrenia is clinically defined as a splitting of thought and feeling: the 'schizophrenia' of Postmodernism can be seen as a fin-de-siècle parody or caricature of a dualism inherent in the Western tradition of thought where the self is defined as a transcendent rationality which necessitates splitting off what is considered to be the irrational, emotion, and projecting it as the 'feminine' onto actual women. It is to see T.S. Eliot's 'dissociation of sensibility' from a feminist rather than a High Tory position. Freud, of course, has taught us that reason and feeling are inextricably bound up with each other, but even he believed that ego could and should master id, that impersonal reason is the basis of personal autonomy. Increasingly in this century, such a contracted 'rational' self cannot make sense of the world:

whether in the fictions of Kafka or Bellow, for example, or in the aetiolated dramas of Samuel Beckett. When transcendence fails, however, the threat of disorder is seen to come from the split off (and therefore uncontrollable) aspects of the psyche, the non-rational projected onto and thus defining women, racial minorities, so-called 'sexual deviants' or even 'the masses'.

Postmodernism may seek to locate the possibility of disruption or 'jouissance' in this space, but in continuing to regard it as 'feminine', whether it speaks of actual women or not, then it simply continues the process of projection and does little to overcome the dualism and psychological defensiveness inherent in it. Often in postmodernist fiction, for example, traditional images of the castrating female, the unknown and therefore uncontrollable woman, are overlaid in a technological age with their representation as machines which have outstripped the controlled and rational dominance of the male (one thinks of V again). The 'emotionality' thus projected onto the feminine or onto women in order to retain rationality and autonomy as the core of masculine identity produces both images of woman as the 'other' of romantic desire and woman who, thus beyond control, threatens annihilation or incorporation. If feminists wish to argue a politics of femininity as avant-garde disruptive desire they should first think about some of the meanings of, for example, V or Nurse Ratched.

In fact, in both modernist and postmodernist writing, when order conceived of as a circumscribed rationality seems no longer to cohere in either the self or in history, then it is projected onto the impersonal structures of language or of history conceived of as myth, a static and synchronic space. Despite the new 'perspectivism' which enters literary history in the early part of the century, the potential for the re-evaluation of the relations between subjectivity and objectivity, so many of the aesthetic manifestoes of the time and later critical accounts of the period emphasize 'impersonality', 'autonomy', 'objectivity', 'universal 'significant form', 'spatial form', 'objective correlative' – even when many of the artefacts, such as *Ulysses*, clearly problematize such notions. The New Critical theorization of literature, in particular the modernist text, as an autonomous linguistic structure, reinforced this. Since then the increasing professionalization of literature has extended this: defamiliarization, systems of signs, the death of the author, the free play of the signifier, simulations...

One can see in much modernist literature both the attempted assertion and the failure of Enlightened modernity's ideal of autonomy. The belief in absolute self-determination, whether that of Stephen Dedalus or Mr. Ramsay, is always discovered to be dependent on the desires of others. Whereas a transcendent being could anchor desire as absolute, to express it in relation to others is always seen to produce delusion, deception, jealousy, a whole variety of epistemological crises which modernist texts explore. The possibility of Art itself as an absolute autonomous realm, however, often comes to take the place of the sacred here. Art, as religion, seems to offer precisely that illusion of utter self-determination and transcendence which relations with other mortals must always shatter. It is interesting how many of the male heroes of modernist literature achieve an apparent self-determination in aesthetic terms through a refusal of social relationship. Hence the figure of the alienated artist who affirms his own autonomy, his independence from the mediation of others at the price of the cessation of human relationship and desire: Marcel writing in his room, Ralph Touchett vicariously living through Isabel, Malone talking to himself, Mann's Leverkühn, Hesse's Steppenwolf. Art as the impersonal focus for desire displaces the possibility of human relationship because it involves no mediation through the desire of the other. Hovering behind these texts is Nietzsche's self-creating and self-affirming artist for whom to recognize the other would be to fall into a slave mentality.

In my view it is the identification of self with an impossible ideal of autonomy which can be seen to produce the failure of love and relationship in so many texts by male modernist and postmodernist writers. Can one rethink the self outside of this concept without abandoning subjectivity to dispersal and language games? Not only do I believe that one can, I also believe that many feminist writers have done so. This is the really 'grand and totalizing' part of my argument. It seems to me that autonomy defined as transcendence, impersonality and absolute independence, whether an idealized goal or a nostalgic nihilism, whether informing the aesthetics of Modernism or those of Postmodernism, is not a mode with which most feminists, nor indeed, most women, can very easily identify. Feminist theory, though drawing on anti-humanist discourses to sharpen its understanding of social processes, has emphasised that 'impersonal' historical determinants are lived out through experience. This distance from anti-humanist discourse has allowed feminist academics to connect with grass roots activists outside the academy. Their own historical experience has tended to develop in women strongly 'humanist' qualities in the broader sense of the term and feminism has always been rooted in women's subjective experience of the conflicting demands of home and work, family and domestic ties and the wider society.

Psychoanalysis, Gender and Aesthetics

Jürgen Habermas has recently suggested that modernity is not exhausted, simply unfinished. His view of this is not incompatible with some of the ideas I am trying to develop here. What he has argued is that instead of abandoning its ideals we need to modify them by redefining the model of Reason which underlies them. His work is part of a tradition of critical thinking which sees Enlightenment reason failing because defined too narrowly in the terms of an instrumental, purposive or utilitarian epistemology. He proposes instead a model of what he calls 'communicative reason', based on speech act theory and emphasizing not individual autonomy but intersubjectivity (1987). Like so many theorists within the postmodern debate, however, he seems singularly unaware of many of the developments in feminist thinking over the last twenty years. It seems to me that many feminists have been working for some time with models which are not fundamentally incompatible with Habermas's whether or not they have used them in specifically theoretical ways. I will now examine some of these ideas and suggest that through them it is possible to arrive not only at an alternative definition of the aesthetic but also of subjectivity itself.

According to most psychoanalytic theories and their popularly disseminated forms, subjecthood is understood as the achievement of separation. Maturity is seen to be reached when the dependent infant comes to regard its primary caretaker (nearly always a woman) as simply an object through which it defines its own identity and position in the world. This is then maintained through the defensive patrolling of boundaries. Implicit then in most theories of identity is the assumption that the 'otherness' analyzed by feminists from de Beauvoir on, is the necessary condition of women – certainly as long as women mother. Separation and objectivity rather than relationship and connection become the markers of identity. Freudian theory has been used to support this view. Both the liberal self and the postmodern 'decentred subject' can be articulated through Freud's notion of the unconscious, dominated by instinctual and universal drives seeking impossible gratification. In the liberal version, ego as rationality can master the drives either intrapsychically or with the help of the silent, impersonal and objective analyst who will be uncontaminated by countertransference. In the postmodern version, rationality breaks down and the anarchy of desire as impersonal and unconscious energy is unleashed either in the freeplay of the signifier of the avant-garde text or that of the marketplace of Late Capitalism. Freud's infant hovers behind both: an autoerotic isolate, inherently aggressive and competitive, its sexuality and identity oedipally resolved only by fear, seeking to discharge libidinal energy which is necessarily in conflict with 'rational' and 'enlightened' concern for others and for society as a whole.

Can we imagine alternative models of subjectivity? If knowledge is inextricably bound up with experience then it seems that we certainly can, for this is not a description of universal experience. In fact Freud himself hints at other possibilities in less familiar parts of his writings. In the paper 'On Narcissism', for example, he says: 'A strong egotism is a protection against falling ill, but in the last resort we must begin to love in order not to fall ill and we are bound to fall ill if in consequence of frustration, we are unable to love' (1914, p.85). In fact, in the development of selfhood, the ability to conceive of oneself as separate from and mutually independent with the parent develops with the ability to accept one's dependency and to feel secure enough to relax the boundaries between self and other without feeling one's identity to be threatened. Why, then, is autonomy always emphasized as the goal of maturity? Why not emphasize equally the importance of maintaining connection and intersubjectivity? As Joan Rivière has argued 'There is no such thing as a single human being pure and simple, unmixed with other human beings ...we are members one of another' (1986). Parts of other people, the parts we have had relationships with, are parts of us, so the self is both constant and fluid, ever in exchange, ever redescribing itself through its encounters with others. It seems to be this recognition of mediation as that which renders total self-determination impossible which so many male modernist and postmodernist writers find unacceptable. Yet much women's, particularly feminist, writing has been different in that it has neither attempted to transcend relationship through the impersonal embrace of Art as formal autonomy or sacred space nor through rewriting its own Apocalyptic sense of an ending.

Returning to psychoanalysis, however, one can see some of the reasons why the definition of subjectivity as transcendence and autonomy has been so powerful and why it has come to be seen not as a description of the experience of most white, Western males, but of universal structures of subjectivity. In psychoanalytic terms, if subjectivity is defined as separateness, its acquisition will involve radical disidentification with women in a society where women are normally the exclusive caretakers of children. This will be true even for girls who, at the level of gender, will also seek to identify with the mother. Fathers are not perceived as threatening non-identity for in classical analysis they are seen as outside the pre-oedipal world of primary socialization with its intense ambivalences and powerful Imagos. They are from the start associated with the clear, rational world of work and secondary socialization. Object relations theorists like Nancy Chodorow (1978), however, have pointed out that the desire for radical disidentification with the mother will be more acute for boys for the perception of women as mothers will be bound up with pre-oedipal issues of mergence and potential loss of identity requiring a culturally reinforced masculine investment in denial and separation. The world of secondary socialization associated with the father comes to be seen as superior and as inherently male. Subjectivity thus comes to be seen as autonomy or as role-definition through work. Truth is defined as objectivity and transcendence. Science in the form of an instrumental technology will be overvalued and defined in terms of objectivity; philosophy comes to deal only with universal and metaphysical truths (whatever the theoretical challenges to these notions). Women (or the 'feminine') come to be identified in Cartesian or post-structuralist philosophy with all that cannot be rationally controlled and thus threatening dissolution or non-identity: mortality, the body, desire, emotionality, nature. Post-structuralist 'femininity' is simply another way of making actual femininity safe, of controlling through a process of naming which in post-structuralist fashion prises the term utterly away from the anatomical body of woman.

If the female sex thus represents, in Sartre's words 'the obscenity...of everything which gapes open' (1985), then men seem to be justified in their instrumental attitude to women and to everything, including nature, which has been 'feminized' and which must therefore be distanced, controlled, aestheticized, subdued (one might call this the Gilbert Osmond syndrome). Women appear threatening in this way because they carry the culture's more widespread fear of the loss of boundaries, of the uncontrollable, more threatening because unconsciously split off in order to retain the purity of a subjectivity, a humanness defined as autonomy, pure reason and transcendence. Cartesian dualism thus persists along with strict empiricism in science and impersonality and formalism in literary theory and criticism.

If women's identity is broadly speaking, and allowing for a range of differences, experienced in terms which do not necessarily valorize separation at the expense of connection, one would expect some expression of this in fictional writing as well as in theory. Women's sense of ego is more likely, for psychological and cultural reasons, to consist of a more diffuse sense of the boundaries of self and their notion of identity understood in relational and intersubjective terms. Virginia Woolf has been so important for feminist literary criticism because both formally and thematically her work articulates a critique of patriarchal institutions through its exploration of the relatedness of subjects and of subjects and objects. Beyond this, however, she simultaneously offers a critique of the exclusive identification of women with relationality through an exploration of its negative effects in characters like Mrs. Dalloway and Mrs. Ramsay. For relationality as the basis of identity in a society where women are perceived as culturally inferior, has often functioned to reinforce their desire to please, to serve others and seek definition through them, internalizing masochistically any anger about this as a failure of (essential) femininity. We are back, therefore, to the contradiction at the heart of feminism expressed at the beginning of this essay: that women have sought recognition for a concept of identity which they simultaneously attempt to change, viewing it as a construction of patriarchy. The formal and thematic expression of identity as mutually defined, the centrality of primary affectional relationships need not, however, be experienced in pathological ways, and, indeed, as writers like Alice Walker, Doris Lessing and Toni Morrison have recently shown us, are essential for the survival of the human race.

Freud emphasized that the development of the ego is the work of culture. If that culture's ideal of selfhood is that of an impersonal, contained rationality, then it seems to me that culture can only produce incomplete and divided human beings. Postmodern beings.

Much feminist writing has, over the last thirty years, explored modes of relational identity, often, indeed, also drawing on postmodern ideas about 'situatedness' or using its techniques of parody, irony, playfulness. Such a relational understanding of identity makes possible, ethically and imaginatively, a new, negative capability which can transform both the Enlightened discourses of emancipation as well as those of subjectivity. A writer whose work is particularly important in this respect, for example, is Doris Lessing. In her novel *Memoirs of a Survivor* (1976), she explores how Utopian impulses fail because they are still tied to a model of human subjectivity based on autonomy, separateness and overvaluation of a particular definition of rationality. The narrator, struggling to preserve an order within her psyche which has disappeared from the world outside, finds herself drawn towards a perception of the fundamental interdependence of human beings, of the persistence in us of an elemental hunger, the need to be fed – the novel abounds with images of eating and orality – to give food and to receive it, which binds us physically and psychologically to one another. She reflects:

> As for our thoughts, our intellectual apparatus, our rationalisms and our deductions, our logics and so on, it can be said with absolute certainty that dogs and cats and monkeys cannot make a rocket or fly to the moon or weave artificial dress materials out of the by-products of petroleum, but as we sit in the ruins of this variety of intelligence it is hard to give it much value. (p.74)

The most frightening aspect of the 'now' of this novel is that its children of violence, the wild, anarchic, semi-humans born out of upheaval and brutality, out of the failures of over-rationalized logic and the denial of human relational need, can no longer recognize their own or other's needs, cannot nurture each other and have, literally, turned cannibal and are consuming each other. For Lessing, salvation can only come through a profound and full recognition of our relational being, which means trying to imagine a world not constructed as an extension of a model of self as isolated, competitive ego nor one where ethics is reduced to nihilistic performance. She may use the formal modes of postmodern art but to articulate an imaginative world which is very far from those which emerge in most postmodern theory. Lessing's novel is apocalyptic in the sense that it is set after a holocaust, but it does not proclaim either the end of modernity nor the end of hope. We can compare this with, for example, Kroker's vision of postmodernity as a 'dead space which will be marked by increasing and random outbursts of political violence, schizoid behaviour and the implosion of all signs of communication, as Western culture runs down toward the brilliant illumination of a final burn out' (1988, p. xvii). If Lessing's 'small personal voice' is heard only as a whisper, it seems to me it can, drawing on postmodern *aesthetic* forms, speak to more people, women and men, but in ways which resist Kroker et al's *theoretically* ubiquitous postmodern Bang.

References

Barth, J. 1980: 'The Literature of Replenishment' *The Atlantic*, 65-71.

Barthelme, D. 1971: *City Life*, London: (1974). *Guilty Pleasures*. New York.

Baudrillard, J. 1983a: *Simulations*, trans. Paul Foss, Paul Patton and Philip Beitchman. New York.

Barthes, R. 1977: *Roland Barthes by Roland Barthes*, trans. Richard Howard. London.

Chodorow, N. 1978: *The Reproduction of Mothering: Psychoanalysis and the Sociology of Gender*. Berkeley and London.

Coover, Robert 1969: *Pricksongs and Descants*. New York.

Fiedler, L. 1975: 'Cross the Border – Close that Gap: Postmodernism', *Sphere History of Literature 9*, ed. Marcus Cunliffe. London.

Freud, S. 1957: 'On Narcissism: an Introduction', *S.E.14*, ed. James Strachey. London.

Habermas, J. 1985: 'Modernity – an Incomplete Project', *Postmodern Culture*, ed. Hal Foster. London and Sydney, 3-16. (1987). *The Philosophical Discourse of Modernity*, Trans. F. G. Lawrence, Cambridge and Oxford.

Jameson, F. 1985: 'Postmodernism and Consumer Society', in Foster, ed.

Jardine, A.A. 1985: *Gynesis: Configurations of Women and Modernity*. Ithaca and London.

Kermode, F. 1967: *A Sense of an Ending*. Oxford.

Kristeva, J. 1982: 'Women's Time', *Feminist Theory: A Critique of Ideology*, ed. Nannerl O. Keohane *et al.*, Brighton, Sussex.

Kroker, A. and Cook, D. 1988: *The Postmodern Scene: Excremental Culture and Hyper-Aesthetics*. London.

Lyotard, J. F. 1984: *The Postmodern Condition: A Report on Knowledge*, trans Bennington and Massumi. Minneapolis.

Newman, C. 1985: *The Postmodern Aura*. Evanston.

Nietzsche, F. 1990: *Twilight of the Idols/ The Antichrist*, trans. R.J. Hollingdale. Harmondsworth. (1990): *My Sister and I*, trans. Ocar Levy, Los Angeles.

Pynchon, T. 1979: *V*. Harmondsworth.

Rivière, J. 1977: 'The Unconscious Phantasy of an Inner World Reflected in Examples from Literature', *New Directions in Psychoanalysis*, ed. Melanie Klein. London.

Sartre, J.P. 1958: *Being and Nothingness*, trans. H.E. Barnes. London.

Sontag, S. 1966: *Against Interpretation*. New York.

SELECT BIBLIOGRAPHY

General Works on Literary Theory

Douglas Atkins, G. and Morrow, Laura (eds.) 1989: *Contemporary Literary Theory*. London: Macmillan.

Eagleton, T. 1983: *Literary Theory: An Introduction*. Oxford: Basil Blackwell.

Eagleton, T. 1990: *The Ideology of the Aesthetic*. Oxford: Blackwell.

Hawthorn, J. 1987: *Unlocking the Text*. London: Edward Arnold.

Jefferson, A. and Robey, D. (ed.) 1982: *Modern Literary Theory: A Comparative Introduction*. London: Batsford Academic and Educational Ltd.

Selden, R. 1985: *A Reader's Guide to Contemporary Literary Theory*. Sussex: Harvester Press.

Russian Formalism

Bann, S. and Bowlt, J.E. (eds.) 1973: *Russian Formalism*. Edinburgh: Scottish Academic Press.

Bennett, T. 1979: *Formalism and Marxism*. London and New York: Methuen.

Erlich, V. 1981 (3rd edn): *Russian Formalism: History-Doctrine*. New Haven and London: Yale UP.

Jameson, F. 1972: *The Prison-House of Language: A Critical Account of Structuralism and Russian Formalism*. Princeton and London: Princeton UP.

Lemon, L.T. and Reis, M.J. 1965: *Russian Formalist Criticism: Four Essays*. Lincoln: University of Nebraska Press.

Matejka, L. and Pomorska, K. (eds.) 1971: *Readings in Russian Poetics: Formalist and Structuralist Views*. Cambridge, Mass. and London: MIT Press.

Medvedev, P.N. and Bakhtin, M.M. 1978: *The Formal Method in Literary Scholarship: An Introduction to Sociological Poetics*. Baltimore and London: Johns Hopkins UP.

Saussure and Structuralism

Barthes, R. 1967a: *Elements of Semiology*. tr. A. Lavers and C. Smith: London: Jonathan Cape.
—— 1967b: *Writing Degree Zero*. tr. A. Lavers and C. Smith: London: Jonathan Cape.
Culler, J. 1975: *Structuralist Poetics: Structuralism, Linguistics and the Study of Literature*. London: Routledge & Kegan Paul.
—— 1976: *Saussure*. London: Fontana/Collins.
—— 1981: *The Pursuit of Signs*. London: Routledge & Kegan Paul.
Eco, U. 1977: *A Theory of Semiotics*. Bloomington and London: Indiana UP.
Genette, G. 1980: *Narrative Discourse*. Oxford: Blackwell.
Hawkes, T. 1977: *Structuralism and Semiotics*. London: Methuen.
Jackson, L. 1991: *The Poverty of Structuralism: Literature and Structuralist Theory*. London and New York: Longman.
Lodge, D. 1977: *The Modes of Modern Writing: Metaphor, metonymy and the Typology of Modern Literature*. London: Edward Arnold.
—— 1981: *Working with Structuralism*. London: Routledge and Kegan Paul.
Macksey, R. and Donato, E. (eds.) 1972: *The Structuralist Controversy: The Languages of Criticism and the Sciences of Man*. Baltimore: Johns Hopkins UP.
Rimmon-Kenan, S. 1983: *Narrative Fiction: Contemporary Poetics*. London: Methuen.
Robey, D. (ed.) 1973: *Structuralism: an Introduction*. Oxford: Clarendon Press.
Saussure, F. de 1974: *Course in General Linguistics*. tr. W. Baskin London: Fontana/Collins.
Scholes, R. 1974: *Structuralism in Literature: An Introduction*. New Haven and London: Yale UP.
Todorov, T. 1975: *The Fantastic: a Structural Approach to a Literary Genre*. tr. R. Howard: Ithaca, NY: Cornell UP.
—— 1977: *The Poetics of Prose*. tr. R. Howard: Oxford: Blackwell.

Marxism

Althusser, L. 1977a: *For Marx*. tr. B. Brewster: London: New Left Books.
—— 1977b: *Lenin and Philosophy and Other Essays*. tr. B. Brewster: London: New Left Books.
Barthes, R. 1972: *Mythologies*. tr. A. Lavers: London: Jonathan Cape.
Bennett, T. 1979: *Formalism and Marxism*. London and New York: Methuen.
Eagleton, T. 1976a: *Marxism and Literary Criticism*. London: Methuen.
Eagleton, T. 1991: *Ideology*: London and New York: Verso.
—— 1976b: *Criticism and Ideology*. London: New Left Books.
Frow, J. 1986: *Marxism and Literary History*. Oxford: Blackwell.

Jameson, F. 1971: *Marxism and Form*. Princeton, NJ: Princeton UP.
Macherey, P. 1978: *A Theory of Literary Production*. tr. G. Wall: London: Routledge & Kegan Paul.
Williams, R. 1977: *Marxism and Literature*. Oxford: Oxford UP.

Reader Theory

Eco, U. 1979: *The Role of the Reader: Explorations in the Semiotics of Texts*. Bloomington: Indiana UP.
Fish, S. 1975: *Is There a Text in This Class?* Cambridge, Mass.: Harvard UP.
Holub, R.C. 1984: *Reception Theory: A Critical Introduction*. London: Methuen.
Ingarden, R. 1973: *The Literary Work of Art*. tr. G.G. Grabowicz: Evanston, Ill.: Northwestern UP.
Iser, W. 1978: *The Act of Reading: A Theory of Aesthetic Response*. Baltimore and London: Johns Hopkins UP.
Jauss, H.R., 1982: *Toward an Aesthetic of Reception*. tr. T. Bahti: Sussex: Harvester Press.
Suleiman, S. and Crossman, I. (eds) 1980: *The Reader in the Text: Essays on Audience and Interpretation*. Princeton, NJ.: Princeton UP.
Tompkins, J.P. (ed) 1980: *Reader Response Criticism: From Formalism to Post-Structuralism*. Baltimore: Johns Hopkins UP.

Feminism

Barrett, M. 1980: *Women's Oppression Today*. London: New Left Books.
Beauvoir, S. de 1974: *The Second Sex*. tr. Parshley, H.M.: Harmondsworth: Penguin.
Brunt, R. and Rowan, C. 1982: *Feminism, Culture and Politics*. London: Lawrence & Wishart.
Eisenstein, H. 1984: *Contemporary Feminist Thought*. London and Sydney: Unwin.
Ellman, M. (ed) 1979: *Thinking about Women*. London: Virago.
Felski, R. 1989: *Beyond Feminist Aesthetics: Feminist Literature and Social Change*. London: Hutchinson.
Greene, G. and Kahn, C. (ed) 1985: *Making a Difference: Feminist Literary Criticism*. London and New York: Methuen.
Humm, M. 1986: *Feminist Criticism: Women as Contemporary Critics*. Sussex: Harvester.
Kaplan, C. 1986: *Sea Changes: Essays on Culture and Feminism*. London: Verso.
Jacobus, M. (ed.) 1979: *Women Writing and Writing about Women*. London: Croom Helm.
Millet, K. 1977: *Sexual Politics*. London: Virago.
Moi, T. 1985: *Sexual/Textual Criticism: Feminist Literary Theory*. London: Methuen.

Showalter, E. 1977: *A Literature of Their Own*. Princeton, NJ: Princeton UP. (1978: London: Virago.)
—— 1986: *The New Feminist Criticism*. London: Virago.
Warhol, R. and Herndl, D.P.: *Feminisms: An Anthology of Literary Theory and Criticism*. New Brunswick and New Jersey: Rutgers UP.
Waugh, P. 1989: *Feminine Fictions: Revisiting the Postmodern*. London and New York: Routledge.
Wolff, J. 1990: *Feminine Sentences: Essays on Women and Culture*. Cambridge: Polity.

Post-Structuralism

Barthes, R. 1975: *S/Z*. tr. Richard Miller: London: Jonathan Cape.
—— 1976: *The Pleasure of the Text*. tr. Richard Miller: London: Cape.
Belsey, C. 1980: *Critical Practice*. London: Methuen.
Harland, B. 1987: *Superstructuralism*. London: Methuen.
Harari, J.V. (ed.) 1979: *Textual Strategies: Perspectives in Post-Structuralist Criticism*. Ithaca, NY: Cornell UP. (1980: London: Methuen.)
Hawthorn, J. (ed.) 1984: *Criticism and Critical Theory*. London: Edward Arnold.
Leitch, V. 1983: *Deconstructive Criticism: An Advanced Introduction*. London: Hutchinson.
Lentricchia, F. 1980: *After the New Criticism*. London: Athlone Press.
Marks, E. and Courtivron, I de (eds.) 1980: *New French Feminisms*, Sussex: Harvester.
Norris, C. 1985: *The Contest of Faculties: Philosophy and Theory after Deconstruction*. London and New York: Methuen.
Sturrock, J. (ed.) 1979: *Structuralism and Since: From Lévi-Strauss To Derrida*. Oxford: Oxford UP.
Young, R. (ed) 1981: *Untying the Text: a Post-Structuralist Reader*. Boston and London: Routledge & Kegan Paul.

The Subject

Belsey, C. 1985: *The Subject of Tradegy*. London: Methuen.
Coward, R. and Ellis, J. 1977: *Language and Materialism: Developments in Semiology and the Theory of the Subject*. London: Routledge & Kegan Paul.
Felman, S. (ed.) 1977: Literature and Psychoanalysis: The Question of Reading: Otherwise. *Yale French Studies* 55/56.
Flax, J. 1990: *Thinking Fragments: Psychoanalysis, Feminism and Postmodernism in the Contemporary West*. Berkeley: California UP.
Grosz, E. 1989: *Sexual Subversions: Three French Feminists*. Sydney: Allen and Unwin.
Lacan, J. 1977a: *Ecrits: a Selection*. tr. A. Sheridan: London: Tavistock.
—— 1977b: *The Four Fundamental Concepts of Psychoanalysis*. tr. A. Sheridan: London: Hogarth Press.

Wright, E. 1984: *Psychoanalytic Criticism: Theory and Practice*. London: Methuen.

Language and Textuality

Attridge, D. 1988: *Peculiar Language: Literature as difference from the Romantics to James Joyce*. London: Methuen.
Derrida, J. 1976: *Of Grammatology*. tr. G. Spivak: Baltimore and London: Johns Hopkins UP.
—— 1978: *Writing and Difference*, tr. A. Bass: London: Routledge & Kegan Paul.
Hartman, G. (ed.) 1979: *Deconstruction and Criticism*. London: Routledge & Kegan Paul.
Norris, C. 1982: *Deconstruction: Theory and Practice*. London: Methuen.
Ryan, M. 1982: *Marxism and Deconstruction: A Critical Articulation*. Baltimore and London: Johns Hopkins UP.

Discourse and the Social

Bakhtin, M.M. 1981: *The Dialohiv Imagination: Four essays*, tr. M. Holquist and C. Emerson: Austin: University of Texas Press.
—— 1986: *Rabelais and his World*. Cambridge Mass.: MIT Press.
Diamond, I. and Quilby, L. 1988: *Feminism and Foucault: Reflections on Resistance*. Boston: Northwestern University Press.
Foucault, M. 1970: *The Order of Things*. London: Tavistock.
Foucault, M. 1988: *Technologies of the Self*, ed., L.H. Martin, H. Gutman, P.H. Hutton. London: Tavistock Press.
Said, E. 1978: *Orientalism*. London: routledge & Kegan Paul.
Stallybrass, P. and White, A. 1986: *The Politics and Poetics of Transgression*. London: Methuen.
Volosinov, V.N. 1973: *Marxism and the Philosophy of Language*. tr. L. Matejka and I.R. Titunik: London and New York: Seminar Press.

New Historicism

Dollimore, J. and Sinfield, A. (eds.) 1985: *Political Shakespeare: New Essays in Cultural Materialism*. Ithaca: Cornell UP.
Goldberg, J. 1983: *James I and the Politics of Literature: Jonson, Shakespeare, Donne, and their Contemporaries*. Baltimore and London: Johns Hopkins.
Greenblatt, S. 1980: *Renaissance Self-Fashioning: From More to Shakespeare*. Chicago: Chicago UP.
Levinson, M. *et al* 1989: *Rethinking Historicism: Critical Readings in Romantic History*. Oxford: Blackwell.
McGann, J. 1988: *The Beauty of Inflections: Literary Investigations in Historical Method and Theory*. Oxford: Clarendon.

Weimann, R. 1977: *Structure and Society in Literary History: Studies in the History and Theory of Historical Criticism*. London: Lawrence and Wishart.

Postmodernism

Baudrillard, J. 1983a: *Simulations*. New York: Semiotext(e).
—— 1983b: *In the Shadow of the Silent Majorities*. New York: Semiotext(e).
Foster, H. (ed.) 1985: *Postmodern Culture*. London: Pluto Press.
Jameson, F. 1989: *The Ideologies of Theory: Essays 1971-86*. New York.
Lyotard, J-F. 1985: *The Postmodern Condition*. Manchester: Manchester UP.
Rorty, R. 1989: *Contingency, Irony and Solidarity*. Cambridge: Cambridge UP.
Waugh, P. 1992: *Practising Postmodernism/Reading Modernism*. London: Edward Arnold.
1992: *Postmodernism: A Reader*. London: Edward Arnold.

INDEX

INDEX